ON YOUR OWN

How to Start, Develop, and Manage a New Business

ON YOUR OWN

How to Start, Develop, and Manage a New Business

Robert D. Hisrich

Michael P. Peters

BUSINESS ONE IRWIN
Homewood, IL 60430

© RICHARD D. IRWIN, INC., 1992

Sponsoring editor: Cynthia A. Zigmund
Project editor: Lynne Basler
Production manager: Diane Palmer
Designer: Larry J. Cope
Compositor: Graphic Composition, Inc.
Typeface: 10/12 Times Roman
Printer: R. R. Donnelley & Sons Company

Library of Congress Cataloging-in-Publication Data

Hisrich, Robert D.
    On your own : how to start, develop, and manage a new business /
Robert D. Hisrich, Michael P. Peters.
      p.   cm.
    Includes index.
    ISBN 1–55623–650–6
    1. New business enterprises.   2. Entrepreneurship.   I. Peters,
Michael P.   II. Title.
HD62.6.H679   1991
658′.041—dc20   91–32699

Printed in the United States of America
1 2 3 4 5 6 7 8 9 0 DOC 8 7 6 5 4 3 2 1

To our wives, Tina and Debbie, and daughters Kary, Katy, Kelly, Christa and Kimberly, and their entrepreneurial spirit.

PREFACE

Starting and operating a new business involves considerable risk. It takes effort to overcome the inertia against creating something new. In creating and growing a new venture, the entrepreneur takes all the responsibility and risks for its development and survival, as well as enjoying the corresponding rewards. The fact that consumers, businesspeople, and government officials are interested in entrepreneurship is shown by: the increasing research on the subject, the growing number of college courses in entrepreneurship, the more than 2 million new enterprises started each year despite a 70 percent failure rate, the increased coverage and focus by the media, and the realization that this is an important topic for developed, developing, and once-controlled economies.

Who is the focus of all this attention—who is willing to accept all the risks and effort involved in creating a new venture? It may be a man or a woman, from an upper-class or lower-class background, a technologist or somebody lacking any degree of technological sophistication, a college graduate or a high school dropout. The person may have been an inventor, manager, nurse, salesperson, engineer, student, teacher, homemaker, or retiree. It is someone able to juggle life between work, family, and civic responsibilities while meeting payroll.

To provide an understanding of this person and the entrepreneurial process, *On Your Own* is divided into five major sections. **Part I—The Entrepreneurial Perspective**—introduces the entrepreneur and the entrepreneurial process. The role and nature of entrepreneurship in creating new ventures and impacting economic development is presented. This is followed by a discussion of the characteristics and background of typical entrepreneurs and some methods you can use to self-assess your entrepreneurial characteristics.

Part II—Starting a New Venture and Developing a Business—focuses on the specific elements in the entrepreneurial process. First, important aspects and methods of creating the business are presented including creating your own idea, obtaining an idea, or buying a business already in existence. Then, an overview of developing and using the all-important business plan is discussed, followed by a chapter devoted to each of its major aspects—the marketing plan, the financial plan, and the organizational plan.

Probably the most difficult aspect of creating and establishing a new venture is the focus of **Part III—Financing a New Venture.** Following a discussion of the alternative sources of capital, in-depth attention is devoted to two primary financing mechanisms—venture capital and public offerings.

Part IV—Managing the New Venture—presents material on establishing, developing, and ending the venture. We pay particular attention to the many aspects of managing the new venture during early operations and expansion. Specific alternatives available to the entrepreneur for extricating him or herself from the venture are presented.

Part V—Special Issues for the Entrepreneur, deals with patents, trademarks, warranties, direct marketing, franchising, internationalizing the venture, and intrapreneurship—establishing entrepreneurship in an existing organization.

To make *On Your Own* as meaningful as possible, each chapter begins with a profile of an entrepreneur whose career is especially relevant to the chapter material. Chapter objectives follow, and numerous specific examples occur throughout, illustrating applications of the material. A comprehensive glossary concludes the book.

Many people—students, business executives, entrepreneurs, professors, and publishing staff—have made this book possible. Of great assistance were the detailed and thoughtful comments of our reviewers: Nancy Bowman-Upton (Baylor University), Robert Brockhaus (St. Louis University), Alan Carsrud (University of Southern California), William Dwyer (Northeastern University), Fred Fry (Bradley University), Wayne Long (University of Calgary), Richard Judy (University of Wisconsin–Stevens Point), and Roderick Powers (Iowa State University).

Particular thanks go to Bill Wetzel for helpful comments on Chapter 10, "Venture Capital" and to Lynn Moore for comments on Chapter 11, "Going Public." Special thanks are given to Sandy Hughes and Haven Muench for preparing the manuscript so competently, and to Cynthia Anderson, Troy Bradley, Holly Donovan, Andrea Prokop, and Shelley Skyrmes for providing research material and editorial assistance for this edition.

We are deeply indebted to our spouses, Debbie and Tina, and to our daughters, Christa, Kary, Katy, Kelly, and Kimberly, whose support and understanding helped bring this effort to fruition. It is to these future entrepreneurs—Christa, Kary, Katy, Kelly, and Kimberly and the generation they represent—that this book is particularly dedicated. May you always beg forgiveness rather than ask permission.

Robert D. Hisrich
Michael P. Peters

CONTENTS

PART IV
Managing the New Venture

PART I *THE ENTREPRENEURIAL PERSPECTIVE*

1

A Historical Perspective

CHAPTER OBJECTIVES

1. To introduce the concept of entrepreneurship and its historical development.

2. To explain the entrepreneurial decision process.

3. To identify the basic types of start-ups.

4. To explain the role of entrepreneurship in economic development.

5. To discuss the future of entrepreneurship.

TED TURNER

Ted Turner, founder of Turner Broadcasting System, is an entrepreneur who loves living life on the edge. Who else would buy an unprofitable Metro-Goldwyn-Mayer film studio for $1.6 billion? Who else would bet on producing the Goodwill Games with U.S. versus Soviet athletes at a cost of about $50 million?

Robert Edward Turner III was born in 1938, and his boyhood was spent primarily in Savannah, Georgia. As a boy he was an enthusiastic reader of books about heroes, from Horatio Hornblower to Alexander the Great.

Unsuccessful in playing any of the major sports, he turned to one that required no special physical attributes but relied on the ability to think, take chances, and compete—sailing. Turner became a fanatic sailor, using a method that earned him such nicknames as the Capsize Kid and Turnover Ted. He loved sailing's competitive frenzy.

Turner graduated from the second military school he attended and applied to Harvard for admission but was rejected. His father insisted that he attend an Ivy League College, so he went to Brown University to study Greek classics. Dismayed by this area of study, Turner's father eventually convinced him to change his major to economics. After two suspensions for infractions involving women, Turner was kicked out of Brown University for setting fire to his fraternity's homecoming float.

After a few years, Turner joined the family business. His father, R. E. Turner, Jr., was an ambitious businessman who had built a $1 million billboard business. However, in a short time, Turner's family disintegrated—his sister, Mary Jane, died, his parents were divorced, and his father killed himself.

Although his father's will left the Atlanta billboard company to Ted, a contract to sell the business had been signed before he died. Showing the deal-making ingenuity that has characterized his business activities, the young Turner convinced the buyers that, by shifting lease sites to another company he had inherited, he would sabotage the company before the deal closed. The buyers backed down, and Turner's career moved forward. At the helm of the company, Turner began to expand, buying up billboard companies and radio stations. Since these constant acquisitions required huge outlays of cash and incurred debt, he learned to maintain a sufficient cash flow to cover payments.

In 1969 he took his company public with a merger that included a small Atlanta television station now called WTBS. In 1976, WTBS was the first station to become a network by beaming its signal to cable systems via satellite. By 1986, WTBS reached 36 million U.S. households and was cable television's most profitable advertising-supported network. The 1986 operating cash flow of the company was $70 million, and 1989 sales topped the $1 billion mark.

Turner does not sit back and watch the cash come in. He is always looking for ways to build his assets. Despite industry skepticism, Turner used the growing cash flow from WTBS to start the Cable News Network (CNN) in 1980. The 24-hour news channel was a success, winning praise from news professionals. This success enabled Turner to create another news network, Headline News. By 1986 the news networks were operating solidly in the black.

Turner's uncanny success in starting high-risk ventures is not accidental. A vigilant and relentless manager, Turner would often sleep on his office couch after working 18-hour days. Until autumn 1986, when Turner established a five-man management committee comprised of veteran TBS executives, he personally supervised company tasks and decisions. One person familiar with Turner's management style was surprised at the formation of the committee: "He (Turner) would never even let the five go out and have a beer together, let alone run the company."

Turner's talents extend beyond the corporate boardroom. A high risk taker, he won the America's cup race in 1977. In 1979 he won the Fastnet race off England's southwest coast, during which 15 competitors died in the violent seas.

In his own view, Turner is a quintessential achiever. He says, "I've got more awards than anybody—anybody my age. I've probably got more debt than anyone in the world. That's something, isn't it?" What makes him keep pushing for more?

Not satisfied with his accomplishments, Turner has a visionary goal: to use his power and his network to influence world issues. He wants to concentrate on issues such as nuclear weapons, environmental abuse, and overpopulation. He speaks proudly of TBS specials, such as one based on Martin Luther King, Jr. When asked if he would want to be president of the United States, Turner said, "The United States is only 5 percent of the world's population. I'm in global politics already."

Turner's view is both global and long run. In 1985, one CNN executive said, "Ted's mind is always 5 or 10 years down the road. Right now he's probably living in 1995." Turner's purchase of the MGM studio was motivated by rising licensing fees for old movies and television shows. Bill Bevins, TBS financial chief executive, projected that higher fees would lower operating profits from 40 percent of sales in 1985 to 10 percent in 1990. But at the end of 1989, gross profits were $631 million and sales were, as stated earlier, over $1 billion. Turner felt that the simple solution was either to increase buyer clout by taking over CBS or to acquire his own program library.

Turner's attempt to take over CBS in 1985 failed, costing him $23 million in lawyer and investment banker fees. But Turner, an undaunted optimist and aggressive competitor, views this attempted hostile takeover defeat as a triumph. Since CBS had to borrow heavily to acquire stock to stop the takeover, Turner feels this set CBS back 10 years.

Turner moved directly from this defeat to the acquisition of MGM. The 3,650-film library offered Turner Broadcasting a solution to rising licensing fees. About 1,000 of these films have enduring commercial value and will be aired on WTBS. Some analysts feel that the price paid—$1.6 billion—was too high, with the deal putting Turner heavily into debt. Another potential debt for TBS may result from Turner's decision to colorize up to 10 percent of the film in this newly acquired library—at an average cost of $300,000 per film and a total cost of $22 million to $55 million. Also, the terms of the contract could affect Turner's majority share position in the company.

The preferred stock issued has strict dividend requirements, including common share payments, which, if not met, could cause Turner to lose control of the company. Yet, despite these problems, people who know Turner well would not bet against him. He has an entrepreneurial spirit that thrives on these kinds of on-the-edge situations.

The saga of Ted Turner reflects that of many entrepreneurs in various industries and various sizes of companies. The historical aspect of entrepreneurship, as well as the decision that Ted Turner and others have made to become entrepreneurs, is reflected in the following quotes from two successful entrepreneurs:

> Being an entrepreneur and creating a new business venture is analogous to raising children—it takes more time and effort than you ever imagine and it is extremely difficult and painful to get out of the situation. Thank goodness you cannot easily divorce yourself from either situation.

> When people ask me if I like being in business, I usually respond: On days when there are more sales than problems, I love it; on days when there are more problems than sales, I wonder why I do it. Basically, I am in business because it gives me a good feeling about myself. You learn a lot about your capabilities by putting yourself on the line. Running a successful business is not only a financial risk, it is an emotional risk as well. I get a lot of satisfaction from having dared it—done it—and been successful.

Do the profile of Ted Turner and these quotes fit your perception of the career of an entrepreneur? Both say a great deal about what it takes to start and operate a successful business. To understand this better, it is important to learn about the nature and development of entrepreneurship, the decision process involved in becoming an entrepreneur, and the role of entrepreneurship in economic development.

NATURE AND DEVELOPMENT OF ENTREPRENEURSHIP

Who is an entrepreneur? What is entrepreneurship? What is an entrepreneur career path? These frequently asked questions reflect the increased national and international interest in the field. Yet, in spite of all this interest, a concise, universally accepted definition has not yet emerged. An overview of the development of the theory of entrepreneurship is illustrated in the development of the term itself (see Table 1–1). The term *entrepreneur* comes from the French and literally translated means "between-taker" or "go-between."

One early example of a go-between is Marco Polo, who attempted to establish trade routes to the Far East. As was the custom, he signed a contract with a money person (forerunner of today's capitalist) to sell his goods. A common contract during this time provided a loan to the merchant-adventurer at a 22.5

TABLE 1–1 Development of Entrepreneurship Theory and the Term *Entrepreneur*

Stems from French; means *between-taker* or *go-between.*

Middle Ages: actor (warlike action) and person in charge of large-scale production projects.

17th century: person bearing risks of profit (loss) in a fixed price contract with government.

1725: Richard Cantillon—person bearing risks is different from one supplying capital.

1797: Beaudeau—person bearing risks, planning, supervising, organizing, and owning.

1803: Jean Baptiste Say—separated profits of entrepreneur from profits of capital.

1876: Francis Walker—distinguished between those who supplied funds and received interest and those who received profit from managerial capabilities.

1934: Joseph Schumpeter—entrepreneur is an innovator and develops untried technology.

1961: David McClelland—entrepreneur is an energetic, moderate risk taker.

1964: Peter Drucker—entrepreneur maximizes opportunities.

1975: Albert Shapero—entrepreneur takes initiative, organizes some social-economic mechanisms, and accepts risk of failure.

1980: Karl Vesper—entrepreneur seen differently by economists, psychologists, businesspersons, and politicians.

1983: Gifford Pinchot—intrapreneur is an entrepreneur within an already established organization.

1985: Robert Hisrich—entrepreneurship is the process of creating something different with value by devoting the necessary time and effort, assuming the accompanying financial, psychological, and social risks, and receiving the resulting rewards of monetary and personal satisfaction.

Source: Robert D. Hisrich. "Entrepreneurship and Intrapreneurship: Methods for Creating New Companies That Have an Impact on the Economic Renaissance of an Area," in *Entrepreneurship, Intrapreneurship, and Venture Capital,* ed. Robert D. Hisrich (Lexington, MA: Lexington Books, 1986), p. 96.

percent rate, including insurance. While the capitalist was a passive risk bearer, the merchant-adventurer took the active role in trading, bearing all the physical and emotional risks. Upon the successful completion of a journey by the merchant-adventurer, the capitalist took most of the profits (up to 75 percent), while the entrepreneur-merchant settled for the remaining 25 percent.

In the Middle Ages, the term entrepreneur was used to describe both an actor and a person who managed large production projects. In such large production projects, this person did not take any risks, but merely managed the project using the resources provided. A typical entrepreneur in the Middle Ages was the cleric—the person in charge of great architectural works, such as castles and fortifications, public buildings, or abbeys and cathedrals.

The connection of risk with entrepreneurship developed in the 17th century, with an entrepreneur being a person who entered into a contractual arrangement with the government to perform a service or to supply stipulated products. Since the contract price was fixed, any resulting profits or losses reflected the efforts of the entrepreneurs. One entrepreneur in this period was John Law, a Frenchman, who was allowed to establish a royal bank, which eventually evolved into an exclusive franchise to form a trading company in the New World—the Mississippi Company. Unfortunately, this monopoly on French trade led to Law's downfall when he attempted to push the company's stock price higher than the value of its assets; this eventually led to the collapse of the company.

Richard Cantillon, a noted economist and author in the 1700s, understood Law's mistake. Cantillon developed one of the early theories of the entrepreneur and is regarded by some as the founder of the term. He viewed the entrepreneur as a risk taker, observing that merchants, farmers, craftsmen, and other sole proprietors "buy at a certain price and sell at an uncertain price, therefore operating at a risk."[1]

Finally, in the 18th century the person with capital was differentiated from one needing capital. In other words, the entrepreneur was distinguished from the capital provider (the present-day venture capitalist). One reason for this differentiation was the industrialization occurring throughout the world. Many of the inventions developed during this time were reactions to the changing world, as was the case with the inventions of Eli Whitney and Thomas Edison. Both Whitney and Edison were entering new technologies and were unable to finance their inventions themselves. While Whitney financed his cotton gin with expropriated British crown property, Edison raised capital from private sources to develop and experiment in the complex fields of electricity and chemistry. Both Edison and Whitney were capital users (entrepreneurs), not providers (venture capitalists). A venture capitalist is a professional money manager who makes risk investments from a pool of equity capital to obtain a high rate of return on the investments.

---

[1]Robert F. Herbert and Albert H. Link, *The Entrepreneur-Mainstream Views and Radical Critiques* (New York: Praeger Publishers, 1982), p. 17.

In the late 19th and early 20th centuries, entrepreneurs were frequently not distinguished from managers and were mainly viewed from an economic perspective:

> Briefly stated, the entrepreneur organizes and operates an enterprise for personal gain. He pays current prices for the materials consumed in the business, for the use of the land, for the personal services he employs, and for the capital he requires. He contributes his own initiative, skill and ingenuity in planning, organizing, and administering the enterprise. He also assumes the chance of loss and gain consequent to unforeseen and uncontrollable circumstances. The net residue of the annual receipts of the enterprise after all costs have been paid, he retains for himself.[2]

Andrew Carnegie is one of the best examples of this definition. Carnegie invented nothing, but instead adapted and formed new technology and products to achieve economic vitality. Carnegie, who descended from a poor Scottish family, made the American steel industry one of the wonders of the industrial world, primarily through his unremitting competitiveness, rather than his inventiveness or creativity.

In the middle of the 20th century, the notion of an **entrepreneur as an innovator** was established:

> The function of entrepreneurs is to reform or revolutionize the pattern of production by exploiting an invention or, more generally, an untried technological possibility for producing a new commodity or producing an old one in a new way, opening a new source of supply of materials or a new outlet for products, by reorganizing a new industry. . . . [3]

The concept of innovation and newness as an integral part of entrepreneurship is at the heart of this definition. Indeed, innovation, the act of introducing something new, is one of the most difficult tasks for the entrepreneur. It takes not only the ability to create and conceptualize but also the ability to understand all the forces at work in the environment. The newness can consist of anything from a new product to a new distribution system for simplifying a new organizational structure. Edward Harriman, who reorganized the Ontario and Southern railroad through the Northern Pacific Trust, or John Pierpont Morgan, who developed his large banking house by reorganizing and financing the nation's industries, are examples of entrepreneurs fitting this definition. These organizational innovations are frequently as difficult to achieve successfully as the more traditional technological innovations (transistors, computers, lasers) that are usually associated with the word.

This ability to innovate is an instinct that distinguishes human beings from other creatures. The instinct can be observed throughout history, from the Egyptians who designed and built great pyramids out of stone blocks weighing many

---

[2]Richard T. Ely and Ralph H. Hess, *Outlines of Economics*, 6th ed. (New York: Macmillan, 1937), p. 488.

[3]Joseph Schumpeter, *Can Capitalism Survive?* (New York: Harper & Rowe, 1952), p. 72.

tons each, to the Apollo lunar module, to laser beams. While the tools have changed with advances in science and technology, the ability to innovate has been present in every civilization.

ENTREPRENEUR DEFINITION

The concept of an entrepreneur is further refined when principles and terms from a business, managerial, and personal perspective are considered. In particular, the aspects of entrepreneurship from a personal and sociological perspective have been explored in this century. This exploration is reflected in more recent definitions of an entrepreneur:

> In almost all of the definitions of entrepreneurship, there is agreement that we are talking about a kind of behavior that includes: (1) initiative taking, (2) the organizing and reorganizing of social/economic mechanisms to turn resources and situations to practical account, (3) the acceptance of risk or failure.[4]
>
> To an economist, an entrepreneur is one who brings resources, labor, materials, and other assets into combinations that make their value greater than before, and also one who introduces changes, innovations, and a new order. To a psychologist, such a person is typically driven by certain forces—need to obtain or attain something, to experiment, to accomplish, or perhaps to escape authority of others. . . . To one businessman, an entrepreneur appears as a threat, an aggressive competitor, whereas to another businessman the same entrepreneur may be an ally, a source of supply, a customer, or someone good to invest in. . . . The same person is seen by a capitalist philosopher as one who creates wealth for others as well, who finds better ways to utilize resources, and reduce waste, and who produces jobs others are glad to get.[5]
>
> Entrepreneurship is the dynamic process of creating incremental wealth. The wealth is created by individuals who assume the major risks in terms of equity, time, and/or career commitment or provide value for some product or service. The product service may or may not be new or unique but value must somehow be infused by the entrepreneur by receiving and allocating the necessary skills and resources.[6]

While each of these definitions views entrepreneurs from a slightly different perspective, each contains similar notions: newness, organizing, creating, wealth, and risk taking. Yet, each definition is somewhat restrictive. Entrepreneurs are found in all professions—education, medicine, research, law, architecture, engineering, social work, and distribution. Therefore, to include all types of entrepreneurial behavior, the following definition of entrepreneurship will be the foundation of this book:

---

[4]Albert Shapero, *Entrepreneurship and Economic Development* (Wisconsin: Project ISEED, LTD., The Center for Venture Management, Summer 1975), p. 187.

[5]Karl Vesper, *New Venture Strategies* (Englewood Cliffs, N.J.: Prentice-Hall, 1980), p. 2.

[6]Robert C. Ronstadt, *Entrepreneurship* (Dover, MA: Lord Publishing Co., 1984), p. 28.

> *Entrepreneurship* is the process of creating something different with value by devoting the necessary time and effort, assuming the accompanying financial, psychic, and social risks, and receiving the resulting rewards of monetary and personal satisfaction.[7]

For the person who actually starts his or her own business, the experience is filled with enthusiasm, frustration, anxiety, and hard work. There is a high failure rate due to such things as poor sales, intense competition, or lack of capital. The financial and emotional risk can be very high. What, then, causes a person to make this difficult decision? This question can be best explored by looking at the decision process involved in becoming an entrepreneur.

THE ENTREPRENEURIAL DECISION PROCESS

Many individuals have difficulty bringing their ideas to the market and creating a new venture. Yet, entrepreneurship and the actual entrepreneurial decision have resulted in several million new businesses throughout the world, even in controlled economies such as China, Hungary, and Poland. While no one knows the exact number, in the United States (which leads the world in company formation) estimates indicate that from 1.1 to 1.9 million new companies were formed in recent years.[8]

Indeed, millions of companies are formed despite recession, inflation, high interest rates, lack of infrastructure, economic uncertainty, and the fear of failure. Each of these companies is formed through a very personal human process that, although unique, has some characteristics common to all. Like all processes, it entails a movement, *from* something *to* something—a movement from a present lifestyle to forming a new enterprise, as indicated in Table 1–2.

Change from Present Life-Style

The decision to leave a career or life-style is not an easy one. It takes a great deal of energy to change and to create something new. While individuals tend to start businesses in familiar areas, two work environments tend to be particularly good for spawning new enterprises: research and development and marketing. Working in technology (research and development), individuals develop new product ideas or processes and often leave to form their own companies when the new ideas are not accepted by their employers. Similarly, individuals in

---

[7]This definition was first developed for the woman entrepreneur. See Robert D. Hisrich and Candida G. Brush, *The Woman Entrepreneur: Starting, Financing, and Managing a Successful New Business* (Lexington, MA: Lexington Books, 1985), p. 18.

[8]This material is taken from an article by the author in Robert D. Hisrich, ed., *Entrepreneurship, Intrapreneurship, and Venture Capital: The Foundation of Economic Renaissance* (Lexington, MA: Lexington Books, 1986).

TABLE 1–2 Decisions for a Potential Entrepreneur

| **Change from present life-style**
Work environment
Disruption | ←——→ | **Form new enterprise**
Desirable
1. Cultural
2. Subcultural
3. Family
4. Teachers
5. Peers
Possible
1. Government
2. Background
3. Marketing
4. Financing
5. Role models |

Source: Robert D. Hisrich, "Entrepreneurship and Intrapreneurship: Methods for Creating New Companies That Have an Impact on the Economic Renaissance of an Area," in *Entrepreneurship, Intrapreneurship, and Venture Capital*, ed. Robert D. Hisrich (Lexington, MA: Lexington Books, 1986), p. 90.

marketing have become familiar with the market and customers' unfilled wants and needs and they frequently start new enterprises to fill these needs.

Perhaps even more incentive to overcome inertia and leave a present life-style to create something new comes from a negative force—disruption. A significant number of companies are formed by people who have retired, who are relocated due to a move by the other member in a dual-career family, or who have been fired. There is probably no greater force than personal dislocation to galvanize a person's will to act. A study in one major city in the United States indicated that the number of new business listings in the Yellow Pages increased by 12 percent during a layoff period. Another cause of disruption that can result in company formation is someone's completion of an educational degree. For example, a student who is not promoted after receiving an MBA degree may decide to start a new company.

Yet, what causes this personal disruption to result in a new company being formed instead of something else? The decision to start a new company occurs when an individual perceives that it is both desirable and possible.

Desirability of New Venture Formation

The perception that starting a new company is desirable results from an individual's culture, subculture, family, teachers, and peers. A culture that values an individual who successfully creates a new business will spawn more company formations than one that does not. The American culture places a high value on being your own boss, having individual opportunity, being a success, and making money—all aspects of entrepreneurship. Therefore, it is not surprising to find a high rate of company formation in the United States. On the other hand, in some countries successfully establishing a new business and making money is not as highly valued, and failure may be a disgrace. Other cultures more closely emulate this attitude than that of the United States.

However, no entire culture is totally for or against entrepreneurship. Many different subcultures that shape value systems are operant within a cultural framework. There are pockets of entrepreneurial subcultures in the United States. While the more widely recognized ones include Route 128 (Boston), Silicon Valley (California), Dallas/Fort Worth, and the North Carolina Triangle, some less-known but equally important entrepreneurial centers are Los Angeles, Indianapolis, Denver, Columbus, and Tulsa. These subcultures support and even promote entrepreneurship—forming a new company—as one of the best occupations. No wonder more individuals actively plan new enterprises in these supportive environments.

There are variations within these subcultures (such as the one in Silicon Valley) caused by family traits. Studies of companies in a variety of industries throughout the United States and the world indicate that 50 to 72 percent of founders of companies had fathers and/or mothers who valued independence. The independence achieved by company owners, professionals, artists, or farmers permeates their entire family life, giving encouragement and value to their children's company-formation activity.

Encouragement to form a company is further gained from teachers, who can significantly influence individuals regarding entrepreneurship as one possible career path. Schools with exciting courses in entrepreneurship and innovation tend to develop entrepreneurs and can actually drive the entrepreneurial environment in an economic area. For example, the number of entrepreneurship courses a person takes increases the probability of starting a venture. Both MIT and Harvard are located near Route 128; Stanford is in the Silicon Valley; the University of North Carolina, North Carolina State, and Duke are the points of the North Carolina Triangle; and the University of Texas facilitates entrepreneurship in the Dallas/Fort Worth area. An area with a strong education base is almost always a prerequisite for entrepreneurial activity and company formation.

Finally, peers are very important in the decision to form a company. An area with an entrepreneurial pool and a meetingplace where entrepreneurs and potential entrepreneurs discuss ideas, problems, and solutions spawns more new companies than an area where this does not occur.

Possibility of New Venture Formation

While the desire generated from the individual's culture, subculture, family, teachers, and peers must be present before any action is taken, the second part of the equation centers around the question: What makes it possible to form a new company? Several factors—government, background, marketing, role models, and finances—contribute to the creation of a new venture (see Table 1–2). The government contributes by providing the infrastructure to support a new venture. It is no wonder that more companies are formed in the United States, given the roads, communication and transportation systems, utilities, and economic stability compared with other countries. Even the U.S. tax rate for companies and individuals is better than in countries such as Ireland or England. Countries that have a repressive tax rate, particularly for individuals, can suppress company formation since a significant monetary gain cannot be achieved even though the social, psychological, and financial risks are still present.

The entrepreneur must also have the needed background. A formal education and previous business experience make a potential entrepreneur feel capable of forming and managing a new enterprise. While educational systems are important in providing the needed business knowledge, individuals still tend to start successful businesses in fields in which they have worked. Entrepreneurs are not born—they develop.

Marketing also plays a critical role in forming a new company. Not only must a market of sufficient size be present but also the marketing know-how to put together the best total package of product, price, distribution, and promotion needed for successful product launching. A company is more easily formed in an area where there is market demand, not technology push.

A role model can be one of the most powerful influences in making company formation seem possible. To see someone else succeed makes it easier to picture yourself engaged in a similar activity—doing better, of course. A frequent comment of entrepreneurs when queried about their motivation for starting their new venture is: "If that person could do it, so can I!"

Finally, financial resources must be readily available. While most of the start-up money for any new company comes from personal savings, credit, friends, and relatives, there is still often a need for seed (start-up) capital. Each venture has a common trait—the need for seed and other types of risk capital. Risk-capital investors play an essential role in the development and growth of entrepreneurial activity. More new companies form when seed capital is readily available.

TYPES OF START-UPS

What types of start-ups result from this entrepreneurial decision process? One very useful classification system divides start-ups into three categories: life-style firms, foundation companies, and high-potential ventures. A **life-style firm** is privately held and usually achieves only modest growth due to the nature of the business, the objectives of the entrepreneur, and the limited money devoted to research and development. This type of firm may grow after several years to 30 or 40 employees and have annual revenues of about $2 million. A life-style firm exists primarily to support the owners and usually has little opportunity for significant growth and expansion.

The second type of start-up—the **foundation company**—is created from research and development and lays the foundation for a new industry. This firm can grow in 5 to 10 years from 40 to 400 employees and from $10 million to $30 million in yearly revenues. Since this type of start-up rarely goes public, it usually draws the interest of private investors only, not the venture-capital community.

The final type of start-up—the **high-potential venture**—is the one that receives the greatest investment interest and publicity. While the company may start out like a foundation company, its growth is far more rapid. After 5 to 10 years the company could employ around 500 employees with $20 to $30 million in revenue. Given its growth and revenues, the high-potential start-up venture will frequently go public or be purchased by a larger company.

Given that the results of the decision-making process need to be perceived as desirable and possible for an individual to change from a present life-style to a radically new one, it is not surprising that the type and number of new business formations vary greatly throughout the United States. Some regions of the country have more support infrastructure and a more positive attitude toward new business creation. For example, in one year, seven of the nine census regions had increases in new corporations with the record total (163,051) being up 1 percent from the previous high a year earlier. In this year, New England had the largest increase (4.6 percent) followed by the East North Center (up 4.3 percent), South Atlantic (up 3.8 percent), West South Central (up 3.5 percent), and East South Central (up 3.1 percent). The Pacific states declined 9 percent and the farm-belt states (West North Central region) 8.9 percent.

ROLE OF ENTREPRENEURSHIP IN ECONOMIC DEVELOPMENT

The role of entrepreneurship in economic development involves more than just increasing per capita output and income; it involves initiating and constituting change in the structure of business and society. This change is accompanied by growth and increased output, which allows more to be divided by the various participants. What in an area facilitates the needed change and development? One theory of economic growth depicts innovation as the key not only in developing new products (or services) for the market but also in stimulating investment interest in the new ventures created. This new investment works on both the demand and supply sides of the growth equation: The new capital created expands the capacity for growth (supply side) and the resultant new spending utilizes the new capacity and output (demand side).

Yet, in spite of the importance of investment and innovation in the economic development of an area, an adequate understanding of the **product-evolution process** is still lacking. This is the process through which innovation develops and commercializes through entrepreneurial activity stimulating economic growth.

The product-evolution process is indicated in Figure 1–1 as a cornucopia, the traditional symbol of abundance. It begins with knowledge in science, thermodynamics, fluid mechanics, electronics, and technology and ends with products or services available for purchase in the marketplace.[9] The critical point in the product-evolution process is the intersection of knowledge and a recognized social need and begins the product development phase. This point, called *iterative synthesis,* often fails to evolve into a marketable innovation.

The innovation can of course be of varying degrees of uniqueness. As indicated in Figure 1–2, most innovations introduced on the market are **ordinary,** that is, with little uniqueness or technology. As expected, there are fewer **technological** and **breakthrough innovations,** with the number of the actual innovations decreasing as the technology involved increases. Regardless of its level of uniqueness or technology, each innovation (particularly the latter two types) evolves and develops to commercialization through one of three mechanisms: the government, intrapreneurship, and entrepreneurship.

Government as an Innovator

The government is one method for commercializing the results of the interaction between a social need and technology. This is frequently called *technology transfer* and has been the focus of a significant amount of research effort. Despite all the effort and findings, to date few inventions resulting from sound scientific research have reached the commercial market. While most of the by-products from this scientific research have little application to any social need, the few products that do require significant modification to have market appeal. Though the government has the financial resources to successfully transfer the technology to the marketplace, it lacks the business skills, particularly marketing and distribution, necessary for successful commercialization. In addition, government bureaucracy and red tape often inhibit the necessary strategic business from being formed in a timely manner.

Intrapreneurship

Intrapreneurship (entrepreneurship within an existing business structure) can also bridge the gap between science and the marketplace. Existing businesses have the financial resources, business skills, and frequently the marketing and distribution system to successfully commercialize innovation. Yet, too often the bureaucratic structure, the emphasis on short-term profits, and a highly structured

---

[9]This process is discussed in Yao Tzu Li, David G. Jansson, and Ernest G. Cravelho, *Technological Innovation in Education and Industry* (New York: Van Nostrand Reinhold, 1980).

FIGURE 1–1 Product Evolution

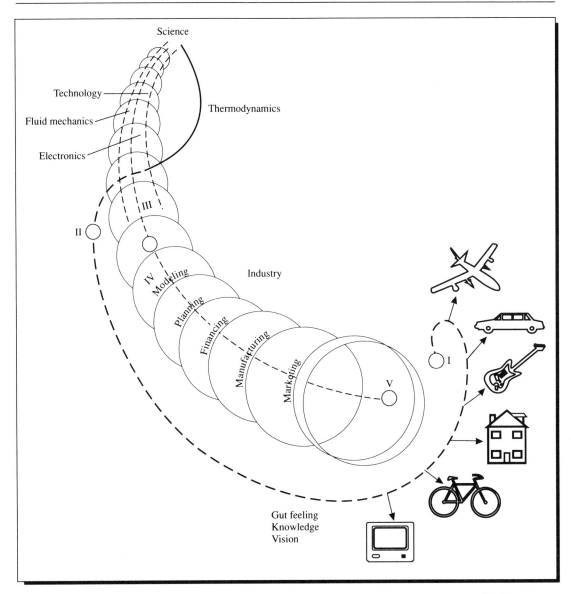

I   Recognition of social need

II Initiation of technological innovation

III Iterative synthesis leading to invention (pressing toward invention)

IV Development phase

V   Industrial phase

Source: Yao Tzu Li, David G. Jansson, and Ernest G. Cravelho, *Technology Innovation in Education and Industry* (New York: Van Nostrand Reinhold, 1980), p. 27.

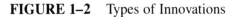

FIGURE 1–2   Types of Innovations

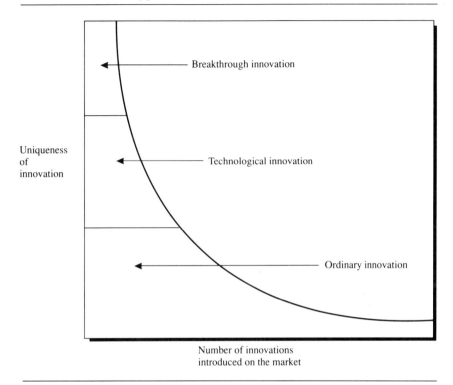

Source: Robert D. Hisrich, "Entrepreneurship and Intrapreneurship: Methods for Creating New Companies That Have an Impact on the Economic Renaissance of an Area," in *Entrepreneurship, Intrapreneurship, and Venture Capital*, ed. Robert D. Hisrich (Lexington, MA: Lexington Books, 1986), p. 73.

organization inhibit creativity and prevent new products from being developed. Corporations recognizing these inhibiting factors and the need for creativity and innovation have attempted to establish an intrapreneurial spirit in their organizations.

Entrepreneurship

Another method for bridging the gap between science and the marketplace is entrepreneurship. Many entrepreneurs have a difficult time bridging this gap and creating new ventures. They frequently lack managerial skills, marketing capability, and finances. Their inventions are frequently unrealistic, needing significant modification to be marketable. And entrepreneurs often do not know how to interface with all the necessary entities such as banks, suppliers, customers, venture capitalists, distributors, and advertising agencies.

Yet, in spite of all these difficulties, entrepreneurship is presently the most effective method for bridging the gap between science and the marketplace, creating new enterprises, and bringing new products and services to market. These entrepreneurial activities significantly affect the economy of an area by building the economic base and providing jobs. Between 1970 and 1980, small businesses increased employment by 20 million new jobs while Fortune 500 companies had a zero net increase in employment. Given the significance of the impact on both the overall economy and the employment of an area, it is surprising that entrepreneurship has not become more of a focal point in economic development.

THE FUTURE OF ENTREPRENEURSHIP

As evidenced by the many different definitions, the term *entrepreneurship* means different things to different people and can be viewed from different conceptual perspectives. However, in spite of the differences there are some common aspects: risk taking, creativity, independence, and rewards. These commonalities will continue to be the driving forces behind the notion of entrepreneurship in the future. One thing is clear—the future for entrepreneurship appears to be bright. We are living in the age of the entrepreneur, with entrepreneurship endorsed by educational institutions, governmental units, society, and corporations. Entrepreneurial education has never been so important in terms of courses and academic research. In 1975, entrepreneurship courses were offered in 104 colleges or universities in the United States; this number had increased to 163 by 1980 and 253 by 1985.[10] Entrepreneurship in these 253 schools was housed in both business administration (212) and engineering (41). This increase in course offerings has been accompanied by an increase in academic research, endowed chairs in the area, entrepreneurship concentration and majors, and centers of entrepreneurial activity. This trend will continue, supported by an increase in Ph.D. activity, which will in turn provide the needed faculty and research effort to support the future increases in course offerings, endowed positions, centers, and research efforts.

The government has also taken an increasing interest in promoting the growth of entrepreneurship. Individuals are encouraged to form new businesses and are provided such government support as tax incentives, buildings, roads, and a communication system—a strong government infrastructure—to facilitate this

---

[10]These and other statistics on entrepreneurship education can be found in Karl H. Vesper, "New Developments in Entrepreneurship Education" in *The Art and Science of Entrepreneurship* (Cambridge, MA: Ballinger Publishing Co., 1986), pp. 379–87.

creation process. The encouragement by the federal and individual state governments should continue in the future as more lawmakers understand that new enterprises create jobs and increase the economic output in an area. Some states are developing their own innovative industrial strategies for fostering entrepreneurial activity and the timely development of the technology of the area. The impact of this strategy is seen in the venture-capital industry, which is always very sensitive to government regulations and policies. The current level and growth in venture-capital funds have resulted primarily in a decrease in the capital gains tax from 49 percent to 28 percent in 1978 and the relaxed rules regarding pension fund investment. Pension funds now contribute about 30 percent of the venture-capital money raised each year.

Society's support of entrepreneurship will also continue. This support is critical in providing both motivation and public support. Never before have entrepreneurs been so revered by the general populace. Entrepreneurial endeavors in the United States are considered honorable and even in many cases a prestigious pursuit. A major factor in developing this societal approval is the media. The media has played and will continue to play a powerful and constructive role by reporting extensively on the general entrepreneurial spirit in the United States, highlighting specific success cases of this spirit in operation. Major articles in such prestigious newspapers as the *New York Times, The Wall Street Journal,* and the *Washington Post* have focused on the pioneer spirit of today's entrepreneurs, describing how this spirit benefits society by keeping the United States in the lead in technology. General business magazines such as *Barron's, Business Week, Forbes,* and *Fortune* have provided similar coverage by adding special columns on entrepreneurship and venturing. New magazines such as *Black Enterprise; Entrepreneur; Inc.; Journal of Venturing;* and *Venture,* which focus on specific issues of the entrepreneurial process; starting new ventures; and small, growing businesses, have built solid and increasing circulation rates. Television on both a national and local level has highlighted entrepreneurship by featuring specific individuals and issues involved in the entrepreneurial process. Not only have local stations covered regional occurrences, but also nationally syndicated shows such as "The Today Show," "Good Morning America," and "20/20" have had special segments devoted to this phenomenon. This media coverage uplifts the image of the entrepreneur and growth companies and focuses on their contributions to society.

Finally, large companies will continue to have an interest in their special form of entrepreneurship—intrapreneurship—in the future. These companies will be increasingly interested in capitalizing on their research and development in the increasingly competitive environment. The largest 15 companies in the United States account for over 20 percent of the total U.S. research and development and over 40 percent of private-sector R&D. General Electric, for example, has created three $1 billion businesses internally in the last 15 years. Other companies, as well, will want to create more new businesses through intrapreneurship in the future.

SUMMARY

The definition of an entrepreneur has evolved over time as the world's economic structure has changed and become more complex. From its beginnings in the Middle Ages, where it was used in relation to specific occupations, the notion of the "entrepreneur" has been refined and broadened to include concepts that are related to the person rather than the occupation. Risk taking, innovation, and creation of wealth are examples of the criteria that have been developed as the study of new business creations has evolved. In this text, entrepreneurship is defined as the process of creating something different with value by devoting the necessary time and effort; assuming the accompanying financial, psychic, and social risks; and receiving the resulting rewards of monetary and personal satisfaction.

The decision to start an entrepreneurial venture consists of several sequential subdecisions:

1. The decision to leave a present career or life-style.
2. The decision that an entrepreneurial venture is desirable.
3. The decision that both external and internal factors make the venture possible.

While the decision-making process is applicable to each of the three types of start-up companies, the emphasis is certainly different. Because of their nature, a foundation company or a high-potential venture requires a more conscious effort to reach a defensible decision on these points than does a life-style firm.

There are both pushing and pulling influences active in the decision to leave a present career: the "push" of job dissatisfaction or even layoff, and the "pull" toward entrepreneurship of seeing an unfilled need in the marketplace. Once the possibility of an entrepreneurial career is acknowledged, it is either accepted or rejected as a valid alternative. The desirability of starting one's own company is strongly influenced by culture, subculture, family, teachers, and peers. Any of these influences can function as a source of encouragement for entrepreneurship, with support ranging from government policies which favor business to strong personal role models of family or friends. Beyond the stage of seeing entrepreneurship as a "good idea," the potential entrepreneur must possess or acquire the necessary education and financial resources for launching the venture.

The study of entrepreneurship has relevance today not because it helps entrepreneurs better fulfill their personal needs but because of the economic function of the new ventures. More than increasing national income by creating new jobs, entrepreneurship acts as a positive force in economic growth by serving as the bridge between innovation and application. While the government gives great support to basic and applied research, there has not been great success in translating the technological innovations to products or services. While intrapreneurship offers the promise of a marriage of research capabilities with the business skills one would expect from a large corporation, the results so far in many companies have been unspectacular. This leaves the entrepreneur, who frequently lacks both technical and business skills, to serve as the major link in the process of economic growth and revitalization. The study of entrepreneurship and the education of potential entrepreneurs are essential parts of any attempt to strengthen this link so essential to our economic well-being.

2

Self-Assessment and the Entrepreneurial Process

CHAPTER OBJECTIVES

1. To identify the general characteristics of an entrepreneur.

2. To explain the aspects of the entrepreneurial process.

3. To explain the differences between the entrepreneurial and managerial domains on five key business dimensions.

4. To discuss the aspects of an entrepreneurial career and entrepreneur's education.

FRANK PHILLIPS

Frank Phillips, the first of nine children, was born November 28, 1873, in Greeley County, Nebraska, to Lucinda and Judge Lewis Franklin Phillips. The Phillipses were farmers in an area largely populated by Crow and Blackfoot Indians. In the summer of 1874, the family's Nebraska farm was ravaged by grasshoppers and, penniless, they moved to Creston, Iowa, to start life over.

As a young boy, Frank displayed an enterprising spirit. After he finished his assigned chores on the farm, he would hire himself out to area farmers, digging potatoes at 10 cents a day. Although the added work left Frank little time for playing games and other activities enjoyed by youngsters his age, he always had more pocket money than any of his friends.

On one of their family trips, young Frank spotted a town barber wearing flashy striped pants that were popular during the period. Frank recalls: "I made up my mind that I wanted to earn enough money so that I could afford to wear striped pants even on weekdays."

At the age of fourteen, Frank became a barber's apprentice. A hard-working quick learner with an engaging personality, he was soon one of the city's most popular barbers and several years later bought his own barber shop. Since barber shops also served as informal town meeting places, Frank stocked cigars and other tobacco products and manufactured a hair tonic called "Mountain Sage." The items sold well and the experience helped Frank develop a basic marketing principle he would later apply to his service station business—the value of catering to customers' wants and needs. Later, each Phillips gas station would carry a complete line of automotive accessories and specialties. In addition, Frank Phillips made the barbers who worked in his shop salesmen by giving them commissions on new customers. These efforts helped Frank Phillips become owner of all three barber shops in the town just 10 years after becoming an apprentice barber.

In 1897, Phillips married Jane Gibson, the daughter of a wealthy banker, sold his three barber shops, and began selling bonds in the New England states and the Chicago area for his father-in-law. On one trip in 1903, he learned about the possibilities of oil exploration in Indian territory. While Phillips, bankrolled by his father-in-law, organized the Anchor Oil and Gas Company in Bartlesville, Oklahoma, his younger brother sold shares of stock in the new company to increase operational revenues. Although the first three wells were unsuccessful, the fourth well, the Anna Anderson (which was to have been their last attempt if unsuccessful) was a huge gusher. Due to the success of the Anna Anderson and subsequent drilling projects, the Anchor Oil and Gas Company prospered.

Frank and his brother sold their interest in Anchor to turn their attention to new ventures, such as the banking industry. In 1906, they founded the Citizen's Bank and Trust with a capital investment of $50,000 and three years later purchased one of their rivals—the Bartlesville National Bank—and consolidated the two banks into the Bartlesville National Bank. During these early banking days, the Phillips brothers organized and promoted drilling ventures, most of which were sold or dissolved within a short time. As Frank was considering getting out of the oil business entirely and establishing a chain of banks throughout the Midwest, the United States entered World War I. Skyrocketing oil prices—from less than 40 cents a barrel to more than one dollar—changed Frank's perspective on the future of the oil industry. In the spring of 1917, 43-year-old Frank Phillips and his brother consolidated all their individual oil holdings into the Phillips Petroleum Company. This consolidation gave the company assets of approximately $3 million, 27 employees, and an array of leases, producing wells, and equipment scattered throughout Oklahoma and Kansas.

Within a few years the new organization began to soar. One key to Phillips's early success was the company's ability to attract investors and obtain loans. While the oil business at that time was considered by many to be only slightly less risky than gambling, Phillips was able to convince investors (including conservative Eastern bankers) otherwise. Making frequent trips to Chicago and New York, he spent as much time in bankers' offices as in the oil fields. Phillips knew firsthand how bankers operated; he knew the information they required and the information they should not get. On several investor trips to his Oklahoma oil fields, Phillips would often "stage" a gusher for the somewhat naive investors—a sight that rarely failed to impress the intended parties.

Needless to say, the Phillips Petroleum Company grew and prospered into one of the largest corporations in the oil industry. There are numerous reasons why Frank Phillips became a successful entrepreneur. Certainly marrying into a wealthy family is one of them, as is luck. However, for Phillips to achieve what he did, he had to have something else: He had a vision of what was and would happen, he knew how to sell himself and his ideas, and he recognized his strengths and weaknesses and hired talent in areas in which he was lacking.

The various entrepreneurial events and stages in the life of Frank Phillips suggest several questions that each potential entrepreneur must answer. These are reflected in the following two quotes of successful entrepreneurs:

> My father started and operated his own business. He was so excited about the venture and provided such a strong role model I never even considered working for anyone else. He also said that you can't really make money or be satisfied unless you are your own boss.

Why did I start my own business? Because I was a professional with experience and I wanted to be independent. Also, there was a market need for my product. There are times, however, I wonder why I did.

Like Frank Phillips did, many other entrepreneurs and future entrepreneurs frequently ask themselves: Am I really an entrepreneur? Do I have what it takes to be a success? Do I have sufficient background and experience to start and manage a new venture? As enticing as the thought of starting and owning a business may be, the problems and pitfalls inherent in the process are as legendary as the success stories. The fact remains that more new business ventures fail than succeed. To be one of the few successful entrepreneurs requires more than just hard work and luck. It requires a hard, honest assessment of both the prospective business viability and, perhaps even more important, your own strengths and weaknesses.

WHO SHOULD START HIS OR HER OWN BUSINESS?

Each day, thousands of individuals ask the difficult question, "Should I start my own business?" When queried, 85 percent of the populace said they would like to be in business for themselves. The driving force behind this desire to start a new venture is the desire to be one's own boss, to be independent. Since there is no definitive measurement that allows an individual to determine if he or she can be a successful entrepreneur, each individual should carefully appraise his or her situation through several different methods and self-assessment models. One way to determine if you have what it takes to be an entrepreneur is to fill out the questionnaire in Table 2–1 and check the answers at the end of this chapter. Keep in mind that the answers develop an average profile of an entrepreneur. There are many exceptions and there is no such person as a typical entrepreneur.

According to the Small Business Administration, the creation of a new business is very risky, with over 1,000 small business firms, most of them less than five years old, failing each day. To help evaluate whether you have some of the abilities necessary to avoid this high failure rate and be a successful entrepreneur, take the entrepreneur Assessment Quiz in Table 2–2 before reading further. Note that this quiz has not been validated statistically. If you score well, however, you may have the ability to be a successful entrepreneur. If you do not, do not be discouraged. Many entrepreneurs describe passion for the idea and the desire to succeed as the most important ingredients for success.

After you have completed this quiz in Table 2–2, count the number of Yes answers. Give yourself one point for each Yes. If you scored above 17 points, you have the drive to be an entrepreneur: the desire, energy, and adaptability to

---

TABLE 2–1   Characteristics of an Entrepreneur

---

1. An entrepreneur is most commonly the _____ child in the family.
   - a. oldest
   - b. middle
   - c. youngest
   - d. doesn't matter

2. An entrepreneur is most commonly:
   - a. married
   - b. single
   - c. widowed
   - d. divorced

3. An entrepreneur is most typically a:
   - a. man
   - b. woman
   - c. either

4. An individual usually begins his or her first significant entrepreneurial business enterprise at which age?
   - a. teens
   - b. twenties
   - c. thirties
   - d. forties
   - e. fifties

5. Usually an individual's entrepreneurial tendency first appears evident in his or her:
   - a. teens
   - b. twenties
   - c. thirties
   - d. forties
   - e. fifties

6. Typically, an entrepreneur has achieved the following educational attainment by the time the *first significant* business venture begins:
   - a. less than high school
   - b. high school diploma
   - c. bachelor's degree
   - d. master's degree
   - e. doctor's degree

7. An entrepreneur's primary motivation for starting a business is:
   - a. to make money
   - b. to be independent
   - c. to be famous
   - d. to create job security
   - e. to be powerful

8. The primary motivation for the entrepreneur's high ego and need for achievement is based upon a relationship with:
   - a. spouse
   - b. mother
   - c. father
   - d. children

9. To be successful in an entrepreneurial venture you need:
   - a. money
   - b. luck
   - c. hard work
   - d. good idea
   - e. all of the above

10. Entrepreneurs and venture capitalists:
    - a. get along well
    - b. are the best of friends
    - c. are cordial friends
    - d. are in conflict

11. A successful entrepreneur relies on which of the following for critical management advice:
    - a. internal management team
    - b. external management professionals
    - c. financial sources
    - d. no one

12. Entrepreneurs are best as:
    - a. managers
    - b. venture capitalists
    - c. planners
    - d. doers

TABLE 2–1 *(concluded)*

---

13. Entrepreneurs are:
    a. high-risk-takers (big gamblers)
    b. moderate-risk-takers (realistic gamblers
    c. small-risk-takers (take few chances)
    d. doesn't matter

14. Entrepreneurs:
    a. are the life of a party
    b. are bores at a cocktail party
    c. will never go to parties
    d. just fit into the crowd at a party

15. Entrepreneurs tend to "fall in love" with:
    a. new ideas
    b. new employees
    c. new manufacturing ideas
    d. new financial plans
    e. all of the above

16. Entrepreneurs typically form:
    a. service businesses
    b. manufacturing companies
    c. financial companies
    d. construction companies
    e. a variety of ventures

Source: This questionnaire is a modified version of one found in Robert D. Hisrich and Candida G. Brush, *The Woman Entrepreneur: Starting, Planning, and Financing a Successful New Business* (Lexington, MA: Lexington Books, 1986).

TABLE 2–2 Entrepreneur Assessment Quiz

---

1. Can you start a project and see it through to completion in spite of a myriad of obstacles?____Yes____No

2. Can you make a decision on a matter and then stick to the decision even when challenged? ____Yes ____No

3. Do you like to be in charge and be responsible? ____Yes ____No

4. Do other people you deal with respect and trust you?
   ____Yes ____No

5. Are you in good physical health? ____Yes ____No

6. Are you willing to work long hours with little immediate compensation?
   ____Yes ____No

7. Do you like meeting and dealing with people? ____Yes ____No

8. Can you communicate effectively and persuade people to go along with your dream? ____Yes ____No

9. Do others easily understand your concepts and ideas?
   ____Yes ____No

10. Have you had extensive experience in the type of business you wish to start?
    ____Yes ____No

11. Do you know the mechanics and forms of running a business (tax records, payroll records, income statements, balance sheets)?
    ____Yes ____No

12. Is there a need in your geographic area for the product or service you are intending to market? ____Yes ____No

---

TABLE 2–2   *(concluded)*

---

13. Do you have skills in marketing and/or finance? ____Yes ____No

14. Are other firms in your industrial classification doing well in your geographic area? ____Yes ____No

15. Do you have a location in mind for your business? ____Yes ____No

16. Do you have enough financial backing for the first year of operations? ____Yes ____No

17. Do you have enough money to fund the start-up of your business or have access to it through family or friends? ____Yes ____No

18. Do you know the suppliers necessary for your business to succeed? ____Yes ____No

19. Do you know individuals who have the talents and expertise you lack? ____Yes ____No

20. Do you really want to start this business more than anything else? ____Yes ____No

---

make a viable business venture a success. However, make sure any business venture you are contemplating is a good one.

If you scored from 13 to 17 points, your entrepreneurial drive is not as apparent. While you may definitely have the ability to be an entrepreneur, make sure that you can accept all the problems and headaches that accompany the joy of being your own boss.

If you scored below 13 points, your entrepreneurial drive is even less apparent. Even though most people say they want to be entrepreneurs, in reality many of them actually prefer to work for someone else.

Regardless of your score, take time to develop and gain experience in your present position while evaluating your real interests and desires before you actually become involved in the entrepreneurial process. Again, keep in mind that the quiz is not a scientifically validated indicator of entrepreneurial drive. Such an instrument has not yet been developed.

THE ENTREPRENEURIAL PROCESS

Perhaps the decision on whether to start your own business is best considered in light of an understanding of the entrepreneurial process.[1] The entrepreneurial process involves more than just problem solving in a typical management position. An entrepreneur must find, evaluate, and develop opportunities by overcoming the strong forces that resist the creation of something new. The actual

---

[1] A highly developed version of this process can be found in Howard H. Stevenson, Michael J. Roberts, and H. Irving Grousbeck, *New Business Ventures and the Entrepreneur* (Homewood, IL.: Richard D. Irwin, 1985), pp. 16–23.

TABLE 2–3   Aspects of the Entrepreneurial Process

Identify and Evaluate the Opportunity	*Develop Business Plan*	*Resources Required*	*Manage the Enterprise*
Creation and length of opportunity	Characteristics and size of market segment	Existing resources of entrepreneur	Management style and structure
Real and perceived value of opportunity	Market plan	Resource gaps and available supplies	Key variables for success
Risks and returns of opportunity	Production requirements	Access to needed resources	Identify problems and potential problems
Opportunity versus personal skills and goals	Financial plan and requirements		Implement control systems
Competitive situation	Form of organization		
	Positioning and strategy for entry		

process itself has four distinct phases: (1) identify and evaluate the opportunity; (2) develop the business plan; (3) determine the resources required; and (4) manage the resulting enterprise created (see Table 2–3). While these phases proceed progressively, none is dealt with in isolation or is totally completed before working on factors in a sequential phase. For example, to successfully identify and evaluate an opportunity (phase 1), an entrepreneur must have in mind the type of business desired (phase 4).

Identifying and Evaluating the Opportunity

Identifying and evaluating a good opportunity is a most difficult task. Most good business opportunities do not suddenly appear but rather result from an entrepreneur being alert to possibilities or, in some cases, by establishing mechanisms to identify potential opportunities. For example, one entrepreneur asks at every cocktail party if anyone is using a product that does not adequately fulfill its intended purpose. This person is constantly looking for a need and opportunity to create a better product. Another entrepreneur always monitors the play and toys of her nieces and nephews. This is her way of looking for any unique toy product niche for a new venture.

Although most entrepreneurs do not have formal mechanisms for identifying business opportunities, some sources are often fruitful: consumers and business associates, members of the distribution system, and technical people. Often, consumers such as business associates purchasing products to fit a certain lifestyle are the best source of ideas for a new venture. How many times have you heard someone comment: "If only there was a product that would. . . ." This comment occasionally results in the creation of a new business. One entrepreneur's evaluation of why so many business executives were complaining about the lack of good technical writing and word-processing services resulted in her creating her own business venture to fill this need. Her technical writing service grew to 10 employees in just two years.

On the basis of their close contact with the end-user, channel members of the distribution system also see product needs. One entrepreneur started a college bookstore after hearing all the students complain about the high cost of books and the lack of service provided by the only bookstore on campus. Many other entrepreneurs have identified business opportunities through a discussion with a retailer, wholesaler, or manufacturer's representative.

Finally, technically oriented individuals often conceptualize business opportunities when working on other projects. One entrepreneur's business resulted from seeing the application of a plastic resin compound in pallets while developing the resin application in another totally unrelated area—its use in casket moldings.

Whether the opportunity is identified from consumers, business associates, channel members, or technical people, each opportunity must be carefully screened and evaluated. This evaluation of the opportunity is perhaps the most critical element of the entrepreneurial process because it allows the entrepreneur to determine whether the specific product or service has the returns needed for the resources required. As indicated in Table 2–3, this evaluation process involves looking at the creation and length of the opportunity; its real and perceived value; its risks and returns; its fit with the personal skills and goals of the entrepreneur; and its differential advantage in the competitive environment.

It is important for the entrepreneur to understand the factor causing the opportunity. Is it technological change, market shift, government regulation, or competition? Each of these factors and the resulting opportunity has a different market size and time dimension.

The market size and the length of the **window of opportunity** are the primary bases for determining risks and rewards. The risks reflect the market, competition, technology, and amount of capital involved. The amount of capital forms the basis for the return and rewards. The methodology for evaluating risks and rewards, the focus of Chapters 7 and 9, frequently indicates that an opportunity does not offer either a financial or personal nonfinancial reward commensurate with the risks involved. The return and reward of the particular opportunity should be viewed in light of any possible subsequent opportunities as well. One company, which delivered bark mulch to residential and commercial users for decoration around the base of trees and shrubs, added loam and shells to their product line. These products were sold to the same customer base using the same distribution (delivery) system. Follow-on products become very important when expanding or diversifying in a particular channel. A distribution channel such as K mart, Caldors, or Target prefers to do business with multiproduct rather than single-product firms.

Finally, the opportunity must fit the personal skills and goals of the entrepreneur. It is critically important that the entrepreneur be able to put forth all the time and effort required to make the venture succeed. Although many entrepreneurs feel that the desire can be developed along with the venture, typically it does not materialize, dooming the venture to failure. An entrepreneur must believe in the opportunity so much that everything will be sacrificed so that the resulting organization will succeed.

Develop a Business Plan

A good **business plan** must be developed in order to exploit the opportunity defined. This is perhaps the most difficult phase of the entrepreneurial process. An entrepreneur usually has never prepared a business plan and often does not have the resources available to do a good job. While the preparation of the business plan is covered in separate chapters (Chapters 5 to 8), it is important to understand the basic issues involved: the characteristics and size of the market segment, the market plan, the production requirements, the financial plan, the organization plan, and the financial requirements. A good business plan is not only important in developing the opportunity but is also essential in determining the resources required, obtaining those resources, and successfully managing the resulting venture.

Resources Required

The resources needed for the opportunity must be assessed. This process starts with an appraisal of the entrepreneur's present resources. Any resources that are critical must be distinguished from those that are just helpful. Care must be taken not to underestimate the amount and variety of resources needed. The downside risks associated with insufficient resources should also be assessed.

Acquiring the needed resources in a timely manner, while giving up as little control as possible, is the next and indeed a most difficult step in the entrepreneurial process. An entrepreneur should strive to maintain as large an ownership position as possible, particularly in the start-up financing stage. As the business develops, more funds will probably be needed, requiring more ownership to be relinquished. Every entrepreneur should give up each piece of the venture only after every other alternative has been explored. Not only must alternative suppliers of these resources be identified but also their needs and desires. By understanding resource supplier needs, the entrepreneur can structure a deal that enables the resources to be acquired at the lowest possible cost and loss of control.

Manage the Enterprise

After the resources are acquired the entrepreneur must put them into action through implementation of the business plan. He or she must also deal with the operational problems of the growing enterprise. This involves implementing a management style and structure, as well as determining the key variables for success (see Table 2–3). Problem areas must be identified and carefully monitored through an implemented control system. Some entrepreneurs have difficulty managing and enlarging the venture they created—one difference between entrepreneurial and managerial decision making.

MANAGERIAL VERSUS ENTREPRENEURIAL DECISION MAKING

The difference between the entrepreneurial and managerial styles of five key business dimensions—strategic orientation, commitment to opportunity, commitment of resources, control of resources, and management structure—is indicated in Table 2–4.[2]

Strategic Orientation

The entrepreneur's strategic orientation depends on his or her perception of the opportunity. This orientation is most important when other opportunities have diminishing returns accompanied by rapid changes in technology, consumer economies, social values, or political rules. When the use of planning systems and measuring performance to control current resources is the strategic orientation, there is more pressure for the administrative domain to be operant, as is the case with many large multinational organizations.

Commitment to Opportunity

In terms of the commitment to opportunity, the second key business dimension, the two domains vary greatly in terms of the length of this commitment. The entrepreneurial domain pressured by the need for action, short decision windows, willingness to assume risk, and few decision constituencies has a short time span in terms of opportunity commitment. While the administrative domain is slow to act on an opportunity, once action is taken the commitment is for a long time span, too long in some instances. There are often no mechanisms in place to stop and reevaluate an initial resource commitment.

Commitment of Resources

An entrepreneur is used to having resources committed at periodic intervals, often based on certain tasks or objectives being reached. These resources, often acquired from others, are usually difficult to obtain, forcing the entrepreneur to

---

[2]The differences are fully delineated in Howard H. Stevenson and William A. Sahlman, "Importance of Entrepreneurship in Economic Development," in *Entrepreneurship, Intrapreneurship, and Venture Capital,* ed. Robert D. Hisrich (Lexington, MA: Lexington Books, 1986), pp. 1–26.

achieve significant milestones using very few resources. This multistage commitment allows the resource providers (such as venture capitalists) to have as small an exposure as possible at each stage of business development and to constantly monitor the track record being established. While funding may also be in stages, the commitment of the resources is for the total amount needed in the administrative domain. Administratively oriented individuals respond to the source of the rewards offered and receive personal rewards by effectively administering the resources under their control.

Control of Resources

Control of the resources follows a similar pattern. Since the administrator is rewarded by effective resource administration, there is often a drive to own or accumulate as many resources as possible. The pressures of power, status, and financial rewards cause the administrator to avoid rental or other periodic use of the resource. The opposite is true for the entrepreneur who, under the pressures of limited resources, risk of obsolescence, need for flexibility, and the risks involved, strives to rent or achieve periodic use of the resources on an as-needed basis.

Management Structure

The final key business dimension—management structure—also diverges significantly between the two domains. In the administrative domain, the organizational structure is formalized and hierarchical in nature because of the need for clearly defined lines of authority and responsibility based on management theory and the reward system. The entrepreneur, true to his or her desire for independence, employs a flat organizational structure with informal networks throughout.

ENTREPRENEURIAL CAREERS

What causes an individual to take all the social, psychological, and financial risks associated with starting a new venture? While there has not been a focus on this aspect of entrepreneurship in the past, since 1985 there has been an increased interest in entrepreneurial careers and education. This increased interest has been fostered by such factors as the recognition that small firms play a major role in job creation and innovation; an increased media coverage of entrepreneurs; an understanding that entrepreneurs are not just the ones heralded in the media but the thousands upon thousands of small, cottage companies as well; the feeling that most large organizational structures do not provide an environment for self-actualization; the shift in women being active participants in the

TABLE 2-4 A Comparison of the Entrepreneurial and Administrative Domains

Entrepreneurial Domain Pressures toward This Side	Key Business Dimension	Administrative Domain Pressures toward This Side
Diminishing opportunity streams Rapidly changing: Technology Consumer economics Social values Political rules	Strategic Orientation Driven by perception of opportunity ⟶ ⟵ Driven by resources currently controlled	Social contracts Performance measurement criteria Planning systems and cycle
Action orientation Short decision windows Risk management Limited decision constituencies	Commitment to Opportunity Revolutionary with short duration ⟶ ⟵ Evolutionary of long duration	Acknowledgment of multiple constituencies Negotiation of strategy Risk reduction Management of fit
Lack of predictable resource needs Lack of long-term control Social need for more opportunity per resource unit International pressure for more efficient resource use	Commitment of Resources Multistaged with minimal exposure at each stage ⟶ ⟵ Single-staged with complete commitment upon decision	Personal risk reduction Incentive compensation Managerial turnover Capital allocation systems Formal planning systems

		Control of Resources	Ownership or employment of required resources	Power, status, and financial rewards Coordination Efficiency measures Inertia and cost of change Industry structures
Increased resource Long resource life compared to need Risk of obsolescence Risk inherent in any new venture Inflexibility of permanent commitment to resources	Episodic use or rent of required resources			
Coordination of key noncontrolled resources Challenge to legitimacy of owners' control Employees' desire for independence	Flat with multiple informal networks	Management Structure	Formalized hierarchy	Need for clearly defined authority and responsibility Organizational culture Reward systems Management theory

Source: Adapted from Howard H. Stevenson and William A. Sahlman, "Importance of Entrepreneurship in Economic Development," in *Entrepreneurship, Intrapreneurship, and Venture Capital: The Foundations of Economic Renaissance*, ed. Robert D. Hisrich (Lexington, MA: Lexington Books, 1986), pp. 18–25.

TABLE 2–5 A Framework for an Entrepreneur's Career Development

Life Space Areas	←————————————TIME————————————→		
	Childhood	*Earlier Adulthood*	*Present Adulthood*
Work/Occupation	Education and child-hood work experi-ence I	Employment history IV	Current work situation VII
Individual/Personal	Childhood influences on personality, val-ues, and interests II	Adult development history V	Individual's current perspective VIII
Nonwork/Family	Childhood family en-vironment III	Adult family/nonwork history VI	Current family/non-work situation IX

Source: Adapted from Donald D. Bowen and Robert D. Hisrich, "The Female Entrepreneur: A Career Development Perspective," *The Academy of Management Review,* 2 (April 1986), pp. 393–407.

work force, with more than 50 percent of families having two incomes; and women entrepreneurs forming new ventures at three times the rate of men.

Yet, in spite of this increase, most people, even entrepreneurs, do not think of entrepreneurship as a career. A conceptual model for understanding entrepreneurial careers, indicated in Table 2–5, views the career stages as dynamic ones, with each stage reflecting and interacting with other stages and events in the individual's life—past, present, and future. This **life-cycle approach** conceptualizes entrepreneurial careers in nine major categories: educational environment, the individual's personality, childhood family environment, employment history, adult development history, adult nonwork history, current work situation, the individual's current perspective, and the current family situation.[3]

While it has been generally felt that entrepreneurs are less educated than the general population, it is clear that this is more myth than truth. Studies have found entrepreneurs overall and female entrepreneurs in particular to be far more educated than the general populace.[4] However, the type and quality of the education received sometimes does not produce specific skills needed in the venture creation and management process. Female entrepreneurs, who frequently suffer from a math anxiety, appear to be at more of a disadvantage than male entrepre-

---

[3]Each of these categories is fully developed, particularly for the female entrepreneur, in Donald D. Bowen and Robert D. Hisrich, "The Female Entrepreneur: A Career Development Perspective," *Academy of Management Review* 2 (April 1986), pp. 393–407; and James D. Brodzinski, Robert F. Sherer, and Frank A. Wiebe, "Entrepreneur Career Selection and Gender: A Socialization Approach," *Journal of Small Business Management* 28, pp. 37–43.

[4]See Robert D. Hisrich and Candida G. Brush, *The Woman Entrepreneur: Starting, Financing, and Managing a Successful New Business* (Lexington, MA: Lexington Books, 1986).

neurs in this respect, with women entrepreneurs frequently majoring in non-business and nonengineering disciplines.

Childhood influences have also been explored, particularly in the area of values and the individual's personality. The most frequently researched personality traits are need for achievement, locus of control, risk taking, and gender identity. Since the personality traits are more thoroughly discussed in Chapter 3, it is sufficient here to indicate that few firm conclusions can be drawn from all the research on universal personality traits of entrepreneurs.

The research on childhood family environment of the entrepreneur has had more definitive results. Entrepreneurs tend to have self-employed fathers, many of whom are entrepreneurs themselves. Many also have entrepreneurial mothers. The family, particularly the father or mother, plays an important role in establishing the desirability and credibility of entrepreneurship as a career path.

Employment history has an impact on entrepreneurial careers in both a positive and negative sense. On the positive side, entrepreneurs tend to have a higher probability of success when the venture created is in their fields of work experience. This success rate makes the providers of risk capital particularly concerned when this work experience is not present. Negative displacement, such as dissatisfaction with various aspects of one's job, being fired or demoted, being transferred to an undesirable location, or having one's spouse take a new position in a new geographic area are some of the major factors encouraging entrepreneurship, not only in the United States but in other cultures as well.

Although no definitive research has been done on adult development history for entrepreneurs, it appears that this would also affect entrepreneurial careers. This should be so particularly for women since they tend to start their businesses at a later stage in life than men, after having experienced significantly more job frustration.

There is a similar lack of data on adult family/nonwork history. Although there is some information on the female entrepreneurs' marital and family situations, the data available adds little to our understanding of entrepreneurial career paths.

On the other hand, the impact of the current work situation has received considerably more research attention. Entrepreneurs are known for their strong work values and aspirations, their long work hours, and a dominant management style. Entrepreneurs tend to fall in love with the organization and will sacrifice almost anything in order for the established organization to survive. This desire is reflected in the individual entrepreneur's current career perspective and family/nonwork situation. The new venture usually takes the highest priority in life and is the source of the entrepreneur's self-esteem and life goal.

ENTREPRENEURIAL EDUCATION

The educational ramifications of this lack of understanding of career paths are significant. While they are in college, few future entrepreneurs realize that they will pursue entrepreneurship as their major life goal. Even among the minority

---

TABLE 2–6 Selected Skills Needed through Entrepreneurship Education

---

1. Fact versus myth about entrepreneurship
2. Reality testing skills
3. Creativity skills
4. Ambiguity tolerance skills and attitudes
5. Opportunity identification skills
6. Venture evaluation skills
7. Venture start-up—action skills
8. Venture strategy skills
9. Career assessment skills
10. Environmental assessment skills
11. Ethical assessment skills
12. Deal-making skills
13. Contacts-networking skills
14. Harvesting skills

Source: Robert C. Ronstadt, "The Educated Entrepreneurs: A New Era of Entrepreneurial Education Is Beginning," *American Journal of Small Business* (Summer 1985), p. 16.

that do, relatively few individuals will start a business immediately after graduation, and even fewer will prepare for a new venture creation by working in a particular position or industry. This mandates that entrepreneurs continually supplement their education through books, trade journals, seminars, or taking courses in weak areas. Generally, skills that need to be acquired through seminars or courses include creativity, financing, control, opportunity identification, venture evaluation, and deal making. A list of the skills needed by most entrepreneurs is indicated in Table 2–6.

SUMMARY

There is more to a successful business than a good idea—there must be a good entrepreneur. Although the "ideal" entrepreneur can not be profiled, there are certain trends and norms that make a good model for the potential entrepreneur. Some of the characteristics and traits commonly found in successful entrepreneurs are examined in Table 2–2. In many respects, traits such as responsibility, tenacity, and the ability to think clearly under stress are more important to success than the product or service being offered. Knowledge of the product and the skills required to run a business are more easily attained.

The entrepreneurial process involves finding, evaluating, and developing opportunities for creating a new venture. Each step is important to the eventual success of the new firm, and each is closely related to the others. For example, before the opportunity identification stage can result in a meaningful search, the potential entrepreneur must have a general idea about the type of company desired. However, the resulting selection criteria employed cannot be too inflexible or a valuable idea may be excluded.

There are both formal and informal mechanisms for identifying business opportunities. Formal mechanisms generally operate within a more established company, thereby emphasizing growth through intrapreneurship. Most entrepreneurs use more informal sources for their ideas, such as being sensitive to the complaints and chance comments of friends and associates.

Once the opportunity is identified, the evaluation process begins. Basic to the screening process is the understanding of the factors creating the opportunity—technology, market change, competition, or changes in government regulations. From this base, the market size and time dimension associated with the idea, which give the necessary inputs to the risk/reward decision, can be estimated. It is important that the idea fit the personal skills and goals of the entrepreneur. Although skills can be developed, the desire to see the opportunity brought to fruition is equally necessary and usually impossible to create. In the process of evaluating an opportunity, the required resources should be clearly defined and obtained at the lowest possible cost.

Managing a new venture differs in many ways from managing an existing operation. Five key dimensions are listed and discussed: strategic orientation, commitment to opportunity, commitment of resources, control of resources, and management structure. The entrepreneurial venture presents the manager with a more ambiguous, more rapidly changing environment than the typical corporate manager faces. A distinctly different set of skills needs to be developed, either through the entrepreneurial experience or education.

Just as there is no distinct entrepreneurial personality profile, there is no specific entrepreneurial career path. A life-cycle approach, focusing on the interaction of past, present, and future events in the individual's life, is more appropriate to the experiences of entrepreneurs than a more conventional time-line career path. Education, personality, childhood family life, employment history, adult development history, adult nonwork history, current work situation, current perspective, and current family situations are all factors in determining the avenue through which an individual approaches entrepreneurship.

The education of potential entrepreneurs is a difficult task because of the lack of clear career patterns. Many potential entrepreneurs are not found in business or engineering schools, or do not know that they are going to be entrepreneurs in the future. The goal of an entrepreneurial studies curriculum should be to offer a program addressing entrepreneurship at different levels—personal assessment, idea generation or selection, and the business skills needed at various stages in the life of an entrepreneurial venture.

CHAPTER

3

Characteristics and Background of Entrepreneurs

CHAPTER OBJECTIVES

1. To identify the key entrepreneurial feelings.

2. To identify key elements in an entrepreneur's background.

3. To explain what motivates an entrepreneur.

4. To discuss the importance of role models and support systems.

5. To identify the similarities and differences between male and female entrepreneurs.

6. To explain the differences between inventors and entrepreneurs.

7. To identify some general entrepreneur profiles.

LILLIAN VERNON KATZ

Lillian Katz was born in Leipzig, Germany, in 1927 to parents she characterizes as hardworking and scrupulously honest. After living briefly in Holland, the family emigrated to the United States in 1937, when Lillian was 10 years old. She found the freedom of her New York City home exhilarating. The dominant figure in her early life was her father, a leather goods manufacturer, who instilled in Lillian the same characteristics of hard work and honesty that her mother possessed. He taught her that girls, no less than boys, could achieve any goal they wished in any field they chose. This unusual paternal guidance (particularly for those days) gave his young daughter confidence in herself and her dreams.

In 1949, after majoring in psychology at New York University for two years, she married Sam Hochberg. Two years later, at 24, she was pregnant with her first child. They were living in a three-room apartment in Mount Vernon on Sam's $75 per week earnings. Feeling they would need an additional $50 per week to support the new baby, Lillian decided to open her own business. Her father's influence on her early life left her with no doubts about her ability to succeed. Because she did not want a 9-to-5 job but something that could be run from her own home, Lillian chose mail order after considering several alternatives.

Using $2,000 of wedding gift money, she launched her venture—Vernon Specialties Company—which offered personalized leather handbags and belts designed by Lillian and made by her father. Her concept for the business was to offer by mail something personalized that could not be readily found at an affordable price. An advertisement in the September 1951 issue of *Seventeen* magazine, costing $495, generated $16,000 in orders in six weeks for the fledgling company. The resulting profits were used to purchase more ads and buy more handbags and belts. Lillian worked during the day in a loft rented from her father, and did the clerical work on her kitchen table at night. The line was soon expanded to include three colors of handbags and belts and personalized bookmarks costing $1. After the birth of her second son, David, she decided to include her own designs. Vernon Products was born.

Since the mid-1950s did not offer a positive environment for female entrepreneurs, Lillian confronted many obstacles. Many bankers would not even bother to talk to her, and neighbors felt she was not being a good mother because she left her sons with a nanny. However, Lillian overcame these problems, using her

AT&T stock as collateral for bank loans and managing her business around her children's schedules. While the nanny did the cleaning, cooking, and laundry, Lillian did the shopping, ran the house, and joined in car pooling. There were times, however, when motherhood took second place, such as one Christmas when she sent her children to her mother's for the holidays due to a backlog of orders. While regretting this instance, Lillian accepts it as part of the cost of success: "I wasn't burdened with the guilt many working mothers have, because being a working mother seemed normal."

In 1956, Sam closed his retail store and turned it into a warehouse for the Vernon Specialities mail-order business. The manufacturing part of the business was worth around $1 million and the mail-order division around $1 million. While the business thrived, the marriage did not; Sam and Lillian were divorced after 20 years of marriage. Lillian chose to retain the mail-order business, a decision that later proved to have been excellent.

A year after her divorce, Lillian married Robbie Katz, a professional engineer and businessman who ran his own Lucite manufacturing business. With both her children in college, Lillian could begin to really devote herself to the company, which grew from $1 million in sales in 1970 to $137 million in sales by 1986—her 35th anniversary in business—to $155 million in 1989.

In developing the company from a million to a multimillion dollar business, Lillian found it necessary to hire professional managers—veterans of large corporate cultures—some of whom were unable to make the timely decisions required in the smaller company's fast-paced competitive situation. This opportunity allowed Lillian to identify both the entrepreneurial process through which the company began and grew and the management process necessary to help it continue to grow: "If I've learned anything over the past 35 years, it is the importance of drawing from the best qualities of both the entrepreneur and the professional manager. These are truly the left and right sides of the business brain, and they must harmonize in a healthy corporation."

With the day-to-day business operations in the hands of competent managers, Lillian concentrates on finding the best products for her catalog. In this search, she travels approximately 16 weeks each year, personally approving every item listed in the catalog. An item usually will not be carried unless someone she knows would like it or use it. Lillian was one of the first to handle goods from mainland China, going there in the 1970s.

Even with the time required for selecting the items in the catalog, Lillian still is personally involved in every aspect of the company's operation. She signs checks, reviews and helps write copy, and approves the catalog photos. The copy accompanying the catalog items is renowned in the industry.

Today, Lillian's sons, David and Fred, are both involved in the company's management. Fred is executive vice president and chief operating officer, and David is director of public affairs. The Lillian Vernon Corporation has grown from an initial investment of $2,000 to a publicly traded company with 1989 sales of approximately $155 million—a profit of $11 million—and includes The

New Company, Inc., a wholesale division making brass items; Lillian Vernon International in Italy and Hong Kong; Lillian Vernon: The Store in New Rochelle, New York; and since May of 1988, a state-of-the-art fully automated 454,000-square-foot fulfillment center, including 123,552 square feet of warehouse space and a mainframe computer used for inventory control.

Lillian Katz adamantly supports other entrepreneurial efforts. Of the 1,500 suppliers of her catalog items, many are owned by fellow entrepreneurs. In a recent speech, she urged the financial community to take a risk on an entrepreneur: "You are investing in potential, which can pay tremendous dividends." She sits on the board of several charities and foundations and is a member of the Women's Forum and the Committee of 200, groups of the brightest "fast-track" female executives in the country.

The success of the company lies primarily in the dedication and hard work of Lillian Katz: "Hard work, long hours, and personal sacrifice are just some of the disciplines necessary to achieve this (success), but the end rewards are worth it!"

Lillian Katz exhibits one profile of an entrepreneur. Other entrepreneurs appearing in this book present different ones. Is there an exact entrepreneurial profile in terms of characteristics and background? This chapter addresses this question by looking at feelings on control, independence, and willingness to take risks; family, education, and occupational backgrounds; motivation; skills; male versus female entrepreneurs; entrepreneurs versus inventors; and general entrepreneurial profiles.

ENTREPRENEURIAL FEELINGS

Before considering the various characteristics and backgrounds of the typical entrepreneur, it should be emphasized that there are significant differences between individual entrepreneurs and any overall general profile established. There is really no such thing as a "true entrepreneurial profile." Entrepreneurs come from a variety of educational backgrounds, family situations, and work experiences. A potential entrepreneur may presently be a nurse, secretary, assembly-line worker, salesperson, mechanic, homemaker, manager, or engineer. A potential entrepreneur can be male or female.

Locus of Control

One concern people have when considering forming a new venture is whether they will be able to sustain the drive and energy required not only to overcome the inertia in forming something new but also to manage the new enterprise and

---

TABLE 3–1 Checklist for Feelings about Control

1. Do you often feel "That's just the way things are and there's nothing I can do about it"?	_____Yes	_____No
2. When things go right and are terrific for you, do you think "It's mostly luck!"?	_____Yes	_____No
3. Do you think you should go into business or do something with your time for pay because everything you read these days is urging you in that direction?	_____Yes	_____No
4. Do you know that if you decide to do something, you'll do it and nothing can stop you?	_____Yes	_____No
5. Even though it's scary to try something new, are you the kind who tries it?	_____Yes	_____No
6. Your friends, husband, and mother tell you that it's foolish of you to want a career. Have you listened to them and stayed home all these years?	_____Yes	_____No
7. Do you think it's important for everyone to like you?	_____Yes	_____No
8. When you do a good job, is your pleasure in a job well done satisfaction enough?	_____Yes	_____No
9. If you want something, do you ask for it rather than wait for someone to notice you and "just give it to you"?	_____Yes	_____No
10. Even though people tell you "it can't be done," do you have to find out for yourself?	_____Yes	_____No

Source: Robert D. Hisrich and Candida G. Brush, *The Woman Entrepreneur: Starting, Financing, and Managing a Successful New Business* (Lexington, MA.: Lexington Books, 1986), p. 6.

make it grow. Are you driven by an inner need to succeed and win? An initial assessment of this can be made by answering the 10 questions in Table 3–1. After answering these questions determine whether you are internally or externally driven by comparing your answers with the responses below. Answering Yes to questions 4, 5, 8, 9, and 10 indicates that you possess the internal control aspect of being an entrepreneur. Yes answers to questions 1, 2, 3, 6, and 7 indicate that you are more geared to external controls, which may inhibit your entrepreneurial tendencies and ability to sustain drive.

In evaluating these results and your internal-external control dimension, keep in mind that research is not conclusive about the role of locus of control in entrepreneurship. For example, only three of the nine research studies of Rotter's internality-externality (I-E) dimension of entrepreneurs depicted them as having a sense of control over their lives, that is, being internals. One study indicated that entrepreneurial intentions were associated with internality and another reported a positive correlation between career success and internality.[1] Two studies of entrepreneurs under stress had mixed results—some entrepreneurs under stress shifted toward greater internality while others shifted toward greater externality. Studies of 31 entrepreneurs in St. Louis indicated that more successful entrepreneurs were more internal and entrepreneurs overall were more internal than the general populace but not more than male managers.[2] While internal beliefs appear to differentiate entrepreneurs from the general public, they do not differentiate entrepreneurs from managers; both have an internality tendency.

Feelings about Independence and Need for Achievement

Closely related to this feeling of control is the **need for independence.** An entrepreneur is generally the type of person who needs to do things in his or her own way and time; each has a difficult time working for someone else. To evaluate your feelings on independence answer the questions in Table 3–2. After completing the questions, compare your answers to those below. Yes answers to questions 1, 4, 5, 8, 9, and 10 indicate that you do not have a strong need for independence.

Of a more controversial nature is the entrepreneur's **need for achievement.** McClelland's work on the need for achievement identified psychological characteristics present in entrepreneurs.[3] He specified three attributes from his overall theory of need for achievement (*n* Ach) as characteristics of entrepreneurs: (1) individual responsibility for solving problems, setting goals, and reaching these goals through their own efforts; (2) moderate risk taking as a function of skill, not chance; and (3) knowledge of results of decision/task accomplishment. McClelland's conclusion that a high *n* Ach leads individuals to engage in entrepreneurial behavior sparked several studies, the results of which are summarized in Table 3–3. The results are inconclusive, as some studies indicate that there is

---

[1]For a review of these nine studies, see D. E. Jennings and C. P. Zietham, "Locus of Control: A Review and Directions for Entrepreneurial Research," *Proceedings* of the 43rd Annual Meeting of the Academy of Management (April 1983), pp. 417–21. A discussion of the concept itself can be found in J. B. Rotter, "Generalized Expectancies for Internal versus External Control of Reinforcement," *Psychological Monographs:* General and Applied Number 80, 1966.

[2]See Robert H. Brockhaus, "Psychological and Environmental Factors Which Distinguish the Successful from the Unsuccessful Entrepreneur," *Proceedings* of the 40th Annual Meeting of the Academy of Management (August 1980), pp. 368–72 and Robert H. Brockhaus and W. R. Nord, "An Exploration of Factors Affecting the Entrepreneurial Decisions: Personal Characteristics versus Environmental Conditions," *Proceedings* of the 40th Annual Meeting of the Academy of Management (August 1979), pp. 364–68.

[3]This is developed in three works of David McClelland: *The Achieving Society* (Princeton, N.J.: Van Nostrand Publishing Co., 1961); "Business Drive and National Achievement," *Harvard Business Review* 40 (July-August 1962): pp. 99–112; and "Achievement Motivation Can Be Developed," *Harvard Business Review* 43 (November-December 1965), pp. 6–24.

TABLE 3–2   Checklist for Feelings about Independence

1. I hate to go shopping for clothes alone.	_____Yes	_____No
2. If my friends won't go to a movie I want to see, I'll go by myself.	_____Yes	_____No
3. I want to be financially independent.	_____Yes	_____No
4. I often need to ask other people's opinions before I decide on important things.	_____Yes	_____No
5. I'd rather have other people decide where to go on a social evening out.	_____Yes	_____No
6. When I know I'm in charge, I don't apologize, I just do what has to be done.	_____Yes	_____No
7. I'll speak up for an unpopular cause if I believe in it.	_____Yes	_____No
8. I'm afraid to be different.	_____Yes	_____No
9. I want the approval of others.	_____Yes	_____No
10. I usually wait for people to call me to go places, rather than intrude on them.	_____Yes	_____No

Source: Robert D. Hisrich and Candida G. Brush, *The Woman Entrepreneur: Starting, Financing, and Managing a Successful New Business* (Lexington, MA.: Lexington Books, 1986), p. 7.

---

a relationship between *n* Ach and entrepreneurs, while others do not. Perhaps a modification of McClelland's concept may result in a better understanding of the relationship between achievement and entrepreneurship.[4]

Risk Taking

Virtually all recent definitions of an entrepreneur indicate a risk-taking component. Indeed, risk taking, whether financial, social, or psychological, is a part of the entrepreneurial process. You can assess your risk-taking behavior by answering the questions in Table 3–4 and then comparing your responses to those below. If you answered Yes to questions 2, 5, and 9, you may need to develop a greater willingness to take risks. Many studies of risk taking in entrepreneurship have focused on the component of general risk-taking propensity, the results of which are summarized in Table 3–5. Since no conclusive causal relationship has been determined, it appears that risk-taking propensity may not be a distinguishing characteristic of entrepreneurs. While this may be a function of the research instrument (Kogan-Wallach CDQ is the research instrument predominantly used), little can still be concluded from the results of the empirical research on the risk-taking propensities of entrepreneurs of either sex.

---

[4]A good discussion of some alternative measurements is found in Alan L. Carsrud and Kenneth W. Olm, "The Success of Male and Female Entrepreneurs: A Comparative Analysis," in *Managing Take-Off in Fast Growth Firms*, Ray M. Smilor and Robert L. Kuhn, eds. (New York: Praeger Publishers, 1986), pp. 147–62.

TABLE 3–3 Need for Achievement Research

Researcher	Instrument	Comparative	Results
McClelland (1961–1965)	TAT	Longitudinal	High *n* Ach associated with entrepreneurs
Schrage (1965)	McClelland's TAT	None	Subjects did not rank consistenly high in *n* Ach
Wainer and Rubin (1969)	McClelland's TAT	None	High *n* Ach associated with high performance
Hornaday and Bunker (1970)	EPPS	Male norms	Entrepreneurs scored considerably higher than norms
Hornaday and Aboud (1971)	EPPS	Male norms	Entrepreneurs scored significantly higher than norms
Komives (1972)	Gordon's SIV	Norms	Entrepreneurs high in achievement and decisiveness categories
DeCarlo and Lyons (1979)	EPPS	Female norms	Entrepreneurs scored significantly higher than norms
Sexton and Bowman (1983)	PRF-E	Business/nonbusiness students	Entrepreneurship students did not score significantly different
Hull, Bosley, and Udell (1980)	Lynn's achievement motivation questionnaire	Business school alumni	*n* Ach did not distinguish between high and low likelihood of starting a business
Smith and Miner (1984)	Miner sentence completion questionnaire	Fast-growth and slow-growth entrepreneurs/nonentrepreneurs	Successful entrepreneurs (fast-growth) scored significantly higher on *n* Ach motives

Source: Adapted from Donald Sexton and Nancy Bowman, "Personality Inventory for Potential Entrepreneurs: Evaluation of a Modified JPI/PRF-E Test Instrument," *Proceedings* 1985 Entrepreneurship Research Conference, pp. 513–29.

TABLE 3–4 Checklist for Willingness to Take Risks

1. Can you take risks with money, that is, invest, and not know the outcome? _____Yes _____No
2. Do you take an umbrella with you every time you travel? A hot water bottle? A thermometer? _____Yes _____No
3. If you're frightened of something, will you try to conquer the fear? _____Yes _____No
4. Do you like trying new food, new places, and totally new experiences? _____Yes _____No
5. Do you need to know the answer before you'll ask the question? _____Yes _____No
6. Have you taken a risk in the last six months? _____Yes _____No

---

TABLE 3–4 *(concluded)*

---

7. Can you walk up to a total stranger and
   strike up a conversation? _____Yes _____No

8. Have you ever intentionally traveled an
   unfamiliar route? _____Yes _____No

9. Do you need to know that it's been done
   already before you're willing to try it? _____Yes _____No

10. Have you ever gone on a blind date? _____Yes _____No

Source: Robert D. Hisrich and Candida G. Brush, *The Woman Entrepreneur: Starting, Financing, and Managing a Successful New Business* (Lexington, MA.: Lexington Books, 1986), p. 7.

ENTREPRENEUR BACKGROUND AND CHARACTERISTICS

Although many aspects of an entrepreneur's background have been explored, only a few have differentiated the entrepreneur from the general populace or managers. The background areas explored include childhood family environment, education, personal values, age, and work history.

Childhood Family Environment

Specific topics in the family environment of the entrepreneur researched include **birth order,** parent's occupation and **social status,** and relationship with parents. The impact of birth order has had conflicting research results since Hennig and Jardim found that female executives tend to be the firstborn.[5] Being the firstborn or an only child is postulated to result in the child receiving special attention and thereby developing more self-confidence. For example, in a national sample of 408 female entrepreneurs, Hisrich and Brush found 50 percent to be firstborn.[6] However, in many studies of male and female entrepreneurs the firstborn effect has not been present. Since the relationship to entrepreneurship has been only weakly demonstrated, further research on the firstborn effect is needed to evaluate if it really does have an effect on an individual's becoming an entrepreneur.[7]

---

[5]M. Henning and A. Jardim, *The Managerial Woman* (Garden City, NY: Anchor Press/Doubleday, 1977).

[6]Robert D. Hisrich and Candida G. Brush, "The Woman Entrepreneur: Management Skills and Business Problems," *Journal of Small Business Management* 22 (January 1984), pp. 30–37.

[7]For a review of some of this research, see C. J. Auster and D. Auster, "Factors Influencing Women's Choices of Nontraditional Careers," *Vocational Guidance Quarterly* 29 (March 1981): 253–63; J. H. Chusmin, "Characteristics and Predictive Dimensions of Women Who Make Nontraditional Vocational Choices," *Personnel and Guidance Journal* 62 (September 1983): 43–47; and D. L. Sexton and C. A. Kent, "Female Executives and Entrepreneurs: A Preliminary Comparison," *Proceedings,* 1981 Conference on Entrepreneurship (April 1981), pp. 40–55.

TABLE 3–5   Risk-Taking Research

Researcher	Instrument	Results
Meyer, Walker, and Litwin (1966)		Entrepreneurial group showed a preference for intermediate risk
Hull, Bosley, and Udell (1980)	Four-item risk questionnaire	Entrepreneurs scored significantly different
Brockhaus (1980)	Kogan-Wallach CDQ	Risk-taking propensity failed to distinguish entrepreneurs from managers
Brockhaus (1980a)	Kogan-Wallach CDQ	Risk-taking propensity failed to distinguish between successful and unsuccessful entrepreneurs
Sexton et al. (1982)	Kogan-Wallach CDQ	Entrepreneurs did not score significantly different
Sexton and Bowman (1983)	Kogan-Wallach CDQ	Potential entrepreneurs scored significantly different
Sexton and Bowlan (1983)	PRF-E	Potential entrepreneurs scored significantly lower on harm avoidance
Sexton and Bowman (1983)	JPI	Potential entrepreneurs scored significantly higher on risk taking

Source: Adapted from Donald Sexton and Nancy Bowman, "Personality Inventory for Potential Entrepreneurs: Evaluation of a Modified JPI/PRF-E Test Instrument," *Proceedings* 1985 Entrepreneurship Research Conference, pp. 513–29.

In terms of the occupation of the entrepreneurs' parents, there is strong evidence that entrepreneurs tend to have self-employed or entrepreneurial fathers. As indicated in Table 3–6, female entrepreneurs are as likely to report self-employed or entrepreneurial fathers as male entrepreneurs. Having a father who is self-employed provides a strong inspiration for the entrepreneur. The independent nature and flexibility of self-employment exemplified by the father is ingrained at an early age. As one entrepreneur stated, "My father was so consumed by the venture he started and provided such a strong example, it never occurred to me to go to work for anyone else." This feeling of independence is often further enforced by an entrepreneurial mother. Although the results are much less consistent, female entrepreneurs appear to have more than their share of entrepreneurial mothers.

The overall parental relationship, whether entrepreneurs or not, is perhaps the most important aspect of the childhood family environment in establishing the desirability of entrepreneurial activity for the individual. Parents can be sup-

TABLE 3–6 Occupations of Entrepreneurs' Parents

Studies of Entrepreneurs in General, or Male Entrepreneurs Only	*Studies of Female Entrepreneurs*
Brockhaus (1982) cities four studies suggesting that entrepreneurs tend to have entrepreneurial fathers.	Hisrich and Brush (1983) report a nationwide sample of 468 female entrepreneurs; 36 percent had entrepreneurial fathers; 11 percent had entrepreneurial mothers.
Brockhaus and Nord (1979) found that 31 St. Louis male entrepreneurs were no more likely than male managers to have entrepreneurial fathers.	Mescon and Stevens (1982) find 53 percent of 108 Arizona real estate brokers had fathers who were entrepreneurs. No mothers were entrepreneurs.
Cooper and Dunkelberg (1984) report that 47.5 percent of 1,394 entrepreneurs had parents who owned a business.	Sexton and Kent (1981)—40 percent of 48 Texas female entrepreneurs had entrepreneur fathers, 13 percent had entrepreneur mothers (versus 13 percent and 11 percent for 45 female executives).
Jacobowitz and Vidler (1983) found that 72 percent of mid-Atlantic state entrepreneurs had parents or close relatives who were self-employed.	Waddell (1983) found that 63.8 percent of 47 female entrepreneurs reported entrepreneurial fathers and 31.9 percent entrepreneurial mothers (versus 42.5 percent and 8.5 percent for female managers and 36.2 percent and 8.5 percent for secretaries).
Shapero and Sokol (1982) report that 50 to 58 percent of company founders in the United States had self-employed fathers (at a time when self-employed were only 12 percent of the work force). Cites data on the same pattern in nine other cultures.	Watkins and Watkins (1983)—37 percent of 58 British female entrepreneurs had self-employed fathers (self-employment in male U.K. labor force is 9 percent); 16 percent of mothers were whole or part owners of businesses (female self-employment is 4 percent).

Source: Donald D. Bowen and Robert D. Hisrich, "The Female Entrepreneur: A Career Development Perspective," *Academy of Management Review* 11 (April 1986), p. 399.

portive and encourage independence, achievement, and responsibility. This supportive relationship of the parents (particularly the father) appears to be most important for female entrepreneurs. Female entrepreneurs tend to grow up in middle- to upper-class environments, where families are likely to be relatively child-centered, and to be similar to their fathers in personality.[8]

---

[8]See Robert D. Hisrich and Candida G. Brush, *The Woman Entrepreneur: Starting, Financing, and Managing a Successful New Business* (Lexington, MA: Lexington Books, 1986).

Education

The educational level of the entrepreneur has received significant research attention (see Table 3–7). While it is frequently stated that entrepreneurs are less educated than the general population, the research findings indicate that this clearly is not the case. Education was important in the upbringing of the entrepreneurs. Its importance is reflected not only in the level of education obtained but in the fact that it continues to play a major role in helping· to cope with problems confronted and correcting deficiencies in business training. Although a formal education is not necessary for starting a new business, as reflected in the success of such entrepreneur high school dropouts as Andrew Carnegie, William Durant, Henry Ford, and William Lear, it does provide a good background, particularly when it is related to the field of the venture. In terms of type and quality of education, female entrepreneurs previously experienced some disadvantage. While nearly 70 percent of all women entrepreneurs have a college degree, many with graduate degrees, the most popular college majors are English, psychology, education, and sociology, with few having degrees in engineering, science, or math.[9] However, a mere count of the number of women in business and engineering schools indicates that the numbers have been significantly increased. Both male and female entrepreneurs have cited an educational need in the areas of finance, strategic planning, marketing (particularly distribution), and management. The ability to deal with people and communicate clearly in the written and spoken word is important in any entrepreneurial activity.

Personal Values

Although there have been many studies indicating that personal values are important for entrepreneurs, frequently these studies fail to indicate that entrepreneurs can be differentiated on these values from managers, unsuccessful entrepreneurs, or even the general populace. For example, while entrepreneurs tend to be effective leaders, this does not distinguish them from successful managers. While personal value scales for leadership as well as support, aggression, benevolence, conformity, creativity, veracity, and resource seeking are important for identifying entrepreneurs, they frequently also identify successful individuals as well. However, studies have shown that the entrepreneur has a different set of attitudes about the nature of the management process and business in general.[10] The nature of the enterprise, opportunism, intuition, and individuality of the entrepreneur diverge significantly from the bureaucratic organization, and

---

[9]Hisrich and Brush, *The Woman Entrepreneur.*

[10]See, for example, Y. Gasse, *Entrepreneurial Characteristics and Practices* (Sherbrooke, Quebec: Rene Prumer Imprimeur, Inc., 1977).

TABLE 3–7 Amount of Education of Entrepreneurs

Studies	Findings	Comments
	1. Entrepreneurs in general	
Brockhaus (1982)	Reviews four studies concluding that entrepreneurs tend to be better educated than the general population, but less so than managers.	All samples small and limited to one geographical area or industry.
Cooper and Dunkelberg (1984)	National survey of 1,805 small-business owners shows that a larger proportion of business starters or purchasers (approximately 64 percent) have less than a college degree compared to those who inherit or are brought in to run the business (57 percent).	
Gasse (1982)	Reports four studies where entrepreneurs are better educated than general public.	Educational level varies with industry (e.g., high-tech).
Jacobowitz and Vidler (1982)	Results of interviews with 430 entrepreneurs shows that they do not prosper in schools. Thirty percent were high school dropouts. Only 11 percent graduated from a 4-year college.	Sample of Pennsylvania and New Jersey entrepreneurs; 11 percent female.
	2. Male versus Female Entrepreneurs	
Humphreys and McClung (1981)	Fifty-four point eight percent of the female entrepreneurs were college graduates. Surpasses rate for males and females in general, and for male managers and administrators.	Oklahoma sample of 86 female entrepreneurs from all areas of the state.
Charboneau (1981)	Quotes 1977 Census Bureau study showing that the average female entrepreneur is a college graduate.	Also quotes SBA study with similar finding.
DeCarlo and Lyons (1979)	Female entrepreneurs have more education than the average adult female.	
	Nonminority female entrepreneurs have more education than minority female entrepreneurs.	122 female entrepreneurs drawn at random in mid-Atlantic states.
Hisrich and Brush (1983)	Sixty-eight percent of nationwide survey of 468 female entrepreneurs were at least college graduates.	
Mescon and Stevins (1982)	Two thirds had attended college; 15 percent had pursued graduate degrees.	Sample of 108 female real estate brokerage owners in Arizona.
Sexton and Kent (1981)	Female entrepreneurs were slightly less educated than female executives (44 percent and 51 percent	Interviewed 93 women (48 female entrepreneurs) from Texas.

TABLE 3–7	*(concluded)*	
Studies	*Findings*	*Comments*
	college graduates, respectively). Younger female entrepreneurs were better educated than female executives of companies.	

Source: Donald D. Bowen and Robert D. Hisrich, "The Female Entrepreneur: A Career Development Perspective," *Academy of Management Review* 11 (April 1986), p. 397.

the planning, rationality, and predictability of its managers. Perhaps all these traits instead of individual ones are encompassed in a winning image that allows the entrepreneur to create and enhance the new venture. In one study, *winning* emerged as the term best describing companies having an excellent reputation.[11] Five consensus characteristics found across consumer and leadership groups were superior quality in products; quality service to customers; flexibility—ability to adapt to changes in the marketplace; high-caliber management; and honesty and ethics in business practices. A successful entrepreneur is frequently characterized as a winner, almost a prerequisite for his or her actually becoming one.

Age

The relationship of age to the entrepreneurial career process has also been carefully researched.[12] In evaluating these results, it is important to differentiate between entrepreneurial age (the age of the entrepreneur reflected in the experience) and chronological age. As discussed in the next section, entrepreneurial experience is one of the best predictors of success, particularly when the new venture is in the same field as this business experience.

In terms of chronological age, most entrepreneurs initiate their entrepreneurial careers between the ages of 22 and 55. Although a career can be initiated before or after these years it is not as likely as an entrepreneur requires experience, financial support, and a high energy level in order to successfully launch

---

[11]For a summary of the results of this study, see "To the Winners Belong the Spoils," *Marketing News* 20 (October 10, 1986): 1 and 13.

[12]Much of this information is based on research findings in Robert C. Ronstadt, "Initial Venture Goals, Age, and the Decision to Start an Entrepreneurial Career," *Proceedings* of the 43rd Annual Meeting of the Academy of Management" (August 1983), p. 472; and Robert C. Ronstadt, "The Decision Not to Become an Entrepreneur," *Proceedings,* 1983 Conference on Entrepreneurship (April 1983), pp. 192–212.

and manage a new venture. While an average age has little meaning, when appropriate training and preparation are present, earlier starts in an entrepreneurial career are better than later ones. Also, there are milestone years that occur in approximately five-year intervals (25, 30, 35, 40, 45, and 50) when an individual is more inclined to start an entrepreneurial career. As one entrepreneur succinctly stated, "I felt it was now or never in terms of starting a new venture when I approached 30." Generally, male entrepreneurs tend to start their first significant venture in their early 30s, while women entrepreneurs tend to do so in their middle 30s.

Work History

Work history not only is a negative displacement in the decision to launch a new entrepreneurial venture but is also important in the growth and eventual success of the new venture. While dissatisfaction with various aspects of one's job—challenge, promotional opportunities, frustration, and boredom—often motivates the launching of a new venture (see Chapter 1), previous technical and industry experience is important once the decision to launch has been made. Experience areas particularly important include obtaining financing, such as bank financing and venture capital; developing the best product or service for the market; establishing manufacturing facilities; developing channels of distribution; and preparing the marketing plan for market introduction.

As the venture becomes established and starts growing, managerial experience and skills become increasingly important. While most ventures start with managing one's own activities and those of a few part- or full-time employees, as the number of employees increases along with the size, complexity, and geographical diversity of the business, the entrepreneur's managerial skills come more and more into play. This is particularly true when the new venture requires the addition of other managers.

In addition to managerial experience, entrepreneurial experience increases as the complexity of the venture increases. Most entrepreneurs indicate that their most significant venture was not their first one. Throughout their entrepreneurial careers, entrepreneurs are exposed to more "corridors" of new venture opportunities than individuals in other career paths.

MOTIVATION

What motivates an entrepreneur to take all the risks and launch a new venture, pursuing an entrepreneurial career against the overwhelming odds for success? Although many people are interested in starting a new venture and even have the background and financial resources to do so, few decide to actually start their own businesses. Individuals who are comfortable and secure in a job situation, have a family to support, like their present life-style and reasonably predictable leisure time often do not want to take the risks associated with venturing out alone.

While the motivations for venturing out alone vary greatly, the reason cited most frequently for becoming an entrepreneur is independence—not wanting to work for anyone else. This desire to be one's own boss is what drives both male and female entrepreneurs to accept all the social, psychological, and financial risks and to work the significant hours needed to create and develop a successful new venture. Nothing less than this motivation would be strong enough to endure all the frustrations and hardships. Other motivating factors differ between male and female entrepreneurs. Money is the second reason for starting a new venture for men while job satisfaction, achievement, opportunity, and money are the reasons in rank order for women. These second-order motivations reflect, in part, the work and family situation as well as the role model of the entrepreneur.

ROLE MODELS AND SUPPORT SYSTEMS

Perhaps one of the most important factors influencing entrepreneurs in their career choices is **role models.**[13] Role models can be parents, brothers or sisters, other relatives, or successful entrepreneurs in the surrounding community or nationally touted entrepreneurs. Successful entrepreneurs are viewed frequently as catalysts by potential entrepreneurs. As one person stated, "After evaluating Ted and his success as an entrepreneur, I knew I was much smarter and could do a better job. So, I started my own business."

Role models can also serve in a supportive capacity as mentors during and after the new venture is launched. Indeed, an entrepreneur needs a strong support and advisory system in every phase of the new venture. This support system is perhaps most crucial during the start-up phase by providing information, advice, and guidance on such matters as organizational structure, obtaining needed financial resources, marketing, and market segments. Since entrepreneurship is a social role embedded in a social context, it is important that an entrepreneur establish connections to these support resources early.

As initial contacts and connections expand, they form a network with similar properties prevalent in a social network—density (extensiveness of ties between the two individuals) and centrality (the total distance of the entrepreneur to all other individuals and the total number of individuals in the network). The

[13]The influence of role models on career choice is discussed in E. Almquist and S. Angust, "Role Model Influences on College Women's Career Aspirations," *Merrill-Palmer Quarterly* 17 (July 1971), pp. 263–97; J. Strake and C. Granger, "Same-sex and Opposite-sex Teacher Model Influences on Science Career Commitment among High School Students," *Journal of Educational Psychology* 70 (April 1978), pp. 180–86; Alan L. Carsrud, Connie Marie Gaglio, and Kenneth W. Olm, "Entrepreneurs—Mentors, Networks, and Successful New Venture Development: An Exploratory Study," *Proceedings,* 1986 Conference on Entrepreneurship (April 1986), pp. 229–35; and Howard Aldrich, Ben Rosen, and William Woodward, "The Impact of Social Networks on Business Foundings and Profit: A Longitudinal Study," *Proceedings,* 1987 Conference on Entrepreneurship (April 1987), pp. 154–68.

strength of the ties between the entrepreneur and any individual in the network is dependent on the frequency, level, and reciprocity of the relationship. The more frequent, the more in-depth, and the more mutually beneficial a relationship, the stronger and more durable is the network between the entrepreneur and the individual.[14]

But how does an entrepreneur establish this needed support-system network? Although a network is usually not a formally organized, directly established structure, an informal network for moral and professional support greatly benefits the entrepreneur.

Moral-Support Network

It is important for each entrepreneur to establish a **moral-support network** of family and friends—a cheering squad. This cheering squad is particularly important during the many difficult and lonely times that occur throughout the entrepreneurial process. Most entrepreneurs indicate that their spouses are their biggest supporters. This support is critical for allowing the excessive amounts of time that must be devoted to the new venture.

Friends also play key roles in a moral-support network. Not only can friends provide advice that is often more honest than that received from other sources, but they also provide encouragement, understanding, and even assistance. Entrepreneurs can confide in friends without fear of criticism.

Finally, relatives (children, parents, grandparents, aunts, and uncles) can also be strong sources of moral support, particularly if they are also entrepreneurs. As one entrepreneur stated: "The total family support I received was the key to my success. Having an understanding cheering squad giving me encouragement allowed me to persist through the many difficulties and problems."

Professional-Support Network

In addition to moral encouragement, the entrepreneur needs advice and counsel throughout the establishment of the new venture. This advice can be obtained from a mentor, business associates, trade associations, or personal affiliations—different members of the **professional-support network.**

A mentor-protegee relationship is an excellent method for securing the needed professional advice as well as being an additional source of moral sup-

---

[14]A thoughtful development of the network concept can be found in Howard Aldrich and Catherine Zimmer, "Entrepreneurship through Social Networks," in *The Art and Science of Entrepreneurship* (Cambridge, MA: Ballinger Publishing Co., 1986), pp. 3–24.

port. Many entrepreneurs indicate that they have mentors. How do you find a mentor? This task sounds much more difficult than it really is. Since a mentor is a coach, a sounding board, and an advocate—someone with whom the entrepreneur can share both problems and successes—the individual selected needs to be an expert in the field. An entrepreneur can start the "mentor-finding process" by preparing a list of experts in various fields such as in the fundamental business activities of finance, marketing, accounting, law, or management. These individuals can provide the practical "how-to" advice needed in the new venture. From this list an individual who can offer the most assistance can be identified and acquainted with the nature of the business. If the selected individual is willing to act as a mentor, he or she should be periodically apprised of the progress of the business so that a relationship can gradually develop.

Another good source of advice can be obtained through establishing a network of business associates. This group can be composed of self-employed individuals who have experienced starting a business; clients or buyers of the venture's product or service; experts such as consultants, lawyers, or accountants; and suppliers of the goods and services to the venture. Clients are a particularly important group to cultivate. This group not only represents the source of revenue to the venture but can also be the best source of word-of-mouth advertising. There is nothing better than word-of-mouth advertising from satisfied customers to help establish a winning business reputation and promote goodwill. Customers, excited about the entrepreneur's concern about the product or service fulfilling their need, happily provide valuable feedback on the present product or service as well as on new products or services being developed.

Suppliers are another important component in a professional-support network, as they help to establish credibility with creditors and customers. A new venture needs to establish a solid track record with suppliers in order to build a good relationship and ensure adequate availability of materials and other supplies. Suppliers can also provide good information on the nature and trends in the industry, as well as on competition.

Besides mentors and business associates, trade associations can provide an excellent mechanism for a professional-support network. Trade association members can be developed into a regional or national network and carefully cultivated to keep the new venture competitive. Trade associations keep up with new developments and can provide overall industry data.

Finally, personal affiliations of the entrepreneur can also be a valuable part of a professional-support network. Affiliations developed with individuals in hobbies, sporting events, clubs, civic involvements, and school alumni groups are excellent potential sources of referrals, advice, and information.

Each entrepreneur needs to establish both a moral- and a professional-support network, regardless of the final composition. These contacts provide confidence, support, advice, and information. As one entrepreneur stated: "In your own business, you are all alone. There is a definite need to establish support groups to share problems with and gain overall support for the new venture."

MALE VERSUS FEMALE ENTREPRENEURS

Even though there has been significant growth in female self-employment, much of what is known about the characteristics of entrepreneurs, their motivations, backgrounds, families, educational background, occupational experiences, and problems is based on studies of male entrepreneurs. This is not surprising since men make up the majority of people who start and own their own businesses, even though women are now starting new ventures at three times the rate of men.

While overall very similar, in some respects female entrepreneurs possess very different motivations, business skill levels, and occupational backgrounds than their male counterparts.[15] Factors in the start-up process of a business for male entrepreneurs are also dissimilar to that of females, especially in such areas as support systems, sources of funds, and problems.[16] The major differences between male and female entrepreneurs are summarized in Table 3–8. As is indicated, men are often motivated by the drive to control their own destinies, to make things happen. This drive often stems from disagreements with their boss or a feeling that they can run things better. In contrast, women tend to be more motivated by the need for independence and achievement arising from job frustration in not being allowed to perform at the level of which they are capable. These factors can cause the man or woman to feel the best solution is to start a new venture.

Departure points and reasons for starting the business are similar for both men and women. Both generally have a strong interest and experience in the area of their venture. However, for men, the transition from a past occupation to the new venture is often facilitated when the new venture is an outgrowth of a present job, sideline, or hobby. Women, on the other hand, often leave a previous occupation with only a high level of job frustration and enthusiasm for the new venture rather than experience, making the transition more difficult.

Start-up financing is another area where male and female entrepreneurs differ (see Table 3–8). While males often list investors, bank loans, or personal loans in addition to personal funds as sources of start-up capital, women usually rely solely on personal assets or savings. This points up a major problem area for both—obtaining financing and lines of credit.

Occupationally, there are also vast differences between male and female entrepreneurs. Although both groups tend to have experience in the field of their ventures, men more often are recognized specialists in their fields or have attained competence in a variety of business skills. In addition, their experience is

---

[15]An interesting comparison is found in Alan L. Carsrud and Kenneth W. Olm, "The Success of Male and Female Entrepreneurs: A Comparative Analysis," in *Managing Take-Off in Fast Growth Firms,* Ray M. Smilor and Robert L. Kuhn, eds. (New York: Praeger Publishers, 1986), pp. 147–62.

[16]This material is also discussed in Robert D. Hisrich and Candida G. Brush, *The Woman Entrepreneur: Starting, Financing, and Managing a Successful New Business* (Lexington, MA: Lexington Books, 1986).

TABLE 3–8 Comparison between Male and Female Entrepreneurs

Characteristic	Male Entrepreneurs	Female Entrepreneurs
Motivation	Achievement—strive to make things happen	Achievement—accomplishment of a goal
	Personal independence—self-image as it relates to status through their role in the corporation is unimportant	Independence—to do it alone
	Job satisfaction arising from the desire to be in control	Job satisfaction arising from previous job frustration
Departure point	Dissatisfaction with present job	Job frustration
	Sideline in college, sideline to present job, or outgrowth of present job	Interest in and recognition of opportunity in the area
	Discharge or layoff	
	Opportunity for acquisition	Change in personal circumstances
Sources of funds	Personal assets and savings	Personal assets and savings
	Bank financing	Personal loans
	Investors	
	Loans from friends or family	
Occupational background	Experience in line of work	Experience in area of business
	Recognized specialist or one who has gained a high level of achievement in the field	Middle-management or administrative-level experience in the field
	Competent in a variety of business functions	Service-related occupational background
Personality characteristics	Opinionated and persuasive	Flexible and tolerant
	Goal-oriented	Goal-oriented
	Innovative and idealistic	Creative and realistic
	High level of self-confidence	Medium level of self-confidence
	Enthusiastic and energetic	Enthusiastic and energetic
	Must be own boss	Ability to deal with the social and economic environment
Background	Age when starting venture 25–35	Age when starting venture 35–45
	Father was self-employed	Father was self-employed
	College educated—degree in business or technical area (usually engineering)	College educated—degree in liberal arts
	Firstborn child	Firstborn child
Support groups	Friends; professional acquaintances (lawyers, accountants)	Close friends
	Business associates	Spouse
	Spouse	Family
		Women's professional groups
		Trade associations
Type of business started	Manufacturing or construction	Service-related—educational services, consulting, or public relations
	Average net income—$7,100/year	Average net income—$2,200/year

often in manufacturing, finance, or technical areas. Most women, in contrast, usually have administrative experience, which is limited to the middle-management level, often in more service-related areas such as education, secretarial work, or retail sales.

In terms of personality, there are strong similarities between male and female entrepreneurs. Both tend to be energetic, goal-oriented, and independent. However, men are often more confident and less flexible and tolerant than women, which can result in very different management styles.

The backgrounds of male and female entrepreneurs tend to be similar, except that most women are a little older when they embark on their ventures (35 to 40 versus 25 to 35) and their educational backgrounds are different. Men often have studied in technical- or business-related areas, while many women have a liberal arts education.

Support groups also provide a point of contrast between the two. Men usually list outside advisors (lawyers, accountants) as most important supporters, with the spouse being second. Women list their spouses first, close friends second, and business associates third. Moreover, women usually rely heavily on a variety of sources for support and information, such as trade associations and women's groups, while men are not as likely to have as many outside supporters.

Finally, businesses started by male and female entrepreneurs differ in terms of the nature of the venture. Women are more likely to start a business in a service-related area—retail, public relations, educational services—whereas men are more likely to enter manufacturing, construction, or high-technology fields. The result is often smaller female-owned businesses with lower net earnings. However, opportunities for women are greater than ever, with women starting businesses at a faster rate than men.

ENTREPRENEURS VERSUS INVENTORS

There is a great deal of confusion about the nature of an entrepreneur versus an inventor and the similarities and differences between the two. An **inventor,** an individual who creates something for the first time, is a highly driven individual motivated by his or her own work and personal ideas. Besides being highly creative, an inventor tends to be well-educated, with college or often postgraduate degrees; has family, education, and occupational experiences that contribute to creative development and free thinking; is a problem solver able to reduce complex problems to simple ones; has a very high level of self-confidence; is willing to take risks; and has the ability to tolerate ambiguity and uncertainty.[17] A typical inventor places a high premium on being an achiever,

---

[17]This and other information on investors and the invention process can be found in Robert D. Hisrich, "The Inventor: A Potential Source for New Products," *The Mid-Atlantic Journal of Business* 24 (Winter 1985/86), pp. 67–80.

measuring achievement by the number of inventions developed and the number of patents granted. An inventor is not likely to view monetary benefits as a measure of success.

As indicated in this profile, an inventor differs considerably from an entrepreneur. While an entrepreneur falls in love with the organization (the new venture) and will do almost anything, including mortgaging house, spouse, dog, or cat, an inventor falls in love with the invention and will reluctantly modify the invention to make it more commercially feasible. The development of a new venture based on an inventor's work often requires the expertise of an entrepreneur—a team approach to new venture creation.

GENERAL NONENTREPRENEURIAL PROFILES

In addition to inventors, there are several other personality types that have a difficult time in successfully creating and managing a new venture. These personality types, which have characteristics that can lead even the brightest entrepreneur with the best idea into bankruptcy, are a concern of resource providers such as venture capitalists, bankers, suppliers, and customers. Eight of these personality types are profiled in Table 3–9: Shotgun Sam, Simplicity Sue, Prima Donna Paul, Ralph the Rookie, Meticulous Mary, Underdog Ed, Hidden Agenda Harry, and Inventor Irving. Each has certain flaws such as the lack of follow-through (Shotgun Sam); making everything much simpler than it really is (Simplicity Sue); falling in love with the idea itself (Prima Donna Paul); lacking real-world experience (Ralph the Rookie); being a perfectionist (Meticulous Mary); lacking the ability to put things into concrete action (Underdog Ed); lacking the right motives (Hidden Agenda Harry); and loving creating more than doing (Inventor Irving). While, in moderation, these tendencies pose no problems, an entrepreneur with an excess of any of these traits may need to modify it in order to have a higher probability in successfully launching a new venture.

SUMMARY

Is there something about an entrepreneur that differentiates him or her from the rest of the population? This chapter outlines the current thinking and research related to identifying the unique characteristics of a person who successfully launches a new venture. Developing an understanding of the factors linked with the initiation and success of a new venture is an important step in encouraging potential entrepreneurs and improving their probability of success.

The study of management techniques and managerial personalities was a springboard for some of the earlier research on entrepreneurs. Rotter's internality-externality locus of control, McClelland's *n* Ach, and various risk measures are examples of this. While the traits measured by these instruments seem intu-

TABLE 3–9   Eight Entrepreneurial Profiles

Profile	Description
Shotgun Sam	An entrepreneurial type who quickly identifies new promising business opportunities but rarely if ever follows through on the opportunity to create a successful new venture.
Simplicity Sue	An entrepreneurial type who always thinks everything is a lot simpler than it is to create a successful business through one or two easy solutions. Usually a great salesperson. This entrepreneur can make even the most improbable deal seem possible.
Prima Donna Paul	An entrepreneurial type so in love with his own idea that he feels everyone is out to take his idea and take advantage of him. This paranoia does not allow any trust to be established and help given.
Ralph the Rookie	An entrepreneurial type who is well grounded in theory but lacks real-world business experience.
Meticulous Mary	A perfectionist entrepreneurial type who is so used to having things under control that he or she cannot manage during a catastrophe and cannot handle periods of ambiguity and chaos.
Underdog Ed	An entrepreneurial type who is not comfortable with actually transforming the invention into a tangible business success. This entrepreneurial type likes to attend seminars and discuss problems but does not like putting things into action so needs a strong managerial team.
Hidden Agenda Harry	An entrepreneur who does not have the right motives and objects for developing and expediting a new enterprise.
Inventor Irving	An inventor more than an entrepreneur who is more concerned about the invention itself rather than creating and expediting a business.

Source: "8 Demons of Entrepreneurship," *Success* (March 1986), pp. 54–57.

itively related to entrepreneurial tendencies, the research to date has been inconclusive. The formalized, quantitative study of entrepreneurial traits is a fairly young discipline that may produce more definitive results as it matures.

A typical entrepreneurial profile in terms of experience and family background has been more clearly defined. Adult encouragement, parents' occupations, and family interpersonal relationships all give indications of affecting entrepreneurial tendencies. The additional adult encouragement, often more available to a firstborn or only child, the role model of a successful entrepreneurial parent, and a supportive relationship which encourages independence and achievement are factors strongly linked with later entrepreneurial behavior. There are personal characteristics and skills frequently present in successful entrepreneurs, such as leadership traits, creativity, opportunism, and intuition, but so far no unique combination of traits, experiences, and acquired skills differentiates a successful entrepreneur from an unsuccessful one or even a manager.

The research clearly indicates that there are many variables involved in the decision to become an entrepreneur. There are many successful corporate businesspeople who fit an entrepreneurial profile and yet choose to remain in their current careers. Perhaps these individuals lack an appropriate role model or support system. Seeing someone else challenge and overcome the risk in a venture start-up is frequently mentioned as a key influence in the entrepreneurial decision process. While an individual can act as an inspiration, a new venture is also in need of support from an individual or group providing information, advice, and guidance. There are many sources of support systems, starting with friends and family and moving into the wider circle of professional contacts, clients, and industry organizations. Since both the entrepreneur and the new business have needs, a network of helpful, supportive contacts should be developed to help meet those needs.

Significant growth in the number of women employed outside the home has created a new field of research: Are female employees, managers, and entrepreneurs different from their male counterparts? What can be learned from studying, defining, or quantifying these differences (if indeed they exist)? It is clear that male and female entrepreneurs have much in common and, at the same time, differ. While some of the background and personality characteristics are quite similar between the sexes, there are striking differences between them in terms of motivation, departure point, and business skills brought to the venture. The difference in type of business started can be attributed in large part to differences in education and work history.

In developing a unique description of an entrepreneur, there are several personality types that only appear to be entrepreneurial. First on this list is the inventor, who can take on the role of an entrepreneur if a business is started around the product invented. Often the business is second in importance to the invention itself. Other character traits present in an individual, such as lack of tenacity, perfectionism, the tendency to oversimplify, and paranoia, must be identified and overcome to be a successful entrepreneur.

PART

II

STARTING A NEW VENTURE AND DEVELOPING THE BUSINESS

4

Creating and Developing the Business

CHAPTER OBJECTIVES

1. To identify various sources of ideas for new ventures.

2. To discuss methods available for generating new ideas.

3. To explain creativity and the various techniques for creative problem solving.

4. To discuss the aspects of the product planning and development process.

5. To identify the aspects involved in creating a business through acquisition.

6. To explain the process of starting a new venture through the use of a joint venture.

7. To discuss the use of leveraged buyouts in new venture creation.

KEN OLSEN

In 1947, a young man with electrical engineering training from the Navy entered MIT. There he joined a student research team building MIT's first computer. Driven by a concept of computing radically different from that underlying the number-crunching ENIAC built by the University of Pennsylvania, this computer was to be interactive, small, and fast. The computer was designed with circuits that allowed quick response, so the programmer would be able to carry on a primitive dialogue with it. Meeting with success, and showing himself to be a first-rate practical engineer, the student moved on to other, bigger projects. Landing a job on a liaison team with IBM, which was involved in manufacturing computers for MIT, he was shocked at the regimentation and production inefficiencies of the rapidly growing computer company. Knowing that he could do a better job on his own because of the management experience he had gained from being a Sunday school superintendent and backed by $70,000 in venture capital, the engineer founded his own company. Today that company has annual revenues of over $9 billion. The MIT engineer, still president and chief executive officer, is indeed one of the most successful entrepreneurs in the history of American business. Kenneth Harry Olsen (known as "Ken" even to the secretaries) has taken Digital Equipment Corporation (DEC) farther, without acquisitions, than Henry Ford took Ford Motor Company, than Andrew Carnegie took U.S. Steel, than J. D. Rockefeller took Standard Oil. What are Ken's secrets?

First, he had a vision. An engineer by training and temperament, Ken knew what engineers needed in a computer. At a time when computers were large mainframes housed in special centers, maintained by experts, and used to process large batches of data, he had a vision of a small, rugged, inexpensive machine that a user-engineer could apply to an endless variety of tasks. Working with a few friends from his lab days, Olsen introduced the PDP-1 in 1960—the world's first "small" computer.

Second, Olsen's engineering vision became integral to his management vision. Cheap and adaptable were the code words in the early years. He liked the freedom he found working in MIT's computer laboratory and worked to develop this openness in DEC. There was no organizational structure, no wall chart, just bands of engineers forming around products. For several years, this approach worked well. Pioneering new ground left room for unstructured growth into many niches; however, the technically more difficult projects were harder to support without more direction. To overcome this hurdle, Olsen reconsidered his management style (or lack thereof), thought about responsibility, and developed an organizational remedy practically unheard of in 1964.

His plan was to make each of his senior people an entrepreneur within the company. Responsibility for a single product line—from development to sales—rested with one person. This manager had to compete with other managers for as much of the company's resources as he could get. Some engineers missed the looseness of early times and soon left, but those remaining rose to the challenge of running their own operations, and DEC grew at a phenomenal rate.

Everyone was happy, inventing computers right and left. But in 1979 the computer technology created by the managerial system once again outgrew its structure. The chief engineers obtained approval to develop a new generation of super minicomputers, capable of automating entire companies. Could DEC marshal its many far-flung managers, each going his or her own direction, and manage the engineering disciplines required to support this multibillion dollar effort?

A challenge indeed, and, once again, Olsen chose to remain faithful to his engineering vision. Feeling that the future in computers was in systems, networks, and computers talking to each other, he knew his engineers were working on the right technology to be correctly positioned in the market. This view molded the management style of the entire company. Olsen spent five years slowly dismantling the product line system, transforming DEC into a unified marketing organization. While no one was fired during this process, many long-time managers quit, unable to perform in the new system. Critics questioned whether the company could emerge healthy from such a struggle. Not understanding the vision during the turmoil, they suggested that Olsen had succumbed to "founder's disease," unable to handle the demands of operating a mature company and unwilling to step down.

In spite of this pessimism, DEC survived. Although putting the new centralized structure in place and having all new products use the same basic computing and communication methods were costly in terms of time and money, the company still managed to leapfrog the competition in introducing networking capabilities. Company sales grew when the industry was mired in a slump, firmly entrenching DEC as number two in the computer industry. In the fiscal year ending July 1, 1989, net sales were $12.7 billion, versus $11.5 billion in 1988. However, net income before taxes decreased to $1.1 billion in 1989 from $1.3 billion in 1988. Will DEC continue to grow? Will Olsen, as he approaches 70, be able to continue to drive the company? Only time will tell.

As was at the heart of the success story of Ken Olsen, the starting point in being an entrepreneur and developing a new venture is the basic product or service to be offered. Yet, this fundamental notion is a difficult one to actualize. What is the origin of this new product or service idea that is so essential for an entrepreneur? It is either internally generated through developing sources of new ideas or creative problem solving or it is externally acquired and developed through acquisitions, hostile takeovers, joint ventures, or leveraged buyouts.

Indeed a wide variety of techniques can be used in either instance. Ken Olsen had his vision working on a government contract project while obtaining his Ph.D. degree. Fred Smith of Federal Express expressed his original idea in a paper he wrote to complete a college course. For others, such as Bob Reis of Final Technology, Inc. and Frank Perdue of Perdue Chickens, the idea came from work experience. No matter how it is arrived at, a sound idea for a new product (or services) is essential to successfully launch a new venture. And, regardless of the source of the idea, proper valuation is needed to successfully establish a new venture.

SOURCES OF NEW IDEAS

As reflected in the stories of the millions of entrepreneurs throughout the world, there are many possible sources of ideas. Some of the more useful sources are consumers, existing companies, distribution channels, the federal government, and internal research and development.

Consumers

Entrepreneurs are paying increasing attention to what should be the focal point of the idea for a new product or service—the consumer. This can take the form of monitoring potential ideas mentioned on an informal basis or formally arranging for consumers to have an opportunity to express their opinions.

Existing Companies

Entrepreneurs should also establish a more formal method for monitoring and evaluating the products and services that existing or new companies offer. Frequently this analysis uncovers ways to improve on these present offerings, resulting in the formation of a new venture.

Distribution Channels

Members of the distribution channels are also excellent sources for new ideas. Because of their familiarity with the needs of the market, channel members frequently have suggestions for completely new products. These channel members can also be a source of help in marketing the entrepreneur's newly developed products.

Federal Government

The federal government can be helpful in finding and developing new product ideas in two ways. First, the files of the Patent Office contain numerous new product possibilities. Although the patents themselves may not be feasible new product introductions, they can frequently suggest other, more marketable, new product ideas. Several government agencies and publications are helpful in this patent monitoring. The *Official Gazette,* published weekly by the U.S. Patent Office, summarizes each patent granted and lists all patents available for license or sale. Also, the Government Patents Board publishes lists of abstracts of thousands of government-owned patents. One good publication is the *Government-Owned Inventories Available for License.* There are other government agencies, such as the Office of Technical Services, that assist entrepreneurs in obtaining specific product information.

Second, new product ideas can come in response to government regulations. For example, the Occupational Safety and Health Act (OSHA), aimed at eliminating unsafe working conditions in industry, mandated that first-aid kits be in business establishments employing more than three people. These kits must contain specific items, depending on the industry. The weatherproofed first-aid kit needed for a construction company, for example, is different than the one needed by a company manufacturing facial cream. In response to OSHA, both established and newly formed ventures marketed a wide variety of first-aid kits. One newly formed company—R&H Safety Sales Company—was successful in helping companies (other than those in the construction industry) comply with the act.

Research and Development

The largest source for new ideas is the entrepreneur's own "research and development department," whether this is a more formal endeavor connected with current employment or an informal lab in the basement or garage. The more formal research and development department is often better equipped to produce successful new product ideas.

METHODS FOR GENERATING IDEAS

Regardless of all these sources, there is frequently a problem in coming up with a new idea. The entrepreneur can use several methods to help generate and test new ideas. These include focus groups, brainstorming, and problem inventory analysis.

Focus Groups

Focus group interviews have been used in many different areas since the 1950s. This method consists of a moderator leading a group of people through an open in-depth discussion rather than simply asking questions to solicit participant response; the moderator focuses the discussion of the group on the new product area in either a directive or a nondirective manner.

In addition to generating new ideas, the focus group is an excellent method for initially screening ideas and concepts. There are several procedures available to analyze and interpret the results more quantitatively. With the availability of such procedures, the focus group is becoming an increasingly useful method for generating new product ideas for an entrepreneur.[1]

Brainstorming

The brainstorming method is based on the fact that people can be stimulated to greater creativity by meeting with others and participating in organized group experiences. The entrepreneur can gather a group of people to discuss and generate new ideas. While, of course, many of the ideas generated are absurd and have no basis for further development, frequently one or two good ideas emerge. This occurs more often when the brainstorming effort focuses on a specific area. When using this method, the following four overall rules need to be followed:

1. No criticism is allowed by anyone in the group—no negative comments.
2. Freewheeling is encouraged—the wilder the idea the better.
3. Quantity of ideas is desired—the greater the number of ideas, the more the likelihood of useful ideas emerging.
4. Combinations and improvements of ideas are encouraged—ideas of others can be used to produce still another new idea.

The brainstorming meeting should be fun and playful, not work-oriented, with no expert in the field present.

---

[1]For a more in-depth presentation on focus group interviews in general and quantitative applications, see "Conference Focuses on Focus Groups: Guidelines, Reports, and 'the Magic Plaque,'" *Marketing News*, May 21, 1976, p. 8; Keith K. Cox, James B. Higginbotham, and John Burton, "Application of Focus Group Interviews in Market," *Journal of Marketing* 40, no. 1 (January 1976), pp. 77–80; and Robert D. Hisrich and Michael P. Peters, "Focus Groups: An Innovative Marketing Research Technique" *Hospital and Health Service Administration* 27, no. 4 (July/ August 1982), pp. 8–21.

Problem Inventory Analysis

Problem inventory analysis, another method of generating new ideas, uses individuals in a manner analogous to focus groups. However, instead of generating new ideas themselves, consumers are provided with a list of problems from a general product category. They are then asked to identify and discuss products in this category that have the particular problem. This method is often very effective as it is easier to relate known products to suggested problems and arrive at a new product idea than to generate an entirely new product idea by itself. This approach is also an excellent way to test a new product idea.

An application of this approach in the food industry is seen in Table 4–1. As indicated, one of the most difficult aspects of this approach is developing an exhaustive list of problems such as weight, taste, appearance, and cost. Once a complete list of problems is developed, individuals can usually associate products with each problem.

Results from product inventory analysis must be carefully evaluated as they may not actually reflect a new business opportunity. For example, General Foods' introduction of a small, compact cereal box in response to the problem that the available boxes did not fit well on the shelf was not successful. The perceived problem of package size appears to have very little effect on actual purchasing behavior. To ensure the best results, problem inventory analysis should be used primarily to identify product ideas for further in-depth study to determine their importance and potential purchase by consumers.

CREATIVE PROBLEM SOLVING

Creativity is an important attribute of a successful entrepreneur identifying a new product and creating the new venture. Unfortunately, creativity tends to decline with age, education, and lack of use. Creativity declines in stages—first when a person starts school, then in the teens, then at ages 30, 40, and 50. In addition, the latent creative potential of an individual can be stifled by perceptual, cultural, emotional, and organizational factors. Creativity can be unlocked and creative ideas and innovations generated by using one of the creative problem-solving techniques such as those in Table 4–2.[2]

---

[2] A discussion of each of these techniques can be found in Robert D. Hisrich and Michael P. Peters, *Marketing Decisions for New and Mature Products* (Columbus, OH: Charles E. Merrill, 1984, pp. 131–46 and Robert D. Hisrich, "Entrepreneurship and Intrapreneurship: Methods for Creating New Companies That Have an Impact on the Economic Renaissance of an Area." In *Entrepreneurship, Intrapreneurship, and Venture Capital* (Lexington, MA: Lexington Books, 1986), pp. 77–104.

TABLE 4–1 Problem Inventory Analysis

Physiological	Sensory	Activities	Buying Usage	Psychological/Social

A. Weight
  fattening
  empty calories
	A. Taste
	  bitter
	  bland
	  salty
		A. Meal planning
		  forget
		  get tired of it
			A. Portability
			  eat away from home
			  take lunch
				A. Serve to company
				  would not serve to guests
				  too much last-minute preparation

B. Hunger
  filling
  still hungry after eating
	B. Appearance
	  color
	  unappetizing
	  shape
		B. Storage
		  run out
		  package would not fit
			B. Portions
			  not enough in package
			  creates leftovers
				B. Eating alone
				  too much effort to cook for oneself
				  depressing when prepared for just one

C. Thirst
  does not quench
  makes one thirsty
	C. Consistency/texture
	  tough
	  dry
	  greasy
		C. Preparation
		  too much trouble
		  too many pots and pans
		  never turns out
			C. Availability
			  out of season
			  not in supermarket
				C. Self-image
				  made by a lazy cook
				  not served by a good mother

D. Health
  indigestion
  bad for teeth
  keeps one awake
  acidity
		D. Cooking
		  burns
		  sticks
			D. Spoilage
			  gets moldy
			  goes sour	

		E. Cleaning
		  makes a mess in oven
		  smells in refrigerator
			E. Cost
			  expensive
			  takes expensive ingredients	

Source: Edward M. Tauber, "Discovering New Product Opportunities with Problem Inventory Analysis," *Journal of Marketing* (January 1975), 69. Reprinted from *Journal of Marketing*, published by the American Marketing Association.

TABLE 4–2 Creativity and Problem-Solving Techniques

- Brainstorming
- Reverse brainstorming
- Synectics
- Gordon method
- Checklist method
- Free association
- Forced relationships
- Collective notebook method
- Heuristics
- Scientific method
- Kepner-Tregoe method
- Value analysis
- Attribute listing method
- Morphological analysis
- Matrix charting
- Sequence-attribute/modification matrix
- Inspired (big-dream) approach
- Parameter analysis

Brainstorming

The first technique—brainstorming—is probably the most well-known and widely used technique for creative problem solving as well as idea generation. It is an unstructured process for generating, through spontaneous contributions of participants, all possible ideas about a problem within a limited time frame. A good brainstorming session starts with a problem statement that is neither too broad (which would diversify ideas too greatly so that nothing specific would emerge) nor too narrow (which would tend to confine responses).[3] Once the problem statement is prepared, 6 to 12 individuals are selected so that a wide range of knowledge is present. No group member should be a recognized expert in the field of the problem. All ideas, no matter how illogical, must be recorded, with participants not being allowed to criticize or evaluate during the brainstorming session.

Reverse Brainstorming

Reverse brainstorming is similar to brainstorming, except that criticism is allowed. In fact, the technique is based on finding fault by asking the question, "In how many ways can this idea fail?" Care must be taken to maintain the group's morale. Reverse brainstorming can be effectively used prior to other

---

[3]For a discussion of this aspect, see Charles H. Clark, *Idea Management: How to Motivate Creativity and Innovation* (New York: ANA Com., 1980), p. 47.

creative techniques to stimulate innovative thinking.[4] The process most often involves the identification of everything wrong with an idea, followed by a discussion of ways to overcome these faults.

Synectics

Synectics is a creative process that forces individuals to solve problems through one of four mechanisms of analogy—personal, direct, symbolic, and fantasy.[5] A group works through two steps. The first step is to make the strange familiar. This involves, through generalizations or models, putting the problem into a readily acceptable or familiar perspective, thereby eliminating the strangeness. Once the strangeness is eliminated, participants engage in the second step, making the familiar strange, which ideally results in a novel, unique solution being developed.

Gordon Method

The Gordon method, unlike many other creative problem-solving techniques, begins with group members not knowing the exact nature of the problem. This ensures that the solution is not clouded by preconceived ideas and habit patterns.[6] The entrepreneur starts by mentioning a general concept associated with the problem. The group responds by expressing a number of ideas. Then a concept is developed, followed by related concepts, through guidance by the entrepreneur. The actual problem is then revealed, enabling the group to make suggestions for implementation or refinement of the final suggestion.

Checklist Method

In the checklist method, a new idea is developed through a list of related issues or suggestions. The entrepreneur can use the list of questions or statements to guide the direction of developing entirely new ideas or concentrating on specific "idea" areas. The checklist may take any form and be of any length. One general checklist is[7]:

---

[4]For a discussion of this technique, see J. Geoffrey Rawlinson, *Creative Thinking and Brainstorming* (New York: John Wiley & Sons, 1981), pp. 124 and 126; and W. E. Souder and R. W. Ziegler, "A Review of Creativity and Problem-Solving Techniques," *Research Management* 20 (July 1977), p. 35.

[5]For a thorough discussion and application of this method, see W. J. Gordon, *Synectics: The Development of Creative Capacity* (New York: Harper & Row, 1961), pp. 37–53.

[6]This method is discussed in J. W. Haefele, *Creativity and Innovation* (New York: Van Nostrand Reinhold, 1962), pp. 145–47; Sidney J. Parnes and Harold F. Harding, *A Source Book for Creative Thinking* (New York: Charles Scribner's Sons, 1962), pp. 307–23; and Souder and Ziegler, *Review of Techniques*, pp. 34–42.

[7]Alex F. Osborn, *Applied Imagination* (New York: The Scribner Book Companies, Inc., 1957), p. 318.

- *Put to Other Uses?* New ways to use as is? Other uses if modified?
- *Adapt?* What else is like this? What other ideas does this suggest? Does past offer parallel? What could I copy? Whom could I emulate?
- *Modify?* New twist? Change meaning, color, motion, odor, form, shape? Other changes?
- *Magnify?* What to add? More time? Greater frequency? Stronger? Larger? Thicker? Extra value? Plus ingredient? Duplicate? Multiply? Exaggerate?
- *Minify?* What substitute? Smaller? Condensed? Miniature? Lower? Shorter? Lighter? Omit? Streamline? Split up? Understated?
- *Substitute?* Who else instead? What else instead? Other ingredient? Other material? Other process? Other power? Other place? Other approach? Other tone of voice?
- *Rearrange?* Interchange components? Other pattern? Other layout? Other sequence? Transpose cause and effect? Change pact? Change schedule?
- *Reverse?* Transpose positive and negative? How about opposites? Turn it backward? Turn it upside down? Reverse roles? Change shoes? Turn tables? Turn other cheek?
- *Combine?* How about a blend, an alloy, an assortment, an ensemble? Combine units? Combine purposes? Combine appeals? Combine ideas?

Free Association

One of the simplest, yet most effective, methods entrepreneurs can use to generate new ideas is free association. This technique is helpful in developing an entirely new slant to a problem. First, a word or phrase related to the problem is written down, then another and another, with each new word attempting to add something new to the ongoing thought processes, thereby creating a chain of ideas with a new product idea emerging.

Forced Relationships

Forced relationships is another technique that asks questions about objects, or ideas, in an effort to develop a new idea from the resulting new combination. The new combination and eventual concept is developed through a five-step process[8]:

1. Isolate the elements of the problem.
2. Find the relationships between these elements.

---

[8]Rawlinson, *Creative Thinking*, pp. 52–59.

3. Record the relationships in an orderly form.
4. Analyze the resulting relationships to find ideas or patterns.
5. Develop new ideas from these patterns.

Collective Notebook Method

In the collective notebook method, a small notebook that easily fits in a shirt pocket is prepared that includes a statement of the problem, blank pages, and any pertinent background data. The entrepreneur then considers the problem and its possible solution, recording resulting ideas at least once a day. At the end of a month, a list of the best ideas is developed, along with any suggestions.[9] This technique can also be used with a group of individuals who record their ideas, giving their notebooks to a central coordinator who synthesizes the data and summarizes all the material. The summary becomes the topic of a final creative focus group discussion by the group participants.

Heuristics

Heuristics relies on the entrepreneur's ability to discover through a progression of thoughts, insights, and learning. The technique is probably used more than imagined, simply because entrepreneurs frequently must settle for an estimated outcome of a decision rather than an assured certainty. One specific heuristic approach is called the heuristic ideation technique (HIT).[10] This involves locating all relevant concepts that could be associated with a given product area and generating a set of all possible combinations of ideas.

Scientific Method

The scientific method, widely used in various fields of inquiry, consists of principles and processes, conducting observations and experiments, and validating the hypothesis. The approach involves the entrepreneur defining the problem, analyzing the problem, gathering and analyzing data, developing and testing potential solutions, and choosing the best solution.

---

[9]For a thorough discussion of the collective notebook method, see J. W. Haefele, *Creativity and Innovation*, p. 152.

[10]See Edward M. Tauber, "HIT: Heuristic Ideation Technique," *Journal of Marketing* 36, no. 1 (January 1972), pp. 58–70.

Value Analysis

Another technique—value analysis—develops methods for maximizing value to the entrepreneur and the new venture.[11] To maximize value, the entrepreneur asks such questions as "Can this part be of lesser quality, since it isn't a critical area for problems?" In a value analysis procedure, regularly scheduled times are established to develop, evaluate, and refine ideas.

Attribute Listing

Attribute listing is an idea-finding technique requiring the entrepreneur to list the attributes of an item or problem and then look at each from a variety of viewpoints. Through this process, originally unrelated objects can be brought together to form a new combination and possible new uses that better satisfy a need.[12]

Matrix Charting

Matrix charting is a systematic method for searching for new opportunities by listing important elements for the product area along two axes of a chart and then asking questions regarding each of these elements. The answers are recorded in the relevant boxes of the matrix. Example questions that can elicit creative new product ideas include: What can it be used for? Where can it be used? Who can use it? When can it be used? How can it be used?

Big-Dream Approach

The big-dream approach to coming up with a new idea requires that the entrepreneur dreams about a problem and its solution—thinking big. Every possibility should be recorded and investigated without regard to all the natives involved or resources required. This should continue until an idea is developed into a workable form.[13]

---

[11]For a discussion of value analysis and its application at General Electric, see "A Study on Applied Value Analysis," *Purchasing* 46 (June 8, 1959), pp. 66–67.

[12]S. J. Parnes and H. F. Harding, eds. *A Source Book for Creative Thinking* (New York: Charles Scribner's Sons, 1962), p. 308.

[13]For a discussion of this approach, see M. O. Edwards, "Solving Problems Creatively," *Journal of Systems Management* 17, no. 1 (January–February 1966), pp. 16–24.

Parameter Analysis

A final method for developing new ideas—parameter analysis—involves two aspects—parameter identification and creative synthesis.[14] In step one (parameter identification), variables involved in the situation are analyzed to determine their relative importance. These variables become the focus of the investigation, with other variables being set aside. After the primary issues have been identified, the relationships between parameters that describe the underlying issues are examined. Through an evaluation of the parameters and relationships, a solution(s) is developed; this solution development is called *creative synthesis.*

PRODUCT PLANNING AND DEVELOPMENT PROCESS

Once ideas emerge from idea sources or creative problem solving, they need further development and refinement into the final product or service to be offered. This refining process—the product planning and development process—is divided into five major stages: idea stage, concept stage, product development stage, test marketing stage, and commercialization (see Figure 4–1).[15]

In the **idea stage,** the entrepreneur obtains and screens suggestions for new products or services to determine which are good enough to receive more detailed evaluation. Screening criteria must be established that reflect the entrepreneur's strengths, weaknesses, and resources.

Ideas that pass the initial screening enter the **concept stage,** where they are developed into more elaborate concepts by considering the needs of potential buyers. The entrepreneur should develop a tentative business plan describing the product features and the needed marketing program. Whenever possible, a sample of potential buyers should evaluate the concept.

Once the concept for the new product has been approved, it is further developed and refined into a prototype and tested—the **product development stage.** In this stage, the technical and economic aspects of the new product are assessed by assigning the necessary specifications to members of research and development. Unless the need for excessive capital expenditures makes it impossible, laboratory-tested products should be created and produced on a pilot-run basis to allow for production control and product testing. This consumer testing determines whether the potential new product has features superior to currently available products.

---

[14] The procedure for parameter analysis is thoroughly discussed in Yao Tzu Li, David G. Jansson, and Ernest G. Cravalho, *Technological Innovation in Education and Industry,* (New York: Reinhold Publishing Company, 1980), pp. 26–49, 277–86.

[15] For a detailed description of this process, see Robert D. Hisrich and Michael P. Peters, *Marketing Decisions for New and Mature Products* (Columbus, OH: Charles E. Merrill Publishing, 1985), pp. 156–78.

FIGURE 4–1   The Product Planning and Development Process

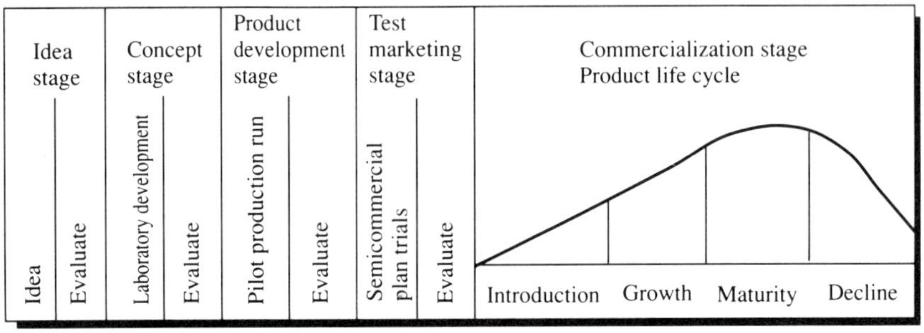

Source: Adapted from Robert D. Hisrich and Michael P. Peters, *Marketing Decisions for New and Mature Products* (Columbus, OH: Charles E. Merrill Publishing, 1984).

While the results of the product development stage provide the basis of the final marketing plan, a market test can be done to increase the certainty of successful commercialization. This last step in the evaluation process—the **test marketing stage**—provides actual sales results, which indicate the acceptance level of consumers. Positive test results indicate the degree of probability of a successful product launch and company formation.

ACQUISITIONS

Another way to start an entrepreneurial career is by acquiring an existing business. Although this does not occur as frequently as the development of an individual's idea, acquisitions can provide the entrepreneur with an excellent way to get into a business. For example, one entrepreneur acquired a chemical manufacturing company after becoming familiar with its problems and operations as an auditor for one of the Big Eight accounting firms. An acquisition is the purchase of a company or a part of it so that the acquired company is completely absorbed and no longer exists as a business entity. An acquisition can take many forms depending on such factors as the goals and position of the parties involved in the transaction, the amount of money involved, and the type of company.

While one of the key issues in buying a business is agreeing on a price, successful purchase of a business actually entails much more. In fact, often the structure of the deal can be more important to the parties involved and the resultant success of the transaction than the actual price. One radio station was successful after being acquired by an entrepreneur primarily because the previous owner loaned the money and took no principal payment (only interest) on the loan until the third year of operation.

From a strategic viewpoint, a prime concern of the entrepreneur is to maintain the focus of the new venture as a whole. Whether the acquisition will become the core of the new business or represents a needed capability, such as a distribution outlet, sales force, or production facility, the entrepreneur must ensure that it fits into the overall direction and structure of the strategic plan for the venture.

Evaluating a Firm

There are three widely used valuation approaches—asset, cash flow, and earnings—that the entrepreneur can use to determine the worth (or value) of an acquisition candidate. Some important ratios helpful in the evaluation process that measure profitability, activity, and liquidity are indicated in Table 4–3. In addition, a glossary of terms used in financial analysis and evaluation is found in the appendix to this chapter. When using the asset valuation method, the entrepreneur is valuing the underlying worth of the business based on its assets. Four methods can be used to obtain this valuation: book value, adjusted book value, liquidation value, or replacement value. While the easiest method for assessing the value of the firm is book value, the figure obtained should be only a starting point since it reflects the accounting practices of the company. A better refinement of this figure is adjusted book value, where the stated book value is adjusted to reflect the actual market value. Another method of valuing the assets of a potential acquisition company is to determine the amount that could be realized if the assets of the company were sold or liquidated and the proceeds used to settle all liabilities. This liquidation value reflects the valuation at a specific point in time. If the company continues operations successfully, the calculated value is low compared to the contribution of the assets. If the company encounters difficulties, a subsequent liquidation would probably yield significantly less than the amount calculated. The final method for valuing assets is the replacement value—the current cost of replacing the tangible assets of the business.

Another way of evaluating a firm, which is particularly relevant for an entrepreneur who is attempting to appraise a return on investment and a return on time, is to calculate the prospective cash flow from the business. There are several different cash flows that are important to the entrepreneur—positive cash flow, negative cash flow, and terminal value. Positive cash flow is cash received from the operation of the business including interest and salary, business-related expenses absorbed by the company, debt repayment, and dividends. Negative cash flow, signifying the company is losing money, can be a benefit to the entrepreneur and the investor in certain tax situations. Frequently the entrepreneur is not in a position to realize these benefits because of a low income; however, the tax benefits can provide substantial value to investors or those entrepreneurs in higher tax brackets. The final cash flow value—the terminal value—is a source of cash when the entrepreneur sells the business.

TABLE 4–3   Critical Financial Ratios in Evaluation

Liquidity: the ability of the company to meet its short-term obligations

Current ratio	$\dfrac{\text{current assets}}{\text{current liabilities}}$
Quick ratio	$\dfrac{\text{current assets-inventory}}{\text{current liabilities}}$

Leverage Ratios: the extent to which the company is financed by debt

Debt to total assets	$\dfrac{\text{total debt}}{\text{total assets}}$
Times interest earned	$\dfrac{\text{earnings before interest and taxes}}{\text{interest charges}}$

Activity Ratios: how well the company is using its resources

Inventory turnover	$\dfrac{\text{Cost of goods sold}}{\text{average inventory}}$ or $\dfrac{\text{sales}}{\text{average inventory}}$
Average collection period	$\dfrac{\text{receivables}}{\text{sales per day}}$
Fixed asset turnover	$\dfrac{\text{sales}}{\text{net fixed assets}}$
Total asset turnover	$\dfrac{\text{sales}}{\text{total assets}}$

Profitability Ratios: management's overall effectiveness

Profit margin	$\dfrac{\text{net profit after taxes (PAT)}}{\text{sales}}$
Return on investment (ROI)	$\dfrac{\text{net profit after taxes}}{\text{total assets}}$
Return on net worth	$\dfrac{\text{net profit after taxes}}{\text{owner equity}}$
Return on sales	$\dfrac{\text{sales}}{\text{owner equity}}$

The last frequently used evaluation method is earnings valuation. This method capitalizes earnings of a company by multiplying the earnings by the appropriate factor (the price earnings multiple). There are two critical issues in this evaluation procedure—the earnings and the multiple. The question of earnings involves determining the appropriate earnings period as well as the type of earnings. The earnings period can be either historical earnings, future earnings under the present management and ownership, or future earnings under new management and ownership. The type of earnings used during the selected period can be earnings before interest and taxes (EBIT), operating income, profit before tax, or profit after tax. The EBIT is used more frequently as it indicates the earning power and value of the basic business without the effects of financing.

After the time period and type of earnings have been established, the final step in earnings evaluation is to select the appropriate price earnings multiple. If the primary return from the investment will be in the form of stock sale at some future time, it is appropriate to select a price earnings multiple of a publicly traded stock similar to the company being evaluated in terms of product, nature of industry, anticipated earnings, growth, and likely stage of the stock market. This can be quite difficult, but usually a value or at least a range of values can be ascertained.

Whether asset, cash flow, or earnings valuation is used, the valuation of a business, though difficult, is vitally important in determining the feasibility of its acquisition. There are also some other important considerations in the acquisition decision process—synergy, legal considerations, and the plan for managing the acquired entity.

Synergy

"The whole is greater than the sum of the parts" is a concept that applies to the integration of an acquisition into the entrepreneur's venture. The synergy reflected in this statement should occur in both the business concept—the acquisition functioning as a vehicle to move toward overall goals—and the financial performance. The acquisition should positively impact the bottom line, affecting long-term gains and future growth. The lack of synergy is one of the most frequent causes of the acquisition failing to meet the anticipated goals of the entrepreneur. An acquisition should be carefully valuated and planned with specific attention given to its integration.

Legal Considerations

The legality of a particular acquisition centers around the type of acquisition and the resulting economic impact. Acquisition activities can be classified as horizontal, vertical, and conglomerate. The entrepreneur must carefully study all legal constraints before acquiring a particular operation.

Managing the Acquired Entity

Of course, the key for success of an acquisition is its management by the entrepreneur—the planning, execution, and postacquisition integration. A profile containing acquisition criteria and prospect data can help guide the search and initial screening. For a good profile, the entrepreneur must construct a checklist that identifies a prospective company, its history, management, product (or service), finances, marketing, production, and labor relations and then briefly evaluates the prospect. Prospects can be identified through internal referrals and external sources such as accountants, brokers, investment bankers, and lawyers. Once the prospect passes the initial checklist, more rigorous analysis is done to further evaluate the viability of the acquisition.

Hostile Takeovers

One form of acquisition, the hostile takeover, has received increased attention through the activities of such corporate raiders as Carl Icahn and T. Boone Pickens. Although hostile takeovers do not create wealth, as the underlying wealth is the assets of the corporation which were created by the company management, they often result in a more accurate appraisal of the company.

Three items make a hostile takeover possible: (1) a low stock evaluation versus performance, (2) a low debt/equity ratio allowing the entrepreneur to use the assets of the company to fund the takeover, and (3) a high percentage of institutional investors holding the company's stock. Since the objective of these institutional investors is to turn a quick profit, they will frequently vote in favor of the hostile takeover by the entrepreneur due to the anticipated gain in stock price and firm evaluation.

The most effective method for the entrepreneur to acquire a company in a hostile takeover is by using a multiple-step junk bond offer. Here the raiding entrepreneur acquires a small percent of the company (around 5 percent), lines up financial backers, and makes a very attractive offer for 51 percent of the company financed through the use of junk bonds. This sets up a situation that enables current shareholders to sell their stock and obtain their fair share of the value. If a stockholder does not tender his or her shares, that individual's stock has less value once the takeover occurs because the greater value of the company has been used to acquire 51 percent of the stock; the remaining 49 percent has less value.

An entrepreneur can also execute a hostile takeover through shareholder action by consent. This less publicized takeover format occurs when the majority of the shareholders are not pleased with the performance of the present management. They agree to back the entrepreneur in voting out the current management and selecting a new management team.

As might be expected, the increase in hostile takeovers has prompted companies to use a variety of defensive measures. One defensive weapon is to stagger the terms of the board of directors by electing only one-third of the board each year. This requires the raiding entrepreneur to go through two annual elections to obtain board control. Another more direct measure is for the company to alter the corporate charter, eliminating shareholder action by consent.

A third defensive measure is for the company to institute a "**poison pill**"—a mechanism to protect values of existing shareholders. With a poison pill in place at the time of an attempted hostile takeover, existing shareholders have the right to additional values. This additional value can be in the form of a provision that automatically increases the value of a current shareholders' stock in the event of a hostile takeover bid. Tendering stock to the raiding entrepreneur would then decrease the shareholder's value.

A fourth defensive measure is to institute **covenants** governing the level of allowable debt debentures. Covenants such as this would totally prohibit or dramatically reduce additional debt that can be incurred by the company, which makes it very difficult for a raider to use the assets of the company for the leverage needed to finance the takeover.

A final defensive weapon against hostile takeovers is "**poison puts.**" These are provisions in a company's bonds that allow the bond's holders to cash in if the insurer of the bond (the company) is taken over. This provision not only discourages takeovers but also helps hold the price of the bonds, which otherwise tend to decrease in takeover activity and the accompanying lower bond ratings.

Even if an entrepreneur does not use the hostile takeover mechanism for acquiring a venture, he or she should know about the activity, particularly the defensive weapons available—such knowledge might prove useful once the entrepreneur's own venture is successful. Perhaps one or more of these defensive measures can be incorporated in the original structure of the new venture to prevent a hostile takeover later when success and increased assets have been accrued.

JOINT VENTURE

Another mechanism for starting a new venture is through a joint venture, where two or more companies form an alliance to reach a goal beneficial to all parties.[16] The classic historical example of a joint venture occurred in 1879, when General Electric founder Thomas A. Edison teamed up with Corning Glass Works to make the experimental incandescent light bulb. Today, joint ventures are increasingly frequent as business risks have soared and start-up financing has become more difficult to obtain.

Historical Perspective

Joint ventures, defined originally in law as partnerships, had their origins in commercial or maritime trading enterprises. Merchants of ancient Egypt and Syria used the device to conduct sizable overseas trading operations. Similar joint venture partnerships were used by merchants in Great Britain in the 15th and 16th centuries.

---

[16]For a comprehensive presentation of joint ventures, see Kathryn Rudie Harrigan, *Strategies for Joint Ventures* (Lexington, MA: Lexington Books, 1985).

Some of the earliest joint ventures in the United States occurred in the late 1800s when railroads used these partnership arrangements for large-scale projects. Their use continued in the early part of the 20th century in order to pool the risks involved in shipping and gold and oil exploration. One of the largest joint ventures involved the development of crude oil reserves in the Middle East by four American oil companies—ARAMCO. Joint ventures were used even more frequently in the 50s and 60s as methods for pooling risks in such adventures as offshore oil explorations, producing motion pictures, televisions, jet engines, and phonograph records, and commercial real estate developments such as theaters or shopping centers. This increased usage set the stage for the joint ventures occurring in the 70s, 80s, and 90s, particularly in international activities.

Recent Joint Venture Activity

Deregulation, technological and economic changes, increasing need for creativity and product innovation, and globalization have precipitated the present high level of joint venture activity. Firms today are more willing than ever before to consider cooperative rather than competitive strategies to develop new technologies or penetrate new markets. A spirit of economic cooperation to meet the global challenges is the new watchword in corporate strategy.

Types of Joint Ventures

What are the types of joint venture arrangements being used in this new approach to establishing and expanding new ventures? When a joint venture is a separate entity with two or more active partners, there are three basic types: mutually operating joint ventures, one-partner-dependent joint ventures, and new-entity-emphasis joint ventures. In the mutually operating joint venture, the new entity created by two or more active partners is an autonomous decision-making unit carrying on some form of economic activity. Examples of this include Satellite Business Systems—a joint venture of IBM and Aetna Life and Casualty—and Tri-Star Pictures—a joint venture of CBS, Columbia Pictures, and Home Box Office. In each of these instances, the founding companies do not have an active decision-making role in the new entity.

In a joint venture where one partner is dependent on the other, a strong parent company can form a series of joint ventures, acting as its hub. A good example of this is recent actions taken by Eastman Kodak Company. As part of a broadscale diversification plan, Kodak has worked through joint ventures to develop a wide array of new products. Gaining a stake in what it hopes is a large and growing health-care market, it recently joined with ICN Pharmaceuticals, Inc.

to develop drugs to treat viral and aging problems. Kodak is supplying its store-house of 500,000 synthesized chemicals and the capital to support ICN's research into possible pharmaceutical uses for these compounds.

When there is a strong emphasis on the new entity created rather than on either of the creating firms, the third type of joint venture occurs. This joint venture is used less frequently as it needs more preinception research to determine its viability, as the nature of the parent firm's relationship to the new entity is crucial to joint venture success.

In structuring the joint venture agreement, the entrepreneur should be cognizant of some typical problems that might develop and the key factors for success. Most problems in joint venture arrangements stem from the lack of sympathy between the partners, the contribution of the resources and their value with respect to other resource contributions, and the autonomy of the new unit and the relative influence of each of the founders.

Although there are many problems associated with making a joint venture work effectively, these can be minimized if the entrepreneur carefully considers three principles in its establishment. The first principle is timing. Timing is critical in starting any new venture, perhaps even more so in formulating an effort with a partner(s). Not only will it probably take longer to develop a new venture with a partner, but the new entity may preclude any further separate company activity in that particular product/market niche. This preclusion can later become a problem, particularly in rapidly changing environments.

In addition to timing, the relationships between the two companies and between the parents and the joint venture must be considered. A joint venture has a greater probability of success when the managers involved can spark enthusiasm. This chemistry is important at the onset and needs to be carefully maintained throughout the effort. A method should be established for determining in advance if the chemistry is failing, along with procedures for handling this major problem when it occurs.

Finally, all the players involved in a joint venture must enter the relationship with reasonable expectations. Problems will indeed occur no matter what the structure, particularly if it is not entirely clear exactly what objectives can be achieved or if the partners have different objectives. Many joint ventures fail because the objectives were unclear or the joint venture partners aspired to achieve more than was possible in the particular industry situation.

LEVERAGED BUYOUTS

A leveraged buyout occurs when an entrepreneur (or any employee group) uses borrowed funds to purchase an existing venture for cash. Most leveraged buyouts (LBOs) occur because the entrepreneur purchasing the venture believes that he or she could run the company more efficiently than the owners have done. The buyout can be from a variety of sellers such as an entrepreneur or other owner who wants to retire; a large corporation desiring to divest itself of a subsidiary that is too small, having problems, or does not fit its long-term strategic plan; or some other group desiring to terminate its ownership position.

The purchaser needs a large amount of external funding since personal financial resources to acquire the firm directly are frequently limited. Since the issuance of additional equity to raise the needed funding is usually not possible, the capital needed is most often in the form of long-term debt financing (five years or more) with the assets of the firm being acquired serving as collateral. Who usually provides this long-term debt financing? Banks, venture capitalists, and insurance companies have been the most active providers for the debt needed in LBOs.

The actual financial package used in an LBO reflects the lender's risk-reward profile. While banks tend to use senior-debt issues, venture capitalists usually use subordinated debt issues with warrants or options. Regardless of the instrument used, the repayment plan established must be in line with the pro forma cash flows expected to be generated. The interest rates are usually variable and are consistent with the current yields of comparable risk investment.

In most leveraged buyouts, the debt capital usually exceeds the equity by 5:1 with some ratios being as high as 10:1. Given this high debt load and the accompanying high level of risk, successful LBOs usually involve a financially sound and stable company. Of course, any time such a high level of borrowed funds is employed in any business transaction there still remains a high risk of default. In a leveraged buyout, there is significantly more debt relative to equity than in a typical firm's capital structure. While this makes the financial risk great, the key to a successful LBO is not the relative debt-to-equity ratio but rather the ability of the entrepreneur taking over to be able to cover the principal and interest payments through increased sales and profits. The ability depends on the skills of the entrepreneur and the strength and stability of the firm.

Given the importance of the characteristics of the firm in a successful leveraged buyout, it is not surprising that most LBOs involve companies with a long track record of solid earnings, a strong management team, and a strong market share position. These factors help reduce the risk of the LBO failing. This risk can be further reduced by requiring the entrepreneur to invest most of his or her personal assets in the equity of the new firm.

How does an entrepreneur determine whether a specific company is a good opportunity for a leveraged buyout? This can be accomplished by following a basic evaluation procedure. First, the entrepreneur must determine whether the present owner's asking price is reasonable. Many subjective and quantitative techniques can be used in this determination. Subjective evaluations need to be made of the competitiveness of the industry and the competitive position of the firm in that industry; the uniqueness of the offering of the firm and the stage in the **product life cycle;** and the abilities of management and other key personal remaining to successfully operate the firm.

In addition to the important information gained from this evaluation, more quantitative techniques are needed to evaluate the fairness of the asking price. Some useful evaluation techniques were presented earlier in this chapter. The price-earnings ratio of the LBO prospect should be calculated and compared with those of comparable companies, as well as the present value of future earnings of the prospect and its book value.

After the proposed purchase price is found to be reasonable, the entrepreneur must assess the firm's debt capacity. This is particularly critical since the entrepreneur wants to raise as much of the capital needed as possible in the form of long-term debt. How much long-term debt can a prospective LBO carry? It depends on the prospect's business risk and the stability of its future cash flows. The cash flow must cover the long-term debt required to finance the LBO. Any financial amount that cannot be secured by long-term debt due to the inadequacy of the cash flow will need to be in the form of equity from the entrepreneur or other investors.

Once the level of long-term debt financing that can be handled is determined, the third step takes place—developing the appropriate financial package. The financial package must meet the needs and objectives of the providers of the funds as well as the situation of the company and the entrepreneur. While each LBO financial package is tailored to the specific situation, there are usually some significant restrictions. Typical restrictions include the payment of dividends, the issuance of stock options, and moving into risky new lines of business. Frequently, an LBO agreement with venture capitalists has warrants that are convertible into common stock at a later date. Also a sinking fund repayment of the long-term debt is frequently required.

There are many instances of both successful and unsuccessful LBOs. One of the most publicized involved R. H. Macy and Co.—a well-known department store chain. Although Macy's was not in bad condition before the merger, in terms of the traditional measures of sales per square foot, profitability, and return on assets, it had experienced a significant drop in profits and was losing talented middle executives. The LBO was accomplished by some 345 executives participating and sharing a 20 percent ownership in the $4.7 billion retailer. Since the acquisition, there has been a new entrepreneurial spirit in management, providing less incentive to leave for another company; a renewed motivation, with middle managers actually selling and earning sales floor bonuses during slack time; and a long-term planning direction for the board of directors, which meets five times a year instead of once a month—all indications that this LBO will be one of the successful ones.

Recently, LBOs have made significant news in terms of both size and the improprieties involved, particularly in the junk bond market in 1989–90. The largest LBO by far was that led by Kohlberg Kravis Roberts in acquiring RJR Nabisco for $25 million, which was 440 percent of book value. Another large LBO during that same year was HCA-Hospital Corporation of American acquiring Hospital Corp. of America for $3.9 million, 241 percent of book value. These and numerous other LBOs occurring during this period were financed in part by junk bonds. With the discontinuance of junk bonds in 1990, LBOs will not be as plentiful as financing will be more difficult to obtain. Some LBOs will still use cash and stock for financing such as the Wings Holdings acquisition of NWA airlines for $3.6 million in cash.

SUMMARY

The starting point for a new venture is the basic product or service to be offered. This idea can be either generated internally as a newly created concept or acquired externally through various acquisition techniques. A wide variety of techniques can be used in either instance.

The possible sources of new ideas range from the comments of consumers to changes in government regulations. Monitoring the comments of acquaintances, evaluating the new products offered by competitors, becoming familiar with the ideas contained in previously granted patents, and becoming actively involved in research and development are all techniques used by existing companies that would be appropriate for an entrepreneur also. There are many specific techniques entrepreneurs can use to generate ideas. For example, a better understanding of the consumer's true opinions can be gained from using a focus group rather than a survey. Another consumer-oriented approach is the problem inventory analysis, during which consumers associate particular problems with specific products and help develop a new product that does not contain identified faults.

Brainstorming is a technique useful in both idea generation and problem solving. The main idea behind this approach is to stimulate creativity by allowing a small group of people to work together in an open, nonstructured environment. Other techniques to enhance the creative process are using a checklist of related questions, free association, keeping an idea notebook, and using the "big-dream" approach. Some techniques are very structured, while others are designed to be more free-form. Each entrepreneur should know the technique best suited to him or her and what other techniques are available if one approach does not work.

Once the idea or group of ideas is generated, the planning and developing process begins. If a large number of potential ideas have been uncovered, they must be screened or evaluated to determine their appropriateness for further development. Ideas showing the most potential are then moved through the concept stage, the product development stage, the test marketing stage, and finally into commercialization. The entrepreneur should constantly evaluate the idea throughout this process.

A very different approach to creating a new business is through acquisition. Buying an existing business requires careful evaluation, on both the subjective and objective levels, of the entrepreneur's goals, the assets and condition of the proposed acquisition, and the potential results of the purchase. Several valuation techniques for determining the worth of a firm have been developed.

There are three ways of acquiring an existing business. Hostile takeovers rely on the entrepreneur being able to raise enough cash to make an offer for the majority of the stock of a publicly held corporation. As this has become a more frequent occurrence, methods for combating such offers have been developed. Joint ventures have also increased in popularity, particularly in fields requiring expensive research and development. The cooperative pooling of resources reduces the risk to both partners.

The last avenue presented, the leveraged buyout, is a frequently used method for beginning an entrepreneurial career. The preacquisition phase involves the identification and evaluation of prospects. The ability of the prospect to carry the long-term debt financing required depends largely on the entrepreneur's managerial talents.

CHAPTER

5

Developing and Using
a Business Plan

CHAPTER OBJECTIVES

1. To define what the business plan is, who prepares it, and who reads it.

2. To understand the scope and value of the business plan to investors, lenders, employees, suppliers, and customers.

3. To identify information needs and sources for business planning.

4. To present a comprehensive outline of an effective plan.

5. To present examples and a step-by-step explanation of the business plan.

6. To present helpful questions for the entrepreneur at each stage of the planning process.

7. To appreciate the importance of monitoring the business plan.

8. To understand the major reasons why business plans fail.

JOHN McCORMOCK

The business plan, although often criticized for being "dreams of glory," is an important requirement for seeking venture capital from banks or investors. The business plan also assists the entrepreneur in defining the goals and objects of the start-up and how they will be achieved. No one understands this better than John McCormock, the founder of Visible Changes Inc., a chain of hair salons.

John McCormock, a former New York City policeman, has created one of the fastest growing businesses in the country. People who are familiar with his achievements compare him to Ray Kroc. The success of Visible Changes Inc. is based on an unusual approach to people and information, which has attracted interest from entrepreneurs all over the world.

What was unusual about McCormock's business plan? The successful entrepreneur has built a hair salon company that gives employees a feeling of paternalism without having to give up equity in the operation. Each employee has to earn every dollar of benefit that he or she receives. How does it work?

Each employee has to achieve a request rate of 25 percent within three months and 50 percent within six months or leave. Commissions are also given for sale of hair-care products, with the commission on the first $120 used to pay health insurance. After the first $120 the employee may earn up to 15 percent. In addition, each employee is rated once a quarter on a scale of 1 to 10 for attitude, customer service, and success in meeting personal goals. A score of 10 every quarter can lead to a bonus of 10 percent. Other bonuses in the form of trips are also given to employees. On top of all this, each employee is involved in a profit-sharing program which is a flat 15 percent of gross pay. As of January 1, 1989, 100 employees will be fully vested in the profit-sharing program.

McCormock's plan certainly was considered unique for this industry. His incentive programs achieved not only an average salary for each employee of $33,000 but also an average revenue for each salon of $855,387 in 1986, more than three times better than the most successful large salon chains.

In addition to the success with sales revenue, the company also has outdistanced the industry in every performance measure including average sales per customer, sales of retail products as a percentage of revenue, and inventory turnover. These results would have been regarded as impossible by anyone in this industry, yet McCormock has not only reached these goals but has done so quite dramatically. All this came about with simply a new concept in running hair salons.

The typical hairdresser is in his or her early 20s. Rather than attending college, he or she went to hairdressing school and then worked for a salon. Usually these individuals average about $12,000 per year with few benefits. This contributed significantly to turnover and general confusion with regard to personnel. The $33,000 average salary of employees of Visible Changes is thus almost three times the average for the industry.

McCormock does not regard himself as being generous. Each employee's bonus, benefit, salary, and so on is tied to some specific action or achievement. In other words—they earn it.

The system has also been effective because employees contribute to many management decisions. For example, standards regarding request rates were set by the employees, not management. In addition to the employee involvement, McCormock has meticulously designed each salon to reflect a message of quality service. All of these quality design decisions make customers comfortable and help them feel they are getting good value for every dollar spent.

In spite of his success, McCormock is not willing to stand pat. With the management pool developed over the years with the incentive program, he is already planning expansion. Many will probably be enthusiastic about owning their own salons with financing and support from McCormock.[1]

As we can see from the example of Visible Changes Inc., the business plan is a meaningful and vital component in the entrepreneur's effort in launching a new venture. It represents long hours of critical assessment and evaluation of all aspects of a proposed venture, including the entrepreneur. The result of these many hours is a comprehensive, written, and well-organized document that will serve the entrepreneur as a guide in the beginning of the venture as well as an instrument to raise necessary capital and financing. In today's environment, where competition is intense and investors very selective in supporting new ventures, the business plan is essential.

WHAT IS THE BUSINESS PLAN?

The business plan is a written document prepared by the entrepreneur that describes all the relevant external and internal elements involved in starting a new venture. It is sometimes referred to as a game plan or a road map that answers the questions, Where am I now? Where am I going? and How will I get there? Potential investors, suppliers, and even customers will request or require a business plan.

---

[1]For more background on the story of Visible Changes Inc., see Bruce G. Posner and Bo Burlingham, "The Hottest Entrepreneur in America," *Inc.* 10, no. 1 (January 1988), pp. 44–58.

If we think of the business plan as a road map we might better understand its significance. Let's suppose you were trying to decide whether to drive from Boston to Los Angeles (mission or goal) in a motor home. There are a number of possible routes, each requiring different time frames and costs. Like the entrepreneur, the traveler must make some important decisions and gather information before preparing the plan.

The travel plan would consider external factors such as emergency car repair, weather conditions, road conditions, sights to see, available camp grounds, and so on. These factors are basically uncontrollable by the traveler but must be considered in the plan just as the entrepreneur would consider external factors such as new regulations, competition, social changes, changes in consumer needs, or new technology.

On the other hand, the traveler does have some idea of how much money is available, how much time he or she has, and the choices of highways, roads, campgrounds, sights, and so forth. Similarly, the entrepreneur has some control over manufacturing, marketing, and personnel in the new venture.

The traveler should consider all of these factors in determining what roads to take, what campgrounds to stay in, how much time to spend in selected locations, how much time and money to allow for vehicle maintenance, who will drive, and so on. Thus, the travel plan responds to the three questions, Where am I now? Where am I going? and How do I get there? Then the traveler in our example or the entrepreneur, the subject of our book, will be able to determine how much money will be needed from existing sources or new sources to achieve the plan.

WHO SHOULD WRITE THE PLAN?

The business plan should be prepared by the entrepreneur; however, he or she may consult with many other sources in its preparation. Lawyers, accountants, marketing consultants, and engineers are useful in the preparation of the plan. Some of the above sources can be found through services offered by the Small Business Administration (SBA), Service Core of Retired Executives (SCORE), Small Business Development Centers (SBDC), universities, and friends or relatives. Where there is doubt, the entrepreneur should consult with the sources being considered to ascertain their availability, scope of expertise, and fees.

To help determine whether to hire a consultant or to make use of other resources, the entrepreneur can make an objective assessment of his or her own skills. Figure 5–1 is an illustration of a rating to determine what skills are lacking and by how much. For example, a sales engineer recently designed a new machine that allows a user to send a 10-second personalized message in a greeting card. A primary concern was how best to market the machine: as a promotional tool a firm could use for its distributors, suppliers, shareholders, or employees or as a retail product for end users. This entrepreneur, in assessing his skills, rated himself as excellent in product design and sales, good in organizing,

FIGURE 5–1 Skills Assessment

Skills	Excellent	Good	Fair	Poor
Accounting/taxes				
Planning				
Forecasting				
Marketing research				
Sales				
People management				
Product design				
Legal issues				
Organizing				

and only fair or poor in all the remaining skills. Through such an assessment, the entrepreneur can identify what skills are needed and from where they could be obtained.

SCOPE AND VALUE OF THE BUSINESS PLAN—WHO READS THE PLAN?

The business plan may be read by employees, investors, bankers, venture capitalists, suppliers, customers, and consultants. Since each of these segments will read the plan for different purposes, it must be comprehensive enough to address all their particular issues and concerns. In some ways the business plan must try to satisfy the needs of everyone, whereas in the actual marketplace the entrepreneur's product will be trying to meet the needs of selected groups of customers.

The depth and detail in the business plan depend on the size and scope of the proposed new venture. An entrepreneur planning to market a new portable computer will need quite a comprehensive business plan, largely because of the nature of the product and market pursued. On the other hand, an entrepreneur who plans to open a retail video store will not need the comprehensive coverage required by a new computer manufacturer. Thus, differences in the scope of the business plan may depend on whether the new venture is a service, involves manufacturing, or is a consumer good or industrial product. The size of the market, competition, and potential growth may also affect the scope of the business plan.

The business plan is valuable to the entrepreneur, potential investors, or even for the review of new personnel. The business plan is important to these people because:

- It helps determine the viability of the venture in a designated market.
- It provides guidance to the entrepreneur in organizing his or her planning activities.
- It serves as an important tool in helping to obtain financing.

Potential investors are very particular about what should be included in the business plan. Even if some of the information is based on assumptions, the thinking process required to complete the plan is a valuable experience for the entrepreneur since it forces him or her to assess such things as cash flow and cash requirements. In addition, the thinking process takes the entrepreneur into the future, leading him or her to consider important issues that could impede the road to success.

The process also provides a self-assessment of the entrepreneur. Usually, he or she feels that the new venture is assured of success. However, the planning process forces the entrepreneur to bring objectivity to the idea and reflect on such questions as Does the idea make sense? Will it work? Who is my customer? Does it satisfy customer needs? What kind of protection can I get against imitation by competitors? Can I manage such a business? Whom will I compete with? This self-evaluation is similar to role-playing, requiring the entrepreneur to think through various scenarios and consider obstacles that might prevent the venture from succeeding. The process allows the entrepreneur to plan ways to avoid such obstacles. It may even be possible that, after preparing the business plan, the entrepreneur realizes the obstacles cannot be avoided or overcome. Hence the venture may be terminated while still on paper. Although this certainly is not the most desirable conclusion, it would be much better to terminate the business endeavor before investing further time and money, then failing.

INFORMATION NEEDS

Before committing time and energy to preparing a business plan, the entrepreneur should do a quick feasibility study of the business concept to see if there are any possible barriers to success. The information, which can be obtained from many sources, should focus on marketing, finance, and production. Before beginning the feasibility study, the entrepreneur should clearly define the goals and objectives of his or her venture. These goals help define what needs to be done and how it will be accomplished. These goals and objectives also provide a framework for the business plan, marketing plan, and financial plan.

Goals and objectives that are too general make the business plan difficult to control and implement. An example might illustrate this point more clearly.

A young woman, Ms. G, and her mother, Mrs. G, had been making Christmas dresses for years for relatives and friends. Both enjoyed sewing and creating a "different" dress for each customer. Responding to continued requests, the two women started their own business and began to explore the distribution of such dresses to major department stores. Access to many seamstresses, under the direction of Mrs. G, would make quantity production feasible. With the slow acceptance of department stores, the two entrepreneurs continued to make dresses on request. However, many requests required customized work that was generally done without much extra charge. In evaluating their costs, both realized they were losing money when they factored in their own charge.

The preceding example illustrates the lack of a business goal and a clear understanding of the business concept. Should the business be custom, volume, or both, and what prices should reflect these different strategies? Because the entrepreneurs did not address these issues, they did not understand where they were going. This confusion led to negative profits until they both realized the importance of clear goals and the need for more information.

We can compare the above example with John McCormock's Visible Changes Inc. For his start-up, McCormock had clearly defined goals that he translated into specific successful marketing strategies. For example, McCormock's goal of having every employee earn his or her benefits had allowed employees not only to receive health benefits but also to set aside funds for retirement. Both these benefits are a rare commodity among hairdressers.

Market Information

One of the initial important elements of information needed by the entrepreneur is the market potential for the product or service. The size of the market can be determined by using secondary sources or by developing a marketing research study. Given the limits of financial resources for most new ventures, the entrepreneur should first explore a number of secondary sources before considering any primary research study.

To assess the total market potential, the entrepreneur should consider trade associations, government reports, and published studies. (See Figure 5–8 for examples of secondary sources). In some instances this information is readily available. For example, an entrepreneur recently developed a new software package called Club-Kit for tennis and racquetball clubs. To determine the size of the potential market, the entrepreneur identified the number of tennis and racquetball clubs from a state directory. Business-to-business telephone books were also available as an alternative source. The total number of clubs thus represented the maximum potential sales for the product. In addition to the product, the company anticipated providing management and marketing consultation to these clubs. The total market potential for the software package was then assessed to be a percentage of the number of hours per year.

The service aspect of the market will be more difficult to project. However, the entrepreneur could contact a sample of clubs and determine how much of this service these clubs would need. Other external sources such as trade associations may publish data on consulting services that could also be used to support any projections.[2]

The information obtained in this market feasibility study will support the entrepreneur's marketing decisions in the business plan. It should also include information on competition, margins for distribution, market trends, and growth potential.

Operations Information Needs

The relevance of a feasibility study of the manufacturing operations depends on the nature of the business. Most of the information needed can be obtained through direct contact with the appropriate source.

The entrepreneur may need information on the following:

- Location—The company's location and its accessibility to customers, suppliers, and distributors need to be determined.
- Manufacturing operations—Basic machine and assembly operations need to be identified, as well as whether any of these operations would be subcontracted and by whom.
- Raw materials—The raw materials needed and suppliers' names, addresses, and costs should be determined.
- Equipment—The equipment needed should be listed and whether it will be purchased or leased.
- Labor skills—Each unique skill needed, the number of personnel in each skill, pay rate, and an assessment of where and how these skills will be obtained should be determined.
- Space—The total amount of space needed should be determined, including whether the space will be owned, leased, and so on.
- Overhead—Each item needed to support manufacturing, such as tools, supplies, utilities, salaries, and so on, should be determined.

Most of the above information will be incorporated directly into the business plan. Each item may require some research but is deemed necessary by those who will assess the business plan and consider funding the proposal.

---

[2]For more information on issues and questions relating to market information needs, see Michael P. Peters, "The Role of Planning in the Marketing of New Products," *Planning Review,* November 1980, 24–28.

Financial Information Needs

Before preparing the business plan, the entrepreneur must have a complete evaluation of the profitability of the venture. The assessment will primarily tell potential investors if the business will be profitable, how much money will be needed to launch the business and meet short-term financial needs, and how this money will be obtained (i.e., stock, debt, etc.).

There are traditionally three areas of financial information that will be needed to ascertain the feasibility of the new venture: (1) expected sales and expense figures for at least the first three years; (2) cash flow figures for the first three years; and (3) current balance sheet figures and pro forma balance sheets for the next three years.

Determination of the expected sales and expense figures for each of the first 12 months and each subsequent year is based on the market information discussed earlier. Each expense item should be identified and given on a monthly basis for the year.

Estimates of cash flow consider the ability of the new venture to meet expenses at designated times of the year. The cash flow forecast should identify the beginning cash, expected accounts receivable and other receipts, and all disbursements on a monthly basis for the entire year.

Current balance sheet figures provide the financial conditions of the business at any particular time. They identify the assets of the business, the liabilities (what is owed), and the investment made by the owner or other partners.

WRITING THE BUSINESS PLAN

The business plan could take more than 200 hours to prepare, depending on the experience and knowledge of the entrepreneur. It should be comprehensive enough to give any potential investor a complete picture and understanding of the new venture. It will also help the entrepreneur clarify his or her thinking about the business.

Many entrepreneurs incorrectly estimate the length of time that an effective plan will take to prepare. Once the process has begun, however, the entrepreneur will realize that it is invaluable in sorting out the business functions of a new venture.

The outline for a business plan is illustrated in Figure 5–2. Each of the items in the outline is detailed in the following paragraphs of this chapter. Key questions in each section are also appropriately detailed.[3]

---

[3]For additional material, see *Business Plan for Small Manufacturers,* 2nd ed. (Lexington, MA: Haley Publications, 1985).

FIGURE 5–2   Outline of a Business Plan

  I. Introductory Page
     A. Name and address of business
     B. Name(s) and address(es) of principals
     C. Nature of business
     D. Statement of financing needed
     E. Statement of confidentiality of report

 II. Executive Summary—Three to four pages summarizing the complete
     business plan

III. Industry Analysis
     A. Future outlook and trends
     B. Analysis of competitors
     C. Market segmentation
     D. Industry forecasts

 IV. Description of Venture
     A. Product(s)
     B. Service(s)
     C. Size of business
     D. Office equipment and personnel
     E. Background of entrepreneurs

  V. Production Plan
     A. Manufacturing process (amount subcontracted)
     B. Physical plant
     C. Machinery and equipment
     D. Names of suppliers of raw materials

 VI. Marketing Plan
     A. Pricing
     B. Distribution
     C. Promotion
     D. Product forecasts
     E. Controls

VII. Organizational Plan
     A. Form of ownership
     B. Identification of partners or principal shareholders
     C. Authority of principals
     D. Management-team background
     E. Roles and responsibilities of members of organization

VIII. Assessment of Risk
     A. Evaluate weakness of business
     B. New technologies
     C. Contingency plans

 IX. Financial Plan
     A. Pro forma income statement
     B. Cash flow projections
     C. Pro forma balance sheet
     D. Break-even analysis
     E. Sources and applications of funds

FIGURE 5–2   *(concluded)*

   X.   Appendix (contains backup material)
      A. Letters
      B. Market research data
      C. Leases or contracts
      D. Price lists from suppliers

Introductory Page

This is the title or cover page that provides a brief summary of the business plan's contents. The introductory page should contain the following:

- The name and address of the company.
- The name of the entrepreneur(s) and a telephone number.
- A paragraph describing the company and the nature of the business.
- The amount of financing needed. The entrepreneur may offer a package, that is, stock, debt, and so on. However, many venture capitalists prefer to structure this package in their own way.
- A statement of the confidentiality of the report. This is for security purposes and is important for the entrepreneur.

   This title page sets out the basic concept that the entrepreneur is attempting to develop. Investors consider it important because they can determine the amount of investment needed without having to read through the entire plan. An illustration of this page can be found in Figure 5–3.

Executive Summary

This section of the business plan is prepared after the total plan is written. About three to four pages in length, the executive summary should stimulate the interest of the potential investor. The investor uses the summary to determine if the business plan is worth reading in total. Thus, it would highlight in a concise and convincing manner the key points in the business plan, that is, the nature of the venture, financing needed, market potential, and support as to why it will succeed.

Industry Analysis

It is important to put the new venture in a proper context. In particular, the potential investor, while assessing the venture on a number of criteria, needs to know which industry the entrepreneur will be competing in. Discussion of the

---

FIGURE 5–3   Sample Introductory Page

KC CLEANING SERVICE
OAK KNOLL ROAD
BOSTON, MA 02167
(617) 969-0100

Co-owners: Kimberly Peters, Christa Peters

Description of Business:

This business will provide cleaning service on a contract basis to small and medium-sized businesses. Services include cleaning of floors, carpets, draperies, and windows, and regular sweeping, dusting, and washing. Contracts will be for one year and will specify the specific services and scheduling for completion of services.

Financing:

Initial financing requested is a $100,000 loan to be paid off over 6 years. This debt will cover office space, office equipment and supplies, two leased vans, advertising, and selling costs.

This report is confidential and is the property of the co-owners listed above. It is intended only for use by the persons to whom it is transmitted and any reproduction or divulgence of any of its contents without the prior written consent of the company is prohibited.

---

industry outlook, including future trends and historical achievements, should be included. The entrepreneur should also provide insight on new product developments in this industry. Competitive analysis is also an important part of this section. Each major competitor should be identified, with appropriate strengths and weaknesses described, particularly as to how they might affect the new venture's potential success in the market.

Who is the customer? The market should be segmented and the target market for the entrepreneur identified. Most new ventures are likely to compete effectively in only one or a few of the market segments. This strategy may be a function of the competition, who may be more vulnerable in one or a few segments of the total market.

Any forecasts made by the industry or by the government should be noted. A high-growth market may be viewed more favorably by the potential investor. Some key questions the entrepreneur should consider are described in Figure 5–4.

Description of Venture

The new venture should be described in detail in this section of the business plan. This will enable the investor to ascertain the size and scope of the business. Key elements are the product(s) or service(s), the location and size of the business, the personnel and office equipment that will be needed, the background of

---

FIGURE 5–4 Critical Issues for Industry Analysis

1. What are total industry sales over the past five years?
2. What is anticipated growth in this industry?
3. How many new firms have entered this industry in the past three years?
4. What new products have been recently introduced in this industry?
5. Who are the nearest competitors?
6. How will your business operation be better than this?
7. Are each of your major competitors' sales growing, declining, or steady?
8. What are the strengths and weaknesses of each of your competitors?
9. What is the profile of your customers?
10. How does your customer profile differ from that of your competition?

FIGURE 5–5 Describing the Venture

1. What are your product(s) and/or service(s)?
2. Describe the product(s) and/or service(s), including patent, copyright, or trademark status.
3. Where will the business be located?
4. Is your building new? Old? In need of renovations? (If renovation needed, state costs.)
5. Is the building leased or owned? (State the terms.)
6. Why is this building and location right for your business?
7. What additional skills or personnel will be needed to operate the business?
8. What office equipment will be needed?
9. Will equipment be purchased or leased?
10. What is your business background?
11. What management experience do you have?
12. Describe personal data such as education, age, special abilities, and interests.
13. What are your reasons for going into business?
14. Why will you be successful in this venture?
15. What development work has been completed to this date?

---

the entrepreneur(s), and the history of the venture. Figure 5–5 summarizes some of the important questions the entrepreneur needs to answer when preparing this section of the business plan.

Location of any business may be vital to its success, particularly if the business is retail or involves a service. Thus, the emphasis placed on location in the business plan is a function of the type of business.

In assessing the building or space the business will occupy, the entrepreneur may need to evaluate such factors as parking, access from roadways to facility, access to customers, suppliers, or distributors, delivery rates, and town regulations or zoning laws. An enlarged local map may help give the location some perspective with regard to roads, highways, access, and so forth.

Recently an entrepreneur considered opening a new donut shop at a location diagonally across from a small shopping mall on a heavily traveled road. Traffic counts indicated a large potential customer base if people would stop for coffee and so forth on their way to work. After enlarging a local map, the entrepreneur noted that the morning flow of traffic required drivers to make a left turn into the donut shop, crossing the outbound lane. Unfortunately, the roadway was divided by a concrete center strip with no break to allow for a left-hand turn. The only possibility for entry into the shop required the customer to drive down about 400 yards and make a U-turn. It would also be difficult for the customer to get back on the roadway traveling in the right direction. Since the town was unwilling to open the road, the entrepreneur eliminated this site from any further consideration.

This simple assessment of the location, market, and so on saved the entrepreneur from a potential disaster. Maps that locate customers, competitors, and even alternative locations for a building or site can be helpful in this evaluation. Some of the important questions that might be asked by an entrepreneur are as follows:

- How much space is needed?
- Should I buy or lease the building?
- What is the cost per square foot?
- Is the site zoned for commercial use?
- What town restrictions exist for signs, parking, and so forth?
- Is renovation of the building necessary?
- Is the facility accessible to traffic?
- Is there adequate parking?
- Will the existing facility have room for expansion?
- What is the economic, demographic profile of the area?
- Is there an adequate labor pool available?
- What are local taxes?
- Are sewage, electricity, and plumbing adequate?

If the building or site decision involves legal issues such as a lease or requires town variances, the entrepreneur should hire a lawyer. Problems relating to regulations and leases can be avoided easily and under no circumstances should the entrepreneur try to negotiate with the town or a landlord without good legal advice.

Production Plan

If the new venture is a manufacturing operation, a production plan is necessary. This plan should describe the complete manufacturing process. If some or all of the manufacturing process is to be subcontracted, the plan should describe the subcontractor(s), including location, reasons for selection, costs, and any contracts that have been completed. If the manufacturing is to be carried out in

---

FIGURE 5–6 Production Plan

 1. Will you be responsible for all or part of the manufacturing operation?
 2. If some manufacturing is subcontracted, who will be the subcontractor(s)? (Give names and addresses.)
 3. Why were these subcontractors selected?
 4. What are the costs of the subcontracted manufacturing? (Include copies of any written contracts.)
 5. What will be the layout of the production process? (Illustrate steps if possible.)
 6. What equipment will be needed immediately for manufacturing?
 7. What raw materials will be needed for manufacturing?
 8. Who are the suppliers of new materials and appropriate costs?
 9. What are the costs of manufacturing the product?
10. What are the future capital equipment needs of the venture?

If a Retail Operation or Service:
 1. From whom will merchandise be purchased?
 2. How will the inventory control system operate?
 3. What are storage needs of the venture and how will they be promoted?

---

whole or in part by the entrepreneur, he or she will need to describe the physical plant layout, the machinery and equipment needed to perform the manufacturing operations, raw materials and suppliers' names, addresses, and terms, costs of manufacturing, and any future capital equipment needs. In a manufacturing operation, the discussion of these items will be important to any potential investor in assessing financial needs.

If the venture is not a manufacturing operation but a retail store or service, this section would be titled as a "merchandising plan" and the purchasing of merchandise, inventory control system, and storage needs should be described. Figure 5–6 summarizes some of the key questions for this section of the business plan.

Marketing Plan

The marketing plan (discussed in detail in Chapter 6) is an important part of the business plan since it describes how the product(s) or service(s) will be distributed, priced, and promoted. Specific forecasts for product(s) or service(s) are indicated in order to project profitability of the venture. The budget and appropriate controls needed for marketing strategy decisions are also discussed in detail in Chapter 6.

Potential investors regard the marketing plan as critical to the success of the new venture. Thus, enough time should be taken to ensure that the strategy outlined can be effectively implemented. Marketing planning will be an annual requirement (with careful monitoring and changes made on a weekly or monthly basis) for the entrepreneur and should be regarded as the road map for short-term decision making.

FIGURE 5–7   Organization Structure

1. What is the form of ownership of the organization?
2. If a partnership, who are the partners and what are the terms of agreement?
3. If incorporated, who are the principal shareholders and how much stock do they own?
4. What type and how many shares of voting or nonvoting stock have been issued?
5. Who are members of the board of directors? (Give names, addresses, and résumés.)
6. Who has check-signing authority or control?
7. Who and what is the background of each member of the management team?
8. What are the roles and responsibilities of each member of the management team?
9. What are the salaries, bonuses, or other forms of payment for each member of the management team?

Organizational Plan

This section of the business plan should describe the venture's form of owner-ship, that is, proprietorship, partnership, or corporation. If the venture is a part-nership, the terms of the partnership should be included. If the venture is a corporation, it is important to detail the shares of stock authorized, share op-tions, names, and addresses and résumés of the directors and officers of the corporation. It is also helpful to provide an organization chart indicating the line of authority and the responsibilities of the members of the organization. Alter-native forms of organization and discussion of the various layouts of an organi-zation are discussed further in Chapter 8.

Figure 5–7 summarizes some of the key questions the entrepreneur needs to answer in preparing this section of the business plan. This information provides the potential investor with a clear understanding of who controls the organization and how other members will interact in performing their management functions.

Assessment of Risk

Every new venture will be faced with some potential hazards, given the partic-ular industry and competitive environment. It is important to the entrepreneur to recognize the potential risks and prepare an effective strategy to deal with them. Major risks for a new venture could result from a competitor's reaction; weak-nesses in the marketing, production, or management team; and new advances in technology that might render the new product obsolete. Even if these factors present no risks to the new venture, the business plan should discuss why that is the case.

It is also useful for the entrepreneur to provide alternative strategies should any of the above risk factors occur. These contingency plans and strategies illus-trate to the potential investor that the entrepreneur is sensitive to important risks and is prepared should any occur.

Financial Plan

The financial plan is discussed further in Chapter 7. This, like the marketing, production, and organization plans, is an important part of the business plan. It determines the potential investment commitment needed for the new venture and indicates whether the business plan is economically feasible.

Generally, three financial areas are discussed in this section of the business plan. First, the entrepreneur should summarize the forecasted sales and the appropriate expenses for at least the first three years, with the first year's projections provided monthly. The form for displaying this information is illustrated in Chapter 7. It includes the forecasted sales, cost of goods sold, and the general and administrative expenses. Net profit after taxes can then be projected by estimating income taxes.

The second major area of financial information needed is cash flow figures for three years, with the first year's projections provided monthly. Since bills have to be paid at different times of the year, it is important to determine the demands on cash on a monthly basis, especially in the first year. Remember that sales may be irregular and receipts from customers may also be spread out, thus necessitating the borrowing of short-term capital to meet fixed expenses such as salaries and utilities. A form for projecting the cash flow needs for a 12-month period can be found in Chapter 7.

The last financial item needed in this section of the business plan is the projected balance sheet. This shows the financial condition of the business at a specific time. It summarizes the assets of a business, its liabilities (what is owed), the investment of the entrepreneur and any partners, and retained earnings (or cumulative losses). A form for the balance sheet and more detailed explanations of the items included are discussed further in Chapter 7. Any assumptions considered for the balance sheet or any other item in the financial plan should be listed for the benefit of the potential investor.

Appendix

The appendix of the business plan generally contains any backup material that is not necessary in the text of the document. Reference to any of the documents in the appendix should be made in the plan itself. Various types of documents that may be included are discussed below.

Letters from customers, distributors, or subcontractors are examples of information that should be included in the appendix. Any documentation of information, that is, secondary data or primary research data used to support plan decisions, should also be included. Leases, contracts, or any other types of agreement that have been initiated may also be included in the appendix. Last, price lists from suppliers and competitors may be added.

USING AND IMPLEMENTING THE BUSINESS PLAN

The business plan is designed to guide the entrepreneur through the first year of operations. It is important that the implementation of strategy contain control points to ascertain progress and to initiate contingency plans if necessary. Some of the controls necessary in manufacturing, marketing, financing, and the organization are discussed in subsequent chapters. Most important to the entrepreneur is that the business plan not end up in a drawer somewhere once the financing has been attained and the business launched.

There has been a tendency among many entrepreneurs to avoid planning. The reason often given is that planning is dull or boring and is something used only by large companies. This may be an excuse; perhaps the real truth is that some entrepreneurs are afraid to plan.[4]

Planning is and should be an important part of any business operation. Without good planning the entrepreneur is likely to pay an enormous price. All one has to do is consider the planning done by suppliers, customers, competitors, and banks to realize that it is important for the entrepreneur. It is also important to realize that without good planning the employees will not understand the company's goals and how they are expected to perform in their jobs. We again point to our example of John McCormock's business, where employees have a clear understanding of what is expected.

Bankers are the first to admit that few business failures result from a lack of cash but, instead, fail because of the entrepreneur's inability to plan effectively.

Intelligent planning is not a difficult or impossible exercise for the inexperienced entrepreneur. With the proper commitment and support from many outside resources, such as those shown in Figure 5–8, the entrepreneur can prepare an effective business plan.

In addition, the entrepreneur can enhance effective implementation of the business plan by developing a schedule to measure progress and to institute contingency plans. These frequent readings or control procedures will be discussed further below.

Measuring Plan Progress

During the introductory phases of the start-up, the entrepreneur should determine the points at which decisions should be made as to whether the goals or objectives are on schedule. Typically, the business plan projections will be made on a 12-month schedule. However, the entrepreneur cannot wait 12 months to see if the plan has been successfully achieved. Instead, on a frequent basis (i.e.,

---

[4]Bruce G. Posner, "Real Entrepreneurs Don't Plan," *Inc.*, November, 1985, 129–35.

FIGURE 5-8   Sources of Information

- Small Business Administration
- Department of Commerce
- Federal information centers
- Bureau of Census
- State and municipal governments
- Banks
- Chambers of Commerce
- Trade associations
- Trade journals
- Libraries
- Universities and community colleges

---

beginning of each month) the entrepreneur should check the profit and loss statement, cash flow projections, and information on inventory, production, quality, sales, collection of accounts receivable, and disbursements for the previous month. This feedback should be simple but be able to provide key members of the organization with current information in time to correct any major deviations from the goals and objectives outlined. A brief description of each of these control elements is given below:

- Inventory control—By controlling inventory, the firm can ensure maximum service to the customer. The faster the firm gets back its investment in raw materials and finished goods, the faster that capital can be reinvested to meet additional customer needs.
- Production control—Compare the cost figures estimated in the business plan against day-to-day operation costs. This will help to control machine time, labor manhours, process time, delay time, and downtime cost.
- Quality control—This will depend on the type of production system but is designed to make sure that the product performs satisfactorily.
- Sales control—Information on units, dollars, specific products sold, price of sales, meeting of delivery dates, and credit terms are all useful to get a good perspective of the sales of the new venture. In addition, an effective collection system for accounts receivable should be set up to avoid aging of accounts and bad debts.
- Disbursements—The new venture should also control the amount of money paid out. All bills should be reviewed to determine how much is being disbursed and for what purpose.

Updating the Plan

The most effective business plan can become out of date if conditions change. Environmental factors such as the economy, customers, new technology, or competition and internal factors such as the loss or addition of key employees can all change the direction of the business plan. Thus, it is important to be sensitive to changes in the company, industry, and market. If these changes are likely to affect the business plan, the entrepreneur should determine what revisions are needed in it. In this manner, the entrepreneur can maintain reasonable targets and goals and keep the new venture on a course that will increase its probability of success.

WHY SOME BUSINESS PLANS FAIL

Generally a poorly prepared business plan can be blamed on one or more of the following factors:

- Goals set by the entrepreneur are unreasonable.
- Goals are not measurable.
- The entrepreneur has not made a total commitment to the business or to the family.
- The entrepreneur has no experience in the planned business.
- The entrepreneur has no sense of potential threats or weaknesses to the business.
- No customer need was established for the purposed product or service.

Setting goals requires the entrepreneur to be well informed about the type of business and the competitive environment. Goals should be specific and not so mundane as to lack any basis of control. For example, the entrepreneur may target a specific market share, units sold, or revenue. These goals are measurable and can be monitored over time.

In addition, the entrepreneur who has not made a total commitment to the business or to his or her family will not be able to meet the demands of a new venture. For example, it is difficult to operate a new venture on a part-time basis while still holding onto a full-time position. And it is also difficult to operate a business without an understanding from family members as to the time and resources that will be needed. Lenders or investors will not be favorably inclined toward a venture that does not have full-time commitment. Moreover, lenders or investors will expect the entrepreneur to make a significant financial commitment to the business even if it means a second mortgage or a depletion of savings.

Generally, a lack of experience will result in failure unless the entrepreneur can either attain the necessary knowledge or team up with someone who already has it. For example, an entrepreneur trying to start a new restaurant without any experience or knowledge of the restaurant business would be disastrous.

The entrepreneur should also document customer needs before preparing the plan. Customer needs can be identified from direct experience, letters from customers, or from marketing research. A clear understanding of these needs and how the entrepreneur's business will effectively meet them is vital to the success of the new venture.

SUMMARY

This chapter has established the scope and value of the business plan and outlined the steps in its preparation. The business plan may be read by employees, investors, lenders, suppliers, customers, and consultants. The scope of the plan will depend on the size and the specific industry for which the venture is intended.

The business plan is essential in launching a new venture. The results of many hours of preparation will represent a comprehensive, written, and well-organized document that will serve as a guide to the entrepreneur and as an instrument to raise necessary capital and financing.

Before beginning the business plan, the entrepreneur will need information on the market, manufacturing operations, and financial estimations. This information should be evaluated based on the goals and objectives of the new culture. These goals and objectives provide a framework for a controlling business plan.

The chapter provides a comprehensive discussion and outline of a typical business plan. Each key element in the plan is discussed and examples are provided. Control decisions are presented to ensure the effective implementation of the business plan. In addition, some insights as to why business plans fail are discussed.

CHAPTER

The Marketing Plan

CHAPTER OBJECTIVES

1. To explain the marketing system and its key components.

2. To compare marketing strategies for a service and product-related business.

3. To define the steps in preparing the marketing plan.

4. To describe the type of information needed to prepare an effective marketing plan.

5. To explain why some marketing plans fail.

FRANK PERDUE

At a time when market planning has become a hot topic across the country, one of the most effective marketers is a slender, whiny-voiced, balding, long-nosed company president, Frank Perdue. His popularity has achieved cultlike significance in the Northeast, where he does most of his business. Without a doubt, Frank Perdue has become the single most important entrepreneur in the history of chickens.

In 1920, the year Frank Perdue was born, his father spent $5 for his first laying hens. At the age of ten Frank was netting, after expenses, almost $20 per week, which during the Depression was a good salary. After two years of college, Frank quit to join his father's business. He also kept his own flock of hens on the side and by 1941 he personally owned 800 hens.

Perdue farms has built its success on a tightly run organization that Frank Perdue attributes to his father. His father never borrowed a cent during the 40 years he was active in the chicken business. In fact, it was not until 1961, when his father was 76 and Frank was 41, that they did borrow any money—a $500,000 loan needed to expand the business.

Since that day, Perdue Farms has never failed to grow. In fact, Perdue has built a business that now employs more than 11,000 people and has achieved more than $500 million in annual sales. This places Perdue Farms in the top 50 of the private firms in the United States.

In 1968, Perdue, with a clear set of goals and objectives as part of his plan, invested in a processing plan in order to market his own branded, freshly dressed poultry. His strategy has been to emphasize to customers the concept of product freshness through the statement "never frozen." Through careful planning and innovations in breeding, nutrition, housing, equipment, rearing, and disease control and management, Perdue Farms now controls the entire production cycle from the genes to the chicken dinner. Continuous new products such as the stuffed roaster, chicken franks, chicken bologna, and fresh breaded nuggets have projected the company into a dominant market position in the Northeast and made it the fifth largest producer of broilers in the United States.

One of the key innovations in the marketing of Perdue products has been Perdue's personal involvement in advertising. During the past 15 years he has appeared in almost every television commercial for his products. One of the great advertising slogans of all times was part of a Perdue Farm ad: "It takes a tough man to make a tender chicken." This slogan's success lies in more than its clever phrasing—it's because of Perdue himself and his not-so-tough appeal.

Advertising, although an important part of the firm's success, is still not the most important marketing variable. According to Perdue, "The quality of the product is the most important variable and advertising is number two. In advertising you have to tell people why they should buy the product. That means you have to have a product that's better than most or if possible the best in your field." This image of quality is exactly what Perdue has been able to accomplish in the television commercials.

Now in his late 60s, Perdue still attends supermarket openings. It is not unusual to find him spending his Sundays at a number of functions. Why does he attend such functions? "Because they ask me," he states. "My father wouldn't do it but I'll do anything it takes for this business because I consider it my baby. I have been totally into it for 20 to 30 years and I've been the principal force in its growth."

Frank Perdue has succeeded by careful market planning of a product that most would argue was undifferentiable. His success has given the chicken business a tremendous boost in sales and profits.

Because the entrepreneur must anticipate the future, it is important for him or her to develop and prepare a marketing plan. Planning, as discussed in the previous chapter, spans a wide assortment and range of activities and is intended to formally detail the business activities, strategies, responsibilities, budgets, and controls to meet specific, designated goals.

The marketing plan represents a significant element in the business plan for a new venture. In addition, market planning is an annual or short-term planning activity that provides action on the marketing-mix variables (product, price, distribution, and promotion). Like the annual budgeting cycle, market planning has become an annual activity all entrepreneurs should incorporate, regardless of the size or type of the business. These marketing plans must be monitored frequently, that is, monthly, to assess if the business is "on plan." If not "on plan," changes in strategy or even in the goals and objectives may be warranted.

UNDERSTANDING MARKET PLANNING

Since the term *market plan* denotes the significance of marketing, it is important to understand the marketing system. The **marketing system** identifies the major interacting components, both internally and externally to the firm, that enable the firm to successfully provide products and/or services to the marketplace.

FIGURE 6–1 The Marketing System

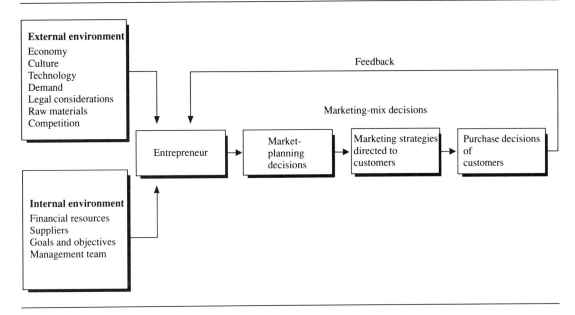

Figure 6–1 provides a summary of the components that comprise the marketing system.[1]

As can be seen from Figure 6–1, both the external and internal environments play very important roles in developing the market plan. Thus, preparation of the market plan should begin with an environmental analysis.

ENVIRONMENTAL ANALYSIS

In general, the external environment is viewed as uncontrollable by the entrepreneur. However, in preparing the market plan the entrepreneur should be aware of changes in the following areas:

- *Economy*—The entrepreneur should consider trends in the gross national product (GNP), unemployment by geographic area, disposable income, and so on.

---

[1]For an in-depth discussion of the marketing system, see Philip Kotler, *Principles of Marketing* (4th ed.). Englewood Cliffs, NJ: Prentice-Hall, 1989.

- *Culture*—In an evaluation of cultural changes, the entrepreneur may consider shifts in the population by demographics, for example, the impact of the Baby Boomers or the growing elderly population. Shifts in attitudes, such as buy American, or trends in safety, health, nutrition, or concern for the environment may all have an impact on the entrepreneur's market plan.
- *Technology*—Advances in technology are difficult to predict. However, the entrepreneur should consider potential technological developments determined from resources committed by major industries or the U.S. government. Being in a market that is rapidly changing due to technological development will require the entrepreneur to make careful short-term marketing decisions and to prepare contingency plans given any new technological developments that may affect his or her product or service.
- *Demand*—Most products or services follow a life cycle. During various stages of the life cycle, demand growth, decline, or stabilization can be expected. Market planning can prepare the entrepreneur for these changes and provide a means for preparing for changes in demand that require specific actions on the product/service, channel of distribution, price, or promotion.

It is also important to recognize the potential life span of any given product or service. This information will help market-planning decisions as well as product development decisions for the entrepreneur.

- *Legal concerns*—There are many important legal issues in starting a new venture; they are discussed in Chapter 11. Legal issues are also important in market planning. The entrepreneur should be prepared for any future legislation that may affect the product or service, channel of distribution, price, or promotion strategy. New legislation, such as the deregulation of prices, restrictions on media advertising (i.e., ban on cigarette ads, or requirement for advertising to children), and safety regulations affecting the product or packaging are a few examples of legal restrictions that can affect any marketing program.
- *Competition*—Most entrepreneurs generally face potential threats from larger corporations. The entrepreneur must be prepared for these threats and should prepare a marketing plan that will outline the most effective strategy within this competitive environment.
- *Raw materials*—It is also quite difficult to predict shortages of raw materials. It is a good idea for the entrepreneur to establish a strong relationship with suppliers and be sensitive to potential threats of shortages. If there is a potential for a shortage of raw materials, the entrepreneur should plan for alternative sources of them. Many start-up ventures were ended with the oil shortages in the early and mid-70s. It may have been impossible to have established alternative sources. In such cases, entrepreneurs aware of the risk could have avoided significant losses in trying to maintain their businesses by either diversifying or closing them out.

The above external factors are generally uncontrollable. However, as indicated, an awareness and assessment of these factors can prevent serious marketing mistakes and can contribute to longer-term profitability.

The internal environment represents variables over which the entrepreneur has some control. Some of the major internal variables are:

- *Financial resources*—The financial plan is discussed in the next chapter and should outline the financial needs for the new venture.

- *Management team*—It is extremely important for organizations to appropriately assign responsibilities for the implementation of the marketing plan. In some cases the availability of a certain expertise may be uncontrollable (i.e., a shortage of certain types of technical managers). In any event, the entrepreneur must build an effective management team and assign the responsibilities to implement the marketing plan.

- *Suppliers*—The suppliers used are generally based on a number of factors such as price, delivery time, quality, management assistance, and so on. In some cases, where raw materials are scarce or there are only a few suppliers of a particular raw material or part, the entrepreneur has little control over the decision. Since the price of supplies, delivery time, and so on are likely to affect many marketing decisions, it is important to incorporate these factors in the marketing plan.

- *Goal and objectives*—Every new venture should establish goals and objectives that will guide the firm through long-term decision making. While these goals and objectives commit management and the marketing program to a defined course, the entrepreneur can change them if necessary, hence they are controllable. However, it should be understood that goals and objectives are meant to be long-term guidelines and constant change may indicate a level of insecurity or instability on the part of management.

THE MARKETING MIX

The marketing mix represents the interaction of four major variables within the marketing system: product/service, pricing, distribution, and promotion. The significance of each of these variables will differ, depending on the industry, company mission, nature of the market, and size of the firm, as well as numerous environmental factors.

For example, entrepreneurs in technical markets find that the channel of distribution to the end user is more direct than do entrepreneurs in the consumer market. In the case of a service, of course, the channel distribution would be even more direct. The goal, or mission, of some firms is to "provide the best value for the price," which may affect all four of the marketing-mix elements, whereas other firms may choose to provide premium quality at a high price. In the latter instance, the firm could focus on a quality product (higher quality ingredients or raw materials), unique channels, higher prices, and perhaps different promotion alternatives.

Each of the four major elements in the marketing mix contains numerous other variables. It is important to recognize these factors as well, since they may also be included in the marketing plan. Each of the four elements in the marketing mix is elaborated further below.

- *Product or service*—This element in the marketing mix may fully describe the nature of the entrepreneur's business since there may be only a single product or service in the initial phases of the new venture. For example, a new venture called Video Van will deliver and pick up videotapes at a price competitive with most video clubs or stores. The service in this case is easily defined and also describes the nature of the entrepreneur's business. If this company later offered videocassette recorders, videocassettes, movies, and so on for sale, the product service would become more diversified.

Within the product/service element there are other variables that must be considered in the marketing plan, such as packaging, branding, new product development, and product design (includes shape, color, etc.). Each of these elements can provide a means to differentiate the product or service from the competition.

A new service venture differs from a product venture. Services, as distinct from a product, are intangible, inseparable, variable, and perishable.[2] Since a service is not something physical that you can touch or feel, it is generally difficult to separate the service itself from the provider of the service. For example, the entrepreneur who starts a computer repair service is really the service. At the same time it is also difficult for the entrepreneur offering a service to maintain consistency in the service performed. Often, the results are variable, which would not be the case for a new product venture, where production can be more easily controlled. Last, in a service venture, lost time cannot be replaced. For example, if a customer fails to show up for an appointment, the time has been lost and cannot be replaced and hence would be regarded as perished. Specific strategies may be used in the marketing plan to lessen the negative impact of these four distinctions. Some of these are discussed in Table 6–1.

- *Pricing*—One of the most difficult decisions for any new venture is determining the appropriate price for the product or service. A quality product or service may necessitate a high price to maintain the proper image. However, with the pricing decision many other factors must be considered, such as costs, discounts, freight, and markups. Determining costs may depend on the demand for the product since the ability to buy materials in larger quantities may reduce the costs.

---

[2]Christopher H. Lovelock, *Services Marketing* (Englewood Cliffs, NJ: Prentice-Hall, 1983), pp. 29–36.

TABLE 6–1 Strategies for Marketing Services

Characteristics	*Strategy*
Intangibility	Try to build tangible representation of service, e.g., plastic card to represent bank service. Can also associate the intangible service with tangible objects, e.g., "I've got a piece of the rock."
Inseparability	Can try to add more service providers and build client confidence in them, e.g., chains or franchises of Health Stops—simple care health care.
Variability	Can develop a good personnel selection and training program. Also need to develop an adequate customer-satisfaction monitoring system such as suggestion and complaint systems, customer surveys, and comparison shopping.
Perishability	Use different pricing to shift demand to off-peak periods. A reminder system to avoid lost appointments can also be effective.

The elements in the marketing mix were earlier described as being interrelated. Thus, a change in price can reflect a different product/service image. Where it is difficult to differentiate his or her product, the entrepreneur will generally have little opportunity to charge a price much different than the competition.

• *Distribution*—This variable provides place utility to the customer, that is, makes a product convenient to purchase when it is needed. For the entrepreneur, the distribution channel or intermediary can be a critical factor since it can reflect price, promotion, and product image. In addition, it is possible that the channel of distribution can assist the entrepreneur in forecasting, market planning and strategy, and product development.

Some of the variables inherent in the distribution element of the marketing mix are type of channel, number of intermediaries, and location of channel member. The type of channel reflects the length of the channel. Since most new ventures are not likely to have access to a large sales force, the entrepreneur may find it useful to hire manufacturers' representatives to sell the product. These representatives do not take title, do not carry competitive products, and work on a commission basis and thus can be an effective substitute for a sales force.[3]

---

[3]For a full discussion of the advantages of manufacturers' representatives, see "Selling Through Independent Representatives: Getting Them to Talk to You," *Sales and Marketing Management*, June 1982, special report.

The number of each type of channel member (i.e., number of representatives, wholesalers, or retailers) may be a function of the product. Those products requiring a very intensive distribution will have a larger number of channel members. More specialized products, on the other hand, require fewer channel members.

For a service, the channel is direct but could include numerous outlets or locations (e.g., Video Van may set up centers throughout a region). The location, of course, will depend on the geographic market sought by the entrepreneur.

The marketing plan must clarify each of the preceding marketing-mix elements as well as the countless factors within each of the elements. Although flexibility may be an important consideration, the entrepreneur needs a strong base to provide direction for the day-to-day marketing decisions. The marketing plan is the framework for guiding these day-to-day actions.

DEFINITION OF THE MARKETING PLAN

The marketing plan may be compared to a road map used to guide a traveler. It is designed to provide three basic pieces of information: Where have you been? Where do we want to go (short term)? How do we get there? These three questions provide the basis for an effective marketing plan.

The marketing plan should be understood by management to be a guide for implementing marketing decision making and not as some generalized superficial document. When entrepreneurs do not take the appropriate time to develop a marketing plan or think that "it is a waste of time," they usually have misunderstood the meaning of the marketing plan and what it can and cannot accomplish. Table 6–2 illustrates some of the things the marketing plan can and cannot do.

The mere organization of the thinking process involved in preparing a marketing plan can help the entrepreneur because, to develop the plan, he or she must formally document and describe as many marketing details as possible that will be part of the decision process during the next year. This process will enable the entrepreneur to not only understand and recognize the critical issues but be prepared in the event any change in the environment occurs. Even though the marketing plan provides a formal vehicle for implementing marketing strategy, there are some problem areas that make accurate market planning difficult.[4] Some of these problems or obstacles to effective market planning are discussed below.

---

[4]David S. Hopkins, *The Marketing Plan* (New York: The Conference Board, Inc., 1981), p. 1.

TABLE 6–2   What Market Planning Can and Cannot Do

Can Do	*Cannot Do*
• It will enhance the firm's ability to integrate all marketing activities so as to maximize efforts toward achieving the corporate goals and objectives.	• It will not provide a crystal ball which will enable management to predict the future with extreme precision.
• It will minimize the effects of surprise from sudden changes in the environment.	• It will not prevent management from making mistakes.
• It establishes a benchmark for all levels of the organization.	• It will not provide guidelines for every major decision. Judgment by management at the appropriate time will still be critical.
• It can enhance management's ability to manage since guidelines and expectations are clearly designated and agreed to by many members of the marketing organzation.	• It will not go through the year without some modification as the environment changes.

Forecasting

The ability of the entrepreneur to set realistic forecasts may be a very difficult task. With competitive environments changing, markets restructuring, and new technology contributing to volatile market conditions, the entrepreneur must be prepared to design plans and make appropriate modifications and adjustments where necessary in order to meet the desired goals and objectives.

The assistance of channel members, industry data, and marketing research can provide some support in forecasting. It is also important to establish control mechanisms in the market plan that allow for the modification of marketing strategy, given that changes do occur.

Obtaining Needed Information

To develop an effective market plan, information regarding market trends, consumer needs, technology, market share changes, competitor reactions, and the like are necessary. Generally, entrepreneurs are unable or not sure how to obtain all the needed information. There are numerous library or secondary sources of information the entrepreneur can utilize. Trade associations, trade journals, and government sources (Department of Commerce) are valuable sources of market information. The information needed and the ability to obtain it will vary, depending on the market and the industry. For example, in a stable predictable

---

TABLE 6–3   Facts Needed for Market Planning

- Who are the users, where are they located, how much do they buy, who do they buy from, and why?
- How have promotion and advertising been employed and which approach has been more effective?
- What are the pricing changes in the market, who has initiated these changes, and why?
- What are the market's attitudes concerning competitive products?
- What channels of distribution supply consumers and how do they function?
- Who are the competitors, where are they located, what advantages/disadvantages do they have?
- What marketing techniques are used by the most successful competitors? By the least successful?
- What are the overall objectives of the company for next year and five years hence?
- What are the company's strengths? Weaknesses?
- What are one's production capabilities by product?

---

market such as institutional vegetable shortening, management may find that the only information needed is competitors' prices. In more volatile markets such as computers, oil, coffee, automobiles, and so on, much more information would be needed, making it more difficult to develop an effective marketing plan. Table 6–3 provides a sample of questions that might generate the kind of information needed for effective planning. The relevance of these questions will vary, depending on the nature of the business. Additional sources of information are described in a later section of this chapter.

Time Constraints

As is often the case with planning decisions, it is difficult to predict how much time will be needed to adequately prepare the market plan. Since time is so critical for the entrepreneur, he or she may spend less time than necessary in preparation, which often results in a superficial market plan. This can lead to incorrect marketing strategy decisions that do not consider all of the appropriate alternatives and their outcomes.

Coordination of the Planning Process

For a new venture, the management team must coordinate the planning process. Since many of the members of the team may lack expertise in market planning, this presents problems in its effective completion. In many cases, the entrepreneur may be the only person involved in preparing the market plan, especially if it is a new venture. In this case, coordination may not be an issue. However, the entrepreneur may still lack the understanding and experience for preparing a market plan. In this instance, the entrepreneur should seek help from any available sources such as the Small Business Association, small business development centers, universities, marketing consultants, and even textbooks.

Implementation of the Marketing Plan

The marketing plan reflects the entrepreneur's commitment to a specific strategy. It is not a formality that serves as a superficial document for outside financial supporters or suppliers. It is meant to be a formal vehicle for answering the three questions posed earlier in this chapter and a commitment to make adjustments as needed or dictated by market conditions.

CHARACTERISTICS OF A MARKETING PLAN

The design of the marketing plan should meet certain criteria. Some of the important characteristics that must be incorporated in an effective marketing plan are as follows:

- It should provide strategy to accomplish the company mission or goal.
- It should be based on facts and valid assumptions. Some of the facts needed are illustrated in Table 6–3.
- It must provide for the use of existing resources. Allocation of all equipment, financial resources, and human resources must be described.
- An appropriate organization must be described to implement the marketing plan.
- It should provide for continuity so that each annual marketing plan can build on it, successfully meeting longer-term goals and objectives.
- It should be simple and short. A voluminous plan will be placed in a desk drawer and likely never used. However, the plan should not be so short that details of how to accomplish a goal are excluded.
- The success of the plan may depend on its flexibility. Changes, if necessary, should be incorporated by including "what if" scenarios and appropriate responding strategies.
- It should specify performance criteria that will be monitored and controlled. For example, the entrepreneur may establish an annual performance criterion of 10 percent of market share in a designated geographic area. To attain this goal, certain expectations should be made at given time periods (i.e., at the end of three months we should have a 5 percent share of market). If not attained, then new strategy or performance standards may be established.

It is clear from the preceding discussion that the market plan is not intended to be written and then put aside. It is intended to be a valuable document, referred to often and providing some guidelines for the entrepreneur during the next time period.

STEPS IN PREPARING THE MARKETING PLAN

Figure 6–2 illustrates the various stages involved in preparing the marketing plan. Each of these stages, when followed, will complete the necessary information to formally prepare the marketing plan. Each of the steps is outlined and discussed, using examples to assist the reader in fully understanding the necessary information and procedure for preparing the marketing plan.

Defining the Business Situation

The **situation analysis** is a review of where the company has been. It responds to the first of the three questions mentioned earlier in this chapter. To fully respond to this question, the entrepreneur should provide a review of past performance of the product and the company. If this is a new venture, the background will be more personal and describe how the product or service was developed and why it was developed (e.g., consumer needs that will be satisfied). If the plan involves an existing product, this stage or section of the marketing plan should contain information on present market conditions and performance of company and industry. Any future opportunities or prospects should also be included in this section of the plan.

Industry analysis should begin with a review of secondary sources at the library. Trade magazines, government publications, or journal or newspaper articles may be useful in determining how attractive the industry is for the entrepreneur. Information on size of market, growth rate, source and availability of suppliers, threat of innovation or new technology, regulations, new entries, and effects of economic conditions should be documented before the marketing strategy is determined.

Video Van, described earlier, would be a new venture; thus, this section of its company's plan would describe the video industry and trends that would support the need for this service.

In this section of the marketing plan, the entrepreneur should provide a detailed assessment of the competitive environment. The assessment should identify each competitor's location, size, market share, sales, profits, strengths, and weaknesses. In addition, it should evaluate such things as their ability to develop new products, management ability, and manufacturing capabilities and financial capabilities. The entrepreneur could actually rate these factors as excellent, good, fair, or poor. This analysis will support the entrepreneur's marketing strategy.

FIGURE 6–2 Sample Flow Chart for a Marketing Plan

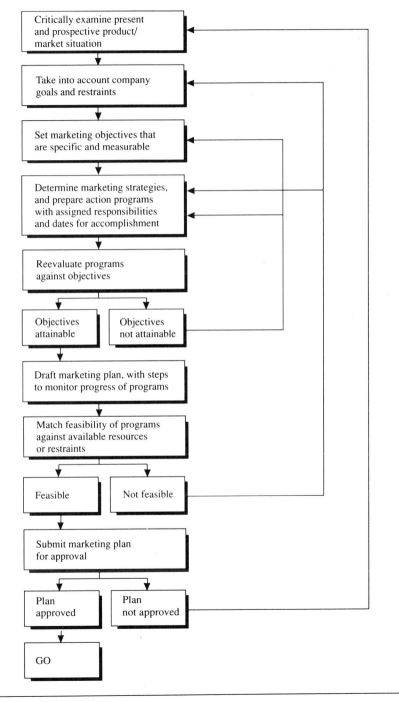

From David S. Hopkins, *The Marketing Plan* (New York: The Conference Board, 1981), p. 17.

Defining The Target Market/Opportunities and Threats

Before learning what consumers to target, the entrepreneur should segment the marketplace. Market segmentation is the process of dividing the market into smaller homogeneous groups. This allows the entrepreneur to respond more effectively to the needs of targeted consumers (the **target market**). Otherwise the entrepreneur would have to identify a product or service that would meet the needs of everyone in the marketplace.

Henry Ford's vision was to manufacture a single product (one color, one style, one size, etc.) for the mass market. His Model T was produced in large numbers on assembly lines, enabling the firm to reduce costs through specialization of labor and materials. His strategy was unique, but any successful mass-marketing strategy employed today would be an exception to the rule.

In 1986, Paul Firestone of Reebok discovered that many consumers who bought running shoes were not athletes. They bought the shoe for comfort and style. From this realization, Firestone developed a marketing plan that directly targeted this segment.

The process of segmenting and targeting customers by the entrepreneur should proceed as follows[5]:

1. Decide what general market or industry you wish to pursue.
2. Divide the market into smaller groups based on characteristics of the customer or buying situations. Consumer characteristics could be one or more of the following:
   a. Geography (e.g., state, country, city, region).
   b. Demographics (e.g., age, sex, occupation, education, income, race, etc.).
   c. Psychographic (e.g., personality, lifestyles, etc.).
   Buying situations that might be considered in segmenting the market are as follows:
   a. Desired benefits (e.g., product features).
   b. Usage (e.g., rate of use).
   c. Buying conditions (e.g., time available, product purpose, etc.).
   d. Awareness or buying intention (e.g., familiarity of product, willingness to buy, etc.).
3. Select segment or segments to target.
4. Develop marketing plan integrating product, price, distribution, and promotion.

Let's assume an entrepreneur has developed a unique liquid cleaner that could clean a restaurant grill at operating temperatures; remove grease from household appliances; clean whitewall tires, bumpers, upholstery, and engines; and clean

---

[5]For more in-depth information on segmentation, see Eric N. Berkowitz, Roger A. Kerin, and William Rudelius, *Marketing,* 2nd ed. (Homewood, IL: Richard D. Irwin Inc., 1989), pp. 185–221.

boats. At least four markets could be identified from its uses: restaurants, households, automobiles, and boats. Each of the markets would then be segmented on the basis of the variables discussed above. The entrepreneur found that in the restaurant market there was little competition, the product's advantages were most evident, and massive marketing resources were not necessary for entry. Thus, on this basis the entrepreneur chose the restaurant market. This market was then segmented by state, by type of restaurant (i.e., fast food, family, etc.), and whether the restaurant was part of a hospital, school, company, or so on. After evaluating each of these segments, the entrepreneur chose to initially target independent family restaurants in a four-state region.

This market offered the greatest opportunity because no existing product could clean a grill at operating temperature without damaging the grill. The threats in this market included ease of entry and potential imitation by major competitors—in fact, a number of large firms such as Colgate-Palmolive and Procter & Gamble may be interested in the market. Regardless of the threats, however, the restaurant grill cleaning segment presented the greatest opportunity; hence, it became the target market.

Strengths and Weaknesses

It is important for the entrepreneur to consider the product's strengths and weaknesses in the target market. For example, referring to the liquid grill cleaner, its primary strength in its market is clearly its unique application: it can be used on a hot operating grill with no discernible odor. Other strengths rest in the fact that the company had experience in the restaurant business and understood the customer.

Weaknesses would include a production capacity limited by space and equipment. In addition, the company lacked a strong distribution system for the product and would have to depend on manufacturers' representatives. Lack of cash to support a heavy promotional effort could also be identified as a weakness.

Establishing Goals and Objectives

Before marketing-strategy decisions can be outlined, the entrepreneur must establish realistic and specific goals and objectives. These marketing goals and objectives should describe where the company is going and should specify such things as market share, profits, sales (by territory and region), market penetration, number of distributors, awareness level, new product launching, pricing policy, sales promotion, and advertising support.

For example, the entrepreneur of a new frozen diet product may determine the following objectives for the first year: 10 percent market penetration, 60 percent of market sampled, and distribution in 75 percent of the market. All of these goals must be considered reasonable and feasible given the business situation described earlier.

Although all of the above goals could be measured for control purposes, not all goals and objectives must be quantified. It is possible for a firm to establish such goals or objectives as complete research of customer attitudes toward product, set up sales training program, improve packaging, change name of product, or find new distributor. It is a good idea to limit the number of goals or objectives to between six and eight. Too many goals make control and monitoring difficult. Obviously, these goals should represent key areas to ensure marketing success.

Defining Marketing Strategy and Action Programs

Once the marketing goals and objectives are established, the entrepreneur can begin to develop the marketing strategy to achieve them. These strategy and action decisions respond to the question, How do we get there? As indicated earlier, it is important that the marketing strategy and action programs be specific and detailed enough to guide the entrepreneur through the next year. Examples of a poor and a good marketing strategy follow.

- Poor strategy—We will increase sales for our product by lowering the price.
- Good strategy—We will increase sales for our product by 6 to 8 percent by (1) lowering the price 10 percent, (2) attending an important trade show in New York, and (3) conducting a mailing to 5,000 potential customers.

Designating Responsibility for Implementation

Writing the marketing plan is only the beginning of the marketing process. The plan must be implemented effectively in order to meet all of the desired goals and objectives. Someone must take the responsibility for implementing each of the strategy and action decisions made in the marketing plan. Typically, the entrepreneur will assume this responsibility since he or she will be interested in controlling and monitoring the venture.

Budgeting the Marketing Strategy

Effective planning decisions must also consider the costs involved in the implementation of these decisions. If the entrepreneur has followed the procedure of detailing the strategy and action programs to meet the desired goals and objectives, costs should be reasonably clear. If assumptions are necessary, they should be clearly stated so that anyone else who reviews the written marketing plan (e.g., a venture-capital firm) would understand the implications.

This budgeting of marketing action and strategy decisions will also be useful in preparing the financial plan. Details of how to develop a financial plan are discussed in Chapter 7.

TABLE 6–4 Outline for a Marketing Plan

Situation Analysis
   Background
   Opportunities and threats
   Strengths and Weaknesses
Objectives and Goals
Marketing Strategy and Action Programs
Budgets
Controls

Monitoring Progress of Marketing Actions

Generally, monitoring of the plan involves tracking specific results of the marketing effort. Sales data by product, territory, representative, and outlet are a few of the specific results that should be monitored. What is monitored depends on the specific goals and objectives outlined earlier in the marketing plan. Any weak signals from the monitoring process will provide the entrepreneur with the opportunity to redirect or modify the existing marketing effort to allow the firm to achieve its initial goals and objectives.

Table 6–4 summarizes the outline for a typical marketing plan. Variations of this outline will depend on the market and nature of the product, as well as the general company mission.

CONTINGENCY PLANNING

Generally, the entrepreneur does not have the time to consider many alternative plans of action should the initial plan fail. However, as stated earlier, it is important for the entrepreneur to be flexible and prepared to make adjustments where necessary. It is unlikely that any marketing plan will succeed exactly as planned.

WHY SOME PLANS FAIL

Marketing plans fail for different reasons. In fact, failure may also be considered a matter of degree since some goals may be met and others missed completely. The overall failure of the plan will be judged by management and may depend on the mere solvency of the organization. Some of the reasons for failure can be avoided if the entrepreneur is careful in preparing the marketing plan. Some of the more common reasons for failure that can be controlled are as follows:

- Lack of a real plan—The marketing plan is superficial and lacks detail and substance, especially regarding goals and objectives.
- Lack of an adequate situation analysis—It is invaluable to know where you are and where you have been, before deciding where you want to go. Careful analysis of the environment can result in reasonable goals and objectives.
- Unrealistic goals—This generally results because of a lack of understanding of the situation.
- Unanticipated competitive moves, product deficiencies, and acts of God— With a good situation analysis, and an effective monitoring process, competitive decisions can be assessed and predicted with some degree of accuracy. Deficiencies in the product often result from rushing the product to the market. For an act of God such as an oil shortage, flood, hurricane, war, and so on, the entrepreneur has no control.

SOURCES OF MARKET INFORMATION

It was stated earlier that information is important in the preparation of the marketing plan. Information is important to the situation analysis and in assessing the needs of the market plan. Table 6–5 summarizes many valuable sources of market information that can be used by the entrepreneur in the preparation of the marketing plan.

TABLE 6–5 Sources of Market Information

- External to company
    - customers
    - competitive literature
    - suppliers
    - trade magazine
    - trade associations
    - professional organizations
- Government
    - census data
    - patent reviews
    - federal publications
- Internal to company
    - market research reports
    - sales calls reports
    - orders
    - complaints
    - informal persons
    - past year's customer correspondence
    - sales meeting summaries
    - technical reports

The annual market planning process should not be an annual exercise in futility. Its purpose is to provide guidance to the entrepreneur through the market decision-making process. The continuity of the annual plan becomes significant for achieving and meeting the long-term company mission.

SUMMARY

Market planning is a critical element in ensuring the long-term sources of any entrepreneurial effort. The marketing plan designates the response to three questions: Where have we been? Where are we going? How do we get there?

To be able to respond effectively to these questions, the elements of the marketing mix must be understood. The major factors or elements are product/service, price, distribution, and promotion. Not only are these elements interrelated but, within each element, there are countless subcategories.

The marketing plan entails a number of major steps. First, it is important to conduct a situation analysis to assess the question "Where have we been?" Market segments must be defined and opportunities identified. This will help the entrepreneur determine a profile of the customer. Goals and objectives must be established. These goals and objectives must be realistic and detailed (quantified if possible). Next, the marketing strategy and action programs are defined. Again these should be detailed so that the entrepreneur clearly understands how the venture is going to get where it wants to go. The action programs should also be assigned to someone to ensure their implementation. If the plan has been detailed, the entrepreneur should be able to assign some costs and budgets for implementing the marketing plan. During the year, the marketing plan will be monitored in order to discern the success of the action programs. Any weak signals will provide the entrepreneur with the opportunity to modify the plan and/or develop a contingency plan.

Careful scrutiny of the marketing plan can enhance its success. However, many plans fail, not because of poor management or a poor product, but because the plan was not specific or had inadequate situation analysis, unrealistic goals, or unanticipated competitive moves, product deficiencies, and acts of God.

The use of market information can assist the entrepreneur in preparing a successful plan, as well as monitoring some of the market decisions. These sources may be internal to the company, external to the company, or from the government.

CHAPTER

7

The Financial Plan

CHAPTER OBJECTIVES

1. To understand why positive profits can result in a negative cash flow.

2. To learn how to prepare monthly pro forma cash flow and income statements for the first year of operation.

3. To understand the preparation of the pro forma balance sheet at the end of the first year of operation.

4. To learn the purpose and preparation of the pro forma sources and applications of funds at the end of the first year.

5. To explain the application and calculation of the break-even point for the new venture.

WILLIAM McGOWAN

Bill McGowan, the tough and cunning chairman of MCI Communication Corporation, in 18 years has not only built a successful company but has created a new industry. MCI has been McGowan's biggest but not his only successful endeavor. An ambitious entrepreneur, he has hustled alligator handbags, raised money for the film industry, and made his first million by selling a small contracting firm he started. MCI's business, which is offering private long distance telephone lines between major cities, was actually someone else's idea. In 1968, John D. Goeken, an entrepreneur from Joliet, Illinois, had been granted a license by the FCC to provide long-distance service from St. Louis and Chicago using microwave transmission rather than conventional cables. This unusual decision by the FCC pried loose some of AT&T's monopoly. In 1968, McGowan joined forces with Goeken and looked for backers for their new venture, Microwave Communications Inc. From investors and a small public offering, McGowan raised much-needed funds. Goeken, more of an investor type and with a large amount of stock, then decided to leave the business to McGowan.

McGowan was not satisfied with a small private-line business. But to attain a bigger percentage of the AT&T business, he needed direct communications to millions of customers through local Bell phone companies.

To achieve this direct connection, McGowan sued AT&T and, after an initial loss at the FCC, finally prevailed in federal court in 1975. McGowan and MCI were now off and running with a new business aimed at the giant AT&T.

McGowan's success was due to persistence, stubbornness, and a strong will. Born in Ashley, Pennsylvania, to a railroad engineer, he worked summers in the local railroad yards before graduating from Harvard Business School. He then spent about 15 years as a consultant in New York, dabbling in a few new ventures and trying to turn around small businesses on the verge of failure. Growing up in a working-class environment seems to have contributed to his sometimes informal and unorthodox management style. Some have described the atmosphere at MCI as institutional chaos with no formal channels. However, McGowan's belief is that managers should be challenged with the independence to make their own decisions.

The success of MCI has required careful financial planning. After the AT&T court decisions, McGowan raised $114 million—$33 million from a common stock issue, $64 million as a line of credit, and $17 million in private funds. All of this was obtained for a firm that was not operational. With careful financial planning, McGowan then began building a long-distance telephone network that in 1990 earned over $8 billion in revenue, an increase of about 25 percent over 1989.

Like many other firms, however, MCI ran into cash flow problems. AT&T refused to accept the government's court decision and would not reach an agreement with MCI on the necessary local connections on their lines. Money was being spent with no revenue being returned to the organization—a common problem among new ventures. In MCI's case it took 10 years to resolve the legal battle with AT&T and 12 years before it achieved its first profit. Fortunately, because competition was slow to enter the market, MCI was able to pay off its debt, return to a positive cash flow, and become the profitable firm it is today. However, this could not have been achieved without careful financial planning— monitoring the profits, cash flow, and funds in the new venture.

MCI still faces an increasingly competitive market that will require the firm to continue its financial planning efforts. In 1987, MCI's earnings per share had dropped 50 percent from the previous year. In 1990, its earnings per share increased to $3.50 from $2.80 in 1989. AT&T, however, in response to competition from MCI, reduced its costs of long-distance business. MCI is staying competitive with AT&T because of its ability to offer its services at a lower price through control of costs and cash flow.[1]

The financial plan provides the entrepreneur with a complete picture of how much and when funds are coming into the organization, where funds are going, how much cash is available, and the projected financial position of the firm. It provides the short-term basis for budgeting control and helps prevent one of the most common problems for new ventures—lack of cash.

The financial plan must explain to any potential investor how the entrepreneur plans to meet all financial obligations and maintain liquidity in order to provide a good return on investment. In general, the financial plan will need three years of projected financial data to satisfy any outside investors. The first year should reflect monthly data.

This chapter discusses each of the major financial items that should be included in the financial plan: pro forma income statements, break-even analysis, pro forma cash flow, pro forma balance sheets, and pro forma sources and applications of funds. Decisions on how to manage and control assets, cash, inventory, and so on are discussed in Chapter 12.

---

[1]"MCI Founder Bill McGowan," *Inc.* (August, 1986), pp. 29–38, and *MCI Communications—Company Report.* Paine Webber Inc. (June 21, 1990).

PRO FORMA INCOME STATEMENTS

The marketing plan discussed in the previous chapter provides an estimate of sales for the next twelve months. Since sales is the major source of revenue and since other operational activities and expenses relate to sales volume, it is usually the first item that must be defined.

Figure 7–1 summarizes all of the profit data during the first year of operations for MPP Plastics. This company makes plastic moldings for such customers as hard goods manufacturers, toy manufacturers, and appliance manufacturers. As can be seen from the pro forma income statement in Figure 7–1, the company begins to earn a profit in the fourth month. Cost of goods sold fluctuates because of the higher costs incurred for materials and labor needed to meet the sales demands in a particular month.

In preparing the pro forma income statement, sales by month must be calculated first. Marketing research, industry sales, and some trial experience might provide the basis for these figures. Forecasting techniques such as a survey of buyers' intentions, a composite of sales force opinions, expert opinions, or time series may be used to project sales.[2] As would be expected, it will take a while for any new venture to build up sales. The costs for achieving these increases can be disproportionately higher in some months, depending on the given situation in any particular period.

The pro forma income statements also provide projections of all operating expenses for each of the months during the first year. Each of the expenses should be listed and carefully assessed to make sure that any increases in them are added in the appropriate month.[3] For example, selling expenses such as travel, commissions, entertainment, and so on should be expected to increase somewhat as firms expand territories and hire new salespeople or representatives. Selling expenses as a percentage of sales may also be expected to be higher initially since more sales calls will have to be made to generate each sale, particularly when the firm is an unknown.

Salaries and wages should reflect the personnel employed by the company and described in the organizational plan in the next chapter. As new personnel are hired to support the increased business, the costs will need to be included in the pro forma statement. In January, for example, a new secretary is added to the staff. Other increases in salaries and wages may also reflect raises in salary.

The entrepreneur should also consider the need to increase insurance, attend special trade shows, or add space for warehousing. As the pro forma statement in Figure 7–1 shows, insurance costs increase in November and again in May. These charges can be determined easily from an insurance company and reflect

---

[2] Douglas J. Dalrymple and Leonard J. Parsons, *Marketing Management: Strategy and Cases,* 5th ed. (New York, John Wiley & Sons, 1990), pp. 241–55.

[3] See E. A. Helfert, *Techniques of Financial Analysis,* 7th ed. (Homewood, Ill.: Richard D. Irwin, Inc., 1991), pp. 135–65.

FIGURE 7–1

MPP PLASTICS, INC.
Pro Forma Income Statement
First Year by Month (000s)

	July	Aug	Sept	Oct	Nov	Dec	Jan	Feb	Mar	Apr	May	June
Sales	40.0	50.0	60.0	80.0	80.0	80.0	90.0	95.0	95.0	100.0	110.0	115.0
Less: cost of goods sold	26.0	34.0	40.0	54.0	50.0	50.0	58.0	61.0	60.0	64.0	72.0	76.0
Gross profit	14.0	16.0	20.0	26.0	30.0	30.0	32.0	34.0	35.0	36.0	38.0	39.0
Operating expenses												
Selling expenses	3.0	4.1	4.6	6.0	6.0	6.0	7.5	7.8	7.8	8.3	9.0	9.5
Advertising	1.5	1.8	1.9	2.5	2.5	2.5	3.0	7.0*	3.0	3.5	4.0	4.5
Salaries and wages	6.5	6.5	6.8	6.8	6.8	6.8	8.0	8.0	8.0	8.3	9.5	10.0
Office supplies	0.6	0.6	0.7	0.8	0.8	0.8	0.9	1.0	1.0	1.2	1.4	1.5
Rent	2.0	2.0	2.0	2.0	2.0	2.0	2.0	2.0	2.0	2.0	3.0	3.0
Utilities	0.3	0.3	0.4	0.4	0.6	0.6	0.7	0.7	0.7	0.8	0.9	1.1
Insurance	0.2	0.2	0.2	0.2	0.3	0.3	0.3	0.3	0.3	0.3	0.6	0.6
Taxes	1.1	1.1	1.2	1.2	1.2	1.2	1.6	1.6	1.6	1.7	1.9	2.0
Interest	1.2	1.2	1.2	1.2	1.2	1.2	1.2	1.5	1.5	1.5	1.5	1.5
Depreciation	3.3	3.3	3.3	3.3	3.3	3.3	3.3	3.3	3.3	3.3	3.3	3.3
Miscellaneous	0.1	0.1	0.1	0.1	0.1	0.1	0.1	0.2	0.2	0.2	0.2	0.2
Total operating expenses	19.8	21.1	22.4	24.5	24.8	24.8	28.6	33.4	29.4	31.1	35.3	37.2
Profit (loss) before taxes	(5.8)	(5.2)	(2.4)	1.5	5.2	5.2	3.4	0.6	5.6	4.9	2.7	1.8
Taxes	0	0	0	0.75	2.6	2.6	1.7	0.3	2.8	2.45	1.35	0.9
Net profit (loss)	(5.8)	(5.2)	(2.4)	0.75	2.6	2.6	1.7	0.3	2.8	2.45	1.35	0.9

*Trade show

the status of the operations at that time. In February, an important trade show increases the advertising budget significantly. Any unusual expenses such as the trade show should be flagged and explained at the bottom of the pro forma statement.

In February of the first year, the company incurs additional debt to finance inventory and additional space, which is added in May. Although no charges are reflected in this statement, any needed additional equipment (i.e., new machinery, cars, trucks, etc.) would increase depreciation expenses in the month incurred.

In addition to the monthly pro forma income statement for the first year, projections should be made for years 2 and 3. Generally, investors prefer to see three years of income projections. Year 1 totals have already been calculated in Figure 7–1. Figure 7–2 illustrates the yearly totals of income statement items for each of the three years. The percent of sales is calculated for the first year. This

FIGURE 7–2

MPP PLASTICS, INC.
Pro Forma Income Statement
Three-Year Summary (dollars in thousands)

		Year 1	*Year 2*	*Year 3*
Sales	100%	995.0	1450.0	2250.0
Less: COGS	64.8%	645.0	942.5	1460.0
Gross profit	35.2%	350.0	507.5	790.0
Operating expenses				
Selling expenses	8.0%	79.6	116.0	180.0
Advertising	3.8%	37.7	72.5	90.0
Salaries, wages	9.2%	92.0	134.0	208.0
Supplies	1.1%	11.3	16.5	25.6
Rent	2.6%	26.0	37.9	58.8
Utilities	0.8%	7.5	11.5	16.5
Insurance	0.4%	3.8	4.5	9.5
Taxes	1.8%	17.4	25.4	39.4
Interest	1.6%	15.9	15.5	14.9
Depreciation		39.6	39.6	39.6
Miscellaneous	0.2%	1.7	2.2	2.7
Total operating expenses	33.4%	332.5	475.6	685.0
Profit (loss) before taxes	1.8%	17.5	31.9	105.0
Taxes	0.9%	8.75	15.95	52.5
Net profit (loss)	0.9%	8.75	15.95	52.5

percentage can then be used as a guide in determining the projected expenses for years 2 and 3.

In year 3, the firm expects to significantly increase its profits as compared to the first year. In some instances, the entrepreneur may find that the new venture does not begin to earn a profit until sometime in year 2 or 3. This often depends on the nature of the business and start-up costs. For example, a service-oriented business may take less time to reach a profitable stage than a high-technology company or one requiring a large investment in capital goods and equipment that will take longer to recover.

In projecting the operating expenses for years 2 and 3, it is helpful to first look at those expenses that will likely remain stable over time. It is easier to determine costs for depreciation, utilities, rent, insurance, and interest if you know the forecasted sales for years 2 and 3. Selling expenses, advertising, salaries and wages, and taxes may be represented as a percentage of the projected net sales. When calculating the projected operating expenses, it is most important to be conservative in initial planning. A reasonable profit that is earned with conservative estimates lends credibility to the potential success of the new venture.

FIGURE 7–3   Determining the Break-Even Formula

By definition break-even is where
Total Revenue (TR)   = Total Costs (TC)
(TR)   = Selling Price (SP) × Quantity (Q)
and (TC)   = Total Fixed Costs (TFC)* + Total Variable Costs (TVC)†

Thus: SP × Q = TFC + TVC
  Where TVC   = Variable Costs/Unit (VC/Unit)‡ × Quantity (Q)
   Thus SP × Q = TFC + (VC/Unit   = TFC × Q)
    (SP × Q) − (VC/Unit × Q)
    Q (SP − VC/Unit)   = TFC

$$Q = \frac{TFC}{SP - VC/Unit}$$

---

*Fixed costs are those costs, which without change in present productive capacity, are not affeected by changes in volume of output.
†Variable costs are those that are affected in total by changes in volume of output.
‡The variable cost per unit is all those costs attributable to producing one unit. This cost is constant within defined ranges of production.

BREAK-EVEN ANALYSIS

In the initial stages of the new venture, it is helpful for the entrepreneur to know when a profit may be achieved. This will provide further insight into the financial potential for the start-up business. Break-even analysis is a useful technique for determining how many units must be sold or how much sales volume must be achieved in order to break even.

We already know from the projections in Figure 7–1 that MPP Plastics will begin to earn a profit in the fourth month. However, this is not the break-even point since the firm must meet obligations for the remainder of the year regardless of the number of units sold. These obligations or fixed costs must be covered by sales volume in order for a company to break even. Thus, break-even is that volume of sales at which the business will neither make a profit nor incur a loss.

The break-even sales point indicates to the entrepreneur the volume of sales needed to cover total variable and fixed expenses. Sales in excess of the break-even point will result in a profit as long as the selling price remains above the costs necessary to produce each unit (variable cost).[4] The break-even formula is derived in Figure 7–3 and is given as:

$$B/E\ (Q) = \frac{TFC}{SP - VC/unit\ (marginal\ contribution)}$$

As long as the selling price is greater than the variable costs per unit, some

---

[4]See Eric Berkowitz, Roger Kerin, and William Rudelius, *Marketing*, 2nd ed. (Homewood, IL: Richard D. Irwin, Inc. 1989), pp. 301–6.

contribution can be made to cover fixed costs. Eventually these contributions will be sufficient to pay all fixed costs, at which point the firm has reached break-even.

The major weakness in calculating the break-even lies in determining whether a cost is fixed or variable. For new ventures these determinations will require some judgment. However, it is reasonable to expect such costs as depreciation, salaries and wages, rent, and insurance to be fixed. Materials, selling expenses such as commissions, and direct labor are most likely to be variable costs. The variable costs per unit can usually be determined by allocating the direct labor, materials, and other expenses that are incurred with the production of a single unit.

If, for example, the firm has fixed costs of $250,000, the variable costs per unit is $4.50, and selling price is $10.00, the break-even is determined as follows:

$$B/E = \frac{TFC}{SP - VC/unit}$$
$$= \frac{\$250,000}{\$10.00 - \$4.50}$$
$$= \frac{250,000}{5.50}$$
$$= 45,454 \text{ units}$$

Any units beyond 45,454 that are sold by the above firm will result in a profit of $5.50 per unit. Sales below 45,454 units will result in a loss to the firm. In those instances where the firm produces more than one product, break-even may be calculated for each product. Fixed costs would have to be allocated to each product or determined by weighting the costs as a function of the sales projections. Thus, it might be assumed that 40 percent of the sales is for product X; hence 40 percent of total fixed costs would be allocated to that product. If the entrepreneur feels that a product requires more advertising, overhead, or other fixed costs, this should be included in the calculations.

One of the unique aspects of break-even is that it can be graphically displayed as in Figure 7–4. In addition, the entrepreneur can try different states of nature (i.e., different selling prices, different fixed costs, and/or variable costs) to ascertain their impact on break-even and subsequent profits.

PRO FORMA CASH FLOW

Cash flow is not the same as profit. Profit is the result of subtracting expenses from sales, whereas cash flow results from the difference between actual cash receipts and cash payments. Cash flows only when actual payments are received or made. Sales are not regarded as cash because payment for a sale might not be made for 30 days. Not all bills are paid immediately. On the other hand, cash payments to reduce the principal on a loan do not constitute a business expense

FIGURE 7–4 Graphic Illustration of Break-Even

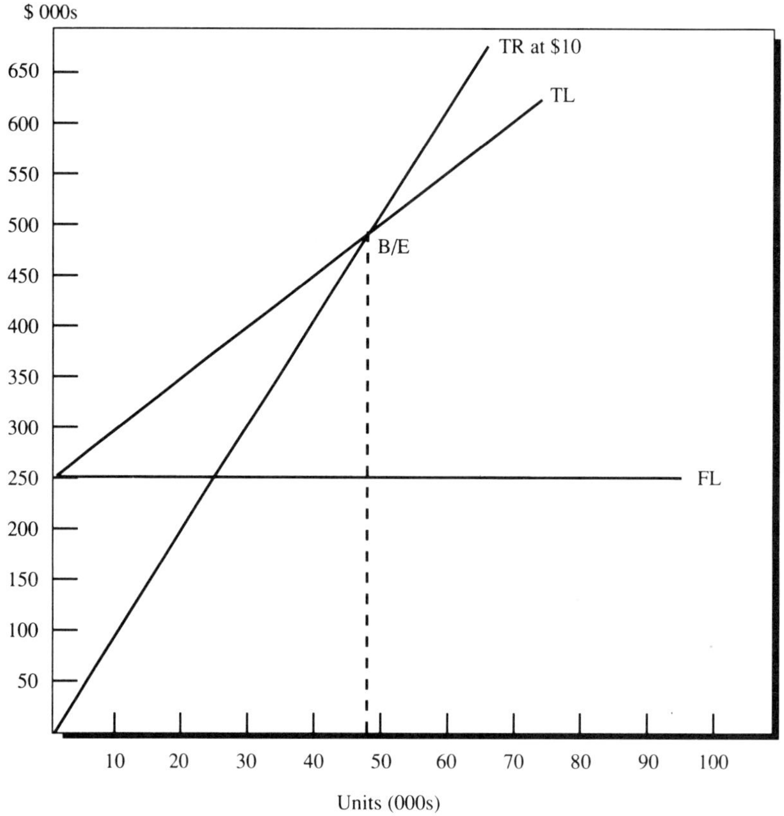

but do constitute a reduction of cash. Also, depreciation on capital assets is an expense, which reduces profits, but not a cash outlay.

As stated earlier, one of the major problems that new ventures face is cash flow. On many occasions, profitable firms fail because of a lack of cash. Thus, using profit as a measure of success for a new venture may be deceiving if there is a significant negative cash flow.

It is important for the entrepreneur to make monthly projections of cash flow similar to the monthly projections made for profits. The numbers in the cash flow projections are calculated from the pro forma income statement with modifications made to account of the expected timing of the changes in cash. If disbursements are greater than receipts in any period, the entrepreneur must either borrow funds or must have cash in a bank account to cover the higher disbursements. Large positive cash flows in any time period may need to be

FIGURE 7–5

MPP PLASTICS, INC.
Pro Forma Cash Flow
First Year by Month (000s)

	July	Aug	Sept	Oct	Nov	Dec	Jan	Feb	Mar	Apr	May	June
Receipts												
Sales	24.0	46.0	56.0	72.0	80.0	80.0	86.0	93.0	95.0	98.0	106.0	113.0
Disbursements												
Equipment	100.0	100.0	40.0	0	0	0	0	0	0	0	0	0
Cost of goods	20.8	32.4	40.8	51.2	50.8	50.0	55.4	61.4	60.2	63.2	70.4	75.2
Selling expenses	1.5	3.55	5.35	5.3	6.0	6.0	6.75	7.65	7.8	8.05	8.55	9.25
Salaries	6.5	6.5	6.8	6.8	6.8	6.8	8.0	8.0	8.0	8.3	9.5	10.0
Advertising	1.5	1.8	1.9	2.5	2.5	2.5	3.0	7.0	3.0	3.5	4.0	4.5
Office supplies	0.3	0.6	0.65	0.75	0.8	0.8	0.85	0.95	1.0	1.1	1.3	1.45
Rent	2.0	2.0	2.0	2.0	2.0	2.0	2.0	2.0	2.0	2.0	3.0	3.0
Utilities	0.3	0.3	0.4	0.4	0.6	0.6	0.7	0.7	0.7	0.8	0.9	1.1
Insurance	0.8	0.8	0.8	0	0.4	0	0	0.5	0	0	0	0
Taxes	0.8	0.8	0.9	1.8	0.9	0.9	2.2	1.3	1.3	2.3	1.5	1.6
Loan principal and interest	2.6	2.6	2.6	2.6	2.6	2.6	2.6	2.9	2.9	2.9	2.9	2.9
Total disbursements	137.1	151.35	112.2	73.35	73.4	72.2	81.5	92.4	86.9	92.15	102.05	109.0
Cash flow	(113.1)	(105.35)	(46.2)	(1.35)	6.6	7.8	4.5	0.6	8.1	5.85	3.95	4.0
Beginning balance	275.0	161.9	56.55	10.35	9.0	15.6	23.4	27.9	28.5	36.6	42.45	46.4
Ending balance	161.9	56.55	10.35	9.0	15.6	23.4	27.9	28.5	36.6	42.45	46.4	50.5

invested in short-term sources or deposited in a bank in order to cover future periods when disbursements are greater than receipts. Usually the first few months of the start-up will require external cash (debt) in order to cover the cash outlays. As the business succeeds and cash receipts accumulate, the entrepreneur can support negative cash periods.

Figure 7–5 illustrates the pro forma cash flow over the first 12 months for MPP Plastics. As can be seen, there is a negative cash flow based on receipts less disbursements for the first four months of operation. The likelihood of incurring negative cash flows is high for any new venture but the amounts and length of time before cash flows become positive will vary, depending on the nature of the business.

The most difficult problem with projecting cash flows is determining the exact monthly receipts and disbursements. The entrepreneur must make some assumptions, but they should be conservative so that enough funds can be maintained to cover the negative cash months. In our example, MPP Plastics anticipated receiving cash for 60 percent of each month's sales, with the remaining 40 percent paid in the subsequent month. Thus, the $46,000 sales total for August reflects a cash receipt of 60 percent of the August sales and 40 percent of the July sales. Similar assumptions can be made for disbursements. For example, from experience it is expected that 80 percent of the cost of goods will be a cash outlay in the month incurred. The remaining 20 percent is paid in the next month. Additional outlays will be made for materials to maintain an inventory.

Using conservative estimates, cash flows can be determined for each month. These cash flows will also assist the entrepreneur in determining how much money he or she will need to borrow. For this firm, $225,000 was borrowed from a bank and $50,000 from the personal savings of the two entrepreneurs. By the end of the year, the cash balance reaches $50,400 as sales build up and cash receipts exceed cash disbursements. This cash surplus can be used to repay any debt, be invested in highly liquid assets as a safety in case of negative cash months, or it can be used to purchase any new capital equipment.

It is most important for the entrepreneur to remember that the pro forma cash flow, like the income statement, is based on best estimates. As the venture begins, it may be necessary to revise cash flow projections to ensure that their accuracy will protect the firm from any impending disaster. The estimates or projections should include any assumptions so that potential investors will understand how and from where the numbers were generated.[5]

In the case of both the pro forma income statement and the pro forma cash flow, it is sometimes useful to provide several scenarios, each based on different levels of success of the business. These scenarios and projections serve not only the purpose of generating pro forma income and cash flow statements but, more important, familiarize the entrepreneur with the factors involved in effecting the operations.

PRO FORMA BALANCE SHEET

The entrepreneur should also prepare a projected balance sheet depicting the condition of the business at the end of the first year. The balance sheet will require the use of the pro forma income and cash flow statements to help justify some of the figures.[6]

The pro forma balance sheet reflects the position of the business at the end of the first year. It summarizes the assets, liabilities, and net worth of the entrepreneurs.

Every business transaction affects the balance sheet but because of the time and expense, as well as need, it is common to prepare balance sheets at periodic intervals (i.e., quarterly, annually). Thus, the balance sheet is a picture of the business at a certain moment in time and does not cover a period of time.

Figure 7–6 depicts the balance sheet for MPP Plastics. As can be seen, the total assets equals the sum of the liabilities and owner's equity. Each of the categories is explained below.

---

[5]See Clyde P. Stickney, *Financial Statement Analysis: Theory, A Strategic Perspective.* (New York: Harcourt Brace Jovanovich, 1990), pp. 275–90.

[6]Ibid., pp. 135–65.

FIGURE 7–6

MPP PLASTICS, INC.
Pro Forma Balance Sheet
End of First Year
Assets

Current assets		
Cash	$ 50,400	
Accounts receivable	46,000	
Merchandise inventory	10,450	
Supplies	1,200	
Total current assets		$108,050
Fixed assets		
Equipment	240,000	
Less depreciation	39,600	
Total fixed assets		200,400
Total assets		$308,450

Liabilities and Owner's Equity

Current liabilities		
Accounts payable	$ 23,700	
Current portion of long-term debt	16,800	
Total current liabilities		$ 40,500
Long-term liabilities		
Notes payable		209,200
Total liabilities		249,700
Owner's equity		
C. Peters, capital	25,000	
K. Peters, capital	25,000	
Retained earnings	8,750	
Total owner's equity		58,750
Total liabilities and owner's equity		$308,450

- *Assets*—These represent everything of value the business owns. Value is not necessarily meant to imply the cost of replacement or what its market value would be but is the actual cost or amount expended for the asset. The assets are categorized as current or fixed. Current assets include cash and anything else that is expected to be converted into cash or consumed in the operation of the business during a period of one year or less. Fixed assets are those that are tangible and will be used over a long period of time.

- *Liabilities*—These accounts represent everything owed to creditors. Some of these amounts may be due within a year (current liabilities) and others may be long-term debts, such as the loan taken by MPP Plastics to purchase equipment and support cash flow.

- *Owner Equity*—This is the excess of all assets over all liabilities. It represents the net worth of the business. The $50,000 the entrepreneurs invested in the business is included in the owner equity or net worth section of the balance sheet. Any profit from the business will also be included in the net

---

FIGURE 7–7

MPP PLASTICS, INC.
Pro Forma Sources and Applications of Cash
End of First Year

Sources of Funds
    Mortgage loan   150,000
    Term loan   75,000
    Personal funds   50,000
    Net income from operations   8,750
    Add depreciation   39,600
Total funds provided $323,350

Applications of Funds
    Purchase of equipment   240,000
    Inventory   10,450
    Loan repayment   16,800
Total funds expended   267,250
Net increase in working capital   56,100
                                       $323,350

---

worth as retained earnings. Thus, all revenue increases assets and owner equity, and all expenses decrease owner equity and either increase liabilities or decrease assets.

PRO FORMA SOURCES AND APPLICATIONS OF FUNDS

The pro forma sources and applications of funds statement illustrates the disposition of earnings from operations and from other financing. Its purpose is to show how net income was used to increase assets or to pay off debt.

It is often difficult for the entrepreneur to understand how the net income for the year was disposed of and the effect of the movement of cash through the business. Questions often asked are: Where did the cash come from? How was the cash used? What happened to asset items during the period?

Figure 7–7 shows the pro forma sources and applications of funds for MPP Plastics after the first year of operation. Many of the funds were obtained from personal savings or loans. Since a profit was earned at the end of the first year, it too would be added to the sources of funds. Depreciation is added back because it does not represent an out-of-pocket expense. Thus, typical sources of funds are from operations, new investments, long-term borrowing, and sale of assets. The major uses or applications of funds are to increase assets, retire long-term liabilities, reduce owner or stockholder's equity, and pay dividends. The sources and applications of funds statement emphasizes the interrelationship of these items to working capital. The statement helps the entrepreneur as well as investors to better understand the financial well-being of the company as well as the effectiveness of the financial management policies of the company.

SUMMARY

Several financial projection techniques were discussed in this chapter. Each of the planning tools is designed to provide the entrepreneur with a clear picture of where funds come from, how they are disbursed, the amount of cash available, and the general financial well-being of the new venture.

The pro forma income statement provides a sales estimate in the first year (monthly basis) and projects operating expenses each month. The break-even point can be determined from projected income. This measures the point where total revenue equals total cost.

Cash flow is not the same as profit. It reflects the difference between cash actually received and cash disbursements. Some cash disbursements are not operating expenses (e.g., repayment of loan principal) and likewise some operating expenses are not a cash disbursement (e.g., depreciation expense). Many new ventures have failed because of a lack of cash, even when the venture is profitable.

The pro forma balance sheet reflects the condition of the business at the end of a particular period. It summarizes the assets, liabilities, and net worth of the firm.

The pro forma sources and applications of funds help the entrepreneur to understand how the net income for the year was disposed of and the effect of the movement of cash through the business. It emphasizes the interrelationship of assets, liabilities, and stockholders' equity to working capital.

CHAPTER

8

The Organizational Plan

CHAPTER OBJECTIVES

1. To understand the importance of the management team's ability and commitment to the new venture.

2. To understand the differences in production, sales, and marketing-oriented organizations.

3. To learn how to prepare a job analysis, job description, and job specification.

4. To understand the legal and tax advantages and disadvantages of a proprietorship, partnership, and corporation.

5. To explain the S corporation as an alternative form of incorporation.

6. To advise the entrepreneur in the use of outside advisors as part of the organization structure.

COMPAQ COMPUTER

In a recent study of high-technology entrepreneurs from 90 firms, two thirds of the sample stated that the management team was the highest priority in operating the business.[1]

A good example of a strong management team was that of Bill Murto, Jim Harris, and Rod Carion, the entrepreneurs of Compaq Computer. Senior managers of Texas Instruments, they had decided to go out on their own in some entrepreneurial endeavor. They considered a number of alternative businesses, such as a Mexican restaurant, manufacturing hard microcomputer disks, and even a beeping device to help locate lost keys. In 1981, however, they decided to develop a portable personal computer that would be compatible with the IBM PC.

The phenomenal success achieved by Compaq Computer ($111 million in sales in the first year) was accomplished by attracting seasoned professionals to manage and focus on building a long-term successful business. The management team of Murto, Harris, and Carion had to be right for such an endeavor that was committed to becoming a Fortune 500 company. The managers were not only seasoned in the high-technology business but, more important, they were committed to taking on collective responsibility for crucial business decisions. This *smart team,* as it has been referred to, was believed to be the only organizational approach that could be successful in an industry where there is little margin of error, evidenced by the large number of entrepreneurs who had already met failure. In fact, it is the opinion of most high-technology CEOs that a strong management team and organization is the most important criterion for success in their business. Compaq has certainly been an example of the validity of this opinion.

The story of Compaq is somewhat different from that of most of the high flyers in Silicon Valley. The entrepreneurs had no technical breakthrough nor did they have any flashes of genius. What they did have, however, was a strong organization of people with one major goal in mind: the start-up of a business that not only would grow quickly but would last.

---

[1]J. Kotin, "The Smart Team at Compaq Computer," *Inc.,* February 1986, pp. 48–56.

The smart team approach used by Compaq is an interdisciplinary approach based on the idea that each member of the team has something valuable to offer other members and that they should share their ideas. Thus, an engineer is expected to have something important to offer to marketing and manufacturing and vice versa. The advantage of this integration is that it has allowed Compaq to compress the development of a new product in this industry from 12 to 18 months to 6 to 9 months.

The strength of this organizational plan was illustrated on many occasions, some resulting in favorable and some unfavorable responses. Early in 1983, one of the members of the management team had become convinced that Compaq should produce a "lap top" computer small enough to fit in a briefcase. Although there seemed to be general support for the idea, a market researcher opposed it; after completing a thorough study, he concluded that there was no market. The researcher persuaded the team, and Carion, who had proposed the idea, agreed to drop it. Consensus had been achieved and the future proved that the decision was correct, as products by Cavilan Computer Corporation and Data General Corporation were market flops.

The introduction of the Deskpro 286 also illustrates the success of the smart team concept. This new product introduction was achieved in record time as IBM was announcing its new super PC. With IBM plagued by production problems, the Deskpro 286 was being shipped to grateful retailers. This product now commands 34 percent of the business computer market, achieved by successful teamwork. A smart team was created from every department of the company with all members working in parallel. As engineers were designing the product, marketers were developing a marketing plan, manufacturers building a factory to produce it, and financial managers working on the financing. All this could not have been achieved without coordination represented by the smart team chosen for the job.

The management team and the type of organization best suited for the entrepreneurs in their chosen ventures must be clearly defined in the business plan. Investors will evaluate the commitment of the management team, their ability to successfully operate the business, and the basic organizational structure that will define job roles and responsibilities. Also, it is necessary to define the legal form of business for the new venture. Each of these legal forms of business offers different advantages and should be assessed carefully.

The organizational plan should begin with a list of each of the members in the management team, their backgrounds, and their roles in the new venture. This background information should highlight accomplishments that demonstrate their ability to perform the necessary tasks to succeed in this venture. The information should focus especially on any success in increasing sales or profit in prior business endeavors, as well as on skills in labor management, manufacturing, or research and development.

MANAGEMENT TEAM COMMITMENT

In any venture assessment by potential investors, one of the primary evaluative criteria is the management team's ability and commitment to the venture. This was clearly evidenced in the example of Compaq. It is also important to investors that the management team not attempt to operate the business as a sideline or part-time while employed full-time elsewhere. The management team must be prepared to operate the business full-time and at a modest salary. It is unacceptable for the entrepreneurs to try to draw a large salary out of the new venture, and investors may perceive any attempt to do so as a lack in psychological commitment to the business.

Generally, the design of the initial organization will be simple. In fact, the entrepreneur may find that he or she performs all of the functions of the organization alone. As the work load increases, however, the organizational structure will need to expand to include additional employees with defined roles in the organization. However, regardless of the number of actual personnel involved in running the venture, the organization must identify the major activities required to operate it effectively.

The design of the organization will be the entrepreneur's formal and explicit indication to the members of the organization as to what is expected of them. Typically these expectations can be summarized in the following five areas[2]:

- *Organization structure*—This defines members' jobs and the communication and relationship these jobs have with each other. These relationships are depicted in an organization chart.
- *Planning, measurement, and evaluation schemes*—All organization activities should reflect the goals and objectives that underlie the venture's existence. The entrepreneur must spell out how these goals will be achieved (plans), a determination of measurement, and an evaluation of the success of these plans.
- *Rewards*—Members of an organization will require rewards in the form of promotions, bonuses, praise, and so on. The entrepreneur or other key managers will need to be responsible for these rewards.
- *Selection criteria*—The entrepreneur will need to determine a set of guidelines for selecting individuals for each position.
- *Training*—Training, on or off the job, must be specified. This training may be in the form of formal education or learning skills.

The organization's design can be very simple, that is, one in which the entrepreneur performs all of the tasks (usually indicative of start-up) or more complex, in which other employees are hired to perform specific tasks. As the or-

---

[2]J. W. Lorsch, "Organization Design: A Situational Perspective," in *Perspectives on Behavior in Organizations,* 2nd ed., eds. J. R. Hackman, E. E. Lawler III, and L. W. Porter (New York: McGraw-Hill, 1983), pp. 439–47.

ganization becomes larger and more complex, the preceding areas of expectation become more relevant and necessary.

Figure 8–1 illustrates two stages of development in an organization. In Stage 1 in this example, the new venture is operated by basically one person, the entrepreneur. This organizational chart reflects the activities of the firm in production, marketing/sales, and administration. Initially, the entrepreneur may manage all of these functions. At this stage there is no need for submanagers; the owner deals with everyone involved in the business and all aspects of the operation. In this example, the president manages production, which may be subcontracted, marketing and sales (possible use of agents or reps), and all administrative tasks such as bookkeeping, purchasing, and shipping. Planning, measurement and evaluation, rewards selection criteria, and training would not yet be critical in the organization.

As the business expands, the organization may be more appropriately described by Stage 2. Here, submanagers are hired to coordinate, organize, and control various aspects of the business. In the example in Figure 8–1, the production manager is responsible for quality control and assembly of the finished product by the subcontractor. The marketing manager develops promotion and advertising strategy and coordinates the efforts of the expanding rep organiza-

FIGURE 8–1   Stages in Organizational Design

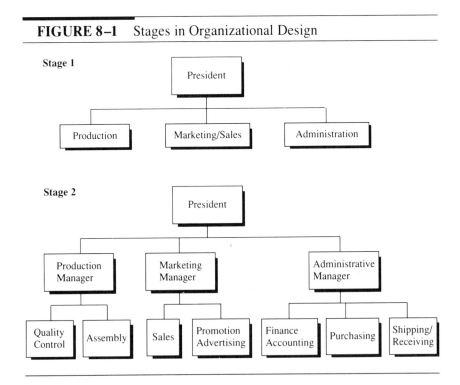

tion. The administrative manager then assumes the responsibility for all administrative tasks in the business operation. Here the elements of measurement, evaluation, rewards, selection, and training become apparent.

A third stage may exist when the firm achieves a much larger size (i.e., 1,000 employees). The activities below each manager in Stage 2 would then be represented by a third level of managers (i.e., quality control manager).

As the organization evolves, the manager or entrepreneur's decision roles also become critical for an effective organization. As entrepreneur, the manager's primary concern is to adapt to changes in the environment and seek new ideas. When a new idea is found, the entrepreneur will need to initiate development either under his or her own supervision (Stage 1 in Figure 8–1) or by delegating the responsibility to someone else in the organization (Stage 2 in Figure 8–1). In addition to the role of adaptor, the manager will also need to respond to pressures such as an unsatisfied customer, a supplier reneging on a contract, or a key employee threatening to quit. Much of the entrepreneur's time in the start-up will be spent "putting out fires."

Another role for the entrepreneur is that of allocator of resources. The manager must decide who gets what. This involves the delegation of budgets and responsibilities. The allocation of resources can be a very complex and difficult process for the entrepreneur since one decision can significantly affect other decisions. The final decision role is that of negotiator. Negotiations of contracts, salaries, prices of raw materials, and so on are an integral part of the manager's job, and since he or she can be the only person with the appropriate authority, it is a necessary area of decision making.[3]

MARKETING-ORIENTED ORGANIZATION

Many entrepreneurs lack understanding of the role of marketing in the organization. Because of insufficient knowledge, the entrepreneur often ignores marketing and focuses on manufacturing and sales. The entrepreneur may believe that marketing is selling and that the key objective of the firm is to sell as much product as possible in order to meet income and/or cash flow needs. This philosophy may lead to serious problems in competitive markets where consumers will select those products that are more likely to satisfy their specific needs. The transition of development by a firm into a marketing-oriented organization may evolve as follows[4]:

- *Production orientation*—Here management concentrates on producing as much as possible since they assume that their product is better than that of their competitors and thus they can sell all that is produced.

[3]H. Mintzberg, "The Manager's Job: Folklore and Fact," in *Perspectives on Behavior in Organizations*, 2nd ed., eds. J. R. Hackman, E. E. Lawler III, and L. W. Porter (New York: McGraw-Hill, 1983), pp. 5–15.

[4]E. N. Berkowitz, R. A. Kerin, & W. Rudelius, *Marketing*, 2nd ed. (Homewood, Il.: Richard D. Irwin, Inc., 1989), pp. 18–19.

- *Sales orientation*—In this situation, the entrepreneur focuses on sales techniques and hard-sell approaches to persuade the consumer to buy the product.
- *Marketing orientation*—This philosophy focuses on the consumer's needs and wants. Management's objective is to determine these needs and develop and deliver products that will effectively meet them.

The entrepreneur often confuses selling and marketing. Selling focuses on the needs of the seller and marketing focuses on the needs of the buyer.[5] Figure 8–2 illustrates the organizational structure differences between production, selling, and marketing organizations. In the production orientation organization, there is no marketing activity outlined. In the selling orientation organization, marketing is confused with sales. Any marketing research or promotion is performed by the sales manager. As the firm becomes marketing-oriented, all of the marketing functions, including sales, report to a higher-level marketing manager or vice president.

BUILDING THE SUCCESSFUL ORGANIZATION

Before writing the organization plan it will be helpful for the entrepreneur to prepare a job analysis. The job analysis will serve as a guide in determining hiring procedures, training, performance appraisals, compensation programs, and job descriptions and specifications. In a very small venture this process would be simple, but as the size and complexity of the venture changes, the process becomes more complex.

The best place to begin the job analysis is with the tasks or jobs that need to be performed to make the venture viable. The entrepreneur should prepare a list of tasks and skills that are needed. Once a list is completed, the entrepreneur should determine how many positions will be necessary to accomplish these needs and what type of person or persons would be ideal. Decisions on where to advertise for employees, how they will be trained, who will train them, how they will be evaluated, and how they will be compensated are important in the early organizational planning for the new venture.

Perhaps the most important issues in the business plan are the job descriptions and specifications, discussed in detail below. Many of the other decisions such as hiring procedures, training, performance appraisals, benefits, and so on can be summarized in a personnel manual that does not need to be part of the business plan. However, the entrepreneur should consider these issues and may at some point find it necessary to hire a consultant to assist him or her in the preparation of such a manual.[6]

---

[5]T. Levitt, "Marketing Myopia," *Harvard Business Review*, July-August 1960, pp. 45–56.

[6]E. S. Ellman, "How to Write a Personnel Manual." *Inc. Special Reports*, 1989, pp. 66–8.

FIGURE 8–2   Production, Selling, and Marketing Organizations

JOB DESCRIPTIONS

The entrepreneur should clarify the roles of employees by preparing job descriptions. These job descriptions should specify the details of the work that is to be performed and any special conditions or skills involved in performing the job.[7] Job descriptions must contain information on what tasks are to be performed, the importance of each task, and the time required for each task. A job descrip-

---

[7]P. Grant, "What Use is a Job Description?" *Personnel Journal*, February 1988, 45–53.

tion communicates to candidates for employment what will be expected of them. It should be written in clear, direct, simple language. Figure 8–3 is an example of a job description for a sales manager.

The entrepreneur with no prior experience may find it difficult writing job descriptions. However, the management team's previous experience may contribute to the preparation of them. As stated earlier, the most effective method when no direct experience exists is to first outline the needs and objectives of the new venture and then work backward to determine the specific activities that will be needed to achieve these goals and objectives. These activities can then be categorized into areas of responsibility, that is, marketing, production, administration, and so on, and job descriptions may then be prepared. As the venture grows, these job descriptions may be upgraded or modified to meet the goals and objectives of the firm.

JOB SPECIFICATIONS

Job specifications should also be clear to the potential employee. The skills and abilities needed to perform the job must be outlined, including prior experience and education requirements. For example, for the sales manager position in Figure 8–3, 3 to 5 years of sales experience, a bachelor's degree in business, experience in sales training, management experience, writing skills, and communication skills may be required.

It is also important for the entrepreneur to stipulate how much travel will be necessary and how much effort will be devoted to developing new business. Reporting responsibilities should also be outlined. Will the sales manager report to the vice president, CEO, or some other designated individual in the new venture? All of this information will help prevent conflicts, misunderstandings, and communication breakdowns in the organization. Time spent deciding on these specifications and requirements before hiring will save the entrepreneur from personnel problems in the long run.

LOCATION OF THE BUSINESS

One of the important preliminary decisions for the entrepreneur is the location of the business. This decision will vary somewhat, depending on whether the business is a service or involves manufacturing. A service will require consideration of and factors such as[8]:

* Lease requirements
* Parking
* Pedestrian flow

---

[8]W. R. Davidson, D. J. Sweeney, & R. W. Stampfl, *Retailing Management*, 5th ed. (New York: John Wiley & Sons, 1984), pp. 179–97.

FIGURE 8–3   Example of Job Description

Sales Manager: Responsible for hiring, training, coordinating, and supervising all sales representatives, internal and external to the firm. Monitor sales by territory in the four-state market area. Call on key accounts in market area once every two weeks to provide sales promotion and merchandising support. Prepare annual sales plan for firm, including sales forecasts and goals by territory.

- Traffic flow
- Public transportation access
- Visibility, signage, ambience
- Affinities (neighbors)
- Entrances/exits
- Profile of trading area
- Nearness to competition

To assess the demographics of the trading area, the entrepreneur should draw a circle around his or her location and then locate competitors, review the traffic routes and public transportation, and determine the demographics or profile of consumers in the area. Local census data should be helpful in developing this profile. Simple observations can detail the traffic and pedestrian flow. Town regulations will provide information on signage and locations of exits and entrances.

In addition to the more obvious sources discussed above, the entrepreneur can also use marketing research to determine the consumer needs of such a service in one or more locations. After reviewing these data, the entrepreneur should be ready to proceed.

For a manufacturer, some of the considerations of location are different. The manufacturing operations may be located in an industrial area where neighbors, signage, pedestrian flow, traffic flow, and the profile of the local residents are unimportant. The manufacturer may consider the following:

- Lease requirements
- Proximity to major highways
- Loading and shipping space
- Access to major distributors
- Access to major suppliers
- Availability of labor

Whatever type of business the entrepreneur is considering, he or she should take some time to assess some of these critical factors. It would be unfortunate and disastrous to find, after locating a business, that consumers cannot conveniently access your business or that there is not enough labor available in the area.

LEGAL FORMS OF BUSINESS

There are three basic legal forms of business formation. There are a number of variations within each of these three forms. The three basic legal forms are (1) **proprietorship,** (2) **partnership,** and (3) corporation. The typical corporation form is also known as **C corporation.** Figure 8–4 describes the legal factors involved in each of these with the differences in the limited partnership and **S corporation** noted where appropriate. These three legal forms of business are compared with regard to ownership, liability, start-up costs, continuity, transferability of interest, capital requirement, management control, distribution of profits, and attractiveness for raising capital.

It is very important that the entrepreneur carefully evaluate the pros and cons of the various legal forms of organizing the new venture. This decision must be made prior to the submission of a business plan and request for venture capital.

The evaluation process requires the entrepreneur to determine the priority of each of the factors mentioned in Figure 8–4 as well as tax factors discussed later in this chapter. These factors will vary in importance, depending on the type of new business.

In addition to these factors, it is also necessary to consider some intangibles. These various types of organizational structures reflect an image to suppliers, existing clients, and prospective customers. For example, suppliers may prefer to deal with profit-making organizations rather than nonprofit companies. This attitude may be reflected in the perceived impressions that nonprofit firms are slow in paying their bills. Customers may sometimes prefer to do business with a corporation. Because of their continuity and ownership advantages, they are sometimes viewed as a more stable type of business. As a customer, it may be desirable to have assurance that the firm will be in business for a long time.

The variations of organizational structure as well as the advantages and disadvantages are many and can be quite confusing to the entrepreneur. The next section of this chapter clarifies some of the confusion and will assist the entrepreneur in making these important decisions.

Ownership

In the proprietorship, the owner is the individual who starts the business. He or she has full responsibility for the operations. In a partnership, there may be owners, some having general partnership ownership and some having limited partnership ownership. In the corporation, ownership is reflected by ownership of shares of stock. Other than the S corporations, where the maximum number of shareholders is 35, there is no limit to the number of shareholders who may own stock.

FIGURE 8–4 Legal Factors in Three Forms of Business Formation

Legal Factors	Proprietorship	Partnership	Corporation
Ownership	Individual	No limitation on number of partners.	No limitation on number of stockholders.
Liability of owners	Individual liable for business liabilities	In general partnership, individuals all liable for business liabilities. In limited partnership, partners are liable for amount of capital contribution.	Amount of capital contribution is limit of shareholder liability.
Costs of starting business	None other than filing fees for trade name	Partnership agreement, legal costs and minor filing fees for trade name. Limited partnership requires more comprehensive agreement, hence higher costs.	Created only by statute. Articles of incorporation, filing fees, taxes, and fees for states in which corporation registers to do business.
Continuity of business	Death dissolves the business	Death or withdrawal of one partner terminates partnership unless partnership agreement stipulates otherwise. In limited partnership, death or withdrawal of one of limited partners has no effect on continuity. Limited partner may be replaced. Limited partner can withdraw capital after six months after notice is provided.	Greatest form of continuity. Death or withdrawal of owner(s) will not affect legal existence of business.
Transferability of interest	Complete freedom to sell or transfer any part of business	General partner can transfer his/her interest only with consent of all other general partners. Limited partner can sell interest without consent of general partners.	Most flexible. Stockholders can sell or buy stock at will. Some stock transfers may be restricted by agreement. In S Corporation, stock may be transferred only to an individual.

FIGURE 8–4 (concluded)

Legal Factors	Proprietorship	Partnership	Corporation
Capital requirements	Capital raised only by loan or increased contribution by proprietor.	Loans or new contributions by partners require a change in partnership agreement.	New capital raised by sale of stock or bonds or by borrowing (debt) in name of corporation. In S Corporation, only one class of stock and limited to 35 shareholders.
Management control	Proprietor makes all decisions and can act immediately.	All partners have equal control and majority rules. In limited partnership, only the general partners have control of the business.	Majority stockholder(s) have most control from legal point of view. Day-to-day control in hands of management who may or may not be major stockholders.
Distribution of profits and losses	Proprietor responsible and receives all profits and losses.	Depends on partnership agreement and investment by partners.	Shareholders can share in profits by receipt of dividends.
Attractiveness for raising capital	Depends on capability of proprietor and success of business.	Depends on capability of partners and success of business	With limited liability for owners, more attractive as an investment opportunity.

Liability of Owners

This is one of the most critical reasons for establishing a corporation rather than any other form of business. The proprietor and general partners are liable for all aspects of the business. Since the corporation is an entity or legal "person," which is taxable and absorbs liability, the owners are liable only for the amount of their investment. In the case of a proprietorship or partnership, no distinction is made between the business entity and the owner(s). Then, to satisfy any outstanding debts of the business, creditors may seize any assets the owners have outside the business.

In a partnership, usually the general partners share the amount of personal liability equally, regardless of their capital contributions, unless there is a specific agreement to the contrary. The only protection for the partners is insurance against liability suits and each putting his or her assets in someone else's name. The government may disallow the latter action if it feels this was done to defraud creditors.

In a limited partnership, the limited partners are liable only for the amount of their capital contributions. This amount, by law, must be registered at a local courthouse, thus making this information public.

Costs of Starting Business

The more complex the organization, the more expensive it is to start. The least expensive is the proprietorship, where the only costs incurred may be for filing for a business or trade name. In a partnership, besides filing a trade name, a partnership agreement is needed. This agreement requires legal advice and should explicitly convey all the responsibilities, rights, and duties of the parties involved. A limited partnership may be somewhat more complex than a general partnership because it must comply strictly with statutory requirements.

The corporation can be created only by statute. This generally means that before the corporation may be legally formed the owners are required to (1) register the name and articles of incorporation and (2) meet the state statutory requirements (some states are more lenient than others). In complying with these requirements, the corporation will likely incur filing fees, an organization tax, and fees for doing business in each state. Legal advice is necessary to meet all the statutory requirements.

Continuity of Business

One of the main concerns of a new venture is what happens if one of the entrepreneurs (or the only entrepreneur) dies or withdraws from the business. Continuity differs significantly for each of the forms of business. In a sole proprietorship, the death of the owner results in the termination of the business. Sole proprietorships are thus not perpetual and there is no time limit on how long they may exist.

The partnership varies, depending on whether it is a limited or a general partnership and on the partnership agreement. In a limited partnership, the death or withdrawal of a limited partner (can withdraw capital six months after giving notice to other partners) has no effect on the existence of the partnership. A limited partner may be replaced, depending on the partnership agreement. If a general partner in a limited partnership dies or withdraws, the limited partnership is terminated unless the partnership agreement specifies otherwise or all partners agree to continue.

In a partnership, the death or withdrawal of one of the partners results in termination of the partnership. However, this rule can be overcome by the partnership agreement. Usually the partnership will buy out the deceased or withdrawn partner's share at a predetermined price based on some appraised value. Another option is that a member of the deceased's family may take over as a partner and share in profits accordingly. Life insurance owned by the partnership is a good solution for protecting the interests of the partnership, along with carefully outlining contingencies in the partnership agreement.

The corporation has the most continuity of all of the forms of business. Death or withdrawal has no impact on the continuation of the business. Only in a closely held corporation, where all the shares are held by a few people, may there be some problems trying to find a market for the shares. Usually the corporate charter requires that the corporation or the remaining shareholders purchase the shares. In a public corporation this, of course, would not be an issue.

Transferability of Interest

There can be mixed feelings as to whether the transfer of interest in a business is desirable. In some cases the entrepreneur(s) may prefer to evaluate and assess any new owners prior to giving them a share of the business. On the other hand, it is also desirable to be able to sell one's interest whenever one wishes. Each of the forms of business offers different advantages as to the transferability of interest.

In the sole proprietorship, the entrepreneur has the right to sell or transfer any assets in the business. The limited partnership provides for more flexibility than the partnership regarding transfer of interest. In the limited partnership, the limited partners can sell their interests at any time without consent of the general partners. The person to whom the limited partner sells, however, can have only the same rights as the previous owner. A general partner in either a limited partnership or partnership cannot sell any interest in the business unless there is some provision for doing so in the partnership agreement. Usually the remaining partners will have the right of refusal of any new partner, even if the partnership agreement allows for transfer of interest.

The corporation has the most freedom in terms of selling one's interest in the business. Shareholders may transfer their shares at any time without consent from the other shareholders. The disadvantage of the right is that it can affect the ownership control of a corporation through election of a board of directors. Shareholders' agreements may provide some limitations on the ease of transferring interest, usually by giving the existing shareholders or corporation the option of purchasing the stock at a specific price or at the price agreed on. Thus, they sometimes can have the right of first refusal. In the S corporation, the transfer of interest can occur only as long as the buyer is an individual.

Capital Requirements

The need for capital during the early months of the new venture can become one of the most critical factors in keeping a new venture alive. As discussed in Chapter 7, the lack of cash flow and need for pro formas emphasizes the likely need for capital in the early stages of the new venture. The opportunities and ability of the new venture to raise capital will vary, depending on the form of business.

For a proprietorship, any new capital can come only from loans by any number of sources or by additional personal contributions by the entrepreneur. In borrowing money from a bank, the entrepreneur in this form of business may need collateral to support the loan. Often an entrepreneur will take a second mortgage on his or her home as a source of capital. Any borrowing from an outside investor may require giving up some of the equity in the proprietorship. Whatever the source, the responsibility for payment is in the hands of the entrepreneur, and failure to make payments can result in foreclosure and liquidation of the business. However, even with these risks the proprietorship is not likely to need large sums of money, as might be the case for a partnership or corporation.

In the partnership, loans may be obtained from banks but will likely require a change in the partnership agreement. Additional funds contributed by each of the partners will also require a new partnership agreement. As in the proprietorship, the entrepreneurs are liable for payment of any new bank loans.

In the corporation, new capital can be raised in a number of ways. The alternatives are greater than in any of the legal forms of business. Stock may be sold as either voting or nonvoting. Nonvoting stock will of course protect the power of the existing major stockholders. Bonds may also be sold by the corporation. This alternative would be more difficult for the new venture since a high bond rating will likely occur only after the business has been successful over time.

Money may also be borrowed in the name of the corporation. As stated earlier, this protects the personal liability of the entrepreneurs.

Management Control

In any new venture, the entrepreneur(s) will want to retain as much control as possible over the business. Each of the forms of business offers different opportunities and problems as to control and responsibility for making business decisions.

In the proprietorship, the entrepreneur has the most control and flexibility in making business decisions. Since the entrepreneur is the single owner of the venture, he or she will be responsible and have sole authority over all business decisions.

The partnership can present problems over control of business decisions if the partnership agreement is not concise regarding this issue. Usually in a partnership, the majority rules unless the partnership agreement states otherwise. It is most important that the partners are friendly toward one another and that delicate or sensitive decision areas of the business are spelled out in the partnership agreement.

The limited partnership offers a compromise between the partnership and the corporation. In this type of organization there is some separation of ownership and control. The limited partners in the venture have no control over business decisions. As soon as the limited partner is given some control over business decisions, he or she then assumes personal liability and can no longer be considered a limited partner.

Control of day-to-day business in a corporation is in the hands of management, who may or may not be major stockholders. Control over major long-term decisions, however, may require a vote of the major stockholders. Thus control is separated based on the types of business decisions. In a new venture there is a strong likelihood that the entrepreneurs who are major stockholders will manage the day-to-day activities of the business. As the corporation increases in size, the separation of management and control becomes more probable.

Stockholders in the corporation can indirectly affect the operation of the business by electing someone to the board of directors who reflects their personal business philosophies. These board members, through appointment of top management, then affect the operation and control of the day-to-day management of the business.

Distribution of Profits and Losses

Proprietors receive all distributions of profits from the business. As discussed earlier, they are also personally responsible for all losses. Some of the profits may be used to pay back the entrepreneur for any personal capital contributions made to keep the business operating.

In the partnership, the distribution of profits and losses depends on the partnership agreement. It is likely that the sharing of profits and losses will be a function of the partners' investments. However, this can vary, depending on the agreement. As in the proprietorship, the partners may assume liability. The limited partnership provides an alternative that protects against personal liability but may reduce shares of any profits.

Corporations distribute profits through dividends to stockholders. These distributions are not likely to absorb all of the profits that may be retained by the corporation for future investment or capital needs of the business. Losses by the corporation will often result in no dividends. These losses will then be covered by retained earnings or through other financial means discussed earlier.

Attractiveness for Raising Capital

In both the proprietorship and the partnership, the ability of the entrepreneurs to raise capital depends on the success of the business and the personal capability of the entrepreneur. These two forms are the least attractive for raising capital, primarily because of the problem of personal liability. Any large amounts of capital needed in these forms of business should be given serious consideration.

The corporation, because of its advantages regarding personal liability, is the most attractive form of business for raising capital. Shares of stock, bonds, and/ or debt are all opportunities for raising capital with limited liability. The more attractive the corporation, the easier it will be to raise capital.

TAX ATTRIBUTES OF FORMS OF BUSINESS

The tax advantages and disadvantages of each of the forms of business differ significantly. Some of the major differences are discussed below. There are many minor differences that, in total, can be important to the entrepreneur. If the entrepreneur has any doubt about these advantages, he or she should get outside advice. Figure 8–5 provides a summary of some of the major tax advantages of these forms of business. These are discussed further below.

Tax Issues for Proprietorship

For the proprietorship, the IRS treats the business as the individual owner. All income appears on the owner's return as personal income. Thus, the proprietorship is not regarded by the IRS as a separate tax entity. As can be seen in Figure 8–5, this treatment of taxes affects the taxable year, distribution of profits to owners, organization costs, capital gains, capital losses, and medical benefits. Each of these is treated as if it is incurred by the individual owner and not the business.

FIGURE 8–5 Tax Attributes of Various Legal Forms of Business

Attributes	Proprietorship	Partnership	Corporation
Taxable year	Usually a calendar year	Usually calendar year but other dates may be used.	Any year end can be used at beginning. Any changes require changes in incorporation.
Distribution of profits to owners	All income appears on owner's return	Partnership agreement may have special allocation of income. Partners pay tax on their pro rata shares of income on individual return even if income not immediately distributed.	No income is allocated to stockholders.
Organization costs	Not amortizable	Amortizable over 60 months	Amortizable over 60 months
Dividends received	$100 dividend exclusion for single return and $200 on joint return.	Dividend exclusion of partnership passes to partner. (conduit)	80% or more of dividend received may be deducted (after 12/31/86)
Capital gains	Taxed at individual level. A deduction is allowed for long-term capital gains.	Capital gain to partnership will be taxed as a capital gain to the partner. (conduit)	Taxed at corporate level. After July 1, 1987 the maximum rate will be 34%.
Capital losses	Carried forward indefinitely	Capital losses can be used to offset other income. Carried forward indefinitely. (conduit)	Carry back three years and carry over five years as short-term capital loss offsetting only capital gains.
Initial organization	Commencement of business results in no additional tax for individual.	Contributions of property to a partnership not taxed.	Acquisition of stock for cash entails no immediate taxes. Transfer of property in exchange for stock may be taxable if stock value greater than contributed property.

Limitations on losses deductible by owners	Amount at risk may be deducted except for real estate activities.	Partnership investment plus share of recourse liability if any. At-risk rules may apply except for real estate partnership.	No losses allowed except on sale of stock or liquidation of corporation. In S Corporation, shareholders' investment to corporation is deductible.
Medical benefits	Itemized deductions for medical expenses in excess of percentage of adjusted gross income on individual's return. No deduction for insurance premium.	Cost of partners' benefits not deductible to business as an expense. Possible deduction at partner level.	Cost of employee-shareholder coverage deductible as business expense if designed for benefit of employee.
Retirement benfits	Limitations and restrictions basically same as regular corporations.	Same as for corporations.	Limitations on benefits from defined benefit plans—lesser of $90,000 or 100% of compensation. Limitations on contributions to defined contribution plans—lesser of $30,000 or 25% of compensation (15% of aggregate for profit-sharing plans).

The proprietorship has some tax advantages when compared to the corporation. First, there is no double tax when profits are distributed to the owner. Another advantage is that there is no capital stock tax or penalty for retained earnings in the business. Again, these advantages exist because the proprietorship is not recognized as a separate tax entity; all profits and losses are part of the entrepreneur's tax return.

Tax Issues for Partnership

The partnership's tax advantages and disadvantages are very similar to those of the proprietorship, especially regarding income distributions, dividends, and capital gains and losses. Limited partnerships can provide some unique tax advantages since the limited partner can share in the profits without being responsible for any liability beyond his or her investment.

Both the partnership and proprietorship are organizational forms that serve as nontaxable conduits of income and deductions. These forms of business do have a legal identity distinct from the partners or owners, but this identity is only for accounting reporting.

It is especially important for partnerships to report income since this serves as the basis for determining the share of each partner. The income is distributed based on the partnership agreement. The owners then report their share as personal income and pay taxes based on this amount.

Tax Issues for Corporation

Since the corporation is recognized by the IRS as a separate tax entity, it has the advantage of being able to take many deductions and expenses that are not available to the proprietorship or partnership. The disadvantage is that the distribution of dividends is taxed twice, as income of the corporation and as income of the stockholder. This double taxation can be avoided if the income is distributed to the entrepreneur(s) in the form of salary. Bonuses, incentives, profit sharing, and so on are thus allowable ways to distribute income of the corporation as long as the compensation is reasonable in amount and payment was for services rendered.

The corporate tax may be lower than the individual rate, although, with the new tax laws effective in 1987, these advantages may be lessened. The entrepreneur is best advised to consider the tax pros and cons and decide on that basis. Projected earnings may be used to calculate the actual taxes under each form of business in order to identify the one that provides the best tax advantage. Remember, the tax advantages may be outweighed by the advantages of liability responsibility in the respective form of business.

S CORPORATION

The S corporation combines the tax advantages of the partnership and the corporation. It is designed so that venture income is declared as personal income on a pro rata basis by the shareholders. In fact, the shareholders benefit from all of the income and the deductions of the business. In order to be an S corporation, the venture must meet following qualifications:[9]

- Must be a domestic corporation
- Cannot be a subsidiary of another corporation
- Can have only one class of stock
- Must have 35 shareholders or less
- Shareholders must be individuals, estates, or certain types of trusts
- No shareholder can be an alien

If all of the above requirements are met, then a corporation may elect S corporation status. This election must have the unanimous consent of all shareholders. If the election of an S corporation is made during the year, then any shareholders prior to the election who have surrendered their shares must also consent to the S corporation status. This rule is designed to prevent gains or losses in that taxable year from being allocated to nonconsenting shareholders. If the decision to elect S corporation status is made after the 15th of the third month of the taxable year, it does not become effective until the following taxable year.

Advantages of an S Corporation

The S corporation offers the entrepreneur some distinct advantages over the typical corporation, or C corporation. However, there are also disadvantages.[10] In those instances when the disadvantages are great, the entrepreneur should elect C corporation form. Some of the advantages of the S corporation are as follows:

- Capital gains or losses from the corporation are treated as personal income or losses by the shareholders on a pro rata basis (determined by number of shares of stock held). The corporation is thus not taxed.
- Shareholders retain limited liability protection of C corporation.
- It is not subject to a minimum tax, as is the C corporation.
- Stock may be transferred to low-income-bracket family members (children must be 14 years or over).

---

[9]S. Jones, M. B. Cohen, & V. V. Coppola, *Growing Your Business* (New York: John Wiley & Sons, 1988), pp. 106–12.

[10]I. L. Blackman, "Pro's and Con's of S Corporations," *National Petroleum News*, November 1988, p. 72.

- Stock may be voting or nonvoting.
- This form of business may use the cash method of accounting.
- Corporate long-term capital gains and losses are deductible directly by the shareholders to offset other personal capital gains or losses.

Disadvantages of an S Corporation

Although the advantages appear to be favorable for the entrepreneur, this form of business is not appropriate for everyone. The disadvantages of the S corporation are as follows:

- There are stringent requirements to quality for this form of business.
- If the corporation earns less than $100,000, then the C corporation would have a lower tax.
- The S corporation may not deduct most fringe benefits for shareholders.
- The S corporation must adopt a calendar year for tax purposes.
- Only one class of stock is permitted for this form of business (common stock).
- The net loss of the S corporation is limited to the shareholder's stock plus loans to the business.

The Tax Reform Act of 1986 added some provisions that affect the allocation of stock to lower-tax-bracket family members and the disposition of assets sold within a 10-year period after the election of an S corporation. With the new tax laws and changing rates, owners need to compare alternative forms before election. This should be done with the advice of a tax attorney, since once a decision is made, it is difficult to change again.

State laws regarding the S corporation vary from state to state. This inconsistency reinforces the need to review all options carefully before deciding on the corporate form.

THE ORGANIZATION AND USE OF ADVISORS

The entrepreneur will usually need to use outside advisors such as accountants, bankers, lawyers, advertising agencies, and market researchers. These advisors can become an important part of the organization and thus will need to be managed just like any other permanent part of it.

The relationship of the entrepreneur and outside advisors can be enhanced by seeking out the best advisors and involving them thoroughly and at an early stage. Advisors should be assessed or interviewed just as if they were being hired for a permanent position. References should be checked and questions asked to ascertain the quality of service as well as compatibility with the management team. Advisors are probably more important in getting the start-up under way. Thus, it is important for the entrepreneur to enlist the work of these advisors very early in the development of the business.[11]

Hiring and managing outside experts can be effectively accomplished by considering them as advice suppliers. Just as no manager would buy raw materials or supplies without knowledge of their cost and quality, the same approval can be used for advisors. Entrepreneurs should ask these advisors about fees, credentials, references, and so on before hiring them.

Even after the advisors have been hired, the entrepreneur should question their advice. Why is the advise being given? Make sure you understand the decision and its potential implications. There are many good sources of advisors such as the SBA, other small businesses, chambers of commerce, universities, friends, and relatives. Careful evaluation of the entrepreneur's needs and the competency of the advisor can make their use a valuable asset to the organization of a new venture.

SUMMARY

The organizational plan for the entrepreneur requires some major decisions that could affect long-term effectiveness and profitability. It is important to begin the new venture with a strong management team that is committed to the goals of the new venture. The management team must be able to work together effectively toward these ends. With pressures from competition, it is important to have an effective organization with clearly defined roles and job descriptions. Decisions are needed on hiring procedures, training, supervising, compensation, evaluation of performance, and so on.

Once the structure and roles of the members of the organization are defined, the entrepreneur(s) must decide on the legal form of business. The three major legal forms of business are the proprietorship, partnership, and corporation. Each differs significantly and should be evaluated carefully before a decision is made. This chapter provides considerable insight and comparisons regarding these forms of business to assist the entrepreneur in this decision.

The S corporation is an alternative form of a corporation. It allows the entrepreneur to retain the protection from personal liability provided by a corporation but the tax advantages of a partnership. There are important advantages as well as disadvantages of this form of business, and entrepreneurs should carefully weigh them before deciding.

Advisors will also be necessary in the new venture. Outside advisors should be evaluated as if they were to be hired as permanent members of the organization. Information on their fees and referrals can help determine the best choices.

---

[11]H. H. Stevenson, & W. A. Sahlman, "How Small Companies Should Handle Advisors," *Harvard Business Review,* March-April 1988, pp. 28–34.

P A R T

III

FINANCING A NEW VENTURE

Sources of Capital

CHAPTER OBJECTIVES

1. To identify the general types of financing available.

2. To explain the role of commercial banks in financing new ventures, specifically, the types of loans available and bank lending decisions.

3. To discuss small business administrative loans.

4. To explain the elements of research and development limited partnership.

5. To discuss government grants, particularly small business innovation research grants.

6. To explain the importance of private placement as a source of funds.

WALT DISNEY

Where does an entrepreneur get the funds to turn his or her dreams into reality? Funds come from a variety of sources. In the case of Walt Disney, it all started with a clandestine paper route.

Born in Chicago and raised on a small farm in Missouri, Walt Disney and his family moved to Kansas City when he was 10 years old. He and his brother worked without pay delivering newspapers for their father's circulation franchise. Whenever Walt found a new customer, however, he bypassed his father, buying the additional papers directly from the newspaper office, thereby establishing his own route. With the profits from his private venture, he was able to satisfy his sweet tooth without the knowledge of his parents, who forbade candy in their home.

From this beginning, Disney's entrepreneurial career branched out. As a teenager, he lied about his age and joined the Red Cross to serve in World War I like his revered older brother, Roy. After he arrived in France with the last of the volunteers, his age quickly became a detriment. Duped by his comrades into picking up a bar bill larger than his first paycheck (which he had yet to receive), Walt was forced to sell his boots on the black market, swearing he would never be conned again. He learned to play a good game of poker and started a con game of his own—"doctoring" German steel helmets he collected from the battlefield rubbish to look as though the previous owner had been shot in the head. He sold them as "genuine war souvenirs" to soldiers passing through the Red Cross station. Walt amassed what he considered a small fortune, which he sent home to his mother for safekeeping.

On returning home at the end of the war, Walt tried to fulfill his childhood dream of being a newspaper cartoonist. Although displaying artistic talent, he could not draw the negative, satirical cartoons wanted by the papers. Discouraged by the cold reception in Chicago, Walt moved to Kansas City with his brother Roy, who found him a job illustrating advertisements and catalogs for a client of one of the local banks. Since it was only a short-term job, following the Christmas rush, Walt was again unemployed and in his brother's hair. Teaming up with a more skilled artist he had met on his first job, Walt convinced a local publisher that his low-budget throwaway paper would be greatly improved by adding illustrated advertisements. Won over by Disney's charm, the publisher allowed the two artists to use a spare room (actually, a bathroom) as their studio.

With $250 from his wartime earnings, Walt purchased enough equipment and supplies to start the business.

Always on the alert for more business opportunities, Walt contracted the service to other printers in town. Before long, "Iwerks & Disney" moved into a real office, and the two had enough money to attend the local movie house, where they were fascinated with the cartoon features. Responding to an advertisement for a cartoonist for the Kansas City Film Ad Company, Disney tried to sell the services of the partnership. When he was informed that the job was available to him alone, he gave his half of the partnership to Iwerks and walked away from the illustration business.

Quickly becoming the star of the artistic staff, Disney stayed with the Film Ad Company for only a short time before founding his own production company, Laugh-O-Gram Films, Inc. To raise capital to branch out from advertising, Walt Disney sold shares in his company to a number of local citizens. With $15,000 in capital, he created two cartoon shorts based on fairy tales, which were distributed nationally. Even though both were extremely popular, Disney did not receive any payments and was soon broke. However, he managed to save a camera and a copy of his most original work, "Alice's Wonderland," from his creditors. After raising some money by taking news photographs for the local papers, Disney headed west to Hollywood to start anew.

While the story now becomes more complicated and the money raised much larger, the theme remains the same. Using his copy of "Alice's Wonderland" and his two fairy tale shorts to demonstrate his talent, he relied on charm, old contacts, and family for financial support: a Laugh-O-Gram client agreed to finance the production of several short "Alice" adventures, his brother Roy helped with the business deals, and some of his old Kansas City supporters renewed their contributions. Disney Productions went through cycles of feast and famine brought on by Walt's drive for perfection. When he got his way, the products were outstanding but expensive, and the Disney brothers often found themselves over their heads in dealing with the motion picture industry. Just when they thought they had a hit, ideas were stolen, profits were not accounted for, and their whole world seemed to be on the verge of collapse. Then, miraculously, a new idea would appear and the studio would flourish again. It was during this time that they added sound and color to their increasingly popular short cartoons, which increased both their artistic impact and their cost. Although its name was known worldwide, Disney Productions found it difficult to turn a profit.

The turning point for a profit was the production of a full-length cartoon feature—"Snow White and the Seven Dwarfs." Premiering in 1937, it was a costly box office success. With a production budget of nearly 10 times that of a "live" feature, the cartoon would have ruined the company had it been a failure. Fortunately, it became one of the most successful motion pictures in history. From the profits realized, Walt Disney started working on three new features and expanded the plant facilities. The new movies, "Pinocchio," "Bambi," and "Fantasia," were each completed well over budget and were not initially successful in the American market. To make matters worse, the outbreak of World War II just as these films were being released destroyed the profitable European market. With construction debts increasing, the only financing alternative appeared to be going public—selling stock. In April 1940, 755,000 units of common stock and preferred shares were sold, raising nearly $8 million in capital, once again saving the company.

However, being a public corporation was not the ultimate salvation for Disney Productions. Walt Disney, like many typical entrepreneurs, was used to controlling everything to the tiniest detail and did not like relegating any responsibilities and duties to the shareholders. Growing weary of cartooning and movies, Walt latched onto another dream—an amusement park. However, Roy did not see this as a money-maker and convinced the board of directors and several bankers to turn down Walt's request for money. Desperate for the cash to fulfill his fantasy, Walt turned to a different source of capital—television. Although television was the newest entertainment rage, Disney Productions had avoided it, judging it too demeaning. However, after all other sources of revenue were blocked, Walt agreed to a joint venture with ABC, the newest and smallest of the broadcasting companies. In return for $5 million in financing for the park, Disney agreed to put "Mickey Mouse" on TV. Things have not been the same since, for ABC, Disney Productions, or the American public.

As was the case throughout Walt Disney's entrepreneurial career, one of the most critical problems confronted by each entrepreneur is securing financing for the venture. While this is a problem throughout the life of the enterprise, it is particularly acute at start-up. From the entrepreneur's perspective, the longer the venture can operate without outside capital, the less will be the cost either in terms of interest rates or equity loss in the company. The same amount of money invested three years following a track record of sales and profit might obtain only a 10 percent equity position, where it might obtain a 30 percent equity position earlier. From the perspective of the provider of the funds, a potential investment opportunity needs to have an appropriate risk/return ratio. A higher return is expected when there is a greater risk involved. An investor will seek to maximize return for a given level of risk or minimize risk for a given level of return. This chapter describes some common (and some not so common) sources of capital and the conditions under which the money is obtained. As was the case with Walt Disney, different sources of capital are generally used at different times in the life of the venture.

AN OVERVIEW

Overall, there are two types of financing available: **internal or external funds**. The type of financing most frequently employed is internally generated financing. Internally generated funds can come from several sources: profits, sale of assets, reduction in working capital, credit from suppliers, and accounts receivable. In every new venture, the start-up years involve plowing all the profits back into the venture—outside equity investors expect no payback in these early years. Sometimes, the needed funds can be obtained by selling little-used assets. To conserve cash wherever possible in a start-up situation, each asset should be on a rental (preferably a lease with an option to buy), not an ownership, basis as long as the terms are favorable. Another short-term internal source of funds can be obtained by reducing short-term assets—inventory, cash, and other working-capital items. Sometimes an entrepreneur can generate the needed cash for 30 to 60 days through credit from suppliers. While care must be taken to ensure good supplier relations and continuous sources of supply, taking a few extra days before paying the bills can also generate needed short-term funds. A final method for internally generating funds is by collecting bills (accounts receivable) more quickly. Care should be taken not to irritate key accounts when implementing this practice as certain customers have unalterable payment practices. Mass merchandisers, for example, pay their bills to supplying companies in 60 to 90 days, regardless of a supplying company's accounts receivable policy, the size of the company, or the discount for prompt payment offered. If a company wants this store to carry its product, it will have to abide by this payment schedule.

The other general category of funds are those external to the firm. Alternative sources of external financing need to be evaluated in terms of length of time the funds are available, the costs involved, and the amount of company control lost. Various sources, from self to government programs, are evaluated along these three dimensions in Table 9–1. As indicated, external financing is one of two

TABLE 9–1   Alternative Sources of Financing

| Source of Financing | Length of Time | | Cost | | | | Control | |
	Short-term	Long-term	Fixed Rate Debt	Floating Rate Debt	Percent of Profits	Equity	Covenants	Voting Rights
Self		X				X	X	X
Family and friends	X	X	X	X		X	X	X
Suppliers and trade credit	X				X			
Commercial banks	X		X	X			X	
Asset-based lenders		X	X	X			X	
Institutions and insurance companies		X	X	X	X		X	
Pension funds		X			X	X	X	
Venture capital		X				X	X	X
Private equity placements						X	X	X
Public equity offerings					X	X		X
Government programs		X						

types—debt financing or equity financing. Debt financing is a financing method involving an interest-bearing loan instrument, the payment for which is only indirectly related to the sales and profits of the new venture. Typically, debt financing (also called asset-based financing) requires that some asset (such as a car, house, machine, or land) be available as collateral. Equity financing, on the other hand, typically does not require collateral and offers the investor some form of ownership position in the venture. The investor shares in the profits of the venture, as well as any disposition of assets on a pro rata basis. Key factors in the use of one type of financing over another are the availability of funds, the assets of the venture, and the prevailing interest rates. Frequently, an entrepreneur meets financial needs by employing a combination of debt and equity financing. The more frequently used sources of funds (commercial banks, Small Business Administration (SBA) loans, R&D limited partnerships, government grants, and private placement) indicated in the table are discussed in depth.

COMMERCIAL BANKS

Commercial banks are by far the most frequently used source of short-term funds by the entrepreneur. The funds provided are in the form of debt financing and as such require some tangible guaranty or collateral—some asset with value. This collateral can be in the form of business assets (land, equipment, or building of the venture), personal assets (house, car, land, stock, or bonds of the entrepreneur), or the assets of a cosigner of the note who will guarantee that the loan will be repaid.

Types of Bank Loans

There are several types of bank loans available. To ensure a reasonable expectation of repayment, these loans are based on assets or cash flow of the venture. The **asset base for loans** includes: accounts receivable, inventory, equipment, or real estate.

Accounts receivable provides a good basis for a loan, especially if the customer base is well known and creditworthy. On determination of the creditworthiness of the customer base through investigation, a bank may finance up to 80 percent of the value of the accounts receivable. When customers such as the government are involved, an entrepreneur can develop a factoring arrangement whereby the factor (the bank) actually "buys" the accounts receivable at a value below the face value of the sale and collects the money directly from the account. In this case, if any of the receivables are not collectible, the factor sustains the loss, not the business. The cost of factoring the accounts receivable is of course higher than the cost of securing a loan against the accounts receivable without factoring being involved since the bank has more risk when factoring. The costs of factoring involve the interest charge on the amount of money advanced until the time the accounts receivable are collected, the commission covering the actual collection, and the protection against possible uncollectible accounts.

Inventory is another of the firm's assets that is often a basis for a loan, particularly when the inventory is very liquid, that is, can be sold easily. Usually about 50 percent of the finished goods inventory can be financed. Trust receipts are a type of inventory loan used to finance floor plans of retailers such as automobile and appliance dealers. In trust receipts, the bank advances a large percentage of the invoice price of the goods and is paid on a pro rata basis as the inventory is sold.

Equipment can be used to secure longer-term financing up to 3 to 10 years. Equipment financing can be of several types: financing the purchase of new equipment, financing used equipment already owned by the company, sale-leaseback financing, or lease financing. When new equipment is being purchased or presently owned equipment is used as collateral, usually from 50 to 80 percent of the value of the equipment can be financed, depending on its salability. Given the entrepreneur's propensity to rent versus own, sale-leaseback or lease financing of equipment are widely used. In the sale-leaseback arrangement, the entrepreneur "sells" the equipment to a lender and then leases it back for the life of the equipment to ensure its continued use. In lease financing, the company acquires the use of the equipment through a small down payment and a guarantee to make a specified number of payments over a period of time. The total amount paid is the selling price plus the finance charges.

Real estate is also frequently used in asset-based financing. This mortgage financing can usually be easily obtained to finance a company's land, plant, or building, usually up to 75 percent of its value.

The other type of debt financing frequently provided by commercial banks and other financial institutions is cash flow financing. These **conventional bank loans** include lines of credit, installment loans, straight commercial loans, long-term loans, and character loans. Lines of credit financing are perhaps the most frequently used form of cash flow financing by entrepreneurs. In arranging for a line of credit to be used as needed, the company pays a "commitment fee" at the start to ensure that the commercial bank will make the loan when requested and then pays interest on any outstanding funds borrowed from the bank. Frequently, the loan must be repaid on a periodic basis at least until it is reduced to a certain agreed-upon level.

Installment loans can also be obtained by a going venture with a track record of sales and profits. These short-term funds are frequently used to cover working capital needs for a period of time such as when seasonal financing is needed. These loans are usually for 30 to 40 days.

A hybrid of the installment loan is the straight commercial loan by which funds are advanced to the company for 30 to 90 days. These self-liquidating loans are frequently used for seasonal financing and building up inventories.

When a longer time is required, long-term loans are used. These loans (usually only available to strong, more mature companies) can make funds available for up to 10 years. The debt incurred is usually repaid according to a fixed interest and principal schedule, although the principal can sometimes start being repaid in the second or third year of the loan.

When the business itself does not have the assets to support a loan, the entrepreneur may need a character (personal) loan. These loans frequently must have the assets of the individual pledged or the loan cosigned by another individual. In extremely rare instances, the entrepreneur can obtain money on an unsecured basis for a short time when a high credit standing has been established.

Bank Lending Decisions

One problem for the entrepreneur (particularly for the woman entrepreneur) is how to successfully secure a loan from the bank. Due to previous bad loan decisions by banks, particularly in some depressed areas of the country, banks are far more cautious in lending money since they cannot afford to incur more bad loans. Regardless of the area, commercial loan decisions are made only after the loan officer and loan committee do a careful review of the borrower and the financial track record of the business. These decisions are based on both quantifiable information and subjective judgments.[1]

The bank lending decisions can be summarized as the five Cs of lending—Character, Capacity, Capital, Collateral, and Conditions. Past financial statements (balance sheets and income statements) are reviewed in terms of key profitability and credit ratios, inventory turnover, aging of accounts receivable, the entrepreneur's capital invested, and the commitment to business, which were discussed in Chapter 4. Future projections on market size, sales, and profitability are also evaluated to determine the ability to repay the loan and the margin surrounding that ability. Several questions are usually raised regarding this ability. Does the entrepreneur expect to be carried by the loan for an extended period? If problems occur, is the entrepreneur committed enough to spend the effort necessary to make the business a success? Does the business have a unique differential advantage in a growth market? What are the downside risks? Is there protection (such as life insurance on key personnel and insurance on the plant and equipment) against extraordinary disasters?

While the answers to these questions and the analysis of the company's records allow the loan officer to assess the quantitative aspects of the loan decision, the intuitive factors, particularly the first two Cs—Character and Capacity—are also taken into account. This part of the loan decision—the gut feeling—is the most difficult part of the decision to assess. The entrepreneur must present his or her capabilities and the prospects for the company in a way that elicits a

---

[1]For a discussion of bank lending decisions, see A. D. Jankowicz & R. D. Hisrich, "Intuition in Small Business Lending Decisions," *Journal of Small Business Management*, July 1987, 45–52; N. C. Churchill & V. L. Lewis, "Bank Lending to New and Growing Enterprises," *Journal of Business Venturing*, Spring 1986, 193–206; R. T. Justis, "Starting a Small Business: An Investigation of the Borrowing Procedure," *Journal of Small Business Management*, October 1982, 22–31; and L. Fertuck, "Survey of Small Business Lending Practices," *Journal of Small Business Management*, October 1982, 42–48.

positive loan response. This intuitive part of the loan decision becomes even more important when there is little or no track record, limited experience in financial management, a nonproprietary product or service (one not protected by a patent or license), or few assets available.

Some of the concerns of the loan officer and loan committee can be reduced by providing a good loan application. While the specific loan application format of each bank differs to some extent, generally the application format is a "mini" business plan consisting of an executive summary, business description, owner/manager profiles, business projections, financial statements, amount and use of the loan, and repayment schedule. This information provides the loan officer and loan committee with the two most important pieces of information—the creditworthiness of the individual and business and the ability of the venture to make enough sales and profit to repay the loan and the interest. The entrepreneur should evaluate several alternative banks, select one, call for an appointment, and then carefully present the case for the loan to the loan officer. Presenting a positive business image and following the established procedure are important in obtaining the needed funds from a commercial bank.

Regardless of the type of commercial bank loan, the entrepreneur should generally use this source of financing to the maximum amount possible, as long as the prevailing interest rates and the terms, conditions, and restrictions on the loan are satisfactory. Care must be taken to ensure that the venture will generate enough cash flow to repay the interest and principal on the loan in a timely manner. The entrepreneur should evaluate the track record and lending procedures of banks in the area to secure the money needed on the most favorable terms available. This "bank shopping procedure" will bear fruit and positively affect the financial returns of the venture.

SMALL BUSINESS ADMINISTRATION LOANS

Frequently an entrepreneur is missing the necessary track record, assets, or some other ingredient to obtain a commercial bank loan. This problem can arise from a lack of communication and differences in objectives and concerns of the two parties. For example, the entrepreneur frequently emphasizes the top line—sales—while the bank loan officer emphasizes the bottom line—profit. Although sales are important, the entrepreneur should be careful to make a balanced presentation, emphasizing the effect of sales growth on the bottom line—profit.

When differences cannot be resolved or there are other factors causing the entrepreneur to be unable to secure a regular commercial bank loan, an alternative is a Small Business Administration (SBA) Guaranty Loan. In this type of loan, the SBA guarantees that 80 percent of the amount loaned to the entrepreneur's business will be repaid to the bank by the SBA—the U.S. Government—if the company cannot make payment. This guarantee allows the bank to make a loan that carries a higher risk than loans it would otherwise make. The process for securing such a loan is outlined in Table 9–2. This procedure is the same as

---
TABLE 9–2 SBA Loan Application Procedure
---

1. Assemble the information outlined below.
2. Take it to your bank and ask your banker to review the information and loan proposal. (It will be necessary for you to locate a bank that is willing to participate with SBA and make the loan since direct loan funds from SBA are quite limited and an unreliable source of financing.)
3. If the bank is willing to participate, ask the bank to forward the information to us for our review, along with their comments.

INFORMATION NEEDED FOR LOAN REVIEW

1. Brief resume of business.
2. Brief resume of management, setting forth prior business experience, technical training, education, age, health, etc.
3. Itemized use of loan proceeds:

Working capital	$_____
Land	$_____
Building	$_____
Furniture and fixtures	$_____
Machinery and equipment	$_____
Automotive equipment	$_____
Other	$_____
Total	$_____

4. Current business balance sheet and profit/loss statement.
5. Year-ending balance sheets and profit/loss statements for the last three years or, if the business has been in existence less than three years, furnish the financial statements for each year it has been in operation. (Copies of the financial statements submitted with the income tax returns are adequate.)
6. If the business is not in existence but is proposed, furnish a projected balance sheet of the business showing its proposed assets, liabilities, and net worth upon commencement of operations, together with projected annual operating statements for the first three years of operation.
7. Furnish a separate personal balance sheet showing all assets owned and liabilities owed outside of the business.

The above information is what a loan officer will need to properly analyze your loan proposal.

that for securing a regular loan, except that government forms and documentation are also required. Usually some banks in a city will specialize in these loans; these banks are better able to assist the entrepreneur in filing out the appropriate forms correctly and minimize the time involved in the government's processing and approving (or disapproving) the loan.

Both long- and short-term loans can be guaranteed by the SBA. If the collateral is of a lasting nature, such as land and buildings, a maximum loan period of 15 years on existing buildings and 20 years on new construction can be obtained. If the loan is for inventory, machinery, equipment, or working capital, a maximum loan period of 10 years is available, although the usual time is 5 years. Once the application has been correctly filled out with all the required supporting materials, it is generally processed within 15 days if no backlog exists. An SBA Guaranty Loan also has additional reporting requirements beyond those that exist with a conventional commercial bank loan. Since there is typically no difference between the interest rates of a conventional bank loan and an SBA guaranteed loan, the former type is usually better, as it has fewer reporting requirements and allows the entrepreneur to establish a good banking relationship based on the merits of the business. Such a relationship will be valuable as the venture grows and matures.

RESEARCH AND DEVELOPMENT LIMITED PARTNERSHIPS

Research and development limited partnerships are another possible source of funds for entrepreneurs in high-technology areas. Instead of using debt from lenders, equity from owners, or cash from internal operations, this method of financing provides funds from investors looking for tax shelters. A typical R&D partnership arrangement contracts the sponsoring company to develop the technology and the limited partnership to provide the funds. R&D limited partnerships are good alternatives for funding, particularly for small entrepreneurial companies lacking access to capital markets. They are particularly good when the project involves a high degree of risk and significant expense in doing the research and development. In R&D limited partnerships, these risks, as well as the ensuing rewards, are shared.

Major Elements

The three major components of any R&D limited partnership are the contract, the sponsoring company, and the limited partnership. The contract involves an agreement between the sponsoring company and the limited partnership whereby the sponsoring company agrees to use the funds provided to do the proposed research and development that will result in a marketable technology for the partnership. The sponsoring company does not guarantee results but rather performs the work on a best-effort basis, being compensated by the partnership on either a fixed-fee or cost-plus arrangement. The typical contract has several key features. The first is that the liability for any loss incurred is borne by the limited partners. Second, there are some tax advantages to both the limited partnership and the sponsoring company. This tax deduction is based on two tax authorizations: Section 174 of the Internal Revenue Code and the *Snow* v. *Commissioner* case of 1974. Section 174 allows a taxpayer to deduct R&D costs as incurred expenses rather than have these costs capitalized as part of the final cost of the product. This regulation was supported by the U.S. Supreme Court ruling in *Snow* v. *Commissioner,* which said that it was sufficient for the taxpayer to incur the expenses of research and development in connection with a trade or business. Limited partners may deduct their investments in the R&D contract under Section 174 in the year their investments are made. Depending on the tax bracket of the limited partner (the higher the bracket the more significant the effect), this deduction significantly increases the rate of return, thereby increasing the compensation for the high risk involved.

The second component involved in this contract is the limited partnership. Like the stockholders of a corporation, the **limited partners** have limited liability but differ in not being a total taxable entity. Income and loss from the partnership are allocated to each individual's tax return. Consequently, any tax benefits of the losses in the early stages of the R&D limited partnership are passed directly to the limited partners, offsetting other income and reducing the partners' total taxable incomes. When the technology is successfully developed in later years, the partners share in the profits. In some instances, these profits are valued for tax purposes at the lower capital gains rate versus ordinary income.

The final component—the sponsoring company—acts as the **general partner** developing the technology. The sponsoring company usually has the base technology but needs to secure limited partners to further develop and modify it for commercial success. It is this base technology that the company is offering to the partnership in exchange for money. The sponsoring company usually exchanges the right to use the technology in the future for a license fee, or else a cross-licensing agreement is established whereby the partnership allows the company to use the technology for developing other products.

Procedure

A R&D limited partnership generally goes through three stages: the funding stage, the development stage, and the exit stage. In the funding stage, a contract is established between the sponsoring company and the limited partners and money is invested for the proposed research and development effort. All the terms and conditions of ownership, as well as the scope of the research, are carefully documented.

In the development stage, the sponsoring company performs the actual research using the funds from the limited partners. If the technology is then successfully developed, the exit stage commences, in which the sponsoring company and the limited partners commercially reap the benefits of the effort. There are three basic types of arrangements for doing this: equity partnerships, royalty partnerships, and joint ventures.

In the typical equity partnership arrangement, the sponsoring company and the limited partners form a new, jointly owned corporation. Based on the formula established in the original agreement, the limited partners' interest can be transferred to equity in the new corporation on a tax-free basis. An alternative is to incorporate the R&D limited partnership itself and then either merge it into the sponsoring company or continue as a new entity.

An alternative to the equity partnership exit arrangement is a royalty partnership. In this situation, a royalty based on the sale of the products developed from the technology is paid by the sponsoring company to the R&D limited partnership. The royalty rates typically range from 6 to 10 percent of gross sales and often decrease at certain established sales levels. Frequently, an upper limit or cap is placed on the cumulative royalties paid.

A final exit arrangement is through a joint venture. Here the sponsoring company and the partners form a joint venture to manufacture and market the products developed from the technology. Usually the agreement allows the company to buy out the partnership interest in the joint venture at a certain time or volume of sales and profit.

Benefits and Costs

In any financing arrangement, the entrepreneur must carefully assess the appropriateness of establishing an R&D limited partnership in terms of the benefits and costs involved. Among the several benefits is that an R&D limited partnership provides the needed funds with a minimum amount of equity dilution while reducing the risks involved. In addition, an increase in business and flexible financial planning occurs. Finally, the sponsoring company's financial statements are strengthened through the attraction of outside capital.

There are some costs to be considered in any financial arrangement. First, there are the time and money involved. An R&D limited partnership frequently takes a minimum of six months to establish (if at all) and $50,000 in professional fees. These can increase to a year and $400,000 in costs for a major effort. And, of course, most R&D limited partnerships offered are unsuccessful. Second, the restrictions placed on the technology can be substantial. To give up the technology developed as a by-product of the primary effort may be too high a price. Third, the exit from the partnership may be too complex and difficult and involve too much fiduciary responsibility. Finally, typically an R&D limited partnership is more expensive to establish than are conventional financing arrangements. All these costs and benefits must be carefully evaluated in light of other financial alternatives available.

Examples

In spite of the many costs involved, there are numerous examples of successful R&D limited partnerships. Syntex Corporation raised $23.5 million in an R&D limited partnership to develop five medical diagnostic products. Genetech was so successful in developing human growth hormone and gamma Interferon products from its first $55 million R&D limited partnership that it raised $32 million through a second one six months later to develop a tissue-type plasminogen activator. Trilogy Limited raised $55 million to develop a high-performance computer. And the list goes on. Indeed, R&D limited partnerships offer a financial alternative to fund the development of a venture's technology.

GOVERNMENT GRANTS

Sometimes the entrepreneur can obtain federal grant money to develop and launch the innovative idea. A program of particular interest designed for the small business is the **Small Business Innovation Research (SBIR)** grant program, created in 1982 as a part of the Small Business Innovation Development Act. The act also requires that all federal agencies with R&D budgets in excess of $100 million award a portion of their R&D funds to small businesses through the SBIR grants program. This act not only provides an opportunity for small businesses to obtain R&D money but provides a uniform method by which each participating agency solicits, evaluates, and selects the research proposals for funding. In the first year of the SBIR program, 730 projects were awarded Phase I grants totaling more than $40 million. The amount of money available varies each year but is usually not less than $40 million.

Eleven federal agencies are involved in the program (see Table 9–3). Each agency develops topics and publishes solicitations describing R&D needs it will fund. Small businesses submit proposals directly to each agency using the format required in the specific solicitation; the format is somewhat standardized, regardless of the agency. Each agency, using its established evaluation criteria, evaluates each proposal on a competitive basis and makes awards through a contract, grant, or cooperative agreement.

TABLE 9–3 Federal Agencies Participating in Small Business Innovation Research Program

- Department of Defense (DOD)
- National Aeronautics and Space Administration (NASA)
- Department of Energy (DOE)
- Health and Human Services (HHS)
- National Science Foundation (NSF)
- U.S. Department of Agriculture (USDA)
- Department of Transportation (DOT)
- Nuclear Regulatory Commission (NRC)
- Environmental Protection Agency (EPA)
- Department of Interior (DOI)
- Department of Education (DOED)

TABLE 9–4   Three Phases of Funding in the SBIR Program

Phase I	*Phase II*	*Phase III*
SBIR funds	SBIR funds	Private-sector funds
(Idea stage)	(Product stage)	(Business stage)

The SBIR grant program has three phases (see Table 9–4). Phase I awards are up to $50,000 for six months of feasibility-related experimental or theoretical research. The objective of this research is to determine the technical feasibility of the research effort and assess the quality of the company's performance with a relatively small monetary commitment. Successful projects are then considered for further federal funding support in Phase II.

Phase II is the principal R&D effort for those projects most promising at the end of Phase I. Phase II awards are up to $500,000 for 24 months of further research and development. The money is to be used to develop prototype products or services. A small business receiving a Phase II award has demonstrated good research results in Phase I, developed a proposal of sound scientific and technical merit, and obtained a commitment for follow-on private-sector financing in Phase III for commercialization.

Phase III does not involve any direct funding from the SBIR program. Funds from the private sector or regular government procurement contracts are used to commercialize the developed technologies in Phase III.

Procedure

Applying for an SBIR grant is a quite straightforward procedure. The government agencies participating (listed in Table 9–3) publish solicitations describing the areas of research they will fund. Each of these annual solicitations contains documentation on the agency's R&D objectives, proposal format, due dates and deadlines, and selection and evaluation criteria. The second step involves the submission of the proposal by a company or individual. The proposal—25 pages maximum—follows the standard proposal format. Each agency screens the proposals it receives. Those passing the screen are evaluated by knowledgeable scientists or engineers on a technological basis. Finally, awards are granted to those projects that have the best potential for commercialization. Any patent rights, research data, technical data, and software generated in the research are owned by the company or individual.

The SBIR grant program is one viable alternative for obtaining funds for a technically based entrepreneurial company that is independently owned and operated and employs 500 or fewer individuals. Not only can the company have any organization structure (corporation, partnership, sole proprietorship), it need not even be formally established before the award is granted.

PRIVATE PLACEMENT

A final source of funds is private investors, who may be family, friends, or wealthy individuals. Individuals who handle their own investments frequently use advisors such as accountants, technical experts, financial planners, or lawyers in their investment decisions.

Type of Investors

An investor usually takes an equity position in the company and can influence the nature and direction of the business to a certain extent. He or she may be involved to some degree in the business. The degree of involvement in the direction or the day-to-day operations of the venture is an important point for the entrepreneur to consider in selecting a particular investor. Some investors want to be actively involved in the business. Others desire at least an advisory role in the direction and operation of the venture and want to share in its profits. Still others are more passive in nature, desiring no active involvement in the venture. Generally this more passive type is primarily interested in recovering his or her investment plus the established rate of return.

Private Offerings

A formalized approach for obtaining funds from private investors is through a private offering. A private offering is different from a public offering or going public (the focus of Chapter 11) in several ways. Public offerings involve a great deal of time and expense, in part to fulfill the numerous regulations and requirements involved. The process of registering the securities with the Securities and Exchange Commission (SEC) is an arduous one requiring a significant number of reporting procedures once the firm has gone public. Since this process was established primarily to protect unsophisticated investors, a private offering is faster and less costly when a limited number of sophisticated investors are involved who have the necessary business acumen and ability to absorb risk. These limited sophisticated investors still need access to material information about the company and its management. What constitutes material information? Who is a sophisticated investor? How many is a limited number? Answers to these questions are provided in Regulation D.

Regulation D

Regulation D contains (1) a number of broad provisions designed to simplify private offerings, (2) general definitions of what constitutes a private offering, and (3) specific operating rules—Rule 504, Rule 505, and Rule 506. Regulation

D requires the issuer of a private offering to file five copies of Form D with the SEC 15 days after the first sale, every 6 months thereafter, and 30 days after the final sale. Also, it provides rules governing the notices of sale and the payment of any commissions involved.

The entrepreneur issuing the private offering carries the burden of proving that the exemptions granted have been met. This involves completing the necessary documentation and research. For example, the degree of sophistication of each potential investor needs to be thoroughly investigated and documented. Each offering memorandum presented to an investor needs to be numbered and must contain instructions that the document should not be reproduced or disclosed to any other individual. The date that the investor (or the designated representative) reviews the company's information—its books and records—and the date(s) of any discussion between the company and the investor should also be recorded. At the close of the offering, it should be noted that no persons other than those recorded were contacted regarding the securities. The book documenting all these events should be placed in the company's permanent file. These general procedures of Regulation D are further broadened by the three rules—504, 505, and 506.

Rule 504 provides the first exemption to a company seeking to raise a small amount of capital from numerous investors. Under Rule 504, a company can sell up to $500,000 of securities to any number of investors, regardless of their sophistication, in any 12-month period. While there is no specific form of disclosure required, the issuing company cannot engage in any general solicitation or advertising. Some states do not allow investors to resell their shares unless the security is registered.

Rule 505 changes both the investors and the dollar amount of the offering. This rule permits the sale of $5 million of unregistered securities in the private offering in any 12-month period. These securities can be sold to any 35 investors and an unlimited number of accredited investors. This eliminates the need for the sophistication test and disclosure requirements called for by Rule 504.

Accredited investors include (1) institutional investors (banks, insurance companies, investment companies, employee benefit plans containing over $5 million in assets, tax-exempt organizations with endowment funds of over $25 million, and private business development companies), (2) investors who purchase over $150,000 of the issuer's securities, (3) investors whose net worth is $1 million or more at the time of sale, (4) investors with incomes in excess of $200,000 in each of the last two years, and (5) directors, executive officers, and general partners of the issuing company.

Companies eligible to issue under Rule 505 have been expanded to include oil and gas companies, partnerships, and non-North American companies. Like Rule 504, 505 permits no general advertising or solicitation through public media. When only accredited investors are involved, no disclosure is required under Rule 505 (similar to the issuance under Rule 504). However, if the issuance involves any unaccredited investors, additional information must be disclosed. Regardless of the amount of the offering, two-year financial statements for the two most recent years must be available unless such a disclosure requires "undue effort and expense." When this occurs for any issuing company other than a limited partnership, a balance sheet as of 120 days prior to the offering can be used instead. All companies selling private-placement securities to both accredited and unaccredited investors must furnish appropriate company information to both and allow any questions to be asked prior to the sale.

Rule 506 goes one step further than Rule 505 by allowing an issuing company to sell an unlimited amount of securities to 35 investors and an unlimited number of accredited investors and relatives of issuers. As is the case with each of the other rules, no general advertising or solicitation through public media can be involved.

In securing any outside funding, the entrepreneur must take great care to disclose all information as accurately as possible. Investors generally have no problem with the company as long as its operations continue successfully and the success is reflected in the valuation. But if the business turns sour, often both investors and regulators scrutinize the company's disclosures in minute detail to determine if any technical or securities law violations occurred. When any violation of security law is discovered, management and sometimes the company's principal equity holders can be held liable as a corporation and as individuals. When this occurs, the individual is no longer shielded by the corporation and is open to significant liability and potential law suits. Suits under securities law by damaged investors have almost no statute of limitations as the time does not begin until the person harmed discovers or should reasonably be expected to discover the improper disclosure. The suit may be brought in federal court in any jurisdiction in which the defendant is found or lives or transacts business. An individual can file suit as a single plaintiff or as a class action on behalf of all persons similarly affected. Courts have awarded large attorney's fees as well as settlements when security law violation occurs. Given the number of law suits and the litigious nature of U.S. society, the entrepreneur should be extremely careful to make sure that any and all disclosures are accurate. If this is not enough of an incentive, it should be kept in mind that the SEC can take administrative, civil, or criminal action as well, without any individual law suit involved. This action can result in fine, imprisonment, or the restoration of the monies involved.

SUMMARY

All business ventures require capital. While capital is needed throughout the life of a business, the new entrepreneur faces significant difficulties in acquiring it for start-up.

Generally, an entrepreneur should explore all methods of internal financing first. These methods include using profits, selling unused assets, reducing working capital, obtaining credit from suppliers, and collecting accounts receivable promptly. However, the entrepreneur may find it necessary to seek additional funds through external financing. External financing can be in the form of debt or equity. When considering external financing, the entrepreneur should examine the length of time, the cost, and the amount of control in each alternative financial arrangement.

Commercial bank loans are the most frequently used source of short-term external debt financing. This source of funding requires collateral that may be asset-based or may take the form of cash flow financing. In either case, banks tend to be cautious about lending, particularly if they have had a recent history of bad loan decisions. They carefully weigh the five Cs of lending: Character, Capacity, Capital, Collateral, and Condition. Not every entrepreneur will qualify under the bank's careful scrutiny. When this occurs, an alternative for an entrepreneur is the SBA Guaranty Loan. The SBA guarantees 80 percent of the loan to the bank, allowing banks to lend money to businesses that might otherwise be refused.

A special method of raising capital for high-technology firms is a research and development (R&D) limited partnership. A contract is formed between a sponsoring company and a limited partnership. The partnership bears the risk of the research, receiving some tax advantages and sharing in future profits, including a fee to use the research in developing any future products. The entrepreneur has the advantage of acquiring needed funds for a minimum amount of equity dilution while reducing his own risk in the venture. However, setting up an R&D limited partnership is expensive and the time factor (at least six months) may be too great for some ventures. Restrictions placed on the technology as well as the complexities of exiting the partnership need careful evaluation.

Government grants are another alternative available to small businesses through the SBIR program. Businesses can apply for grants from 11 agencies. Phase I awards carry a stipend of up to $50,000 for six months of initial research. The most promising Phase I projects may qualify for Phase II support of up to $500,000 for 24 months of research.

Finally, the entrepreneur can seek private funding. Individual investors frequently require an equity position in the company and some degree of control. A less expensive and less complicated alternative to a public offering of stock is found in a private offering. By following the procedures of Regulation D and three specific rules—504, 505, and 506—an entrepreneur can sell private securities. When making a private offering, the entrepreneur must exercise care in accurately disclosing information and adhering precisely to the requirements of the SEC. Securities violations can lead to law suits against individuals as well as the corporation.

The entrepreneur should consider all possible sources of capital and select the one that will provide the needed funds with the minimal cost and loss of control. Usually, different sources of funds are used at various stages in the growth and development of the venture, as occurred in the case of Walt Disney, a successful entrepreneur indeed.

Venture Capital

CHAPTER OBJECTIVES

1. To explain the three basic stages of venture funding.

2. To discuss the three risk-capital markets.

3. To discuss the informal risk-capital market.

4. To discuss the nature of the venture-capital industry and the venture-capital decision process.

5. To explain all aspects of valuing your company.

6. To identify several valuation approaches.

7. To explain how to structure a deal.

FREDERICK W. SMITH

Who would think that an entrepreneur with a $10 million inheritance would need more capital to get his company off the ground? The business world is filled with stories of companies, large and small, that started in a garage with an initial investment of a few hundred dollars. But none of those companies needed a nationwide distribution system in place, complete with a fleet of airplanes and trucks, before accepting its first order. And, none of those garage start-ups grew up to be Federal Express, either.

Frederick W. Smith, a Memphis native whose father made his fortune after founding a bus company, first conceived the idea for his air cargo company while he was an economics student at Yale in the 60s. A certain professor was a staunch supporter of the current system of air freight handling, whereby the cargo packages literally hitched rides in any unused space on a passenger flight. Fred Smith saw things differently and, in a paper, described the concept of a freight-only airline, which would fly all packages to one central point, where they would be distributed and flown out again to their destinations. This operation could take place at night, when the airports were less crowded, and with proper logistical control, the packages could be delivered the next day. Whether it was the novelty of the idea, the fact that it went against the professor's theories, or the fact that it was written in one night and was turned in late, the first public display of Smith's grand idea earned him a C.

It was more than just a novel idea for a term paper, though. Smith had seen how the technological base of the country was changing. More companies were becoming involved in the production and use of small, expensive items such as computers, and Smith was convinced they could use his air cargo idea as a way to control their inventory costs. Overnight delivery from a single distribution center to anywhere in the country could satisfy a customer's needs without a duplicate investment in inventory stored in regional warehouses. Smith even thought of the Federal Reserve bank as a potential customer, with vast quantities of checks that had to be delivered to all parts of the country every day. But the Vietnam War and a family history of patriotic service intervened. Smith joined the Marine Corps and was sent to Vietnam, first as a platoon leader and then as a pilot.

After nearly four years of service and 200 ground support missions as a pilot, he left Vietnam, ready to start building something. He went to work with his stepfather, managing a struggling aircraft modification and overhaul shop. Difficulty in getting parts to the shop in Little Rock, Arkansas, revived his interest in the air cargo concept. He commissioned two feasibility studies, both of which returned favorable results based on a high initial investment. The key to this company would be the ability to serve a large segment of the business community from the very beginning, and the key to the required level of service was cash. Full of optimism, Smith went to Chicago and New York, confident that he would be returning with basketloads of investment checks. The progress turned out to be slower than anticipated. Through his boundless energy, belief in his idea, and technical knowledge of the air freight field, he was finally able to get enthusiastic backing (and $5 million in capital) from New Court Securities, a Manhattan-based, Rothschild-backed venture-capital investment bank. This helped the rest of the financing fall into place. Five other institutions, including General Dynamics and Citicorp Venture Capital, Ltd., got involved, and Smith went back to Memphis with $72 million. This was the largest venture-capital start-up deal in the history of American business.

Federal Express first took to the skies in April of 1973, carrying 18 packages the first night. Volume picked up rapidly and service was expanded—it looked as though Federal Express was a true overnight success. Smith's understanding of a market need had been accurate, but he had not counted on OPEC causing a massive inflation of fuel costs just as his company was getting started. By mid-1974, the company was losing more than $1 million a month. His investors were not willing to keep the company going, and his relatives were suing him for mismanaging the family fortune (nearly $10 million of Smith money was invested). Smith never lost faith in his idea, and finally won enough converts in the investment community to keep the doors open long enough to straighten out the pricing problems caused by OPEC. After losing $27 million in the first two years, Federal Express turned a profit of $3.6 million in 1976.

The development and growth of Federal Express was tightly regulated. Due to old laws designed to protect the early pioneers of the passenger airline industry, Smith was required to obtain approval for operating any aircraft with a payload in excess of 7,500 pounds. Since the major airlines—the giants of industry—were not ready to share the cargo market, he was not able to obtain this needed approval and had to operate a fleet of small Falcon jets instead. While this worked well at start-up, by 1977 his operation had reached the capacity of these smaller planes. Since they were already flying several planes on the most active routes, it did not make sense to buy more Falcons. Smith took his salesmanship to Washington and, with the help of a grass-roots Federal Express employee effort, was able to obtain legislation creating a new class of all-cargo carriers. This gave Smith the operating latitude he needed.

Although Smith had the approval to operate large jets, he needed to find a way to purchase them. The corporate balance sheet of the company was still in a mess from early losses, and there was a need to reward the long-suffering early investors. Smith took his company public on April 12, 1978, raising enough money to purchase used Boeing 727s from ailing passenger airlines. The investors were indeed richly rewarded, with General Dynamics watching their $5 million grow to more than $40 million by the time Federal Express was first traded on the New York Stock Exchange in December 1978.

As was the case with Fred Smith, many entrepreneurs often use venture capital as the source of outside funds and yet do not understand the venture-capital process and particularly how to evaluate a proposed deal. This chapter addresses these concerns by looking at overall business development, financing, the informal risk-capital market, the venture-capital industry, and valuing a company in structuring the final deal.

FINANCING THE BUSINESS

In evaluating the appropriateness of venture-capital financing, an entrepreneur must determine the amount and the timing of the funds required, as well as the projected company sales and growth rates. Conventional small businesses and privately held middle-market companies tend to have a more difficult time obtaining external equity capital, especially from the venture-capital industry. Venture-capital firms like to invest in high-potential ventures like Fred Smith's Federal Express. The three basic stages of funding as the business develops are indicated in Table 10–1. The funding problems, as well as the costs of the funds, differ in each stage. **Early-stage financing** is usually the most difficult and costly to obtain. Two types of financing occur during this stage—seed capital and start-up. Seed capital, the most difficult financing to obtain through outside funds, is usually a relatively small amount of funds needed to prove concepts and finance feasibility studies. Since venture capitalists usually have a minimum funding level of $400,000 and higher, they are rarely involved in this type of funding except in the case of a high-technology venture proposed by an entrepreneur with a successful track record needing a significant amount of capital. The second type of funding in this early-stage category is start-up financing. As the name implies, start-up financing is involved in developing and testing some initial products to determine if commercial sales are feasible. These funds are also difficult to obtain.

Expansion or **development financing** (the second basic financing type) is easier to obtain than early-stage financing. Venture capitalists play an active role in providing funds here. As the firm develops in each stage, the funds for expansion are less costly. Generally, funds in the second stage are used as working capital to support initial growth. In the third stage, the company is at break-even or a positive profit level and uses the funds for major sales expansion. Funds in the fourth stage are usually used as bridge financing in the interim period as the company prepares to go public.

TABLE 10–1   Stages of Business Development Funding

Early-Stage Financing

• Seed capital	Relatively small amounts to prove concepts and finance feasibility studies
• Start-up	Product development and initial marketing, but with no commercial sales yet; funding to actually get company operations started

Expansion or Development Financing

• Second stage	Working capital for initial growth phase, but no clear profitability or cash flow yet
• Third stage	Major expansion for company with rapid sales growth, at break-even or positive profit levels but still private company
• Fourth stage	Bridge financing to prepare company for public offering

Acquisitions and Leveraged Buyout Financing

• Traditional acquisitions	Assuming ownership and control of another company
• Leveraged buyouts (LBOs)	Management of a company acquiring company control by buying out the present owners
• Going private	Some of the owners/managers of a company buying all the outstanding stock, making the company privately held again

---

The final type—**acquisition** or **leveraged buyout financing**—is more specific in nature. It is used for such activities as traditional acquisitions, leveraged buyouts (management buying out the present owners), and going private (a publicly held firm buying out existing stockholders, thereby becoming a private company).

An overview of the three **risk-capital markets** and their involvement in financing stages of a firm's growth is indicated in Figure 10–1. The three types of risk-capital markets are the **informal risk-capital market, venture-capital market,** and the **public-equity market**. Each can play a role in the financing needed for a firm to grow. While all three risk-capital markets can be a source of funds for stage-one financing, the public-equity market is available only for high-potential ventures, particularly when high technology is involved. Recently, some biotechnology companies raised their first-stage financing through the public-equity market as investors were excited about the potential prospects and returns in this high-interest area. Similar funding occurred in the areas of oceanography and fuel alternatives when they were "hot areas." Venture-capital firms also provide some first-stage funding. However, the venture must require a minimum level of capital set by the firm—$400,000 on up. As discussed later in this chapter, a venture-capital company establishes this minimum level of

FIGURE 10–1   Risk-Capital Markets and Financing for the Venture

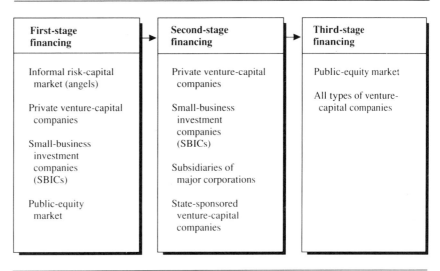

First-stage financing	Second-stage financing	Third-stage financing
Informal risk-capital market (angels)	Private venture-capital companies	Public-equity market
Private venture-capital companies	Small-business investment companies (SBICs)	All types of venture-capital companies
Small-business investment companies (SBICs)	Subsidiaries of major corporations	
Public-equity market	State-sponsored venture-capital companies	

investment since the due diligence in evaluating a deal and the effort in monitoring one once the funds are committed is about the same for a $100,000 as for a $1 million investment. By far the best source of funds for first-stage financing is the informal risk-capital market—the third type of risk-capital market.

INFORMAL RISK-CAPITAL MARKET

The informal risk-capital market is by far the most misunderstood and inefficient type of risk capital since it is composed of a virtually invisible group of wealthy investors—often called "**business angels**"—who are looking for equity-type investment opportunities in a wide variety of entrepreneurial ventures. Typically investing anywhere from $10,000 to $500,000, these angels provide the funds needed in all stages of financing, but particularly start-up (first-stage) financing. Firms funded from the informal risk-capital market frequently raise second- and third-round financing from professional venture-capital firms or the public-equity market.

Despite being misunderstood by and virtually inaccessible to many entrepreneurs, the informal investment market contains the largest pool of risk capital in the United States, about $50 billion compared to the professional venture-capital market with a pool of about $25 billion. Although there is no verification on the size of this pool of money or on the total amount of financing provided by these business angels, some related statistics provide indications. A 1980 survey of a sample of issuers of private placements by corporations, reported to the Securities and Exchange Commission under Rule 146, found that 87 percent of those buying these issues were individual investors or personal trusts, with $74,000 as the average amount invested.[1] Private placements filed under Rule 146 average over $1 billion per year. Another indication is found on examination of the filings under Regulation D—the regulation exempting certain private and limited offerings from the registration requirements of the Securities Act of 1933 discussed in Chapter 11. In its first year, over 7,200 filings, worth $15.5 billion, were made under Regulation D. Corporations accounted for 43 percent of the value ($6.7 billion), or 32 percent of the total number of offerings (2,304). Corporations filing limited offerings (under $500,000) raised $220 million, an average of $200,000 per firm. The typical corporate issuers tended to be small, with fewer than 10 stockholders, revenues and assets less than $500,000, stockholders' equity of $50,000 or less, and five or fewer employees.[2]

Similar results were found in an examination of the funds raised by small technology-based firms prior to making initial public offerings. The study revealed that unaffiliated individuals (the informal investment market) accounted for 15 percent of these funds while venture capitalists accounted for only 12 percent. During the start-up year, unaffiliated individuals provided 17 percent of the external capital.[3]

Similar results were found in a study of angels in New England. The 133 individual investors studied reported risk-capital investments totaling over $16 million in 320 ventures between 1976 and 1980. These investors averaged one deal every two years, with an average size of $50,000. Although 36 percent of these investments averaged less than $10,000, 24 percent averaged over $50,000. While 40 percent of these investments were start-ups, 80 percent involved ventures less than five years old.[4]

The size and number of these investors has increased dramatically, due in part to the rapid accumulation of wealth in various sectors of the economy. In 1986, *U.S. News and World Report* stated that there were over 833,000 millionaires in

[1]*Report of the Use of the Rule 146 Exemption in Capital Formation*. Directorate of Economic Policy Analysis, Securities and Exchange Commission, Washington, DC, 1983.

[2]*An Analysis of Regulation D*. Report by the Directorate of Economic and Policy Analysis, Securities and Exchange Commission, Washington, DC, 1984.

[3]Charles River Associates, Inc. *An Analysis of Capital Market Imperfections*. National Bureau of Standards, Washington, DC, February 1976.

[4]W. E. Wetzel, Jr., "Entrepreneurs, Angels, and Economic Renaissance," in R. D. Hisrich, ed., *Entrepreneurship, Intrapreneurship, and Venture Capital*, 119–40. (Lexington, MA: Lexington Books, 1986), pp. 119–40. Other information on angels and their investments can be found in W. E. Wetzel, Jr., "Angels and Informal Risk Capital," *Sloan Management Review* 24 (Summer 1983), 23–24, and W. E. Wetzel, Jr., "The Informal Venture Capital Market: Aspects of Scale and Market Efficiency," *Journal of Business Venturing* (Fall 1987), 299–314.

the United States at the end of 1985. This number increased to over 1 million in 1989. The millionaires ranged in net worth up to $4.5 billion. The Forbes 400 richest people in America represented a combined net worth of about $150 billion. These individuals are just a few of the numerous individuals and families with substantial means. One study of consumer finances found that the net worth of 1.3 million U.S. families was over $1 million.[5] These families, representing about 2 percent of the population, accumulated most of their wealth from earnings, not inheritance. These research findings indicate that about 311,000 families have invested over $151 billion in nonpublic businesses in which they have no management interest. Each year, over 100,000 individual investors finance between 30,000 and 50,000 firms with a total dollar investment of between $7 billion and $10 billion. What are the characteristics of these angels and why do they invest this amount of money?

The characteristics of these informal investors, or angels, are indicated in Table 10–2. They tend to be well educated, with many having graduate degrees. While they will finance firms anywhere in the United States (and a few in other parts of the world), most of the firms receiving investment are within one day's travel. The majority of the angels expect to play an active role in the affairs of the business. They will make one to two deals each year, with individual firm investments ranging from $10,000 to $500,000, the average being $175,000. If the opportunity is right, angels might well invest from $500,000 to $1 million. In some cases, angels will join with other angels, usually from a common circle of friends, to finance larger deals.

Is there a preference in the type of ventures in which they invest? While angels invest in every type of investment opportunity, from a small retail store to a large oil exploration operation, generally they prefer manufacturing, of both industrial and consumer products; energy; service; and retail/wholesale trade. The returns expected decrease as the number of years the firm has been in business increases, from a median five-year capital gain of 10 times for start-ups to 3 times for established firms over five years old. These investing angels are more patient in their investment horizons, having no problem with a 7-to-10-year time period before cashing out, in contrast to the more predominant 5-year time horizon in the formal venture-capital industry. Investment opportunities are rejected when there is an inadequate risk/return ratio, an inadequate management team, a lack of interest in the business area, or the principals are not sufficiently committed to the venture.

Where do these angel investors generally find their deals? Deals are found through referrals by business associates, friends, active personal research, investment bankers, and business brokers (see Table 10–3). However, even though

---

[5]R. B. Avery & G. E. Elliehausen, "Financial Characteristics of High Income Families," *Federal Reserve Bulletin*, Washington, DC, March 1986.

TABLE 10–2   Characteristics of Informal Investors

Demographic Patterns and Relationships
- Well educated with many having graduate degrees
- Will finance firms anywhere in United States
- Most firms financed within one-day's travel
- Majority expect to play an active role in ventures financed
- Have clusters of 9–12 other investors

Investment Record
- Range of investment: $10,000–$500,000
- Average investment: $175,000
- One to two deals each year

Venture Preference
- Most financings in start-ups or ventures less than five years old
- Most interest in financing:
  - Manufacturing—industrial/commercial products
  - Manufacturing—consumer products
  - Energy/natural resources
  - Services
  - Retail/wholesale trade

Risk/Reward Expectations
- Median 5-year capital gains of 10 times for start-ups
- Median 5-year capital gains of 6 times for firms under 1 year old
- Median 5-year capital gains of 5 times for firms 1–5 years old
- Median 5-year capital gains of 3 times for established firms over 5 years old

Reasons for Rejecting Proposals
- Risk/return ratio not adequate
- Inadequate management team
- Not interested in proposed business area
- Unable to agree on price
- Principals not sufficiently committed
- Unfamiliar with area of business

---

these **referrals sources** provide some deals, most angel investors are not satisfied with the number and type of investment referrals. As indicated in Figure 10–2, 51 percent of the investors surveyed were either partially or totally dissatisfied with their referral systems and indicated that at least moderate improvement is needed.

One method for improving this referral process has been successful at the University of New Hampshire and the University of Tulsa. Each of these universities has a sort of a computer dating service for money—a computerized system that matches entrepreneurs with investing angels on a confidential basis. The two institutions also make this resource available to affiliated universities. Entrepreneurs enter the system—the Venture Capital Network (VCN) at the University of New Hampshire and the Venture Capital Exchange (VCE) at the University of Tulsa—by filling out questionnaires on their business and funding needs.

TABLE 10–3 Referral Sources for Deals of Angels

	Frequency of Classification		
	Frequent Source	*Occasional Source*	*Not a Source*
Business associates	62	37	18
Friends	59	44	15
Active personal search	46	29	36
Investment bankers	17	28	66
Business brokers	12	36	62
Commercial bankers	9	30	68
Other	7	5	46
Attorneys	3	50	55
Accountants	2	41	66

Source: W. E. Wetzel, Jr., Venture Capital Network, Inc: An Experiment in Capital Formation. *Proceedings*, 1984 Conference on Entrepreneurship, April 1984, p. 114.

FIGURE 10–2 Angels' Satisfaction with Referral Sources

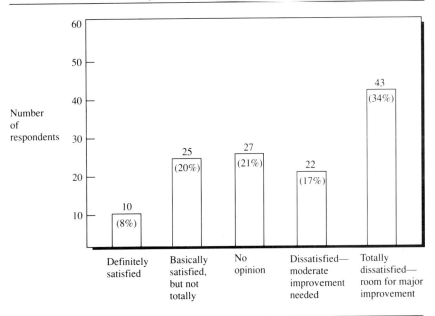

Source: W. E. Wetzel, Jr., Venture Capital Network, Inc: An Experiment in Capital Formation. *Proceedings*, 1984 Conference on Entrepreneurship, April 1984, p. 115.

These requests are matched with the investors on each system who have indicated an interest in the entrepreneur's area of business. After reviewing the information provided by the entrepreneur (the answers to the questions and supporting material), the investor decides whether to be identified to him or her so that more in-depth discussion between the two parties can take place. The Securities and Exchange Commission's rules and regulations prohibit the systems from advising either the investor or entrepreneur or having any involvement in the final negotiations between the two parties. Both the VCE and VCN have linked entrepreneurs to their investment capital in a wide variety of companies.[6]

VENTURE CAPITAL

The important and little-understood area of venture capital will be discussed in terms of its nature, the venture-capital industry in the United States, and the venture-capital process.

Nature of Venture Capital

Venture capital is one of the least-understood areas in the entrepreneurship. Some think that venture capitalists do the early-stage financing of relatively small, rapidly growing technology companies. While true, this is a narrow definition; it is better to view venture capital more broadly as a professionally managed pool of equity capital. Frequently, the **equity pool** is formed from the resources of wealthy limited partners. Other principal investors in venture-capital limited partnerships are pension funds, endowment funds, and other institutions, including foreign investors. The pool is managed by a general partner—the venture-capital firm—in exchange for a percentage of the gain realized on the investment and a fee. The investments are in early-stage deals as well as second- and third-stage deals and leveraged buyouts. In fact, venture capital can best be characterized as a long-term investment discipline, usually over a five-year period, in the creation of early-stage companies, the expansion and revitalization of existing businesses, and the financing of leveraged buyouts of existing divisions of major corporations or privately owned businesses. In each investment, the venture capitalist takes an **equity participation** through stock, warrants, and/or convertible securities and has an active involvement in the monitoring of each portfolio company bringing investment, financing planning, and business skills to the firm.[7]

---

[6]D. C. Foss, "Venture Capital Network: The First Six Months of the Experiment," *Proceedings*, Babson Entrepreneurial Research Conference, Philadelphia, April 1985, 314–24.

[7]Aspects of venture capital are discussed in J. Timmons & W. D. Bygrave, "Venture Capital's Role in Financing Innovation for Economic Growth," *Journal of Business Venturing* 1 (Spring 1986), 161–76; R. B. Robinson, Jr., "Emerging Strategies in the Venture Capital Industry," *Journal of Business Venturing* 2 (Winter 1987), 53–78; and H. H. Stevenson; D. F. Muzyka; & J. A. Timmons, "Venture Capital in Transition: A Monte Carlo Simulation of Changes in Investment Patterns," *Journal of Business Venturing* 2 (Winter 1987), 103–22.

Overview of the Venture-Capital Industry

While the role of venture capital was instrumental throughout the industrialization of the United States, it did not become institutionalized until after World War II. Before World War II, venture investment activity was a monopoly of wealthy individuals, investment banking syndicates, and a few family organizations with a professional manager. The first step toward institutionalizing the venture-capital industry began in 1946 with the formation of the American Research and Development Corporation (ARD) in Boston. The ARD was a small pool of capital from individuals and institutions put together by General Georges Doriot to make active investments in selected emerging businesses. One of its best investments was in Digital Equipment Corporation.

The next major development in institutionalizing the venture-capital industry was the Small Business Investment Company Act of 1958. This act married private capital with government funds to be used by professionally managed small business investment companies (**SBICs**) to infuse capital into start-up and growing small businesses. With the tax advantages, government funds for leverage, and a private capital company, SBICs were the start of the now formal venture-capital industry. The 1960s saw a significant expansion of SBICs with approximately 585 SBIC licenses approved, involving more than $205 million in private capital. Many of these early SBICs failed due to inexperienced portfolio managers, unreasonable expectations, focus on short-term profitability, and an excess of government regulations. These early failures caused the SBIC program to be restructured, eliminating some of the unnecessary government regulations and increasing the amount of capitalization needed. There are approximately 527 SBICs operating today, of which 144 are minority small business investment companies (MESBICs) funding minority enterprises (see Table 10–4).

During the late 1960s, small **private venture-capital firms** emerged.[8] The private venture-capital companies were usually formed as limited partnerships, with the venture-capital company acting as the general partner, receiving a management fee and a percentage of the profits earned on any single deal. The limited partners supplied the funding. The limited partners were frequently institutional investors such as insurance companies, endowment funds, bank trust departments, pension funds, and wealthy individuals and families. There are about 200 private venture-capital firms today.

The third type of venture-capital firm also developed during this time—the venture-capital division of major corporations. These firms, of which there are approximately 100, are usually associated with banks and insurance companies, although companies such as 3M, Monsanto, and Xerox are also involved. Corporate venture-capital firms are more prone to invest in windows on technology or new market acquisition than private venture-capital firms or SBICs. Some of

---

[8]For the role of SBICs, see Farrell K. Slower, "Growth Looms for SBICs," *Venture* (October 1985), 46–47, and M. H. Fleischer, "The SBIC 100—More Deals for the Bucks," *Venture* (October 1985), 50–54.

TABLE 10–4 Overview of Venture-Capital Market

	Private Venture-Capital Firms	*Small Business Investment Companies (SBICs)*	*Corporate/Industrial Venture Capitalists*
Estimated number	200	527 (383 SBICs) (144 MESBICs)	100 in business with 20–30 active (Exxon, G.E., Monsanto, 3M, Allstate Insurance, Xerox, Citicorp, First Chicago Corporation)
Principal objectives and motives	Capital gains 25%–40% compounded after tax per year; 5–10 times original investment in 5–10 years	Capital gains same range as private	Capital gains same range as SBICs: Invest in cutting-edge technology and new market acquisition
Typical size	$300,000 to $4 million Average: $813,000		$10–$15 million average
Stage of ventures sought	Usually second and third stage financing; 25%–35% in start-ups		Emphasize third stage more
Outside approval	Only needed in about 10% of firms		Usually needed at least in 75% of decisions; review by boards and directors

these corporate venture-capital firms have had very disappointing results, causing some corporations to invest in independent, professionally managed venture-capital funds instead of managing their own fund.

In response to the need for economic development, a fourth type of venture-capital firm has emerged—the **state-sponsored venture-capital fund**. These state-sponsored funds have a variety of formats. While the size and investment thrust vary from state to state, from $2.2 million in Colorado to $42 million in Michigan, each fund typically is required to invest a certain percentage of capital in companies in the particular state. Generally, the funds professionally managed by the private sector, outside the states' bureaucracy and political processes, have performed better.

There has been significant growth in the venture-capital industry in both size and number of firms. The number of venture-capital firms increased from 225 in 1979 to 674 in 1989 and the average capital under management during this same period increased from $18 million to $49.5 million (see Figure 10–3). The total pool of venture capital during this period therefore grew from $2.9 billion to $33.4 billion. This growth in fund size is reflected in the increase in annual commitment of funds to the venture-capital industry and the annual disbursements to portfolio companies. The commitment of funds peaked at $4.2 billion in 1987, decreasing to $2.4 billion in 1989. These funds came mostly from institutional investors, led by pension funds which contributed 36 percent of the

FIGURE 10–3 Number and Size of Venture-Capital Firms

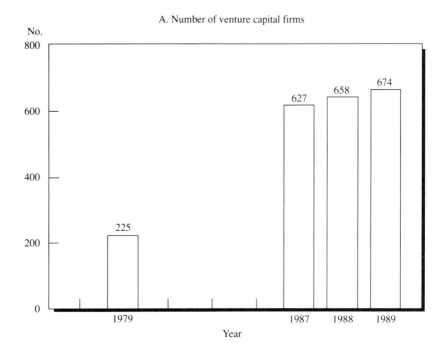

A. Number of venture capital firms

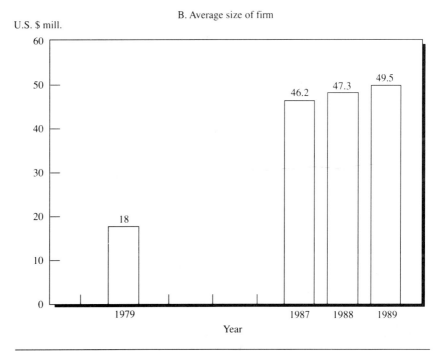

B. Average size of firm

Source: Venture Capital Journal.

new funds in 1989. As is indicated in Figure 10–4, this was a significant change in new funds from previous years. In 1978, 32 percent of the new funds in the venture-capital industry were supplied by individuals and families. In spite of the change in the capital gains tax in 1986, which supposedly was to stimulate this sector, individuals and families only contributed 6 percent of the new funds in 1989. Pension funds, insurance companies, and endowments significantly increased in 1989 from 1978, contributing 30, 13, and 12 percent of the $2.4 billion new funds available (see Figure 10–4).[9]

This growth in funds and the change in their sources has affected the structure of the venture-capital industry. Venture-capital firms can be classified into groups of small, medium, large, and super (extra-large) funds. Each fund, regardless of its size, tends to specialize in its portfolio companies by investment stage, degree of technology, type of product, and geographic region. In 1978, the $2.9 billion in venture capital was managed primarily by private venture firms (45%), followed by corporate venture-capital firms (34%) and others, including SBICs (21%). By 1989 this shifted radically, with 81 percent of the $33.4 billion in venture-capital funds managed by private venture-capital firms. Corporate venture-capital firms managed only 19 percent of this money and others, including SBICs, only 1 percent. During this period, changes also occurred in the size and product preference area of venture-capital firms. In 1989, the largest 95 venture-capital firms controlled 59 percent of the total pool of funds under management, while the smallest 205 firms controlled only 2.4 percent of these funds.

The industry-investment preferences by venture-capital firms also changed during this period. While the consumer and medical/health segments accounted for only 14 percent of the investment dollars in 1978–80, their total increased to 25 percent in 1987–89 (see Figure 10–5). The significant investment in energy and natural resources (9%) in 1978–80, declined to 1 percent in 1987–89. Although the biotechnology segment was being heralded as receiving so much venture-capital attention, the amount invested in it was moderate, increasing from 6 to 8 percent during this time. It appears that the venture-capital industry is shifting toward lower-technology investments across a wide variety of industries.

As would be expected, there is a significant difference in the size of the various venture-capital firms. About 400 of the 600 venture-capital firms of all four types use from 70 to 80 percent of the capital. The size of venture-capital firms varies significantly, with some funds in the $200 to $300 million range. For example, Citicorp has $39.8 million invested, First Chicago Venture $36.7 million, TA Associates $35 million, and First SBIC of California $7.5 million.

---

[9]For a discussion of this change in investors and the impact of the 1986 change in capital gains tax on the venture capital industry see W. D. Bygrave, and J. M. Shulman, "Capital Gains Tax: Bane or Boon for Venture Capital?" *Proceedings*, Babson Research Conference, April 1988, pp. 324–38; and T. Soja and J. E. Reyes. *Investment Benchmarks: Venture Capital* (Needham, MA: Venture Economics, 1990).

FIGURE 10–4 Distribution Source of New Funds for the
Venture-Capital Industry (1978 and 1989)

**A. Source - distribution
of new funds, 1978 —
$ 216 million**

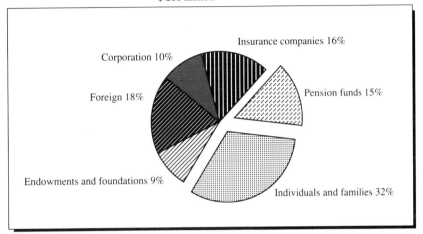

**B. Source - distribution
of new funds, 1989 —
$ 2.40 billion**

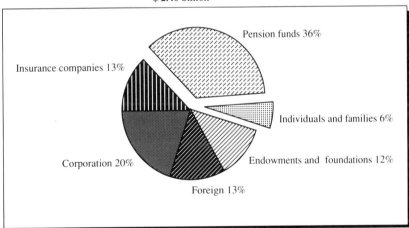

Source: Venture Capital Journal.

FIGURE 10–5   U.S. Venture-Capital Investment by Industry
Sector (1978–1980 and 1987–1989)

A. 1978-1980 $ 1.354 invested

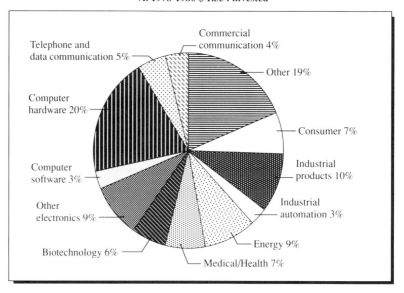

B. 1987-1989 $10.855 billion invested

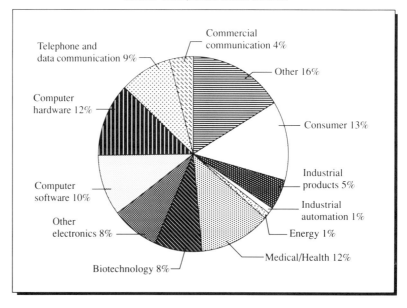

Source: Venture Economics, Inc.

Venture-Capital Process

To be in a position to secure the needed funds, the entrepreneur needs to understand the philosophy and objectives of a venture-capital firm, as well as the venture-capital process. An overview of venture capitalists in terms of the evaluation criteria and process, portfolio, and deal pricing is given in Table 10–5. The objective of a venture-capital firm is to generate long-term capital appreciation through debt and equity investments, typically in young, high-growth ventures. To achieve this objective, the venture capitalist is willing to make any changes or modifications necessary in the business investment. Since the objective of the entrepreneur is the survival of the business, the objectives of the two are frequently at odds, particularly when problems are encountered.

The portfolio objective in terms of return criteria and risk involved of a typical venture-capital firm is shown in Figure 10–6. Since there is more risk involved in financing a business earlier in its development, more return is expected from early-stage financing (50% ROI) than from acquisitions or leveraged buyouts (30% ROI), the late stage in development. The significant risk involved and the pressure venture-capital firms feel from their investors (limited partners) to make safer investments with higher rates of return have caused these firms to

---

TABLE 10–5   Venture Capitalists

Evaluation Criteria
- Strong management team
- Unique opportunity
- Appropriate return in terms of capital appreciation

Evaluation Process
- Initial screening
- Initial agreement of terms
- Due diligence (industry, market, players)
- Go or no-go decision
- Document deal and close
- Monitor deal

Venture Portfolio Goal
- 20% early stage—50–60% ROI
- 40% development financing—40% ROI
- 40% acquisitions and leverage buyouts—30% ROI

Typical Venture Portfolio of 10 Deals
- 4 belly-up
- 3 walking wounded (or living dead)
- 2 hits
- 1 home run

Factors in Pricing a Deal
- Return
- Amount of money needed now and later
- Quality of deal
- Quality of team
- Amount entrepreneur is investing
- Prospects of company in future
- Upside potential
- Downside potential
- Liquidity
- Exit avenues

Guiding "Rules" of Venture Capitalists
- It costs more than you think
- It takes longer than you have planned
- Anything you think won't happen, will

FIGURE 10–6   Venture-Capital Financing—Risk and Return Criteria

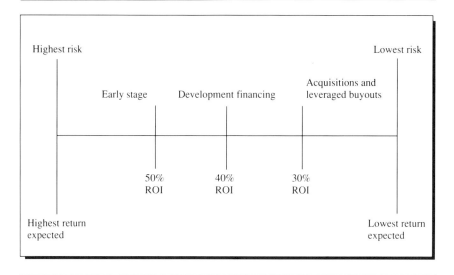

invest even greater amounts of their funds in later stages of financing. In these late-stage investments, there are lower risks, faster returns, less managerial assistance needed, and fewer deals to be evaluated. As is indicated in Figure 10–7, 44 percent of venture-capital investments in 1980 were in seed, start-up, or other early-stage ventures. By 1989, the percentage amount decreased to 28 percent. Even with this decrease, the absolute amount increased from $12 million in 1980 to $144 million in 1989.

Another change has occurred in the amount invested in present portfolio companies versus new ones. The 59 percent invested in new companies in 1979 decreased to 22 percent in 1989. Again, the investment strategy can reduce the risks and increase the return for the venture capitalists.

In most cases, the venture capitalist does not seek control of a company and would rather have the firm at more risk than him- or herself. Once the decision to invest is made, the venture capitalist will do anything necessary to support the management team so that the business and the investment prosper. While venture capitalists expect a seat on the board of directors, the management team is expected to direct and run the daily operations of the company. A venture capitalist will support the management team with investment dollars, financial skills, planning, and expertise in any specific area needed.

Since the venture-capital investment in the company is for a long time (typically five years or more), it is important that there is mutual trust and understanding between the entrepreneur and the venture capitalist. There should be no surprises in the firm's performance. Both good and bad news should be shared, with the objective of taking the necessary action to allow the company

FIGURE 10–7   U.S. Venture-Capital Investment by Stage

A. Portion invested by stage, 1980—$608 million

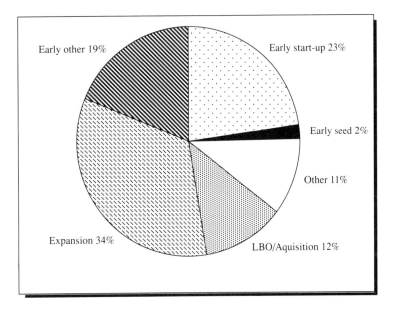

B. Portion invested by stage, 1989—$3.26 billion

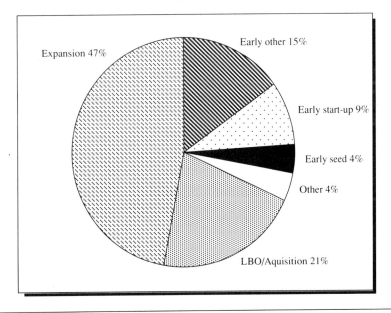

Source: Venture Economics, Inc

to grow and develop in the long run. The venture capitalist should be available to the entrepreneur to discuss problems and develop strategic plans.

In making an investment, the venture capitalist uses three general criteria. First, the company must have a **strong management team**, with the individuals having solid experience and background, commitment to the company, capabilities in their specific areas of expertise, the ability to meet challenges, and the flexibility to scramble whenever necessary. A venture capitalist would rather invest in a first-rate management team and a second-rate product than the reverse. The management team's commitment should be reflected in dollars invested in the company. While the amount is somewhat important, more important is the size of this investment relative to their ability to invest. The commitment of the management team should be backed by the support of the family, particularly the spouse, of each key team player. A positive family environment and spousal support allow team members to spend the 60 to 70 hours per week necessary to ramp up the company. One successful venture capitalist makes it a point to have dinner with the entrepreneur and spouse and even visit the entrepreneur's home before making an investment decision. As this individual said, "I find it difficult to believe an entrepreneur can successfully run and manage a business and put in the necessary time when the home environment is running amok."

The second criterion is that the **product/market opportunity** must be unique, having a differential advantage in a growing market. Having a unique market niche is absolutely essential since the product or service must be able to compete and grow over the five-year investment period. This uniqueness needs to be carefully spelled out in the marketing portion of the business plan and is even more favorably viewed when it can be protected by a patent or a trade secret.

The final criterion for investment is that the business opportunity must have significant capital appreciation. The exact amount of capital appreciation varies, depending on such factors as the size of the deal, the stage of development of the company, the upside potential, the downside risks, and the available exits. The venture capitalist typically expects a 40 to 60 percent return on investment in most situations.

The venture-capital process implementing these criteria is both an art and a science.[10] The art part consists of the venture capitalist's intuition and gut feeling and the creative thinking involved in the process. The science part is the systematic approach and data gathering involved in the assessment; this requires both analysis and discipline.

[10]For a thorough discussion of the venture-capital process, see A. D. Silver, "The Venture Capital Process," *Venture*, December 1983, pp. 86–9; B. Davis, "Role of Venture Capital in the Economic Renaissance of an Area," in R. D. Hisrich, (ed.) *Entrepreneurship, Intrapreneurship, and Venture Capital* (Lexington, MA: Lexington Books, 1986) pp. 107–18; M. Gorman & W. Sahlman, "What Do Venture Capitalists Do?" *Proceedings*, Babson Research Conference, April 1986, pp. 414–36; and Robert D. Hisrich & A. D. Jankowicz, "Intuition in Venture Capital Decisions: An Exploratory Study Using a New Technique," *Journal of Business Venturing* 5, (January 1990), pp. 49–63.

The process starts with the investment objectives and philosophy of the venture-capital firm. The firm must decide on the composition of its portfolio mix, including the number of start-ups, expansion companies, and management buyouts; the types of industries; the geographic region for investment; and any product or industry specializations.

The venture-capital process can be broken down into four primary stages: preliminary screening, agreement on principal terms, due diligence, and final approval. The **preliminary screening** begins with the receipt of the business plan. A good business plan is absolutely essential in the venture-capital process. Most venture capitalists will not even talk to an entrepreneur who doesn't have one. As the starting point, the business plan must have a clear-cut mission and clearly stated objectives, which are supported by an in-depth industry and market analysis and pro forma income statements. The executive summary is the most important part of this business plan as it is used for initial screening in this preliminary evaluation. Many business plans are never evaluated beyond the executive summary. When evaluating the business plan, the venture capitalist first determines if he or she has seen the deal or similar deals before. The investor then determines if the proposal fits his or her long-term policy and short-term cash needs in order to develop an appropriate portfolio balance. In this preliminary screening, the venture capitalist investigates the economy of the industry and evaluates whether he or she has the appropriate knowledge and ability to invest in that industry. The investor reviews the numbers presented to determine if the business can reasonably deliver the ROI required. In addition, the credentials and capability of the management team are evaluated to determine if they can carry out the plan presented.

The second stage is the agreement on principal terms between the entrepreneur and the venture capitalist. The venture capitalist wants a basic understanding of the principal terms of the deal at this stage of the process before making the major commitment of time and effort involved in the due diligence process.

The third stage—detailed review and **due diligence**—is by far the longest, involving anywhere from one to three months. There is a detailed review of the company's history, the business plan, the résumés of the individuals, their financial history, and target market customers. The upside potential and downside risk are assessed. There is a thorough evaluation of the markets, industry, financial analysis, customers, and management.

In the last stage—final approval—a comprehensive, internal investment memorandum is prepared. This document reviews the venture capitalist's findings and details the investment terms and conditions of the investment transaction. This information is used to prepare the formal legal documents that both the entrepreneur and venture capitalist will sign to conclude the transaction.[11]

---

[11]A discussion of some of the important sectors in this decision process can be found in I. MacMillan, L. Zemann, and Sabba Navasimaha, "Criteria Distinguishing Successful from Unsuccessful Ventures in the Venture Screening Process," *Journal of Business Venturing* 2, Spring 1987, pp. 123–38; J. B. Roure and M. A. Meidique, "Linking Prefunding Factors and High-Technology Venture Success," *Journal of Business Venturing* 1 (3), Fall 1986, pp. 295–306; and E. H. Buttner and B. Rosen, "Funding New Business Ventures: Are Decision Makers against Women Entrepreneurs?" *Journal of Business Venturing* 4, Winter 1987, pp. 249–62.

Locating Venture Capitalists

One of the most critical decisions for the entrepreneur is selecting which venture-capital firm to approach. Since venture capitalists tend to specialize either geographically by industry (manufacturing industrial products or consumer products, high-technology, or service) or by size and type of investment, the entrepreneur should approach only those who may have an interest in the investment opportunity. Where do you find this venture capitalist?

While venture capitalists are located throughout the United Sates, there are several traditional centers of concentration: Boston, Chicago, New York, and San Francisco. More recently, several new centers have emerged: Atlanta, Dallas, Los Angeles, and Washington, D.C.[12] An entrepreneur should carefully research the names and addresses of prospective venture-capital firms that might have an interest in the particular investment opportunity. Accountants and lawyers are good sources for introductions to prospective venture capitalists. There are also venture-capital associations in various regions of the country, as well as national associations. These associations will frequently send the entrepreneur a directory listing their members, the types of businesses their members invest in, and any investment restrictions for a nominal fee or none at all.

Approaching a Venture Capitalist

The entrepreneur should approach a venture capitalist in a professional business manner. Since venture capitalists receive hundreds of inquiries and are frequently out of the office working with portfolio companies or investigating potential investment opportunities, it is important to begin the relationship positively. The entrepreneur should call any potential venture capitalist to ensure that the business is in an area of the individual's investment interest. Then the business plan should be sent along with a short professional letter.

Since venture capitalists receive many more plans than they are capable of funding, they screen out as many plans as possible. They tend to focus and put more time and effort on those plans that were referred. In fact, one venture-capital group said that 80 percent of their investments over the last five years were in referred companies. It is well worth the entrepreneur's time to seek out an introduction to the venture capitalist. Typically this can be obtained from an executive of a portfolio company, an accountant, lawyer, banker, or business school professor.

There are some basic rules of thumb that the entrepreneur should be aware of before implementing the actual approach. (Some more detailed guidelines are presented in Table 10–6.) First, take great care in selecting the right venture

---

[12]A complete listing of venture capital firms in the United States and throughout the world can be found in *Venture's Guide to International Venture Capital* (New York: Simon and Schuster, 1985); and E. S. Pratt, *Guide to Venture Capital Sources* (Wellesley, MA: Capital Publishing Corporation, 1988).

TABLE 10–6 Guidelines for Dealing with Venture Capitalists

- Carefully determine the venture capitalist to approach for funding the particular type of deal. Screen and target the approach. Venture capitalists do not like deals that have been excessively "shopped."
- Once a discussion is started with a venture capitalist, do not discuss the deal with other venture capitalists. Working several deals in parallel can create problems unless the venture capitalists are working together. Time and resource limitations may require a cautious simultaneous approach to several funding sources.
- It is better to approach a venture capitalist through an intermediary who is respected and has a preexisting relationship with the venture capitalist. Limit and carefully define the role and compensation of the intermediary.
- The entrepreneur or manager should lead the discussions with the venture capitalist, not an intermediary. Do not bring a lawyer, accountant, or other advisors to the first meeting. Since there are no negotiations during this first meeting, it is a chance for the venture capitalist to get to know the entrepreneur without interference from others.
- Be very careful in what is projected or promised. The entrepreneur will probably be held accountable for these projections in the pricing, deal structure, or compensation.
- Disclose any significant problems or negative situations in this initial meeting. Trust is a fundamental part of the long-term relationship with the venture capitalist; subsequent discovery by the venture capitalist of an undisclosed problem will cause a loss of confidence and probably prevent a deal.
- Reach a flexible, reasonable understanding with the venture capitalist regarding the timing of a response to the proposal and the accomplishment of the various steps in the financing transaction. Patience is needed as the process is complex and time-consuming. Too much pressure for a rapid decision can cause problems with the venture capitalist.
- Do not sell the project on the basis that other venture capitalists have committed themselves. Most venture capitalists are independent and take pride in their own decision making.
- Be careful about glib statements such as "There is no competition for this product," or "There is nothing like this technology available today." These statements can indicate a lack of homework, or that a perfect product has been designed for a nonexistent market.
- Do not indicate an inordinate concern for salary, benefits, or other forms of current compensation. Dollars are precious in a new venture. The venture capitalist wants the entrepreneur committed to an equity appreciation similar to that of the venture capitalist.
- Eliminate to the extent possible any use of new dollars to take care of past problems such as payment of past debts or deferred salaries of management. New dollars of the venture capitalist are for growth, to move the business forward.

---

capitalist to approach. Venture capitalists tend to specialize in certain industries and will rarely invest in a business outside these areas, regardless of the merits of the business proposal and plan. Second, venture capitalists tend to know each other, particularly in a specific region of the country. When a large amount of money is involved, they will invest in the deal together, with one venture-capital firm taking the lead. Since this degree of familiarity is present, a venture-capital firm will probably find out if others have seen your business plan. Therefore it is not advised to shop around among venture capitalists as even a good business plan can quickly become "shop worn." Third, when meeting the venture capitalist, particularly the first time, bring only one or two key members of the management team. A venture capitalist is betting on your management team and its track record, not on outside experts. Any experts can be called in as needed.

Finally, be sure to develop a brief, well-thought-out, oral presentation. This should cover the company's business, the uniqueness of the product or service, the prospects for growth, the major factors behind achieving the sales and profit objectives, the backgrounds and track records of the key managers, the amount of financing required, and the returns anticipated. The first presentation is very critical. As one venture capitalist stated, "I need to sense a competency, a capability, a chemistry within the first half hour of our initial meeting. The entrepreneur needs to look me in the eye and present his story clearly and logically. If a chemistry does not start to develop, I start looking for reasons not to do the deal."

Following a favorable initial meeting, the venture capitalist will do some preliminary investigation of the plan. If favorable, another meeting between the management team and venture capitalist will be scheduled. This meeting is also critical, as both parties will ask questions in order to assess the other and to determine if a good working relationship can be established and if a feeling of trust and confidence is evolving. During this mutual evaluation, the entrepreneur should be careful not to be too inflexible about the amount of company equity he or she is willing to share. If the entrepreneur is too inflexible, the venture capitalist might end negotiations. The next step in the venture-capital process is establishing an initial agreement of terms. If turned down by one venture capitalist, do not become discouraged. Select the next most probable candidate and repeat the procedure. One study found that a significant number of companies denied funding by one venture capitalist were able to obtain funds from other outside sources, including other venture capitalists.[13]

VALUING YOUR COMPANY

A problem confronting the entrepreneur when obtaining outside equity funds, whether from the informal investor market (the angels) or the formal venture-capital industry, is determining a value for the company. This valuation is at the core of the entrepreneur's major concern and anxiety—how much ownership is an investor entitled to for funding the venture? The amount of ownership should be determined by first considering the factors in valuation.

---

[13]A. V. Brune & T. T. Tyebjee, "The One That Got Away: A Study of Ventures Rejected by Venture Capitalists," *Proceedings,* 1983 Babson Research Conference, Wellesley, MA, 1983, pp. 289–306.

Factors in Valuation

Although they may vary depending on the situation, there are eight factors the entrepreneur should consider when valuing the venture. The first factor, and the starting point in any valuation, is the nature and history of the business. The characteristics of the specific venture and the industry in which it operates are fundamental in every evaluation process. The history of the company from its inception provides information on the strength and diversity of the company's operations, the risks involved, and the company's ability to withstand any adverse conditions.

Valuation must also consider the outlook of the economy in general as well as that of the particular industry. This, the second factor, involves an examination of the financial data of the venture compared to that of other companies in the industry. Management's capability now and in the future, as well as the future market for the company's products, is assessed. Will these markets grow, decline, or stabilize, and in what economic conditions?

The third factor is the book value (net value) of the stock and the overall financial condition of the business. The book value (often called owner's equity) is the acquisition cost (less accumulated depreciation) minus liabilities. Frequently the book value is not a good indication of fair market value, as balance sheet items are almost always carried at cost, not market value. The value of plant and equipment, for example, carried on the books at cost less depreciation may be low due to the use of an accelerated depreciation method or other market factors, making the assets more valuable than indicated in the book value figures. Land, particularly, is usually reflected lower than fair market value. For valuation, the balance sheet must be adjusted to reflect the higher values of the assets, particularly land, so that a more realistic company worth is determined. A good valuation should also value operating and nonoperating assets separately and then combine the two into the total fair market value. A thorough valuation includes comparative annual balance sheets and profit and loss statements for the past three years when available.

Even though book value develops the benchmark, future earning capacity of the company, the fourth factor, is the most important factor in valuation. Previous years' earnings are generally not simply averaged but weighted, with the most recent earnings receiving the highest weighting, reflecting their importance. Income by product line should be analyzed to judge future profitability and value. Special attention should be paid to depreciation, nonrecurring expenses, officers' salaries, rental expense, and historical trends.

A fifth valuation factor is the dividend-paying capacity of the venture. Since the entrepreneur in a new venture typically pays little if any dividends, it is the future capacity to pay dividends rather than actual dividend payments made that is important. The dividend-paying capacity should be capitalized.

An assessment of goodwill and other intangibles of the venture is the sixth valuation factor. Frequently, these intangible assets cannot be valued without reference to the tangible assets of the venture.

The seventh factor in valuation involves assessing the previous sale of stock. Previous stock sales better represent future sales if the sales are recent. Motives regarding the new sale (if other than arriving at a fair price) and any change in economic or financial conditions during the intermittent period should be considered.

The final valuation factor is the market price of stocks of companies engaged in the same or similar lines of business. This factor is used in the specific valuation method discussed later in this section. The critical issue is the degree of similarity between the publicly traded company and the one being valued.

General Valuation Approaches

There are several valuation approaches that can be used in valuing the venture. One of the most widely used approaches is assessing comparable publicly held companies and the prices of these companies' securities. This search for a similar going concern is both an art and a science. First, the company must be classified in an industry since companies in the same industry share similar markets, problems, economies, and potential for sales and earnings. The review of all publicly traded companies in this industry classification should evaluate size, amount of diversity, dividends, leverage, and growth potential until the most similar company is identified. This method is often inaccurate as it is very difficult to find a truly comparable company. When a large privately held company is involved, better results are usually obtained, as the relative sales price of this company is generally related to the stock price of a publicly held company in the same industry in the given time period.

A second widely used valuation approach is the **present value of future cash flow**. This method adjusts the value of the cash flow of the business for the time value of money and the business and economic risks. Since only cash (or cash equivalents) can be used in reinvestment, this valuation approach generally gives more accurate results than profits. In using this method, the sales and earnings are projected back to the time of the valuation decision when shares of the company are offered for sale. The period between the valuation and sale dates is determined. The potential dividend payout and the expected price-earning ratio or liquidation value at the end of the period must be calculated. Finally, a rate of return needed by investors must be established, less a discount rate for failure to meet these expectations.

Another valuation method, used only for insurance purposes or in very unique circumstances, is **replacement value**. This method is used, for example, when there is a unique asset involved that the buyer really wants. The valuation of the venture is based on the amount of money it would take to replace (or reproduce) that asset or another important asset or system of the venture.

The **book value** approach uses the adjusted book value or net tangible asset value to determine the firm's worth. Adjusted book value is obtained by making the necessary adjustments to the stated book value by taking into account any depreciation (or appreciation) of plant and equipment and real estate, as well as needed adjustments to inventory resulting from the accounting methods employed. The following basic procedure can be used:

Book value	$_____
Add (or subtract) any adjustments such as appreciation or depreciation to arrive at figure on next line—the fair market value	_____
Fair market value (the sale value of the company's assets)	_____
Subtract all intangibles that cannot be sold, such as goodwill	_____
Adjusted book value	$_____

Being simple to calculate, the book valuation approach is particularly good in a relatively new business, in businesses where the sole owner has died or is disabled, and in businesses with speculative or highly unstable earnings.

The **earnings approach** is the most widely used method of valuing a company as it provides the potential investor with the best estimate of the probable return on investment. The potential earnings are calculated by weighting the most recent operating year's earnings after they have been adjusted for any extraordinary expenses that would not have normally occurred in the operations of a publicly traded company. Then an appropriate price-earnings multiple is selected based on norms of the industry and the investment risk. A higher multiple will be used for a high-risk business and a lower multiple for a low-risk business. For example, a low-risk business in an industry with a seven times earnings multiple would be valued at $4.2 million if the weighted average earnings over the past three years was $0.6 million (7 times $0.6 million).

An extension of this approach is the **factor approach** where three major factors are used to determine value: earnings, dividend-paying capacity, and book value. Appropriate weights for the particular company being valued are developed and multiplied by the capitalized value, resulting in an overall weighted valuation. An example is indicated below:

Approach (in 000s)	Capitalized Value	Weight	Weighted Value
Earnings: $40 × 10	$400	0.4	$160
Dividends: $15 × 20	300	0.4	120
Book value: $600 × 0.4	240	0.2	48
Average			328
10% discount			33
Per share value			$295

A final valuation approach that gives the lowest value of the business is **liquidation value**. Liquidation value is often difficult to obtain, particularly when cost and losses must be estimated for selling the inventory, terminating employees, collecting accounts receivable, selling assets, and other closing-down activities. Nevertheless, it is also good for an investor to obtain a downside risk value in appraising a company.

General Valuation Method

One approach an entrepreneur can use to determine how much of his company a venture capitalist will want for a given amount of his investment can be calculated using the formula below:

$$\text{Venture capitalist ownership (\%)} = \frac{\text{VC \$ investment} \times \begin{array}{c} \text{VC investment} \\ \text{multiple desired} \end{array}}{\begin{array}{c} \text{Company's projected} \\ \text{profits in year 5} \end{array} \times \begin{array}{c} \text{Price earnings multiple} \\ \text{of comparable company} \end{array}}$$

For example, a company needing $500,000 of venture-capital money, anticipating profits of $650,000, where the venture capitalist wants an investment multiple of 5 times and the price earnings multiple of a similar company is 12, would have to give up 32 percent of the company to obtain the needed funds as calculated below:

$$\frac{\$500,000 \times 5}{\$650,000 \times 12} = 32\%$$

A more accurate method for determining this percentage is given in Table 10–7. The step-by-step approach takes into account the time value of money in determining the appropriate investor's share. The following hypothetical ex-

---

TABLE 10–7   Steps in Valuing Your Business and Determining Investors' Share

---

1. Estimate the earnings after taxes based on sales in the fifth year.
2. Determine an appropriate earnings multiple based on what similar companies are selling for in terms of their current earnings.
3. Determine the required rate of return.
4. Determine the funding needed.
5. Calculate using the following formulas:

$$\text{Present value} = \frac{\text{Future valuation}}{(1 + i)^n}$$

where:

future valuation = total estimated value of company in 5 years
i = required rate of return
n = number of years

$$\text{Investors' share} = \frac{\text{Initial funding}}{\text{Present value}}$$

---

ample uses this step-by-step procedure in determining the investor's share. H&B Associates, a start-up manufacturing company, estimates it will earn $1 million after taxes on sales of $10 million. The company needs $800,000 now to reach that goal in five years. A similar company in the same industry is selling at 15 times earnings. A venture-capital firm, Davis Venture Partners, is interested in investing in the deal and requires a 50 percent compound rate of return on investment. What percentage of the company will have to be given up to obtain the needed capital?

$$\text{Present value} = \frac{\$1,000,000 \times 15 \text{ times earning multiple}}{(1 + 0.50)^5}$$

$$= \$1,975,000$$

$$\frac{\$800,000}{\$1,975,000} = 41\% \text{ will have to be given up}$$

DEAL STRUCTURE

In addition to valuating the company and determining the percent of the company that may have to be given up to obtain the needed funding, a critical concern for the entrepreneur is the nature of the deal—the terms of the transaction between the entrepreneur and the funding source.[14] In order to make the venture look as attractive as possible to potential sources of funds, the entrepreneur must understand the needs of the investors as well as his or her own needs. The needs of the funding sources include: the rate of return required, the acceptable level of risk, the timing and form of return, the amount of control desired, and the perception of the risks involved in the particular funding opportunity. While certain investors are willing to bear a significant amount of risk to obtain a significant rate of return, others want less risk and are willing to settle for less return. Still other investors are more concerned about the amount of influence and control they will be able to exert once the investment has been made.

The entrepreneur's needs revolve around similar concerns, such as degree and mechanisms of control, amount of financing needed, and the goals for the particular firm. Before negotiating the terms and structure of the deal with the venture capitalist, the entrepreneur should assess the relative importance of these concerns in order to make appropriate trade offers if needed. Since the final deal structure reflects the circumstances involved as well as what is in vogue at the time, both the venture capitalist and entrepreneur should feel comfortable with it. A good working relationship needs to be established to ease any differences that might arise later. This open, honest relationship will be needed to deal with problems that will occur with the growth of the company.

---

[14]For a discussion of some problems with venture capital deals, see "Why Smart Companies Are Saying No to Venture Capitalists," *Inc.*, August 1984, pp. 65–75.

SUMMARY

In financing a business, the entrepreneur determines the amount and timing of needed funds. In the first stage, seed or start-up capital is the most difficult to obtain, with the most likely source being the informal risk-capital market (angels). These investors are wealthy individuals who average one to two deals per year, ranging from $10,000 to $500,000. Generally, they find their deals through referrals.

Although venture capital may be used in the first stage, it is primarily used in the second or third stage to provide working capital for growth or expansion. Venture capital is broadly defined as a professionally managed pool of equity capital. Since 1958, small business investment companies (SBICs) have combined private capital and government funds to finance the growth and start-up of small businesses. Private venture-capital firms have developed since the 1960s, with limited partners supplying the funding. At the same time, venture-capital divisions operating within major corporations began appearing. More recently, some states have begun to sponsor venture-capital funds to foster economic development.

To achieve the venture capitalist's primary goal of generating long-term capital appreciation through investments in business, three criteria must be met. First, the company must have strong management. Second, the product/marketing opportunity must be unique. Third, the capital appreciation must be significant, offering a 40 to 60 percent return on investment.

The process of obtaining venture capital includes preliminary screening, agreement on principal terms, due diligence, and final approval. Through a referral, entrepreneurs need to approach a potential venture capitalist with a professional business plan and a good oral presentation. After a successful initial presentation, the entrepreneur and investor agree on principal terms before the due diligence process is begun. This stage involves a detailed analysis of the markets, industry, and finances and can take one to three months. The final stage requires a comprehensive documentation of the details of the transaction.

The problem of placing value on the company is of concern to the entrepreneur. The determination of how much ownership the investor is entitled to for funding the venture can be made through the valuation process. Eight factors can be used as a basis for valuation: the nature and history of the business, the economic outlook, book value, future earnings, dividend-paying capacity, intangible assets, sales of stock, and market price of stocks of similar companies. Numerous valuation approaches can also be used. These include assessment of comparable publicly held companies, present value of future cash flow, replacement value, book value, earnings approach, factor approach, and liquidation value. A formula to determine the percentage of ownership a venture capitalist will want is the venture capitalist's investment times the multiple desired divided by the company's projected profits in year five times the price earnings multiple of a comparable company.

In the end the entrepreneur and investor must agree on the terms of the transaction, known as the deal. In negotiation, the entrepreneur should assess his or her own priorities in order to prioritize offers if needed. If care is taken in structuring the deal, both the entrepreneur and investor will maintain a satisfactory relationship while achieving their goals through the business' growth and development.

Going Public

CHAPTER OBJECTIVES

1. To identify the advantages and disadvantages of going public.

2. To identify some alternatives to going public.

3. To discuss the timing of going public and underwriter selection.

4. To explain the registration statement and timetable for going public.

5. To discuss the legal issues of going public and blue sky qualifications.

6. To discuss some important issues for a venture after going public.

SAM WALTON

Sam Walton, the Wal-Mart magnate, has been frequently identified as the richest man in America. He is well known for his marketing strategy of introducing discount stores to the smaller cities and towns ignored by the other chains, but that is not the only foundation for his success. In large part, the growth of his company and the concurrent growth of his personal wealth can be directly attributed to his judicious use of the equity markets.

Walton got his start in retailing in 1940 as a salesman and management trainee at J. C. Penney's. He was one of the best shirt salesmen in the organization, but he knew that it was just a training ground for his real calling as a store owner. In 1945, along with his brother Bud, he began operating a Ben Franklin five-and-dime store in Newport, Arkansas. After five successful years, they moved to a store in Bentonville, Arkansas, where he still lives. The Walton brothers began expanding, buying other variety stores in the area. Utilizing all of his knowledge about sales, Sam set up his own buying office and applied advertising and other marketing principles to his group of stores that others thought were applicable only to bigger ventures. Moving into the 1960s, the Waltons owned enough stores to be the most successful Ben Franklin franchisees in the country.

A new concept was developing in the retail business in the early 60s—discounting. When Gibson's, a Texas-based discounter, opened a store in Fayetteville, where the Waltons had a variety store, Sam decided to try an experiment. Starting with a single department, his discounting attempt soon grew into a complete store. Despite Walton's success with this experiment, and the growing threat of discounting to the local variety stores, the Ben Franklin executives were not receptive to changing the positioning of their chain. Sam decided to strike out on his own. After a brief tour around the country in search of new ideas, he developed a plan to begin operating his own discount stores in towns with a population of less than 25,000. The first Wal-Mart was opened in Rogers, Arkansas, in 1962.

Sam's profits dictated the growth rate of his business. This make-do-with-what-you-have philosophy carried over to the new Wal-Mart stores. To open the first store, Sam and Bud pooled all their available resources and planned the size and location of the store based on that amount of capital. There was no room in the tight budget for fancy displays or large offices if they were to offer quality merchandise at competitive prices in small towns. Evidently, the pipe-rack displays and bare floors were only a minor inconvenience to the shoppers, because Wal-Mart was a success from the start.

Early in the development of the Wal-Mart concept, Sam realized the vital role of distribution in determining profitability. He knew he needed the same low-cost, efficient delivery methods used by his larger counterparts. Rather than build warehouses to serve existing outlets, he clustered his expansion outlets around existing distribution points. At this point, Sam considered a public offering of stock. In 1970, after eight years in the discount store business, there were about 30 Wal-Mart Discount City stores. It became apparent to Walton that he needed his own warehouse to be able to buy in the volume necessary to support new openings. Yet, he did not feel the company could afford to incur the heavy debt burden needed. In the midst of a boom in new issues and on the strength of his impressive growth record, Walton sold a small part of his business to the public for $3.3 million. This cash helped pay for a $5 million distribution center, big enough to serve 80 to 100 stores.

With his distribution center in place, Sam was ready to grow. Two years later, with 51 stores and $78 million in sales, Wal-Mart was listed on the New York Stock Exchange. Original investors who paid $16.50 a share now have shares worth over $900. Sam tapped the public equity market several additional times when he needed to expand or upgrade his system, managing to keep his overall capital costs well below those of his competitors by his careful planning and tight budgeting. To this day, the heart of Wal-Mart's success lies in the fact that most stores are less than a six-hour drive away from one of the company's five warehouses, each of which was built before Wal-Mart expanded its territory.

Sam Walton judiciously decided when to use the public equity market for money to finance the expansion of his business—Wal-Mart. The decision to "go public"—a phrase used to describe the transformation of a closely held corporation into one where the general public has proprietary interest—should be carefully thought out. To some entrepreneurs, going public is the ultimate rite, signaling entry into the most exclusive legitimate business community; but before doing so there are several issues the entrepreneur must carefully address, as Sam Walton did. These include assessing the advantages and disadvantages of going public, evaluating the alternatives to going public, determining the timing of doing so, selecting the underwriter, preparing the registration statement and timetable, and understanding the blue sky qualifications and the resulting reporting requirements.

ADVANTAGES AND DISADVANTAGES

Going public occurs when the entrepreneur and other equity owners of the venture offer and sell some part of the company to the public through a registration statement filed with the Securities and Exchange Commission (SEC) pursuant to the Securities Act of 1933. The resulting capital infusion to the company and the large numbers of stockholders and outstanding shares of stock provide the company with financial resources for its business plan and a relatively liquid investment vehicle for the public investors. Consequently, the company will theoretically have greater access to capital markets in the future and a more objective picture of the public's perception of the value of the business. However, given the reporting requirements, the large number of stockholders, and the costs involved, the entrepreneur must carefully evaluate the advantages and disadvantages of going public before initiating the process. A list of the advantages and disadvantages is given in Table 11–1.

Advantages

There are four primary advantages of going public: obtaining new equity capital, obtaining value and transferability of the organization's assets, enhancing ability to obtain future funds, and acquiring prestige. Whether it be first-stage, second-stage, or third-stage financing, a venture is in constant need of capital to finance its start-up and growth. The new capital provides the needed working capital, plant and equipment, or inventories and supplies necessary for the venture's growth and survival. Going public is often the best way to obtain this needed capital on the best possible terms.

Going public also provides a mechanism for valuing the company and allowing this value to be easily transferred among parties. Many family-owned or other privately held companies may need to go public so that the value of the company can be disseminated among the second and third generations. Venture capitalists view going public as the most beneficial way to attain the liquidity necessary to exit a company with the best possible return on their earlier-stage funding. Other investors as well can more easily liquidate their investment since the company's stock takes on value and transferability. Because of

---

TABLE 11–1   Advantages and Disadvantages of Going Public

Advantages
- Obtaining capital with less dilution to founders
- Enhanced ability to borrow
- Enhanced ability to raise equity
- Liquidity and valuation
- Prestige
- Personal wealth

Disadvantages
- Expense
- Disclosure of information
- Pressures to maintain growth pattern
- Loss of control

---

this liquidity, the value of a publicly traded security frequently is higher than shares of one that is not publicly traded. In addition, publicly traded companies often find it easier to acquire other companies by using their securities in the transactions.

The third primary advantage is that publicly traded companies usually find it easier to raise additional capital, particularly debt. Money can be borrowed more easily and on more favorable terms when there is value attached to a company and that value is more easily transferred. Not only debt financing but future equity capital is more easily obtained when a company establishes a track record of increasing stock value.

A final advantage, prestige, occurs because a publicly traded company is more widely known. This prestige can facilitate obtaining good suppliers as well as other support services.

Disadvantages

While the advantages of going public are significant for a new venture, they must be carefully weighed against the numerous disadvantages. There is a tendency today for entrepreneurs to keep their companies private, even in times of a hot stock market.[1] For example, only 17 of 1987's 500 fastest growing companies took advantage of good stock market conditions and went public. Why did so many of these companies avoid the supposed gold rush of an **initial public offering (IPO)**?

One of the major reasons is the public exposure and potential loss of control of a publicly traded company. To stay on the cutting edge of technology, companies frequently need to sacrifice short-term profits for long-term innovation. This can require reinvesting in technology that in itself may not produce any bottom-line results, even in the long run. Making long-term decisions is increasingly difficult in publicly traded companies where sales/profit evaluations indicate the capability of management as reflected in the value of the stock. The evaluation mechanism accompanying publicly traded companies can partially affect decision making; and when enough shares are sold to the public, the company can lose control of decision making. This loss of control can eventually result in the company being acquired by an unfriendly tender offer, as was discussed in Chapter 4.

Some of the most troublesome aspects of being public are the loss of flexibility and increased administrative burdens that result. The company must make decisions in light of the fiduciary duties owed to the public shareholders, and it is obliged to disclose to the public all material information regarding the company, its operations, and its management. One publicly traded company had to retain a more expensive investment banker than would have been required by a

---

[1]Kotkin, J., "What I do in private is my business," *Inc.* (November 1986), pp. 66–81.

privately held company in order to obtain an "appropriate" fairness opinion in a desired merger. The investment banker increased the expenses of the merger by $150,000, in addition to causing a three-month delay in the merger proceedings. Also, the management of a publicly traded company spends a significant amount of additional time addressing queries from shareholders, press, and financial analysts.

If all these disadvantages have not caused the entrepreneur to look for alternative financing rather than an IPO, the expenses involved may. The major expenses of going public include accounting fees, legal fees, underwriter's fees, registration and blue sky filing fees, and printing costs. The accounting fees involved in going public vary greatly, depending in part on the size of the company, the availability of previously audited financial statements, and the complexity of the company's operations.

Generally the costs of going public (undertaking an IPO) are $300,000 to $600,000, although they can be much greater when significant complexities are involved. Additional reporting, accounting, legal, and printing expenses can run anywhere from $50,000 to $250,000 per year, depending on the company's past practices in the areas of accounting and shareholder communications. In addition to the SEC reports that must be filed, a proxy statement and other materials must be submitted to the SEC for review before distribution to the stockholders. These materials contain certain disclosures concerning management, its compensation, and transactions with the company, as well as the items to be voted on at the meeting. Public companies must also submit an annual report to the shareholders containing the audited financial information for the prior fiscal year and a discussion of any business developments. The preparation and distribution of the proxy materials and annual report are some of the more significant items of additional expense incurred by a company after it is public.

Accounting fees for an initial public offering fluctuate widely but are typically $50,000 to $100,000. Fees are at the lower end of this range if the accounting firm has regularly audited the company over the past several years. They are at the higher end of the range if the company has had no prior audits or if it engages a new accounting firm. The accounting fee covers the preparation of financial statements, the response to SEC queries, and the preparation of "cold comfort" letters for the underwriters described later in this chapter.

Legal fees will also vary significantly, typically ranging from $60,000 to $175,000. This fee generally covers preparing corporate documents, preparing and clearing the registration statement, negotiating the final underwriting agreement, and closing the sale of the securities to these underwriters. Frequently, additional legal fees are involved in a company going public. This so-called housekeeping work can be extensive, particularly if a major reorganization is involved. A public company also pays legal fees for the work involved with the National Association of Securities Dealers, Inc. (NASD) and the state blue sky filings. The legal fees for NASD and state blue sky filings range from $8,000 to $30,000, depending on the size of the offering and the number of states in which the securities will be offered.

The underwriters' fees include a cash discount (or commission), which usually ranges from 7 to 10 percent of the public offering price of the new issue. In some IPOs, the underwriters can also require other compensation, such as warrants to purchase stock, reimbursement for some expenses—most typically legal fees—and the right of first refusal on any future offerings. The NASD regulates the maximum amount of the underwriter's compensation and reviews the actual amount for fairness before the offering can take place. Similarly, any underwriter's compensation is also reviewed in blue sky filings.

There are other expenses in the form of SEC, NASD, and state blue sky registration fees. Of these, the SEC registration fee is quite small—one-fiftieth of 1 percent of the maximum aggregate public offering price of the security. For example, the SEC fee would be $4,000 on a $20 million offering. The minimum fee is $100. Regardless of the amount, the SEC fee must be paid by certified or cashier's check. The NASD filing fee is also small in relation to the size of the offering—$100 plus one-hundredth of 1 percent of the maximum public offering price. In the above example of a $20 million offering, this would be $2,100. The maximum NASD fee is $5,100. The amount of the state blue sky fees depends entirely on the number of states in which the offering is registered. If the initial public offering is registered in all states, the total blue sky filing fees can be more than $15,000, depending on the size of the offering.

The final major expense—printing costs—typically ranges from $50,000 to $200,000. The registration statement and prospectus discussed later in this chapter account for the largest portion of these expenses. The exact amount of expenses varies, depending on the length of the prospectus, the use of color or black and white photographs, the number of proofs and corrections, and the number printed. It is important for the company to use a good printer because accuracy and speed are required in the printing of the prospectus and other offering documents.

THE ALTERNATIVES TO GOING PUBLIC

Since most of the alternatives to going public were presented in Chapter 9, only the most widely used ones will be briefly discussed here. The two most commonly used alternatives are private placements and bank loans. A private placement of securities, particularly with institutional investors—insurance companies, investment companies, or pension funds—is one way to obtain the needed funds with minimum effort. These funds are frequently in the form of intermediate or long-term debt, often carrying a floating interest rate, or preferred stock with specific dividend requirements. In addition, most private placement transactions also carry certain **restrictive covenants.** These covenants are not intended to hamper the operations of the venture but to protect the investor and allow the investment to be profitably liquidated at a later date. The **liquidation covenant** usually contains a provision allowing the investor to require registration of a sale or other disposition of its securities at any time. The entrepreneur must evaluate whether this or any of the other covenants impose too many restrictions on the successful operation of the company before selecting private placement as an alternative source of funds.

To qualify for a private placement under the Securities and Exchange Act of 1933, a company must have a limited number of investors, each of whom has enough sophistication in financial and business matters to be capable of evaluating the risks and merits of the investment. This requires that the investors have available all the information that would be included in a registration statement. In addition, the investors have to agree to hold the securities for a specified period following the purchase. As a rule of thumb, equity securities issued in a private placement will be sold at 20 to 30 percent less than the company might receive for the same securities in a public offering.

In addition to private placement, a bank loan is a viable alternative to going public. Bank loans are a common way to raise additional funds. However, this additional capital is in the form of debt, not equity, and therefore often must have some collateral of the company or the guaranty of the entrepreneur behind it. This collateral is typically in the form of contracts, accounts receivable, machinery, inventory, land, or buildings—some tangible asset. Even when some assets are available for collateral, bank loans are typically made on a short-, or at best, medium-term basis. The interest, which is usually at a floating rate, must also be considered when evaluating this alternative source of funds. The repayment schedule and rigidity of this financial alternative may preclude its use.

Other debt financing can be obtained from nonbank lenders such as equipment leasing companies, mortgage bankers, trade suppliers, or inventory and accounts receivable financing companies. This money has either fixed or fluctuating interest rates and established payment periods similar to bank loans. Usually these loans offer the entrepreneur a greater degree of flexibility than bank loans, although not nearly as much as equity capital.

TIMING OF GOING PUBLIC AND UNDERWRITER SELECTION

Probably the two most critical issues in a successful public offering are the timing of the offering and the firms involved—the underwriting team. An entrepreneur should seek advice from several financial advisors as well as other entrepreneurs who are familiar with the process.

Timing

Am I ready to go public? This is the critical question that entrepreneurs must ask themselves before launching this effort. In answering this question, the entrepreneur should evaluate several critical factors.

First, is the company large enough? While it is not possible to establish rigid minimum size standards that must be met before an entrepreneur can go public, large New York investment banking firms prefer at least a 500,000 share offering at a minimum $10 per share. This means that the company would have to have a past offering value of at least $12.5 million in order to support this $5 million offering, given that the company is willing to sell shares representing not more than 40 percent of the total number of shares outstanding after the offering is completed. This company valuation will be obtained only with significant sales and earnings performance or solid prospects for future growth and earnings.

Second, what is the amount of the company's earnings, and its financial performance? Not only is this performance the basis of the company valuation previously discussed, but it also determines both if a company can successfully go public and the type of firm willing to underwrite the offering. While the exact criteria vary from year to year, reflecting the market conditions, generally a company must have at least one year of good earnings and sales before its stock offering will be acceptable to the market. Larger underwriting firms have more stringent criteria, some as high as sales of $15 to $20 million, $1 million or more net income, and a 30 to 50 percent annual growth rate.

Third, are the market conditions favorable for an initial public offering? Underlying the sales and earnings, as well as the size of the offering, is the prevailing general market condition. Market conditions affect both the initial price that the entrepreneur will receive for the stock and the aftermarket—the price performance of the stock after its initial sale. Some market conditions are more favorable for IPOs than others. Unless there is such an urgent need for money that delay is impossible, the entrepreneur should attempt to take his company public in the most favorable market conditions.

Fourth, how urgently is the money needed? As previously indicated, the entrepreneur must carefully appraise both the urgency of the need for new money and the availability of outside capital from other sources. Since the sale of common stock decreases the ownership position of the entrepreneur and other equity owners involved in the start-up, the longer the time before going public, given profits and sales growth, the less percentage of equity the entrepreneur will have to give up per dollar invested.

Finally, what are the needs and desires of the present owners? Sometimes the present owners lack confidence in the future viability and growth prospects of the business or they have a need for liquidity. Going public is frequently the only method for present stockholders to obtain the cash needed. This occurs particularly when venture-capital money is involved. The goal of the typical venture capitalist is to liquidate the investment within 5 to 10 years.

Underwriter Selection

Once the entrepreneur has determined that the timing for going public is favorable, he or she must carefully select a **managing underwriter,** who will take the lead in forming the **underwriting syndicate.** The underwriter is of critical importance in establishing the initial price for the stock of the company, supporting the stock in the aftermarket so that the price stabilizes and, one hopes, rises, and creating a strong following among security analysts.

Although most public offerings are conducted by a syndicate of underwriters, the entrepreneur needs to select only the lead or managing underwriter(s). The managing underwriters will then develop the strongest possible syndicate of underwriters for the initial public offering. An entrepreneur should ideally develop a relationship with several potential managing underwriters (investment bankers) at least one year before going public. Frequently this occurs during the first- or second-round financing, where the advice of an investment banker helps structure the initial financial arrangements to position the company to go public later.

Since selecting the investment banker is a major factor in the success of the public offering, the entrepreneur should approach one through a mutual contact. Commercial banks, attorneys specializing in securities work, major accounting firms, providers of the initial financing, or prominent members of the company's board of directors can usually provide the needed suggestions and introductions. Since the relationship will be ongoing, not ending with the completion of the offering, the entrepreneur should employ several criteria in the selection process. These include reputation, distribution capability, advisory services, experience, and cost.

An initial public offering rarely involves a well-known company; hence, the managing underwriter needs a good reputation to develop a strong syndicate team and provide confidence to both individual and institutional investors. This confidence and respect in financial circles of the managing underwriter helps sell the public offering and supports the stock in the aftermarket.

The success of the offering is also a function of the underwriter's distribution capability. An entrepreneur wants the stock of his company distributed to as wide and varied a base as possible. Since each investment banking firm has a different client base, the entrepreneur should compare client bases of possible managing underwriters. Is the client base strongly institutional, individual investors, or balanced between the two? Is the base more internationally or domestically oriented? Are the investors long-term or speculators? What is the geographic distribution—local, regional, or nationwide? A strong managing underwriter and syndicate with a quality client base will help the stock sell well and perform well in the aftermarket.

Some underwriters are better able than others to provide financial advisory services. While this factor is not as important as the previous two in selecting an underwriter, financial counsel is frequently needed before and after the IPO. An entrepreneur should address such questions as: Can the underwriter provide sound financial advice? Has the underwriter given good financial counsel to previous clients? Can it render assistance in obtaining future public or private financing? The answers to these questions will indicate the degree of ability among various possible managing underwriters.

As reflected in the previous questions, the experience of the investment banking firm is important. The firm chosen should have experience in underwriting issues of companies in the same or at least very similar industries. This experience will give the managing underwriter credibility, the capability to explain the company to the investing public, and the ability to price the IPO accurately.

TABLE 11–2   Costs of Underwriters

The Most Expensive Underwriters
(These underwriters exacted the highest price for taking lower-quality deals public)

Underwriter*	Average Total Expense as Percent of Offering†	Average Gross Spread as Percent of Offering‡	Average Size of Offering	Total Number of Deals
1. Vanderbilt Securities Inc.	29.1%	10.0%	$468,590	7
2. Alpine Securities Corp.	27.2	14.4	260,000	5
3. Western Capital and Securities Inc.	25.4	13.2	481,600	5
4. Patten Securities Corp.	22.7	10.0	1,027,125	9
5. Stuart-James Co.	20.9	10.0	2,201,875	8
6. Rooney, Pace Inc.	20.1	9.9	4,349,600	7
7. Steinberg & Lyman Investment Bankers	19.8	10.0	3,565,500	5
8. Blinder, Robinson & Co.	19.5	10.0	2,428,571	7
9. D. H. Blair & Co.	18.5	9.9	4,772,065	17
10. Dillon Securities Inc.	18.5	10.2	851,820	5

*Includes only underwriters that completed five or more IPOs
†Average total expenses include legal, accounting, and printing fees that don't go to the underwriter; it also include non-accountable expenses that do go to the underwriter
‡Average gross spread includes underwriting fees, management fees, and selling concessions to the underwriter
Source: Securities Data Co., Venture

The final factor to be considered in the choice of a managing underwriter is cost. As was discussed previously, going public is a very costly proposition. And, as indicated in Table 11–2, costs do vary greatly among underwriters. This table reflects the highest price obtained by underwriters for taking lower-quality deals public. The average gross spread as a percentage of the offering was around 10 percent. Costs associated with various possible managing underwriters must be carefully weighed against the other four factors. At this stage, the entrepreneur should not try to cut corners, given the stakes involved in a successful initial public offering.

REGISTRATION STATEMENT AND TIMETABLE

Once the managing underwriter has been selected, a planning meeting is set that includes company officials responsible for preparing the registration statement, the company's independent accountants and lawyers, and the underwriters and their counsel. At this important meeting, frequently called the "all hands" meeting, a timetable is prepared, indicating dates for each step in the registration process. This timetable establishes the effective date of the registration, which determines the date of the final financial statements to be included. The company's end of the year, when regular audited financial statements are routinely prepared, is taken into account to avoid any possible extra accounting and legal work. The timetable should indicate the individual responsible for preparing the various parts of the registration and offering statement. Problems often arise in an initial public offering when the timetable is not carefully developed and agreed to by all parties involved.

After preliminary preparation has been completed, the first public offering normally requires six to eight weeks to prepare, print, and file the registration statement with the SEC. Once the registration statement has been filed, the SEC generally takes four to eight weeks to declare the registration effective. Delays frequently occur in this process during the heavy periods of market activity; during peak seasons such as March when the SEC is reviewing a large number of proxy statements; when the company's attorney is not familiar with federal or state regulations; when a complete and full disclosure is resisted by the company; or when the managing underwriter is inexperienced.

In reviewing the registration statement, the SEC is charged with attempting to ensure only that the document makes a **full and fair disclosure** of the material reported. The SEC has no authority to withhold approval of or require any changes in the terms of an offering that it deems unfair or inequitable, so long as all material information concerning the company and the offering are fully disclosed. The NASD will review each offering, principally to determine the fairness of the underwriting compensation and its compliance with NASD bylaw requirements.

While certain states will review an application for registration in the same manner as the SEC (i.e., solely concerned with full and fair disclosure), others review it to determine whether the offering is "fair, just, and equitable" to the investors in its state. These states actually have the authority to reject an offering on the basis of the perceived merits. Some of the matters which the blue sky examiners focus on most often are the percentage of ownership retained by the promoters and the amount of capital invested by them for those shares (the amount of "cheap stock" outstanding); the underwriting compensation; the existence of transactions between the officers, directors, or other promoters of the enterprise and the issuer itself (i.e., loans or sales to management and other sorts of self-dealing); and the financial performance and stability of the issuer. Once the effective date has been established by the SEC, the underwriters will immediately offer the shares to the public.

An example summary of the key dates for an initial public offering for the KeKaKa Corporation is given in Table 11–3. The company's fiscal year ends March 31 and audited financial statements have been prepared for each prior year of the company's existence. This year's audited financial statements are being prepared in the usual timely manner.

The registration statement itself consists primarily of two parts: the **prospectus** (a legal offering document normally prepared as a brochure or booklet for distribution to prospective buyers) and the **registration statement** (supplemental information to the prospectus, which is available for public inspection at the office of the SEC). Both parts of the registration statement are governed principally by the Securities and Exchange Act of 1933 (the "1933 Act"), a federal

---

TABLE 11–3 Summary of Key Dates for KeKaKa Corporation

All hands meeting	May 15
First draft of S-1 distributed	June 15
All hands meeting	June 22
All hands meeting	July 1
Registration filing date	July 15
Public offering effective	September 8
Closing of offering	September 17

---

statute requiring the registration of securities to be offered to the public. This act also requires that the prospectus be furnished to the purchaser at or before the making of any written offer or the actual confirmation of a sale. Specific SEC forms set forth the informational requirements for a registration. Most initial public offerings will use **form S–1** or, in the case of smaller offerings, **form S–18.** The appropriate form to be used depends on the company's business, the amount of public information already available on the company, the type of security to be offered, the company's size and past financial performance, and, in some instances, the proposed type of purchasers.

The Prospectus

This part of the registration statement is almost always written in a highly stylized narrative form as it is the selling document of the company. While the exact format is left up to the company, the information must be presented in an organized, logical sequence and an easy-to-read, understandable manner in order to obtain SEC approval. Some of the most common sections of a prospectus include the cover page, prospectus summary, the company, risk factors, use of proceeds, dividend policy, capitalization, dilution, selected financial data, the business, management and owners, type of stock, underwriter information, and the actual financial statements.

The cover page includes such information as company name, type and number of shares to be sold, a distribution table, date of prospectus, managing underwriter(s), and syndicate of underwriters involved. There is a preliminary prospectus and then a final prospectus once approval by the SEC is granted. The cover page of a preliminary prospectus booklet and the final prospectus booklet are shown in Tables 11–4 and 11–5, respectively. The preliminary prospectus is used by the underwriters to solicit investor interest in the offering while the registration is pending. The final prospectus contains all of the changes and additions required by the SEC and blue sky examiners and the information concerning the price at which the securities will be sold. The final prospectus must be delivered with or prior to the written confirmation of purchase orders from investors participating in the offering.

TABLE 11–4 Preliminary Prospectus Dated May 1, 1987

800,000 Shares

XETA CORPORATION

Common Stock

Of the 800,000 shares of Common Stock offered hereby, 600,000 shares are being offered and sold for the account of the Company and 200,000 shares are being offered and sold for the account of the Selling Shareholders. See "Principal and Selling Shareholders." The Company will not receive any of the proceeds from the sale of shares by the Selling Shareholders.

Prior to this offering, there has been no public market for the Common Stock and there can be no assurance that such a market will develop. It is anticipated that the Common Stock will be traded in the over-the-counter market and that prices will be reported on the National Association of Securities Dealers Automated Quotation System ("NASDAQ"). The initial public offering price per share will be determined by negotiations among the Company, the Selling Shareholders and the Underwriters. It is currently estimated that the initial public offering price will be in the range of $8.00 to $10.00 per share. See "Underwriting" for a description of the factors considered in determining the public offering price of the shares.

**THESE SECURITIES INVOLVE A HIGH DEGREE OF RISK.
SEE "RISK FACTORS" and "DILUTION."**

THESE SECURITIES HAVE NOT BEEN APPROVED OR DISAPPROVED BY THE SECURITIES AND EXCHANGE COMMISSION NOR HAS THE COMMISSION PASSED UPON THE ACCURACY OR ADEQUACY OF THIS PROSPECTUS. ANY REPRESENTATION TO THE CONTRARY IS A CRIMINAL OFFENSE.

	Price to Public	Underwriting Discounts(1)	Proceeds to Company(2)	Proceeds to Selling Shareholders(2)
Per Share	$	$	$	$
Total(3)	$	$	$	$

(1) See "Underwriting" for information concerning indemnification and other arrangements with the Representative and the several Underwriters.

(2) Before deducting expenses estimated at $, of which $ will be paid by the Company and $ will be paid by the Selling Shareholders.

(3) Certain of the Selling Shareholders have granted to the Underwriters the right to purchase, within 30 days after the date of this Prospectus, up to 120,000 additional shares of Common Stock at the initial public offering price, less the underwriting discount, to cover over-allotments, if any. If such additional shares are purchased by the Underwriters, the total Price to Public, Underwriting Discounts and Proceeds to Selling Shareholders will be $, $ and $, respectively. See "Underwriting."

The Common Stock is offered by the several Underwriters named herein, subject to prior sale, when, as and if delivered to and accepted by the Underwriters, subject to the right to reject orders in whole or in part and subject to certain other conditions. It is expected that certificates for the Common Stock will be available for delivery on or about June , 1987, at the offices of Eppler, Guerin & Turner, Inc., Dallas, Texas, or through the facilities of The Depository Trust Company, New York, New York.

Eppler, Guerin & Turner, Inc.

The date of this Prospectus is May   1987.

TABLE 11–5 Final Prospectus

800,000 Shares

Common Stock

Of the 800,000 shares of Common Stock offered hereby, 600,000 shares are being offered and sold for the account of the Company and 200,000 shares are being offered and sold for the account of the Selling Shareholders. See "Principal and Selling Shareholders." The Company will not receive any of the proceeds from the sale of shares by the Selling Shareholders.

Prior to this offering, there has been no public market for the Common Stock and there can be no assurance that such a market will develop. See "Underwriting" for a description of the factors considered in determining the public offering price of the shares.

THESE SECURITIES INVOLVE A HIGH DEGREE OF RISK.
SEE "RISK FACTORS" and "DILUTION."

THESE SECURITIES HAVE NOT BEEN APPROVED OR DISAPPROVED BY THE SECURITIES AND EXCHANGE COMMISSION NOR HAS THE COMMISSION PASSED UPON THE ACCURACY OR ADEQUACY OF THIS PROSPECTUS. ANY REPRESENTATION TO THE CONTRARY IS A CRIMINAL OFFENSE.

	Price to Public	Underwriting Discounts(1)	Proceeds to Company(2)	Proceeds to Selling Shareholders(2)
Per Share	$7.00	$0.56	$6.44	$6.44
Total(3)	$5,600,000	$448,000	$3,864,000	$1,288,000

(1) See "Underwriting" for information concerning indemnification and other arrangements with the Representative and the several Underwriters.

(2) Before deducting expenses estimated at $530,000, of which $450,000 will be paid by the Company and $80,000 will be paid by the Selling Shareholders.

(3) Certain of the Selling Shareholders have granted to the Underwriters the right to purchase, within 30 days after the date of this Prospectus, up to 120,000 additional shares of Common Stock at the initial public offering price, less the underwriting discount, to cover over-allotments, if any. If such additional shares are purchased by the Underwriters, the total Price to Public, Underwriting Discounts and Proceeds to Selling Shareholders will be $6,440,000, $515,200 and $2,060,800, respectively. See "Underwriting."

The Common Stock is offered by the several Underwriters named herein, subject to prior sale, when, as and if delivered to and accepted by the Underwriters, subject to the right to reject orders in whole or in part and subject to certain other conditions. It is expected that certificates for the Common Stock will be available for delivery on or about June 24, 1987, at the offices of Eppler, Guerin & Turner, Inc., Dallas, Texas, or through the facilities of The Depository Trust Company, New York, New York.

Eppler, Guerin & Turner, Inc.

June 17, 1987

The prospectus starts with a table of contents and summary. The prospectus summary highlights the important features of the offering, similar to the executive summary of a business plan discussed previously.

A brief introduction of the company follows, which describes the nature of the business, the company's history, major products, and location.

Then a discussion of the risk factors involved is presented. Such issues as a history of operating losses, a short track record, importance of certain key individuals, dependence on certain customers, significant level of competition, or lack of market uncertainty are presented so that the purchaser is aware of the speculative nature of the offering and the degree of risk involved in purchasing.

The next section—use of proceeds—needs to be carefully prepared as the actual use of the proceeds must be reported to the SEC following the offering. This section is of great interest to potential purchasers as it indicates the reason(s) the company is going public and its future direction.

The dividend policy section details the company's dividend history and any restrictions on future dividends. Of course, most entrepreneurial companies have not paid any dividends but have retained their earnings to finance future growth.

The capitalization section indicates the overall capital structure of the company both before and after the public offering.

Whenever there is significant disparity between the offering price of the shares and the price paid for shares by officers, directors, or founding stockholders, a dilution section is necessary in the prospectus. This section describes the dilution, or decrease, of the purchaser's equity interest that will occur.

Form S–1 requires that the prospectus contain, at the end, selected financial data for each of the last five years of company operation to highlight significant trends in the company's financial condition. This analysis of the results of the company's operations and their impact on the financial conditions of the company covers at least the last three years of operation. It provides information that potential purchasers can use to assess the company's cash flow from internal and external sources.

The next section—the business—is the largest in the prospectus. It provides information on the company, its industry, and its products, such as historical development of the company; principal products, markets, and distribution methods; new products being developed; sources and availability of raw materials; backlog orders; export sales; number of employees; and nature of any patents, trademarks, licenses, franchises, and physical property owned.

Following the business section is a discussion of management and key security holders. The section covers background information, ages, business experience, total remuneration, and stock holdings of directors, nominated directors, and executive officers. Also any stockholder (not in the above categories) who beneficially owns more than 5 percent of the company must be indicated.

The description of capital stock section, as the name implies, describes the par and stated value of the stock being offered, dividend rights, voting rights, liquidity, and transferability if more than one class of stock exists.

Following this, the underwriter information section explains the plans for distributing the stock offering, such as the amount of securities to be purchased by each underwriting participant involved, the underwriters' obligations, and the indemnification of the company.

The prospectus part of the registration statement concludes with the actual financial statements. Form S–1 requires audited balance sheets for the last two fiscal years, audited income statements and statements of retained earnings for last three fiscal years, and unaudited interim financial statements as of within 135 days of the date the registration statement becomes effective. It is this requirement that makes it so important to pick a date for going public in light of year-end operations and to develop a good timetable to avoid the time and costs of preparing additional interim statements.

Part II

This section of Form S–1 contains specific documentation of the issue in an item-and-answer format, including such exhibits as the articles of incorporation, the underwriting agreements, company bylaws, stock option and pension plans, and contracts. Other items presented include indemnification of directors and officers, any sale of unregistered securities within past three years, and expenses related to going public.

Form S–18

In April 1979, the SEC adopted a simplified form of the registration statement—Form S–18—for companies planning to register no more than $7.5 million of securities. This form was designed to make going public easier and less expensive by requiring less vigorous reporting requirements. Form S–18 requires less detailed descriptions of the business, officers, directors, and legal proceedings; requires no industry segment information; allows financial statements to be prepared in accordance with generally accepted accounting practices rather than under the guidelines of Regulation S–X; and requires an audited balance sheet at the end of the last fiscal year (rather than the last two years) and audited changes in financial positions and stockholders equity for the last two years (rather than the last three years). While Form S–18 can be filed for review with the SEC's Division of Corporation Finance in Washington, D.C., as all form S–1s are, it can also be filed with the SEC's regional office.

Procedure

Once the preliminary prospectus is filed, it can be distributed to the underwriting group. This preliminary prospectus is called a **red herring,** because a statement printed in red ink appears on the front cover.

The registration statements are then reviewed by the SEC to determine if adequate disclosures have been made. Some deficiencies are almost always found and are communicated to the company either by telephone or a **deficiency letter.** This preliminary prospectus contains all the information contained in the final prospectus except that which is not known until shortly before the effective date—offering price, underwriters' commission, and amount of proceeds. These items are filed through a **pricing amendment** and appear in the final prospectus (see Table 11–5). To see the difference between a red herring and a final prospectus, compare the two Xeta Corporation documents shown in Table 11–4 and Table 11–5. This time, usually around a month between the initial filing of the registration statement and its effective date, is called the waiting period, during which time the underwriting syndicate is formed and briefed.

LEGAL ISSUES AND BLUE SKY QUALIFICATIONS

In addition to all the legal issues surrounding the actual preparation and filing of the prospectus, there are several other important legal concerns. Perhaps the one that is of the most concern to the entrepreneur is the **quiet period**—the period of time from when the decision to go public is made to 90 days following the date of becoming effective. Care must be taken during this period regarding any new information about the company or key personnel. Any publicity effort designed to create a favorable attitude about the securities to be offered is illegal. The guidelines established by the SEC regarding the information that can and cannot be released should be understood not only by the entrepreneur but by everyone in the company as well. All press releases and other printed material should be cleared with the attorneys involved as well as the underwriter. The entrepreneur and key personnel must curtail speaking engagements and television appearances to avoid any possible problematic response to interviewer or audience questions. One entrepreneur whose company was in the process of going public had to postpone a guest appearance on the "Today Show," during which she was to discuss "Women Entrepreneurs," a video scheduled for release after the quiet period was over.

Blue Sky Qualifications

The securities of the company going public must also be qualified under the **blue sky laws** of each state in which the securities will be offered, unless the state has an exemption from the qualification requirements. These blue sky laws cause additional delays and costs to the company going public, as was discussed earlier in this chapter. Many states allow their state securities administrators to prevent the offering from being sold in the state on such substantive grounds as past stock issuances, too much dilution, or too much compensation to the underwriter, even though all required disclosures have been met and clearance has been granted by the SEC.

It is the responsibility of the managing underwriter to determine the states and the number of securities that will be sold in each. The number of securities to be qualified in each state and the offering price are important, as the blue sky laws and qualification fees in many states vary, depending on the number and price. Only after the company has qualified in a particular state and the overall registration statement has been cleared by the SEC can the underwriters sell the number of shares that have been allowed in that particular state. Most states require the company to file sales reports following the offering so that the number of sales sold in the state can be determined and any additional fees assessed if necessary.

AFTER GOING PUBLIC

After the initial public offering has been sold there are still some areas of concern to the entrepreneur. These include aftermarket support, relationship with the financial community, and reporting requirements.

Aftermarket Support

Once the stock has been issued, the underwriting firm and the entrepreneur should monitor its price, particularly in the initial weeks following its offering. Generally, the managing underwriting firm will be the principal market maker in the company's stock and will be ready to purchase or sell stock in the interdealer market. To stabilize the market, preventing the price from going below the initial public offering price, this underwriter may enter bids to buy the stock in the early stages following the offering. This support is important in allowing the stock not to be adversely affected by a precipitous drop in price.

Relationship with the Financial Community

Once a company has gone public, the financial community will take a greater interest in it. An entrepreneur will need an increasing portion of time to develop a good relationship with this community. The relationship established has a significant effect on the market interest and therefore the price of the company's stock. Since many investors rely on analysts and brokers for investment advice, the entrepreneur should attempt to meet these individuals as much as possible. Regular appearances before societies of security analysts should be a part of establishing this relationship, as well as public disclosures through formal press releases. Frequently, it is best to designate one person in the company to be the information officer, ensuring that the press, public, and security analysts are dealt with in a friendly, efficient manner. There is nothing worse than a company not responding in a timely manner to information requests from security brokers and analysts, the trade, the press, and the general public.

Reporting Requirements

As discussed at the beginning of this chapter, one of the negative aspects of going public is the new reporting requirements. One of the first requirements is the filing of a Form SR sales report, which the company must do within 10 days after the end of the first three-month period following the effective date of the registration. This report includes information on the amount of securities sold and still to be sold and the proceeds obtained by the company and their use. A final Form SR sales report must be filed within 10 days of the completion or termination of the offering.

The company must file annual reports on Form 10–K, quarterly reports on Form 10–Q, and specific transaction reports on Form 8–K. The information in Form 10–K on the business, management, and company assets is similar to that in Form S–1 of the registration statement. Of course, audited financial statements are required.

The quarterly report on Form 10–Q contains primarily the unaudited financial information for the most recently completed fiscal quarter. No 10–Q is required for the fourth fiscal quarter.

A Form 8–K report must be filed within 15 days of such events as the acquisition or disposition of significant assets by the company outside the ordinary course of business; the resignation or dismissal of the company's independent public accountants; or a change in control of the company.

The company must also follow the proxy solicitation requirements regarding holding a meeting or obtaining the written consent of security holders. The timing and the type of materials involved are detailed in the Securities and Exchange Act of 1933.

These are but a few of the reporting requirements required of public companies. All the requirements must be carefully observed since even inadvertent mistakes can have negative consequences on the company. Of course the reports must be filed on time.

SUMMARY

Going public—the transformation of a closely held corporation to one where the general public has a proprietary interest—is indeed arduous. An entrepreneur must carefully assess whether the company is ready to go public as well as whether the advantages outweigh the disadvantages. In assessing readiness, the entrepreneur must take into account the size of the company, earnings and performance, market conditions, urgency of monetary need, and the desires of the current owners. The entrepreneur needs to consider the primary advantages of going public—new capital, liquidity and valuation, enhanced ability to obtain funds, and prestige—along with the disadvantages—expense, disclosure of information, loss of control, and pressure to maintain growth.

Once the decision is made to proceed, a managing investment banking firm must be selected and the registration statement prepared. The expertise of the investment banker is a major factor in the success of the public offering. In selecting an investment banker, the entrepreneur should employ the following criteria: reputation, distribution capability, advisory services, experience, and cost. To prepare for the registration date, the entrepreneur must organize an "all hands" meeting of company officials, the company's independent accountants and lawyers, and the underwriters and their counsel. A timetable must be established for the effective date of registration and for the preparation of necessary financial documents, including the preliminary and final prospectus. Following the registration and review of the SEC, the entrepreneur must carefully observe the 90-day quiet period and qualify under the blue sky laws of each state in which the securities will be offered.

After the initial public offering, the entrepreneur needs to maintain a good relationship with the financial community and to adhere strictly to the reporting requirements of public companies. The decision to go public requires much planning and consideration. Going public, indeed, is not for every entrepreneurial venture.

PART IV

MANAGING THE NEW VENTURE

Managing during Early Operations

CHAPTER OBJECTIVES

1. To describe the important procedures for financial control ducontrol during the early stages of the new venture's operation.

2. To understand the differences between the accrual and cash method of accounting.

3. To discuss the important issues in managing cash, expenses, assets, debt, profits, and taxes.

4. To understand the problems that can result from rapid growth of the new venture.

5. To explain how the entrepreneur can collect primary and secondary information to assist in the management of early operations.

6. To understand how to promote the new venture effectively through publicity and advertising.

WILLIAM GATES

William Gates III, cofounder of Microsoft, have proven himself to be an atypical entrepreneur. While other contemporaries of the fast-track computer business, such as Steven Jobs of Apple Computer Inc. and Mitchell Kapor of Lotus Development Corporation, were being forced out or voluntarily dropping out, Gates was not only staying in control of Microsoft but he was turning it into one of the fast-growing successes of the high-flying computer software market. How did he make it through the early years of operation? By using good business sense and careful management of Microsoft during this critical time.

Gates inherited his talent for running a business from his parents. His father, a successful law partner in Shidler, McBroom, Gates, and Lucas, and his mother, a former schoolteacher and director of United Way International, were often engaged in lively business discussions at home. This rich home environment provided much stimulation for Gates to develop his business skills. At age 14, he became hooked on computers when the Lakeside Mothers Club in his hometown put the data on its rummage sale proceeds in a terminal linked by phone to a computer. Soon Bill and three of his friends started the Lakeside Programming Group. Along with one of his friends, Paul Allen, he would sneak away in the middle of the night or during gym classes to work at the computer center. His fascination with the applications eventually led him to develop a payroll system for the school and a system to monitor highway traffic. His friends in the Lakeside Programming Group at one point kicked him out of the organization because he was much younger than the others. However, the organization found out it could not function without him and eventually asked him to return as president.

In 1973, while at Harvard, Gates and Allen wrote a language for a company called MITS, which had been selling a computer kit with a new microprocessor from Intel. Their experience in high school had given them the knowledge to eventually start Microsoft. Then, after some ups and downs caused by MITS's financial problems, Gates found an opportunity to develop an operating system, MS-DOS, for IBM personal computers. That deal with IBM thrust Microsoft into the major leagues of computer software when, in 1981, the firm reached sales revenues of $16 million. The early years were critical for the survival of

Microsoft. Careful financial planning and analysis thrust the firm into a public corporation with Gates's net worth reaching about $1 billion.

The success of Microsoft, however, would not have been sustained without careful management and decision making in the highly competitive computer software market. Long hours in the development of new operating systems, as well as meeting schedules, gave the company a special reputation among its constituents. As the firm grew, Gates learned to delegate authority while still maintaining some control with his hard-nosed, perfectionist management style. The environment of Microsoft, however, could be considered informal with a definite family orientation. The careful management of Microsoft through its early years has led to a few critical new products such as Windows, which is expected to grow about 25 percent and account for about 37 percent of 1991 revenues.

Gates's efforts have not gone without criticism. Many feel that he has large gaps in his knowledge of computer science, yet he continues to find new business to sustain the growth of his company. In 1990, Microsoft's revenues and net profits rose by 40 and 80 percent, respectively. Profits in 1990 were $280 million on sales of $1.2 billion, making it one of the largest computer software companies in the United States.[1]

In this chapter, important management-decision areas are reviewed and discussed. Financial and marketing decisions, which are recognized by entrepreneurs such as Wiliam Gates as very important during the early years, are discussed in detail.

FINANCIAL CONTROL

The financial plan, as an inherent part of the business plan, was discussed in Chapter 7, including how to prepare pro forma income and cash flow statements for the first three years. The entrepreneur will also need some knowledge of how to provide appropriate controls to ensure that projections and goals are met. Some financial skills are thus necessary for the entrepreneur to manage the venture during these early years. The cash flow statement, income statement, and balance sheet are key financial elements that will need careful management and control, the focus of this chapter.

---

[1]See "The Billion-Dollar Whiz Kid," *Business Week,* April 13, 1987, pp. 68–76 and The First Boston Corp., *Microsoft Company Report.* June 18, 1990, pp. 1–3.

ACCRUAL VERSUS CASH ACCOUNTING

It is important that the entrepreneur establish an accounting procedure that will effectively enhance his or her ability to control the finances of the new venture. The accrual method is not very desirable for the new venture. It is utilized mostly by large businesses that do not have problems with short-term cash flows.

Table 12–1 compares the accrual method of accounting with the cash method. As can be seen, in the **accrual method** actual cash inflows and outflows are ignored. Thus, sales may have been incurred but no payments received, or expenses incurred but no disbursements made.

The **cash method** is much more consistent with cash flow, giving the entrepreneur much tighter control over cash. However, even using the cash method, the entrepreneur must be aware that some cash outflows are not expense items and hence a profitable venture may not necessarily be liquid. For example, a large capital expenditure in any year for equipment is not considered an expense in its entirety because of depreciation over time; and the repayment of the principal on a loan is not an expense at all.

We can see the relationship of the accrual and cash methods by using an example. Let's suppose that in August the entrepreneur sells $10,000 worth of merchandise in a clothing store. A total of $6,000 of this is received in cash and the remainder is charged by the customers. An additional $2,000 in payment for merchandise purchased on credit in July is received in August. In the same month, the entrepreneur purchases $8,000 worth of merchandise ($2,000 each from four suppliers). All of this merchandise is to be paid in 30 days (September). The entrepreneur paid $10,000 in August for merchandise purchased in July. There was also $1,000 repayment of the principal on a personal loan from a family member.

We can see the distinction in the two approaches on page 390. The cash method shows a $2,000 loss in August; the accrual method shows a $2,000 profit. Cash flow is further affected by the repayment of the loan principal of $2,000, which is not an expense. Thus, for cash purposes the entrepreneur has a cash outflow of $12,000 and a cash inflow of only $8,000 during August. The

---

TABLE 12–1   Accrual versus Cash Basis

	Accrual Method	*Cash Method*
Sales	Accounted for when sales are made	Not counted until cash is actually received
Expenses	Accounted for when the expense is actually incurred	Not counted until cash is actually paid out

$4,000 that has been charged in August will be included as revenue when the cash is actually received.

August	Cash Method	Accrual Method
Revenue	$ 8,000	$10,000
Expenses	10,000	8,000
Net Income	($ 2,000) loss	$ 2,000

The cash basis, although it may not properly reflect net income, does give the entrepreneur a better picture of the cash position. Either method is acceptable by the IRS. Control over money owed to the entrepreneur (accounts receivable) can be critical if cash flow becomes a problem. To balance the problem of slow receivables, the entrepreneur may try to delay payments of debts (accounts payable), but if this becomes a chronic problem, suppliers may refuse to deliver except on a cash basis.

Managing Cash Flow

Since cash outflow may exceed cash inflows, the entrepreneur should try to have an up-to-date assessment of his or her cash position. This can be accomplished by preparing monthly cash flow statements such as that found in Figure 12–1 and comparing the budgeted or pro forma statements with the actual results. The July budgeted amounts are taken from the pro forma cash flow statement of MPP Plastics (see Figure 7-5). The entrepreneur can indicate the actual amounts next to the budgeted amounts. This will be useful for adjusting the pro forma for remaining months, as well as providing some indication as to where cash flow problems may exist.

Figure 12-1 shows a few potential problem areas. First, sales receipts were less than anticipated. Whether this was due to nonpayment by some customers or an increase in credit sales needs to be assessed. If the lower amount is due to nonpayment by customers, the entrepreneur may need to try enforcing faster payment by sending reminder letters or making telephone calls to delinquent customers. If the lower receipts are due to higher credit sales, the entrepreneur may need to either consider short-term financing from a bank or extend the terms of payment to his or her suppliers.

Cash disbursements for some items were greater than budgeted, indicating a possible need for tighter cost controls. For example, cost of goods was $22,500, which was $1,700 more than budgeted. The entrepreneur may find that suppliers increased their prices, which may require a search for alternative sources or even raising the prices of the products/services offered by the new venture. If the

FIGURE 12–1

MPP PLASTICS INC.
Statement of Cash Flow
July Year 1 (000s)

	July	
	Budgeted	*Actual*
Receipts		
Sales	$ 24.0	$ 22.0
Disbursements		
Equipment	100.0	100.0
Cost of goods	20.8	22.5
Selling expenses	1.5	2.5
Salaries	6.5	6.5
Advertising	1.5	1.5
Office supplies	0.3	0.3
Rent	2.0	2.0
Utilities	0.3	0.5
Insurance	0.8	0.8
Taxes	0.8	0.8
Loan principal and interest	2.6	2.6
Total disbursements	$ 137.0	$ 140.0
Cash flow	(113.1)	(118.0)
Beginning balance	275.0	275.0
Ending balance	161.9	157.0

higher cost of goods (assuming cash basis of accounting) resulted from the purchase of more supplies, the entrepreneur should assess the inventory costs from the income statement. It is possible that the increased cost of goods resulted from the purchase of more supplies because sales were higher than expected. However, if these additional sales resulted in more credit sales, the entrepreneur may need to plan to borrow money to meet short-term cash needs. Conclusions can be made once the credit sales and inventory costs are evaluated.

The higher selling expenses may also need to be assessed. If the additional selling expenses were incurred in order to support increased sales (even if they were credit sales), there is no immediate concern. However, if no additional sales were generated, the entrepreneur may need to review all of these expenses and perhaps institute tighter controls.

Comparison of budgeted or expected cash flows with actual cash flows can provide the entrepreneur with an important assessment of potential immediate cash needs and indicate possible problems in the management of assets or control of costs. These items are discussed further in the next sections.

Management of Assets

Figure 12-2 illustrates the balance sheet for MPP Plastics after the first three months of operation. In the asset section of the balance sheet are items that all need to be managed carefully by the entrepreneur in the early months of the new venture. We have already discussed the importance of cash management using cash flow projections. Other items such as the accounts receivable, inventory, and supplies also need to be controlled to ensure maximum cash flow and effective use of funds by the new venture.

The increasing use and number of credit cards indicate that many consumers will consider buying on credit. Some ventures may even consider providing their own credit to avoid paying fees to the credit card company. There are some trade-offs in using internal credit rather than accepting such cards as Mastercard, Visa, American Express, and Discover.

FIGURE 12–2

MPP PLASTICS INC.
Balance Sheet
First Quarter Year 1

Assets

Current assets		
Cash	$ 13,350	
Accounts receivable (40% of $60,000 in sales the previous month)	24,000	
Merchandise inventory	12,850	
Supplies	2,100	
Total fixed assets		$ 51,300
Fixed assets	$240,000	
Equipment		
Less depreciation	9,900	
Total fixed assets		$230,100
Total assets		281,400

Liabilities and Owner's Equity

Current liabilities		
Accounts payable (20% of 40 CGS)	$ 8,000	
Current portion of L-T Debt	13,600	
Total current liabilities		$ 21,600
Long-term liabilities		
Notes payable		223,200
Total liabilities		244,800
Owner's equity		
C. Peter's capital	$ 25,000	
K. Peter's capital	25,000	
Retained earnings	(13,400)	
Total owner's equity		$ 36,600
Total liabilities and owner's equity		281,400

If the new venture accepts outside credit cards, it shifts the risk involved in accounts receivable collections to the credit card companies. Shifting the risk, however, costs the entrepreneur a fee of about 3 to 4 percent. With that in mind, firms often offer customers lower prices for cash sales. Customers opting for credit cards will pay a higher price for the privilege of using them, a price that offsets the fee paid by the company.

If customers are allowed to buy on internal credit, the entrepreneur will be responsible for collecting any delinquent payments. Delays in payments can also be problematic since, as we have seen in cash flow analysis, they can cause negative cash flows. Any nonpayment of accounts receivable will become an expense (bad debt) on the income statement at the end of the fiscal year. In any event, the entrepreneur will need to be sensitive to major changes in accounts receivable and should always compare actual with budgeted amounts (generally estimated to be a percentage of gross sales) as a means for controlling and managing this important asset.

Inventory control is also important to the entrepreneur. Since inventory is an expensive asset, the entrepreneur must maintain just enough of it to meet demand for finished goods. If inventory is low and the firm cannot meet demand on time, sales could be lost. On the other hand, carrying excess inventory can be costly, either because of excessive handling and storage costs or because it becomes obsolete before being sold. Growing ventures typically tie up more cash in their inventory than in any other part of the business.

Skolnik Industries, a $10 million manufacturer of steel containers for storage and disposal of hazardous materials, recently developed an inventory control system that allows them to ship products to their customers within 24 to 48 hours. This was accomplished with a very lean inventory, thanks to the installation of a computerized control system that allows the firm to maintain records of inventory on a product by product basis. In addition to this capability, the system allows the company to monitor gross margin return on investment, inventory turnover, percentage of orders shipped on time, length of time to fill back orders, and ratio of customer complaints to shipped orders. Software to accomplish these goals is readily available and in many cases can even be modified to meet the exact needs of the business. The reports from this system are generated every two to four weeks in normal sales periods and weekly in heavy sales periods. This system not only provides Skolnik with an early warning system, but it has freed up cash normally invested in inventory and improved the overall profitability of the firm.[2]

From an accounting point of view, the entrepreneur will need to determine the value of inventory and how it affects the cost of goods sold (income statement). For example, assume that an entrepreneur made three purchases of inventory for manufacturing a finished product. Each purchase of inventory involved a different price. The issue will be what to use as a value for cost of

---

[2]J. Fraser, "Hidden Cash," *INC.*, February 1991, pp. 81–2.

goods sold. Generally either a **FIFO** (first-in, first-out) or **LIFO** (last-in, first-out) will be used. Most firms use a FIFO system since it reflects truer inventory and cost-of-goods-sold values. However, there are good arguments for using the LIFO method in times of inflation. This issue will be discussed later in this section.

The following table shows the differences in using FIFO or LIFO and how inventory affects cost of goods sold. Using either FIFO or LIFO,

| | | Cost of Goods | |
Inventory	*Units Sold*	*FIFO*	*LIFO*
1,000 units @ $1.00	800	$800.00	$800.00
500 units @ $1.10	600	$640.00	$650.00
1,000 units @ $1.15	950	$1,037.50	$1,092.50

the first 800 units sold would be valued at $1. The next 600 units sold under FIFO would result in a cost of goods sold of $640,200 units sold at $1 and 400 at $1.10. Under the LIFO method, the 600 units would have a cost of goods of $650. This is determined by 500 units at $1.10 and 100 at $1. The next 950 units sold under FIFO would have a cost of goods sold of $1,037.50, or 100 units at $1.10 and 850 at $1.15. For LIFO, cost of goods sold would be $1,092.50, which results from 950 units costed at $1.15.

As stated above, there are occasions when the entrepreneur might find that the LIFO method actually increases cash flow. A case in point is the Dacor Corporation, a manufacturer of scuba-diving equipment. In 1983, the venture switched from FIFO to LIFO and incurred average annual increases in cash flow of 10 percent, until 1989, when inflation increased so much that the company showed an increase of 25 percent in its cash flow. Such a decision can be implemented in the following manner.

First, the firm must decide whether to group inventory into categories or to cost each item individually. These costs must be pinpointed both at the beginning and end of the year or must be based on an annual average. Large inventories should be categorized or pooled; for those ventures with limited product lines each item or product can be costed individually. Because of the wide variety of products sold, Dacor chose to categorize their inventory for costing purposes. The firm must carefully assess these options, because once the decision is made, it is very difficult to change back without incurring penalties from the IRS.

Second, the firm must cost all inventory by searching through historical records. The amount of effort required for a venture will depend again on the breadth of the product line.

After ascertaining the inventory cost for each category or product, the firm must calculate an average inventory cost. For a new venture with only one or a few products this is relatively easy. For a firm with a wide product line, like Dacor, this requires the assistance of an accounting firm. After all the calculations are made, management must notify the IRS (Form 970) that it is converting to the LIFO method.

The decision to convert from a FIFO to a LIFO system is not simple; thus, it is important for the entrepreneur to carefully evaluate his or her goals before making any commitment. Conversion to LIFO can typically be beneficial if the following conditions exist.[3]

1. Rising labor, materials, and other production costs are anticipated.
2. The business and inventory are growing.
3. The business has some computer-assisted inventory-control capability.
4. The business is profitable. There is no point in converting if the start-up is losing money.

Regardless of the method of inventory costing used, the entrepreneur must keep careful records of inventory. Perpetual inventory systems can be structured using computers or a manual system. As items are sold, inventory should be reduced. A periodical physical count of the inventory can help in maintaining a good balance.

Fixed assets generally involve long-term commitments and large investments for the new venture. These fixed assets, such as the equipment appearing in Figure 12–2, will have certain costs related to them. Equipment will require servicing and insurance and will affect utility costs. The equipment will also depreciate over time, which will be reflected in the value of the asset.

Long-Term versus Short-Term Debt

To finance the assets and ensure that the new venture can meet its cash needs, the entrepreneur may need to borrow funds. Generally, to finance fixed assets the entrepreneur will assume long-term debt by borrowing from a bank. The collateral for such a loan will be the fixed asset itself. The alternatives to borrowing from a bank are to borrow from a family member or friend, or, in the case of a partnership, to have each partner contribute more funds to the business. A corporation may sell stock in the new venture. This decision, however, may require the entrepreneur(s) to give up some equity in the business. The entrepreneur should consider the pros and cons of all options.

Managing Costs and Profits

Although the cash flow analysis discussed earlier in the chapter can assist the entrepreneur in assessing and controlling costs, it is also useful to compute the net income for interim periods during the year. The most effective use of the

---

[3]J. Fraser, "Taking Stock," *INC.*, November 1989, pp. 161–62.

interim income statement is to establish cost standards and compare the actual with the budgeted amount for that period. Costs are budgeted based on percentages of net sales. These percentages can then be compared to actual percentages and assessed over time to ascertain where tighter cost controls may be necessary.

Figure 12–3 compares actual and expected (standard) percentages on MPP Plastic's income statement for its first quarter of operation. This analysis gives the entrepreneur the opportunity to manage and control costs before it is too late. The figure shows that costs of goods sold is higher than standard. This may be partly because some initial small purchases of inventory did not include quantity discounts. If this is not the case, the entrepreneur should consider finding other sources or raising prices.

Most of the expenses appear to be reasonably close to standard or expected percentages. The entrepreneur should assess each item to determine whether these costs can be reduced or whether it will be necessary to raise prices to ensure future positive profits.

As the venture begins to evolve into the second and third years of operation, the entrepreneur should also compare current actual costs to prior incurred costs. For example, in the second year of operation the entrepreneur may find it useful to look back at the selling expenses incurred in the first year of operation. Such comparisons can be done on a month-to-month basis (i.e., January, year 1 to January, year 2) or even quarterly or yearly, depending on the volatility of the costs in the particular business.

FIGURE 12–3

MPP PLASTICS INC.
Income Statement
First Quarter Year 1 (000s)

		Actual (%)	Standard (%)
Net sales	$150.00	100	100
Less cost of goods sold	100.00	66.7	60
Gross margin	(50.0)	32.3	40
Operating expenses			
Selling expenses	11.7	7.8	8.0
Salaries	19.8	13.2	12.0
Advertising	5.2	3.5	4.0
Office supplies	1.9	1.3	1.0
Rent	6.0	4.0	3.0
Utilities	1.3	0.9	1.0
Insurance	0.6	0.4	0.5
Taxes	3.4	2.3	2.0
Interest	3.6	2.4	2.0
Depreciation	9.9	6.6	5.0
Miscellaneous	0.3	0.2	0.2
Total operating expenses	$ 66.3	42.6	38.7
Net profit (loss)	(13.3)	(9.3)	1.3

When expenses or costs are much higher than budgeted, the entrepreneur may need to analyze the account to determine the exact cause of the overrun. For example, utilities represent a single expense item yet may include a number of specific payments for such things as heat, electricity, gas, hot water, and so on. Thus, the entrepreneur should retain a running balance of all these payments if it is necessary to ascertain the cause of an unusually large utility expense. In Figure 12–1 we see that the utility expense was $500, which was $200 over the budgeted amount, or a 67 percent increase. What caused the increase? Was any particular utility responsible for the overrun, or was it a result of higher oil costs, which affected all of the utility expenses? These questions need to be resolved before the entrepreneur accepts the results and makes any needed adjustments for the next period.

Comparisons of the actual and budgeted expenses in the income statement can be misleading for those new ventures that have multiple products or services. For financial reporting purposes to shareholders, bankers, or other investors, the income statement would summarize expenses across all products and services. This information, although helpful to get an overview of the success of the venture, does not indicate the marketing cost for each product, the performance of particular managers in controlling costs, or the most profitable product(s). For example, selling expenses for MPP Plastics (Figure 12–3) was $11,700. These selling expenses may apply to more than one product, in which case the entrepreneur would need to ascertain the amount of selling expense for each product. He or she may be tempted to prorate the expense across each product, which would not provide a realistic picture of the relative success of each. Thus, if MPP Plastics produced three different products, the selling expense for each might be assumed to be $3,900 per product, when the actual selling expenses could be much more or less.

Some products may require more advertising, insurance, administrative time, transportation, storage, and so on, which could be misleading if the entrepreneur chooses to allocate these expenses equally across all products. To mitigate this problem, the entrepreneur should allocate expenses by product as effectively as possible. It important to evaluate these costs for each product and to evaluate them by region, customer, distribution channel, department, and so on.[4] To get a real profit perspective of every product marketed by the new venture, the entrepreneur should avoid arbitrary allocation of costs.

Taxes

The entrepreneur will be required to withhold federal and state taxes for his or her employees. Each month or quarter (depending on the size of the payroll), the venture must make deposits or payments to the appropriate agency for funds withheld from wages. Generally, federal taxes, state taxes, and social security

---

[4]R. Kaplan, "Accounting Critic, Robert Kaplan," *INC.*, April 1988, pp. 54–67.

are withheld from employees' salaries and then deposited later. The entrepreneur should be careful not to use these funds since, if payments are late, there will be high interest and penalties assessed. In addition to withholding taxes, the new venture may be required to pay state and federal unemployment taxes. The exact amount and procedures can be determined by contacting the unemployment agency for the federal government and the appropriate state.

The federal and state governments will also require the entrepreneur to file end-of-the-year returns of the business. If the venture is incorporated, there may be state corporation taxes to be paid regardless of whether the venture earned a profit. The filing periods and tax responsibilities will vary for other types of organizations. Chapter 8 discusses the tax responsibilities of a proprietorship, partnership, or corporation. As stated earlier, a tax accountant can help avoid any errors and provide advice in handling these expenses.

RAPID GROWTH AND MANAGEMENT CONTROLS

When the new venture begins to reach a rapid-growth phase, the entrepreneur should be sensitive to some of the resultant management problems. Usually the entrepreneur sees rapid growth as a positive sign of success and abandons any attempt to establish important management controls, for the sake of doing more and more business. However, rapid growth can quickly change the status of a new venture from profitable to bankrupt if the entrepreneur is not sensitive to certain growth issues. What are these issues? How can growth quickly turn a business into a failure? How should growth be managed? These are a few of the important questions that will be addressed in this section.[5]

First, let's look at some of the growth problems that can affect the management of the new venture. These are summarized in Table 12–2. Before rapid growth occurs, the new venture is usually operating with a small staff and a limited budget. Hence, less time is spent in evaluating management, personnel planning, and cost controls because cash seems to be plentiful.

Rapid growth can also dilute the leadership abilities of the entrepreneur. Shared vision and purpose becomes difficult as the entrepreneur has to devote so much time to the short-term growth demands on his or her time. As a result, communication diminishes and goals become more compartmentalized. Training and development of personnel is overlooked and eventually the entrepreneur and all of the employees begin to feel pressure and stress. The entrepreneur's unwillingness to delegate responsibility can lead to even greater delays in decision making and less emphasis on the long-term survival of the business.

The entrepreneur can avoid these problems through preparation and sensitivity of how to handle rapid growth. If the entrepreneur cannot resolve these issues internally, he or she should hire an outside consultant to provide an objective view of how to manage the venture during this stage of its life cycle.

---

[5]M. Henricks, "The Bigger the Better," *Entrepreneur,* December 1990, pp. 131–37.

TABLE 12–2   Problems during Rapid Growth

- It can cover up weak management, poor planning, or wasted resources.
- It dilutes effective leadership.
- It causes the venture to stray from its goals and objectives.
- It leads to communication barriers between departments and individuals.
- Training and employee development are given little attention.
- It can lead to stress and burnout.
- Delegation is avoided and control is maintained by only the founders, creating bottlenecks in management decision making.
- Quality control is not maintained.

It may also be necessary to put a limit on the venture's growth. This may sound like blasphemy, but a new venture must try to stay within its capabilities. Standing back and reflecting on the goals and objectives of the venture is an important part of the control of growth. The future financial well-being of the venture may necessitate a more controlled growth rate. The limits to the growth of any venture will depend on the availability of a market, capital, and management talent. Growth that is too rapid can stretch these limits and lead to serious financial problems and possible bankruptcy.

MARKET ANALYSIS

The need for information has been emphasized throughout this book. One area for which information is critical is the marketplace. To objectively evaluate the needs of consumers and to assess potential opportunities to improve the profitability of the new venture, the entrepreneur may need to collect secondary or primary data. He or she can use this information in writing the marketing plan, developing new products, promotion, pricing, or forecasting sales.

Secondary Data

Information that already exists is called *secondary data*. Thus, the entrepreneur can avoid costly surveys or having to hire someone to carry out the primary data collection. Examples of secondary data sources are listed in Table 12–3. Many of the publications, particularly those published by government agencies, trade associations, or private firms, are generally available at a local library or university.

Secondary data most often provide general information for the entrepreneur on market trends, industry activities, competitor activities, and demographic profiles of geographically defined segments of the population. What they do not provide is information specifically related to the entrepreneur's problem. Thus, secondary data provide a starting point for marketing research. If there is need for more information, the entrepreneur should consider primary data.

TABLE 12–3   Sources of Secondary Data

- Internal Sources—Includes all financial records, sales reports, invoices, inventory records, memos, and past research reports.
- Government Publications—Examples are *Statistical Abstract, County and City Data Book, U.S. Industrial Outlook, Census of Manufacturers,* and *Population Census.* Each provides a variety of data on demographics, industry activity, and trends.
- Government Agencies—The Small Business Administration, Better Business Bureau, and the Commerce Department have publications with information on various industries and markets.
- Periodicals and Books—Trade publications, *Business Periodical Index, Moody's,* and *Standard & Poor's* all provide important industry statistics. Business magazines and newspapers such as *Business Week, Fortune, Inc., Forbes,* and *The Wall Street Journal* can provide insight on industry and market trends.
- Commercial Data—There are many services (most are very expensive) such as A. C. Nielsen, Simmons, Dun and Bradstreet, Market Research Corporation of America, SAMI, Starch, and so on. Libraries will often subscribe to some of these services.

Primary Data

Information that is obtained for a specific need or purpose is called *primary data.* This is new information can help the entrepreneur in addressing specific issues such as the reaction of customers to a new package, the effect of an advertising campaign, the consumer's intention to buy, the needs of consumers, and so on.

Primary data collection requires the entrepreneur to make decisions regarding the research methodology, methods of contacting respondents, and the sampling plan. Figure 12–4 lists the steps in collecting primary data. Assuming that secondary data have been collected, the primary data needs may be more clearly determined. For example, an entrepreneur is trying to determine the need for a replacement glass business in the suburbs of a major metropolitan area. The service would replace fogged or clouded double-pane windows. This generally is caused by wind and moisture that breaks the seal and makes the window inefficient and visually undesirable. Secondary data on the age and types of homes and demographics would identify communities that should be surveyed. The entrepreneur would then use the primary data to determine if there would be a market for this service and to learn how to most effectively market to this segment.

After identifying two or three communities, the entrepreneur must determine which sampling procedure to use. This, as indicated in Figure 12–4, will be affected by the surveying method and the questionnaire, considering such factors as time and costs. The entrepreneur in our example, keeping in mind his low budget, would then evaluate the following options.

FIGURE 12–4   Steps in Collecting Primary Data

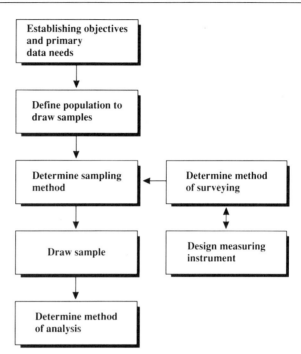

• *Personal Interviews*—These are usually the most expensive of all survey methods. There is an advantage of face-to-face contact and flexibility to ask probing questions. However, the entrepreneur in our example could satisfy the objectives of the survey using another method.

• *Telephone Interviews*—Taking a random sample from the telephone book or using a random-digit dialing system could be very effective for the new glass venture.[6] The major problem will be that interviewees will suspect that the interviewer is trying to sell them something. The only costs in this approach are time and long-distance telephoning.

• *Mail Surveys*—This probably results in the lowest cost per interview if there is an adequate response rate. Many mail surveys result in poor return rates (less than 10%), which can bias the result. However, with the availability of good mailing lists, this method can provide a specific focus on those individuals most likely to purchase the service.

---

[6]See G. A. Churchill, Jr., *Marketing Research: Methodological Foundations*, 4th ed. (New York: The Dryden Press, 1987), pp. 243–46.

In our example, the entrepreneur can probably most effectively, and at little cost, conduct a telephone survey of one or two of the selected communities. At this point, he or she would have to design a questionnaire to address the major issues, but it must be short and concise enough to be completed on the telephone.[7]

Once collected, the data would then be analyzed. For most purposes, the entrepreneur can calculate percentages and frequency distributions for each question. Cross tabulations of key variables can then help provide the market and identify the most appropriate marketing strategy.

PROMOTING THE NEW VENTURE

In the early stages of a new venture, the entrepreneur should focus his or her effort in trying to develop an awareness of the products or services offered. Thus, the initial emphasis of a new venture should be to get some publicity in local media.

Publicity is free advertising in which a trade magazine, newspaper, magazine, radio, or T.V. program finds it of public interest to do a story on the new venture. Local media such as newspapers, radio, or cable T.V. encourage entrepreneurs to participate in their programs or stories. The entrepreneur can increase the opportunity for getting this exposure by preparing a news release and sending it to as many possible media sources as he or she can.

In issuing a news release, the entrepreneur should follow these steps:[8]

1. Identify the news release as such when mailing it to the editor.

2. Begin the release with the service or product to be marketed.

3. List the features and benefits of the product or service to the customer.

4. Make the written news release about 100 to 150 words. This is especially important for print media.

5. Include a high-quality, glossy photograph of the product or of the service being performed.

For radio or T.V., the entrepreneur should identify programs that may encourage local entrepreneurs to participate. A telephone call and follow-up with written information enhance the opportunity to appear on any of these programs.

Free publicity can only introduce the company and its services in a general format. Advertising, however, can be focused to inform specific potential customers of the service—what they will receive, why they should buy it, where they can buy it, and how much it may cost. The entrepreneur may need to hire an advertising agency to effectively develop the advertising program.

---

[7]For assistance in designing a questionnaire, see W. Dillon, T. Madden, and N. Firtle, *Marketing Research in a Marketing Environment*, 2nd ed. (Homewood, IL: Richard D. Irwin, 1990), pp. 376–423.

[8]R. D. Hisrich, and M. P. Peters, *Marketing Decisions for New and Mature Products*, 2nd ed. (New York: Macmillan Publishing Company, 1991), pp. 392–94.

Selecting an Advertising Agency

An advertising agency can provide many promotional services to the entrepreneur. The agency itself may even cater to new ventures or specialize in the specific market the entrepreneur is trying to target. Traditionally, the advertising agency has been perceived as an independent business organization composed of creative and business people who develop, prepare, and place advertising in media for its customers. The agency can even assist the entrepreneur in marketing research or in developing the strategy needed to market the product or service.

Before selecting an agency, the entrepreneur might find it useful to obtain recommendations from friends or agencies such as the SBA. Local chambers of commerce or trade associations can also be of some assistance. In any event, regardless of what agency is considered, the entrepreneur should determine whether it can fulfill all of the needs of the new venture.

Table 12-4 provides a checklist of items the entrepreneur may consider in evaluating an agency. It is especially important to meet the agency staff and to talk with some of its clients to be sure that it is the right choice. All of the items in the checklist could be evaluated subjectively or by assigning some scale value (i.e., 1 to 7) in order to identify the best agency for the new venture.

TABLE 12–4   Checklist for Selecting an Advertising Agency

Item	*Value*
1. Location of agency	_____
2. Organizational structure of agency	_____
3. Public relations department services	_____
4. Research department and facilities	_____
5. Creativity of agency's staff	_____
6. Education and professional qualifications of agency's top management	_____
7. Media department's qualifications and experience	_____
8. Qualifications and experience of account executives (if identifiable)	_____
9. Interest or enthusiasm shown toward firm and new product	_____
10. Copywriters' qualifications and experience	_____
11. Art director's qualifications and experience	_____
12. Recommendations by other clients	_____
13. Experience and success with new products	_____
14. Ability of agency to work with the company's advertising department	
15. Extra services provided	_____
16. Accounting and billing procedures	_____
17. Overall formal presentation	_____

The advertising agency should support the marketing program and assist the entrepreneur in getting the product or service effectively launched. The costs or budget for advertising may be small initially, but certain agencies are willing to invest their resources because of the potential growth of the venture and hence the advertising budget.

HIRING EXPERTS

Most of this chapter focuses on areas such as financial analysis, marketing research, and promotion that the entrepreneur may have no expertise in. If that is the case, he or she should hire outside experts. Trying to save money by performing these tasks alone could end up costing the entrepreneur more than the experts' fees.

There are usually accountants, financial experts, marketing researchers, and advertising agencies that cater to new ventures and small businesses. These firms can usually be identified from local business contacts, the SBA, trade associations, or even the Yellow Pages.

SUMMARY

This chapter deals with some of the key managerial areas of expertise that will be required to keep the business going in the growth phases of the start-up. These areas, such as financial analysis, marketing research, and advertising, may necessitate the hiring of outside experts if the entrepreneur cannot fulfill these managerial needs.

In the area of financial analysis, the entrepreneur must be concerned with managing cash, assets, debt, and profits. Cash flows must be monitored on a regular basis (usually monthly). Budgeted and actual cash flows should be evaluated when they vary significantly.

Assets can be managed by using the balance sheet. In addition, the entrepreneur will need to control accounts receivable and inventory. If accounts receivable are late or delinquent, the entrepreneur will need to tighten collection procedures. Increases in accounts receivable because of increased credit sales may require short-term financing of receivables to meet short-term cash needs.

Expenses need to be controlled in two ways. First, the entrepreneur must understand that expenses should be allocated by product, region, department, and so on. Otherwise, he or she may inaccurately assess the profitability of any product or service. Accuracy can help the entrepreneur understand which products or services are a problem and perhaps even explain which department, region, or manager is responsible.

Inventory also must be controlled. Too much inventory can be costly to the venture and too little can result in fewer sales because delivery dates cannot be met. FIFO or LIFO accounting may be used to cost inventory (cost of goods). FIFO will generally provide a more realistic value of cost of goods sold unless the cost of inventory is increasing by an abnormal rate or the economy is in a cycle of inflation.

Fixed assets such as equipment may require long-term debt. Long-term debt can be obtained from bank loans, loans from friends or relatives, or, in the case of a corporation, the sale of stock. The sale of stock may require the entrepreneur to give up some equity in the business and hence must be weighed carefully.

Comparing actual costs from the income statement with standard percentages (percentages related to net sales) will be useful in managing the costs and profits of the new venture. The entrepreneur should carefully evaluate costs that are higher than anticipated so that he or she is not surprised later.

Rapid growth brings a number of unique problems to the new venture. These problems usually arise because of weak planning, poor communication, no training or employee development, poor quality control, and a general lack of leadership. The entrepreneur can minimize them through preparedness and sensitivity of how to handle rapid growth when it occurs.

Marketing research may help the entrepreneur ascertain the market potential for the business. First, secondary data should be considered. If primary data are needed, the entrepreneur will take the following steps: establish research objectives, define the population, determine the sampling method, select the method of surveying, design the questionnaire, draw the sample, and determine the method of analysis.

The entrepreneur should consider any free publicity opportunities for the new venture. In addition to publicity, the entrepreneur may need to consider some advertising. Generally, the decision to advertise will require the hiring of an agency unless the entrepreneur has expertise in this area.

13

Managing a More Established Company

CHAPTER OBJECTIVES

1. To discuss the need, benefits, and principles of time management.

2. To identify the factors affecting the growth of the venture.

3. To explain the aspects of negotiation.

4. To discuss the types of joint ventures and their uses.

5. To explain the concepts of acquisitions and mergers.

6. To discuss the appropriateness and uses of leveraged buyouts.

STEVE JOBS

Steve Jobs, the adopted son of Paul and Carla Jobs, grew up near San Francisco, California. When he was in junior high school, his family moved to Los Gatos, south of San Francisco, in the heart of what would be called "Silicon Valley." From an early age, Steve showed an interest in figuring out how things worked, and by high school was obsessed with electronics. He went to weekly talks given for teenagers by local Hewlett-Packard engineers, and when he needed parts for a class electronics project, Steve decided to call Bill Hewlett directly. Impressed with Job's single-mindedness, the CEO gave him the necessary parts and helped arrange summer employment.

Steve's single-mindedness did not extend to academic matters, however. After graduating from high school, Steven spent one semester at Reed College in Oregon and then two years hanging out—"wandering through the labyrinths of post-adolescent mysticism and post-Woodstock culture," as he later described it. Out of money and no longer supported by his family, he returned home to find a job. Answering an ad that read "Have fun and make money," Steve became the 40th employee of a new company called Atari.

Although designing video games was "fun" and the atmosphere of Atari was laid back, Steve couldn't fit in. Since he was an idea man, not an engineer, the other engineers thought he was brash and arrogant as he championed his visions. Eventually Steve worked only at night to avoid them and started spending time with the Homekrew Computer Club, of which his former high school friend, Steve Wozniak, was a member. Wozniak was a calculator chip engineer at Hewlett-Packard (HP) who in his spare time had developed a video game called Breakout. Accepting a challenge from Atari's president to design a game using fewer than 50 computer chips, the two Steves modified Breakout to claim the $700 prize. Atari got what became one of its best-selling games and the world got its first taste of the duo that would drive Apple Computers.

Wozniak had been tinkering with computer designs since his high school days and, with the help of ideas passed around at the Homekrew Computer Club, he was able to design and build the first easy-to-use personal computer. When HP said they were not interested in a hobby project that connected to a home TV,

Wozniak accepted their verdict. It was Jobs who saw the potential and thought: Why give away the schematics at a club meeting when they could be selling a finished product?

With Homekrew members and a local computer store showing interest, Jobs sold his Volkswagen microbus and Wozniak his HP calculator to raise $1,300 to open a primitive production line. Apple I was born. Building computers in Jobs's parents' garage out of parts hustled on credit, they sold about 200 of the primitive computers in 1976. "I didn't even know what '30 days net' meant," Jobs later admitted.

As back orders began to pile up, Jobs discovered his true calling—being a wheeler-dealer, a dynamo, an energy source. He repeatedly visited the area's top public relations specialist, Regis McKenna, until McKenna broke down and accepted Apple as a client. In attempting to raise capital, Jobs approached Don Valentine, a well-known investor in new firms; Valentine dismissed the sandals-and jeans-clad Jobs as a "renegade from the human race." However, A. C. Markkula, a former marketing manager for Intel, pledged his expertise and $250,000 of his own money for an equal partnership. Through Mr. Markkula, Apple was able to establish a line of credit with the Bank of America and obtain financing from two venture-capital firms.

When it became apparent that the Apple I was really only a gadget, Wozniak added a typewriter-style keyboard, video terminal, disk drive, and power supply—the Apple II. But it was Jobs who conceptualized what the machine should be able to do and how it should look. He insisted on designing an attractive housing and writing thorough and concise operating manuals. The Apple II was an immediate success when it was first sold in 1977, essentially creating its own market.

Apple dominated the business market by default, with sales growing to over $200 million by 1980. Then two catastrophic blows were dealt: The Apple III was a failure when released (14,000 had to be recalled because of serious mechanical problems) and IBM introduced its PC. Almost overnight the IBM PC became the industry standard and by 1984 it had almost twice the market share of Apple. The personal computer market defined by Apple was changing without Apple responding.

During the rapid growth years of the late 70s, Apple had come to depend more and more on the marketing and management skills of experts hired from other industries. Feeling that the Apple II and the IBM PC were boring and technologically clumsy machines, Jobs assembled a group of Apple employees to work on a project sometimes called his "back-to-the-garage fantasy." As chairman of the board of directors as well as project head, he got few arguments from his co-workers. The MacIntosh was introduced in late 1983 as a "computer for the rest of us." Targeted for the business market, the Mac had several drawbacks as an office machine: it was not easy to use; the internal software was complicated and slow; it could not be customized; little software was written for it; and it was not IBM-compatible. The Mac sold well to individuals but not to business customers.

Job's obsession with following his own vision of what a personal computer should be created problems within the company. He refused to allow Apple II to be marketed as a business computer and insulted managers working for other divisions. Finally, in 1985, Jobs was asked to resign from the company he helped found.

Although his career at Apple is over, his computer dreams are not dead. In an interview shortly after leaving Apple, he said, "What I'm best at doing is finding a group of talented people and making things with them. You have to set double goals, but you still have to have a very lofty vision. You need a well-articulated vision that people can follow."

Jobs is once again back at it with a new dream partially funded from the sale of $21 million in Apple Computer stock. According to him, "Passion is what drives an entrepreneur," and his passion is a great product. "You have to go hide away with people that really understand the technology but also really care about the customers, and dream up the next breakthrough."

Steve's newest company, NeXT, Inc., hopes they have come up with that next breakthrough in the computer industry: an aesthetically pleasing machine with the power of a workstation in a package the size of a PC. The target market for this new machine has changed from colleges to business. Various factors influenced this change during the development of the NeXT machine. One was the price. By the time the machine was introduced, it was doubtful that colleges could afford it. Also factoring into the decision were the new allies (including some former enemies like IBM) and new enemies (including some former allies like John Sculley) that Steve made while creating NeXT, Inc. Now Jobs has more than just a new machine, he has a second chance to prove that he can manage an established corporation.

As was the case with Steve Jobs and the turbulent growth of Apple Computer, it is frequently difficult for an entrepreneur to both manage and expand the venture created. While some entrepreneurs are able to bridge the gap and successfully manage an expanding company, others cannot. An entrepreneur needs to assess his or her liabilities in the management area, identifying when it is necessary to turn the reins over to someone else in order for the venture to expand, grow, and in some cases even survive. As a new venture grows there can be a need for more and more administrative domain. At times, a new infusion of the entrepreneurial spirit that formed the venture is needed. This infusion, called *intrapreneurship* (entrepreneurship in an existing organization), is the focus of Chapter 17. Sometimes an entrepreneur forgets the basic axiom in every business—the only constant is change. An entrepreneur who understands this axiom will effectively manage change by continually adapting organizational culture, structure, procedures, strategic direction, and products. This requires above all an effective monitoring of the environment by tracking the tasks and needs of the marketplace.

But how does an entrepreneur accomplish this and effectively manage an expanding company? Are there any management methods or procedures needed for growth and expansion? This chapter looks at some of the issues in managing an expanding company—time management, control, and negotiations—as well as some of the actual techniques for expansion—joint ventures, mergers, acquisitions, and leveraged buyouts.

IMPACT OF NEW VENTURE CREATION AND GROWTH

In the past, economists have felt that large corporations had the most significant impact on economic development through job creation and new product introduction. Recently, this conventional wisdom has been challenged by research indicating that the small business/entrepreneurial sector is the main component of any economic unit, whether that be an area of a country or the entire country itself. Of the 20 million firms in the United States, 25 percent are farms, 25 percent are part-time, 25 percent are self-run with no employees, and only 25 percent have employees. Revenues for these firms have a similar skewed distribution: 12 million firms have revenues less than $25,000, 6 million firms have revenues between $25,000 to $100,000, 1.2 million have revenues from $100,000 to $1 million, and .8 million have revenues $1 million and above. Of these 20 million firms, 65,000 generate 93 percent of all net new jobs, while approximately 500,000 new ventures are started each year. Most of these start-ups are small, part-time, or temporary businesses.

Many of these small start-up firms will remain small as some firms are not growth-oriented. Some entrepreneurs do not want to grow their venture, choosing instead to pursue other interests, spend more time with the family, or develop other businesses activities.

The growth of a new entrepreneurial venture is a function of both market and management factors. The pervasive market factors are the nature and size of the target market and the window of opportunity. The window of opportunity reflects the existing competitive conditions, the degree of technological advancement, and the amount of protection in the form of patents, copyrights, and trade secrets.

The management factors affecting growth involve the ability to manage growth and the psychological propensity for growth. A useful system for looking at growth appears in Figure 13–1, where firms are classified high or low in terms of their degree of propensity and degree of ability for growth. Statistics for the United States indicate that most new entrepreneurial ventures are life-style or marginal small firms. Few firms have the ability or propensity to achieve solid growth, and several factors affect the entrepreneur's management of those that do. The first, and perhaps most important, factor is changing the job of the CEO. In the start-up phase, the entrepreneur/CEO needs to be involved in almost all areas of the venture's operation from production, marketing, finance, accounts receivable, sales, and receiving. As the venture grows, the entrepreneur's participation and primary decision making in all these areas is no longer possible. He

FIGURE 13–1 New Venture Classification System Based on Growth

		Ability to Grow	
		Low	High
Propensity for Growth	High	Life-style small firms	High-growth firms
	Low	Marginal small firms	Successful small growing firms

or she must delegate decision making to others in the venture and spend more time in planning the venture's strategy and overall direction. This can be a difficult task, as some people have problems relinquishing control over something they have created, something they have invested a significant amount of time and energy in creating. Nevertheless, for a new venture to grow, the entrepreneur must delegate authority and responsibility throughout, allowing and even encouraging decision making and creativity at the lowest possible decision level.

This change in the job of the CEO affects the second growth management factor—change in the entrepreneur's behavioral style. Some entrepreneurs feel at ease in their new roles and are excited about stimulating entrepreneurial behavior in others. Others only reluctantly, if at all, accept this new orientation. Companies have an easier time growing if the entrepreneur readily embraces this new behavioral pattern and encourages entrepreneurship, or more appropriately, intrapreneurship, to permeate the entire venture.

A third factor affecting growth is the difficulty of managing a more complex company. A typical start-up venture is very flat, with all the strategic decisions concentrated, short-run, and episodic in nature. With only scarce resources available, such ventures rent necessary equipment as much as possible and make financing decisions on a requested sequential basis. As the small entrepreneurial venture grows, a bureaucratic, hierarchical organizational structure tends to develop. Such a structure has a developed and detailed reporting system, requiring that certain rules and procedures be followed when a certain set of circumstances occurs. This bureaucratic structure can stifle the entrepreneurial spirit that actually helped grow the venture.

The final factor affecting growth is the age of both the entrepreneur and the venture. As previously discussed, most entrepreneurs start their first significant venture in their 30s, and there is only so much energy available to start and grow new ventures. Some entrepreneurs find that a venture ceases to be the fun experience it once was after it has been in existence for some years. Instead of an entrepreneurial philosophy, a management philosophy is needed to direct and grow the venture. At this stage, many entrepreneurs leave and start a new venture with its own new entrepreneurial excitement.

Several strategies are possible to successfully grow a new venture.[1] One of these is that the entrepreneur immediately sees his new venture as a large entity. From the beginning of the venture, the entrepreneur makes decisions that promote the eventual emergence of a large company. There is no small-firm philosophy guiding any management decisions. Another success strategy is for the entrepreneur to hire and train the individuals in anticipation of the needs for growth. Care must be taken in implementing this strategy to avoid having costly resources on board without the needed sales and revenues to support them. A third strategy for successful growth is to avoid establishing a bureaucratic structure. Keeping decision making at the lowest possible level and operating units small and versatile helps to preserve the entrepreneurial spirit. This strategy is probably the easiest to implement as it requires only minimal change from the original operation of the venture.

A final success strategy is to give employees a stake in the future performance of the company. The founding entrepreneur should realize that some of his or her motivations for starting the new venture may also exist in some employees. Giving these employees an ownership position in the company can motivate them to work even harder for the success of the company. This increased effort and initiative can help grow the venture successfully through the new intrapreneurial spirit.

TIME MANAGEMENT

One of the most frequently mentioned problems of entrepreneurs is encapsulated in the phrase, "If I only had more time." This is a common concern for all busy people. It seems that no one has enough time. Time is the entrepreneur's most precious yet most limited resource. It is a unique quantity—an entrepreneur cannot store it, rent it, hire it, or buy it. With its supply being inelastic, it is totally perishable and irreplaceable. Everything requires it and it passes at the same rate for everyone. While important throughout the life of the venture, time is particularly critical at start-up and during growth and expansion of the venture. No matter what an entrepreneur does, today's ration of time is 24 hours, and yesterday's time is already history.

Even so, entrepreneurs typically spend their time (as we all do) with a prodigality that would shame even the laziest individual. Few entrepreneurs use time effectively and no one ever reaches perfection. Entrepreneurs can always make better use of their time, and the more they strive to do so, the more it will enrich their venture as well as their personal lives.

---

[1]These and other success strategies are discussed in D. C. Hambrick & L. M. Crozier, "Stumblers and Stars in the Management of Rapid Growth," *Journal of Business Venturing* 1, no. 1 (Winter 1985), pp. 31–46.

Generally, the typical individual can be three or four times more productive without ever increasing the number of working hours. This reflects the basic principle that it is more important to do the right things than to do things right. This principle implies the key to effective time management—prioritizing the items that should be accomplished in any given day. Either consciously or by default, an entrepreneur necessarily establishes priorities that reflect his or her personality and values.

How does one get more out of the time spent? How does one effectively manage time? **Time management** means investing time to get what you decide you want out of life, including what you want out of the venture created. This definition assumes that entrepreneurs know what they want out of life—making time management a goal-oriented action. It implies that they have focused values about their ventures, work, family, social activities, possessions, and selves.

Why does the problem of time management exist for the entrepreneur? It is basically due to a lack of information and a lack of motivation. The entrepreneur must want to manage his or her time effectively and then spend the time necessary to acquire the information necessary to accomplish this. Effective time management starts with an understanding of some benefits that will result.

Benefits of Time Management

The entrepreneur reaps numerous benefits from effectively managing his or her time, some of which are listed in Table 13–1. The first of these—increased productivity—reflects the fact that there is always enough time to accomplish the most important things. Through a conscious effort and increased focus, the entrepreneur can determine what is most important to the success and growth of the venture and focus on these rather than on less important or more enjoyable ones; an entrepreneur must learn to focus on the majors, not the minors.

TABLE 13–1   Time Management for the Entrepreneur

Typical Payoffs from Time Management

Increased productivity
More job satisfaction
Improved interpersonal relations
Reduced time anxiety and tension
Better health

Basic Principles of Time Management

The Principle of Desire
The Principle of Effectiveness
The Principle of Analysis
The Principle of Teamwork
The Principle of Prioritized Planning
The Principle of Reanalysis

This overt action will lead to the second benefit—increased job satisfaction. Getting more important things done and being more successful at helping the venture grow will give the entrepreneur more job satisfaction.

There will also be an improvement in the esprit de corps of the venture as the entrepreneur experiences less time pressure, better results, and more job satisfaction. While the total time the entrepreneur spends with other individuals in the company may in fact decrease, it will be of better quality, allowing him or her to improve interrelations. Also, more time becomes available for the entrepreneur to spend with family and friends.

A fourth benefit is that the entrepreneur will experience less time anxiety and tension. Worry, guilt, and other emotions tend to reduce mental effectiveness and efficiency, making decisions less effective. Effective time management reduces concerns and anxieties, allowing better and faster decisions to be made.

All of these benefits culminate in a final one for the entrepreneur—better health. Large amounts of energy and persistence are needed for the growth as well as for the start of a venture, as was discussed in Chapter 1. High energy levels and long working hours require good health, and poor control of time often leads to mental and physical fatigue, poor eating habits, and curtailment of exercise. If there is one thing an entrepreneur needs to help the venture grow, it is good health. And good health is a by-product of good time management.

Basic Principles

How does an entrepreneur develop good time management? By first recognizing that he or she is a time waster—wasting the most important time of all, his or her own. This insight leads the entrepreneur to value time and to change any personal attitudes and habits as needed. This is embodied in the Principle of Desire (see Table 13–1). Like effective dieting, effective time management depends on willpower and self-discipline. It requires that the entrepreneur have a real desire to optimize his or her time.

Second, the entrepreneur should adhere to the Principle of Effectiveness; that is, he or she should automatically focus on the most important issues, even when under pressure. Whenever possible, an entrepreneur should try to complete each task in a single session. This requires that he or she sets aside enough time to accomplish the task correctly. For example, a report should not be drafted until all the necessary data is at hand. While quality is of course important, perfectionism is not and often leads only to procrastination. The entrepreneur must take care not to take time trying to make a small improvement in one thing when time could be better spent on something else.

To manage time effectively, the entrepreneur needs to know how his or her time is presently being spent. Following the Principle of Analysis will help accomplish this. Using a time sheet with 15-minute intervals, the entrepreneur should record and analyze the time spent during the past two weeks. This analysis will reveal some areas of wasted time and provide the basis for prioritizing the tasks to be accomplished. It is particularly important for the entrepreneur to develop methods for handling recurrent situations. Checklists should be developed and kept handy. Handouts on the company and its operation should be prepared for visitors and the press. Standardized forms and procedures should be developed for all recurring events and operations.

The essence of time management is embodied in an important principle that the entrepreneur employed in starting the venture—the Principle of Teamwork. During the time analysis, one thing will become very apparent to the entrepreneur—the small amount of time that is totally under his or her control. The entrepreneur needs to help members of the management team become more sensitive to the time management concept when dealing with other individuals in the organization. Each team member should try to employ the same effective practices of time management.

The Principle of Prioritized Planning includes elements of all the previously mentioned principles of effective time management. Each day, an entrepreneur needs to list the things to be accomplished and indicate the degree of importance, perhaps by using a simple scale such as 1 being most important, 2 somewhat important, and 3 moderately important. By indicating on a 3 × 5 card the most important items to be accomplished that day, the entrepreneur can focus on them, getting to the ones of lesser importance as time permits. This preordination, planning, and focus on the key issues is fundamental to time management as it allows each individual to accomplish the most important things. Some entrepreneurs are most efficient in the morning, some during the afternoon, and some at night. The most efficient period of the day should be set aside to address the most important issues.

As with any procedure implemented, the entrepreneur should periodically review the objectives and the achievement of them. This is the Principle of Reanalysis. Tasks should be delegated whenever possible. The secretary and close assistants should be well trained and encouraged to take initiative. The secretary should sort out all correspondence and draft routine letters for the entrepreneur's signature. The office system should be well organized with a daily diary, a card index, reminder list, operation board, and an efficient pending file. All incoming calls should be filtered and a time set for making and receiving calls except for those most critical. All meetings should be analyzed to see if they are being run effectively. If not, the person who runs the meetings should be trained in how to conduct them. Finally, any committee in the venture should be carefully scrutinized in terms of its results. Committees tend to tie up personnel, slow down decisions, and have the habit of multiplying themselves beyond their need. Through all these efforts the entrepreneur will become a time-saver, not a time-server. This efficient use of time enables the entrepreneur to expand the venture properly, increasing productivity and lessening encroachment of the venture on his or her private life.

NEGOTIATION

Developing and expanding a new enterprise requires the ability to negotiate. Even though it is important, negotiation is usually not a skill well developed by the entrepreneur, particularly women entrepreneurs. As one woman entrepreneur stated, "A woman entrepreneur should develop her negotiating skills as quickly as possible. It is so important in starting and particularly in expanding a business. Women tend to be weaker in negotiating skills than men. This may reflect the level of issues typically negotiated at home versus in a business situation. These skills can be learned and then must be practiced."

Negotiation is often a misunderstood and ill-defined process. What is negotiation? Negotiation is the process by which parties attempt to resolve a conflict by agreement. While a resolution is not always possible, the process of negotiation identifies the critical issues in the disagreement and is therefore central to business dealings. In learning and developing negotiation skills, it is important to understand the underlying motivations, the two types of negotiation (distributive and **integrative bargaining**), the tactics involved, and the skills required.[2]

Underlying Motivation

The underlying motivation of negotiation often involves one party attempting to get another to do something the first desires. At times, this second party will not act unless he or she will obtain something in return that suits his or her interests. This motive for a return must be understood in the negotiation process, whether the negotiation is cooperative or competitive.

Another underlying motive of negotiation is habit. Many behavioral patterns can be attributed to a subconscious drive to continue to do things in the same way. Some individuals, for example, feel the need to negotiate even though they are happy with the present terms of the arrangement. This drive to negotiate just for negotiation's sake makes the process more important to the individual than the actual outcome. Some individuals develop a reputation for such behavior. The entrepreneur must be careful to avoid such negotiations as well as to avoid his or her own predictability in a negotiation process. Periodic "non sequitur" behavior ensures that predictability will not occur.

Cooperative Negotiation—Integrative Bargaining

Integrative bargaining involves **cooperative negotiation** between the negotiating parties. In this situation, the entrepreneur is willing to let the other side achieve its desired outcome while maintaining a commitment to his or her own

---

[2]A thorough discussion of negotiation can be found in R. E. Walton, & R. B. McKersie, *A Behavioral Theory of Labor Negotiations* (New York: McGraw-Hill, 1965).

goals. In a sense, integrative bargaining is actually joint problem solving based on the concept of rational decision making. A model of this process depicts the negotiation flow moving from establishing objectives, to establishing criteria, to analyzing cause-and-effect relationships involved, to developing and evaluating alternatives, to selecting an alternative and an action plan (see Figure 13–2). To be complete, this rational decision process requires that the outcomes be measured once implementation begins. The effectiveness of the decisions made through this process depends on the technical adequacy of such things as information and the commitment of the parties involved to implement the decision reached.

The implementation of this **rational decision model** in an integrative bargaining situation involves several steps. First, the problem must be clearly identified. All the parties in the negotiation should exchange their views on the problem instead of blaming the other parties or demanding a specific outcome. Each party involved must be genuinely interested in solving the problem and understanding the underlying concerns of the others involved. Meetings need to be rescheduled frequently, with each person involved having the ability to convene a meeting whenever necessary. Advance notice of each meeting must be given to allow all participants to prepare. Each meeting should have an agenda of items, the majority of which should have a high probability of resolution. Each agenda item should be stated in a way that allows for open discussion and integrative bargaining to reach a mutually agreeable solution. In other words, it should be stated in terms of the problem, not a proposed solution.

The second step in effective integrative bargaining is searching for alternative solutions. In so doing, the entrepreneur and other parties involved should remember that it is as important to uncover areas of agreement as areas of diver-

FIGURE 13–2 The "Rational" Model for Decision Making

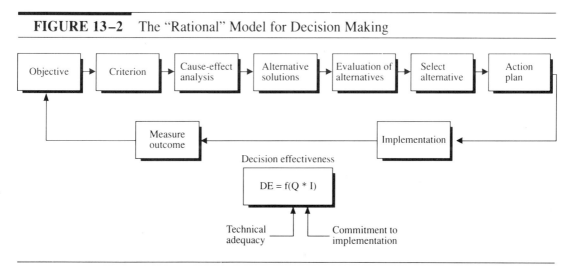

Source: C. Jackson, Working paper, University of Tulsa, October 1987.

gence. This requires that concrete terms be used and appropriate ground rules be established. It is much easier to find a solution to a problem stated in specific rather than general terms. Similarly, it is much easier to develop alternatives under ground rules that encourage trust and respect. Through frequent preliminary discussions, all parties can air tentative solutions and ideas; they can then develop and refine those ideas before formally considering them. This informal, exploratory discussion of a possible solution reduces the likelihood of immediate rejection. Since a solution to one problem may affect solutions to others, all parties involved must maintain flexibility, placing limited emphasis on the order and sequencing of the items discussed. The techniques and frameworks used should differ depending on the specific problem at hand. Integrative bargaining occurs more quickly when the parties involved sense a high likelihood of success. This requires that easier items are dealt with first, with any difficult items being laid aside temporarily if an impasse is reached. Negotiators should not follow a rigid formula in developing this atmosphere for success. Creative solutions do not come from following a systematic procedure since the creative process is unpredictable and spontaneous.

Finally, as indicated in the model of rational decision making, the best alternative solution must be selected. This requires the establishment of an open, honest relationship that allows each party to indicate when something is wrong and accurately report his or her preferences and range of latitude in each problem area. This is the area most susceptible to distortion and further problems. Inadvertent distortion can be most easily avoided by using as much specific data as is available. Specificity not only helps eliminate selective perception but builds an atmosphere of trust between participants. Also, it should be remembered that a problem item divided into parts is more easily solved than one in total.

Competitive Negotiation—Distributive Bargaining

Probably even more central for the successful expansion of a business is the entrepreneur's effectiveness in distributive bargaining. Distributive bargaining is essential to the successful start-up of a company as well as its expansion through joint ventures, mergers, acquisitions, and leveraged buyouts. In contrast to integrative bargaining, distributive bargaining does not allow the other party to achieve his or her goals. There is a fixed pie to be divided, which means that the larger the opponent's share, the smaller the entrepreneur's. Since there is no trust between the parties involved, they can reach a solution only through a series of modified positions of compromise and concession. In this competitive adversarial bargaining arena, the agenda items and their positioning are issues as each party tries to discover the other's goals, values, and perceptions. Of course, some problems involve more conflict of interest than others. The amount of conflict usually revolves around the differing economic objectives and attitudes of the parties involved. When the entrepreneur and the other party have conflicting economic objectives, successful distributive bargaining requires that each must compromise somewhat his or her objective. The directly competing claims on a fixed, limited economic resource (such as the amount of the 100 percent equity in the venture) requires concessions in allocating the shares. Since each party brings to the table different attitudes shaped by the prevailing social, economic, organizational, and technological forces, the disparity in them is often more difficult to overcome than differences in economic objectives.

The key to successful distributive bargaining is for the entrepreneur to discover the goals and perceptions of the other party through direct and/or indirect methods. Indirect methods include discussing the person with anyone who has had previous contact with him or her, such as your employees, the party's employees, or outside individuals; carefully reviewing all previous written and verbal correspondence with the party; and walking around the party's business to get a feel of its vitality and direction. The entrepreneur should employ each of these indirect methods whenever possible to get a feel for the other party's goals and drives so that a strategy can be planned before the actual negotiation commences.

The entrepreneur should also use more direct methods to obtain some insight into the other party. Whenever possible, he or she should meet informally with representatives of the other company, probing them to determine their levels of preparation. Particular emphasis should be directed to the weakest member of the team. Frequently, great insight can be obtained from this individual's responses to laid-back, almost innocent questions.

Several other direct methods employed during the negotiation process can also reveal significant clues. One of these is for the entrepreneur to exaggerate his level of impatience. This often forces the other party to prematurely reveal the amount of bargaining room left. Another method employs the principle of "nonsequiturization." In other words, at a crucial moment in the negotiation the entrepreneur should take on an entirely different posture than he or she has employed throughout. This can be accomplished by making a sudden shift in manners, argument, or demands. For example, this shift can take the form of an attack if a laid-back approach had been maintained previously.

Whether direct or indirect methods are used, an entrepreneur skillful at negotiation attempts to determine the **settlement range** of the other party. The settlement range is the area of values in which a mutually agreeable bargain can be reached. This area is between the resistance points of the parties involved and can be either positive or negative, as indicated in the example in Figure 13–3. In the positive settlement range, the resistance points of the two parties are compatible. In this situation, both parties would rather be involved in the deal than have a work stoppage as in the case of the union settlement in Figure 13–3. The opposite is true when a negative settlement range exists. In this situation, the resistance points are not compatible and it will be difficult to reach an agreement that would be even minimally acceptable to the two parties.

The key to good negotiation is the ability to manipulate the other party's perception of the likely settlement point to a more favorable position for you. This can be accomplished through several strategies. One of these calls for the

---

FIGURE 13–3   Settlement Ranges in Distributive Bargaining

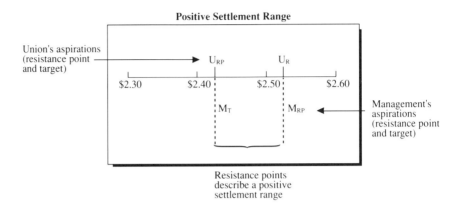

Positive Settlement Range

Union's aspirations (resistance point and target) →

U_{RP} U_R

$2.30 $2.40 $2.50 $2.60

M_T M_{RP}

Management's aspirations (resistance point and target) ←

Resistance points describe a positive settlement range

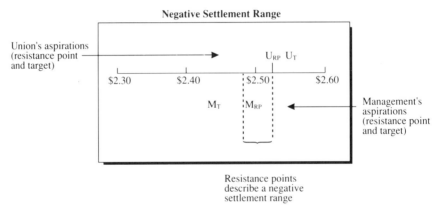

Negative Settlement Range

Union's aspirations (resistance point and target) →

U_{RP} U_T

$2.30 $2.40 $2.50 $2.60

M_T M_{RP}

Management's aspirations (resistance point and target) ←

Resistance points describe a negative settlement range

Source: R. E. Walton & R. B. McKerse, *A Behavior Theory of Labor Negotiations* (New York: McGraw-Hill, 1965), p. 43.

entrepreneur to indicate higher initial demands than he or she actually desires. These high demands, along with a consistent image, can often move the other party to a different, more favorable, position. Similar results can often be achieved by the entrepreneur indicating an overly strong commitment to a particular position. This position needs to be clearly stated, usually through public statements; implied needs should be clearly stated, again usually through public statements that also have implied threats of backing out if this position is not achieved. Another strategy involves focusing on the other party. This means either minimizing this party's opportunity to develop a fixed position or enabling the party to easily revise a previously committed position. The former strategy involves avoiding written documentation and media coverage and not being available for communication between formal negotiation sessions. The second tactic—making it easy for the other party to revise a previous position—can be accomplished by establishing that conditions have changed, making the present situation an entirely new one. This change in circumstances can be augmented by appealing to the public good or presenting the new data.

Perhaps the best strategy for the entrepreneur is to bargain in good faith—indicating a willingness to bargain and be flexible. This will mean that the entrepreneur will make concessions throughout the negotiation process where warranted, particularly when his or her position is further away from a possible solution than the other party's. Any concessions should be linked to the other party's change or at least to an understanding that certain issues are critical in securing an agreement. This strategy often leads to obtaining a settlement point that is acceptable to both parties, completing the negotiation faster than by using other strategies.

Negotiation Approach

There are many different strategies the entrepreneur can use in negotiations, but it is essential that he or she takes an approach to them. One negotiation approach that is easy to implement has eight steps: prepare, discuss, signal, propose, respond, bargain, close, and agree.[3]

Probably the most critical and yet most often overlooked step in the process is preparation. With all the time pressures, an entrepreneur frequently fails to set aside the necessary time to define what has to be done and to develop objectives, the settlement range, and alternative strategies for accomplishing these objectives before the negotiation commences. The objectives need to be prioritized and back-off positions developed.

The second step is the initial meeting. Here, as well as throughout the negotiation process, it is critical that the entrepreneur listen to the other party in order to determine its direction and goals.

Signaling is one aspect of negotiation that tests the other party's willingness to move toward a solution. Through signaling, the entrepreneur can discern real objections and assess the other party's willingness to change his or her original position. This is accomplished through using a phrase such as "I could never agree to that the way it is stated." The entrepreneur must carefully develop the art of signaling and reading the other party's signals.

Once an agreement to move forward to a closure is reached, a proposition must be laid out for discussion. The proposition serves as the basis for developing the final agreement.

---

[3]This process is adapted from G. Kennedy, J. Benson, & J. McMillan, *Managing Negotiations* (London: Business Books Ltd., 1980) and is discussed in R. D. Hisrich & C. G. Brush, *The Woman Entrepreneur* (Lexington, MA: Lexington Books, 1986), pp. 150–55.

The negotiation approach involves responses to the other party's suggestions. These responses are particularly important once a proposition has been put forth. While a response should take into account the interests and limitations of the other party, it does not necessarily contain concessions. Any concessions granted should reflect the priorities and points of inflexibility of the other party.

Besides response and signaling, another difficult aspect of the negotiation approach is bargaining. In bargaining, the entrepreneur gives up something for something else. At first, to help develop this ability, an entrepreneur can state all bargaining items on a conditional basis: "If I . . . then you. . . ."

Every negotiation needs a closure. Closing the agreement frequently is based on a concession or on a summary. A summary is used when a multitude of issues have been discussed and resolved.

The ideal closing ends in a mutually satisfactory agreement—the ultimate goal of negotiation. This is, after all, the objective of most negotiations—reaching an agreement. Any verbal agreement reached should be detailed in writing as specifically as possible.

Through negotiation, an entrepreneur can expand the original venture. The actual expansion can take the form of a joint venture, merger, acquisition, or leveraged buyout.

JOINT VENTURES

With the increase in business risks, competition, and failures, joint ventures have occurred with increased regularity, involving a wide variety of players.[4] This increase should be no great surprise since joint ventures have been used for a long time by entrepreneurial firms to expand into new businesses and enter new markets. The activity has occurred with significant frequency in newly industrialized areas and in international markets.

What is a joint venture? A joint venture is a separate entity involving two or more active participants as partners. Sometimes called strategic alliances, they involve a wide variety of partners, including universities, other not-for-profit organizations, businesses, and the public sector.[5] Joint ventures have occurred between such rivals as General Motors and Toyota or General Electric and Westinghouse. They have occurred between U.S. and foreign concerns in order to penetrate the international market. A unique example of this type of joint venture was AT&T becoming venture partners with such countries as Italy, Japan, Spain, South Korea, and Thailand.

---

[4]For some different perspectives on joint ventures, see J. McConnell & T. J. Nantell, "Corporate Combinations and Common Stock Returns: The Case of Joint Ventures," *Journal of Finance* 40 (June 1985), pp. 519–36; "Corporate Odd Couples," *Business Week*, July 21, 1986, pp. 100–14; R. Thompson, "Joint Ventures with Industry May Solve Shortage of Education Funds," *Modern Healthcare*, July 15, 1985, p. 224.

[5]For a discussion of some different types of joint ventures, see R. M. Cyert, "Establishing University-Industry Joint Ventures," *Research Management* 28 (January–February 1985), pp. 27–28; F. K. Berlew, "The Joint Venturer—A Way into Foreign Markets," *Harvard Business Review*, July–August 1984, pp. 48–49 and 54.

Historical Perspective

Joint ventures were one of the earliest ways of transacting business. Used by ancient merchants of Babylonia, Phoenicia, and Egypt, they served as a vehicle to conduct commercial trading operations. The use of joint ventures by merchants continued and was particularly prevalent in the 15th and 16th centuries; Great Britain used joint ventures to obtain the resources of distant areas, specifically in India and North America.

Joint ventures were first used in the United States in large-scale projects in mining and the railroads in the 1800s. Their use continued in the 1900s in shipping, oil exploration, and gold. Probably the best-known and largest joint venture in this period was the formation of ARAMCO by four oil companies to develop crude oil reserves in the Middle East. By 1959, about 345 joint ventures were being operated in the United States by some of the largest U.S. corporations.[6] Frequently, these domestic joint ventures are vertical arrangements made between competitors. A joint venture of this type (such as the sharing of a primary aluminum reduction plant as a supply facility) allowed the large economies of scale needed for cost-effective plant operation. From 1960 to 1968, the Federal Trade Commission reported that over 520 domestic joint ventures were formed, primarily in the manufacturing sector by over 1,131 U.S. firms.[7] In the 1980s there was an increase in the formation of joint ventures of various types, particularly on an international basis. For example, in 1983 alone, the number of joint ventures in communications systems and services exceeded the total number of previous joint ventures in that industrial sector. This willingness of entities in the public and private sectors to consider joint venture arrangements as a vehicle for growth is an important breakthrough in strategic planning and thinking.

Types of Joint Ventures

While there are many different types of joint venture arrangements, the most common is still between two or more private-sector companies. For example, Boeing/Mitsubishi/Fuji/Kawasaki entered into a joint venture for the production of small aircraft in order to share technology and cut costs. Agreements in order to cut costs were made between Ford and Measurex in the area of factory automation and General Motors and Toyota in automobiles. Other private-sector joint ventures have had different objectives such as entering new markets (Corning and Ciba-Geigy and Kodak and Cetus), entering foreign markets (AT&T and Olivetti), and raising capital and expanding markets (U.S. Steel and Pohong Iron and Steel).

---

[6]S. E. Boyle, "The Joint Subsidiary: An Economic Appraisal," *Antitrust Bulletin* 5 (1960), pp. 303–18.

[7]S. E. Boyle, "An Estimate of the Number and Size Distribution of Domestic Joint Subsidiaries," *Antitrust Law and Economics Review* 1 (1968), pp. 81–82.

New types of joint ventures are also occurring. A current trend is to form a joint venture for cooperative research. Probably the best known of these is the Microelectronics and Computer Technology Corporation (MCC), formed in 1983 in Austin, Texas. Supported by 13 major U.S. corporations, this for-profit corporation does long-range research with a yearly budget of over $75 million. Individual researchers and scientists are loaned to MCC for up to four years and then return to their competing companies to apply the results of their research activities. MCC retains title to all the resulting knowledge and patents, making them available for license by the companies participating in the program.

A different type of joint venture for research development is the Semi-Conductor Research Corporation, located in Triangle Park, North Carolina. A not-for-profit research organization, it began with the participation of 11 U.S. chip manufacturers and computer companies. The number has grown to over 35 since its inception in 1981. The goal of the corporation is to sponsor basic research and train professional scientists and engineers to be future industry leaders. The major drawback to the organization is that it has no formal mechanism for the transfer of people or the technology, so the results usually end up as published research available to the general public.

Industry-university agreements for the purpose of doing research is another type of joint venture agreement that has seen increasing activity. Two major problems have kept this type of joint venture from proliferating even faster. First, a profit corporation has the objective to obtain tangible results, such as a patent, from its research investment, and many universities also want to share in the possible financial returns from the patent. The second problem revolves around proprietary results versus knowledge dissemination. While the corporation wants the competitive edge offered by retaining all proprietary data found in the research effort, university researchers want to make the knowledge available through research papers. In spite of these problems, numerous industry-university teams have been established. In one joint venture agreement in robotics, for example, Westinghouse retains the patent rights, while Carnegie-Mellon receives a percentage of any license royalties. The university also has the right to publish the research results as long as it withholds from publication any critical information that might adversely affect the patent.

The joint venture arrangement between Celanese Corporation and Yale University for researching the composition and synthesis of enzymes took a somewhat different form. Although the agreement specifies the type of research to be accomplished, the partners share the costs. While Celanese assumes the expense of any needed supplies and equipment for the research, as well as the salaries of the post-doctoral researchers, Yale pays the salaries of the professors involved. The research results can be published only after a 45-day waiting period.

Terms of the joint research venture between Monsanto and Rockefeller University are different from the previous two. Monsanto funds the research to develop knowledge about plant molecular biology. While Rockefeller University retains patent rights and is free to publish the results, Monsanto has the right to further develop the knowledge into marketable products under the applicable licensing agreements.

A more coordinated joint research effort was established for the study of microbiology by W. R. Grace Company and Massachusetts Institute of Technology (MIT). Under this joint venture agreement, researchers at MIT propose research projects for funding to a committee consisting of four managers from W. R. Grace and four MIT professors. While W. R. Grace established the research fund covering all the expenses, MIT, at its sole discretion, can use 20 percent of it to do research in microbiology. MIT can publish the results of the research after a review by W. R. Grace managers for proprietary information. In addition, MIT retains the patents, while W. R. Grace gets a royalty-free license on the research results. MIT, however, can license to other companies for a royalty fee.

As these four examples illustrate, joint ventures between universities and corporations take on a variety of forms, depending on the parties involved and the subject of the research. These and new types of research arrangements should continue to proliferate, particularly as long as government support for university research remains at a minimum level.

A discussion of joint ventures would not be complete without a look at international joint ventures. Since these are discussed in Chapter 18, only an overview will be presented here. The advantages of international joint ventures are fourfold. First, both companies can share in the earnings and growth, even when the venture involves sales and earnings beyond the initial technology or product. Second, the joint venture can have a low cash requirement if the knowledge or patents is capitalized as a contribution to the venture. Third, the joint venture provides ready access to new international markets that otherwise may not be easily attained. Finally, since talent and financing come from all the parties involved, an international joint venture causes less drain on a company's managerial and financial resources than a wholly owned subsidiary.

There are several drawbacks in establishing an international joint venture. First, the business objectives of the joint venture partners can be quite different, which can cause problems in the direction and growth of the new entity. In addition, cultural differences in each company can create managerial difficulties in the new joint venture. Finally, U.S. government policy sometimes can have a negative impact on the direction and operation of the international joint venture.

In spite of these problems, the benefits usually outweigh the drawbacks, as evidenced in the frequency rate of establishing international joint ventures. For example, an international joint venture between General Motors and Fanuc Ltd., a Japanese firm, was established to develop the 20,000 robots needed by GM by 1990 to automate its plants. In this 50–50 joint venture partnership, GM supplied the initial design and Fanuc supplied the engineering and technology to develop and produce the car-painting robots.

Cy/Ro, another example, is an international joint venture between Cyamid (United States) and Rochm (Germany) in the area of acrylic plastics. Cyamid supplied the distribution network and plant space for the new technology, and Rochm had the newest technology in the acrylic plastic field. While both partners want to allow Cy/Ro a high degree of operational autonomy, the high turnover rate has been a problem for German executives, who expect their employees to be well trained in their procedures.

Another type of international joint venture was established between Dow Chemical (United States) and Asaki Chemicals (Japan) to develop and market chemicals on an international basis. Asaki provided the raw materials and was a sole distributor, and Dow provided the technology and obtained distribution in the Japanese market. The arrangement eventually dissolved because of the concerns of the Japanese government and the fundamental difference in motives between the two partners. While Dow was primarily concerned with the profits of the joint venture, Asaki was primarily concerned with having a purchaser for its basic petrochemicals.

Even though there are many instances of international joint ventures dissolving, others are still being established to take advantage of production, technology, and marketing advantages of the partners involved. In any internaional arrangement, care should be taken to ensure that the primary objectives of the two partners are compatible and the overall arrangement has the approval of the governments involved.

Factors in Joint Venture Success

Clearly, not all joint ventures succeed. An entrepreneur needs to assess this method of growth carefully before use. In order to use joint ventures effectively, an entrepreneur needs to understand the factors that help ensure success, as well as the problems involved. One of the most critical factors for success is the accurate assessment of the parties involved and how best to manage the new entity in light of the ensuing relationships. The joint venture will be more effective if the managers involved can work well together. Without this chemistry the joint venture has a high probability of encountering great difficulties and perhaps failure.

A second factor for success involves the symmetry between the partners. This symmetry goes beyond that of management chemistry to objectives and resource capabilities. When one partner feels that he or she is bringing more to the table, or one wants profits and the other product outlet (as was the case in the Asaki Dow international joint venture), problems arise. For a joint venture to be successful, the managers in each parent company, as well as those in the new entity, must concur on the objectives of the joint venture and the level of resources that will be provided. Good relationships must be nurtured between the managers in the joint venture and those in each parent company.

A third factor for success is that the expectations about the results of the joint venture must be reasonable. Far too often, at least one of the partners feels a joint venture will be the cure-all for other corporate problems. Expectations for a joint venture must be realistic.

The final factor for the successful establishment of a joint venture is also essential for the successful start-up of any new business entity—timing. With environments constantly changing, industrial conditions being modified, and markets evolving, a particular joint venture could be a success one year and a failure the next. Intense competition provides a hostile environment and increases the risks of establishing a joint venture. Some environments are just not conducive to success. The entrepreneur must determine whether the joint venture will offer opportunities for growth, or whether it will penalize the company such as by preventing it from entering certain markets.

A joint venture is not a panacea for expanding the entrepreneurial venture. Rather, it should be considered as one of many options for supplementing the resources of the firm and responding faster to competitive challenges and market opportunities. The effective use of joint ventures as a strategy for growth and expansion requires the entrepreneur to carefully appraise the situation and the potential partner(s).

Concerns in Establishing Joint Ventures

Since a joint venture allows the entrepreneur to expand the business through sharing equity, control, and risks with a partner, there is always concern that the new entity will not be able to achieve its strategic objective. The entrepreneur must evaluate whether or not to cooperate in a particular situation and, if so, what type of partner should be involved. The resource contribution of each partner is clearly a concern; perhaps even more problematical is how these resources and other contributions should be valued. The degree of autonomy for the new entity must also be established. Other strategic alternatives to the joint venture such as acquisitions, mergers, and leveraged buyouts should also be considered.

ACQUISITIONS

One method the entrepreneur can use in expanding the business is acquisition. Acquisition is defined as the purchase of an entire company or part of it so that the acquired entity is completely absorbed by the acquiring company and no longer exists as a separate business. This is a different expansion method than mergers, joint ventures, or leveraged buyouts. The act of acquiring a business entails far more than agreement on a price between the parties involved. It also involves evaluating a candidate business and structuring the final deal.

Evaluating the Firm

Gone are the days when an entrepreneur could determine whether a company is a good candidate for acquisition by merely tearing down the company's financial statements and asking a few pointed questions. Shrewd evaluation in today's changing environment focuses not only on management and market potential but also on the company's upside potential, downside risks, and vulnerability to changes in markets and technology. Some of the key factors the entrepreneur should consider in evaluating an acquisition candidate include poor corporate communications, few management tools being used, poorly prepared financial statements, and a low number of new products and new markets entered (see Table 13–2). These indicate the degree to which the candidate firm is ready for the future as well as the amount of work that will be needed following the acquisition.

The evaluation process must begin with financial analysis—analyzing the profit and loss figures, operating statements, and balance sheets for the years of the company's operation, concentrating on the more recent years. Past operating results, particularly those occurring in the last three years, indicate the potential for future performance of the company. Solid ratios and operating figures indicate that the company is healthy and has been well managed. Areas of weakness, such as too much leverage, too little financial control, dated and slowly turning inventory, and poor credit ratings and bad debts should also be carefully evaluated. A firm's financial record does not tell the entire story. Sometimes a firm with an unimpressive financial record is on the verge of a technological breakthrough that will send its sales and profits skyrocketing. Conversely, a company with a good financial record may have problems in the future due to its somewhat obsolete products in its highly competitive or shrinking markets.

In evaluating a firm's product lines, the entrepreneur should study the past, present, and future. The strengths and weaknesses of the firm's past products

---

TABLE 13–2   Key Factors in Evaluating a Firm

- One-person management
- Poor corporate communications
- Few management tools being used
- Insufficient financial controls
- Highly leveraged—thinly capitalized
- Variations and poorly prepared financial statements
- Sales growth with no increase in bottom line
- Dated and poorly managed inventory
- Aging accounts receivable
- No change in products or customers

---

should be investigated, particularly in terms of design features, quality, reliability, unique differential advantage, and proprietary position. The life cycle and present market share of each of the firm's present products should also be evaluated. Is this market share diversified or concentrated among a small number of customers? How do past, present, and potential customers regard the firm's products? What is happening with the market in respect to competition, prices, and margins? The entrepreneur must carefully consider the compatibility of the firm's product lines from a marketing, engineering, and manufacturing perspective. The future of the firm's product lines must be assessed in terms of their rate of market growth or contraction. What are the developing trends in the number of competitors, degree of competition, number of new products being introduced, and the rate of technology? Is there any vulnerability to business cycle changes?

One method for evaluating the product line is to plot sales and margins for each product over time. Known as S or life-cycle curves, they indicate the life expectancy of the product and any developing gaps. For example, even though a firm is highly profitable today, it may not have provided for the future. The S-curve analysis could reveal that all products of this firm are at or near their period of peak profitability.

The future of the firm's products and market position is affected by its research and development. The entrepreneur should carefully probe the nature and depth of the candidate firm's research and development department and engineering capability, assessing their strengths and weaknesses. How can this important yet difficult area be evaluated? Conventional wisdom says to look at the total amount of dollars spent on research and development; however, because of the inefficiencies that usually occur in these expenditures, this only indicates the amount invested and does not present a very accurate picture. The evaluation should instead determine whether the R&D expenditures and programs are directed by the firm's long-range plans and whether the firm has allocated enough money to accomplish the tasks outlined. The output and success of the new products developed should be compared with the expenditures. What is the quantity and quality of the patents produced? How much has R&D contributed to lowered break-even points through improved materials and methods? How much has R&D contributed to increased sales and profits?

Similarly, the entrepreneur should carefully evaluate the firm's entire marketing program and capabilities. While all areas of marketing should be assessed, particular care should be taken in evaluating the quality and capability of the established distribution system, sales force, and manufacturers' representatives. One entrepreneur acquired a firm primarily because of the quality of its sales force. Another acquired a firm to obtain its established distribution system, which allowed access to new markets. The entrepreneur can gain insight into the market orientation and sensitivity of the firm by looking at its marketing research efforts. Does the firm have facts about customer satisfaction, trends in the market, and the state of the art of the technology of the industry? Is this and other information forwarded to the needed managers in a timely manner? Is there a marketing information system in place?

The nature of the manufacturing process—the facilities and skills available—is also important in deciding whether to acquire a particular firm. Are the facilities obsolete? Are they flexible, and can they produce output at a quality and price that will compete over the next three years? The increasing pace of technology requires a more careful appraisal of the manufacturing operation than ever before.

Finally, the entrepreneur must rate the management and key personnel of the candidate firm. The individuals who have contributed positively to the past success in sales and profits of the firm should be identified. Will they stay once the acquisition occurs? Have they established good objectives and then implemented plans to successfully reach these objectives? By comparing previous plans, the entrepreneur can determine whether results have been directed or randomly achieved. Insight into management capability and the firm's morale can be gained through an examination of the turnover in executive ranks. Is it large or concentrated in a given area or type of individual? Has the firm implemented any executive development programs? Is there a strong management team in place?

Structuring the Deal

Once the entrepreneur has identified a good candidate for acquisition, an appropriate deal must be structured. Many techniques are available for acquiring a firm, each having a distinct set of advantages to the buyer and seller. The deal structure involves the parties, the assets, the payment form, and the timing of the payment. For example, all or part of the assets of one firm can be acquired by another for some combination of cash, notes, stock, and/or employment contract. This payment can be made at the time of acquisition, throughout the first year, or extended over several years.

The two most common means of acquisition are the entrepreneur's direct purchase of the firm's entire stock or assets or the bootstrap purchase of these assets. In the direct purchase of the firm, the entrepreneur obtains funds from an outside lender or the seller of the company being purchased. The money is repaid over time from the cash flow generated from the operations. While this is a relatively simple and clear transaction, it usually results in a long-term capital gain to the seller and double taxation on the funds used to repay the money borrowed to acquire the company.

In order to avoid these problems, the entrepreneur can make a bootstrap purchase, acquiring a small amount of the firm, such as 20 to 30 percent, for cash. He or she then purchases the remainder of the company by a long-term note that is paid off over time out of the acquired company's earnings. This type of deal results in more favorable tax advantages to both the buyer and seller.

FIGURE 13–3 Merger Motivations

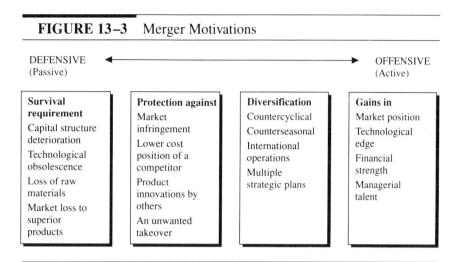

Source: F. T. Haner, *Business Policy, Planning and Strategy* (Cambridge, MA: Winthrop, 1976), p. 399.

MERGERS

Another method for expanding a venture is through a merger—a transaction involving two (or more) companies in which only one company survives. Acquisitions are so similar to mergers that at times the two terms are used interchangeably. In each of the last several years, merger and acquisition activity has been at the $180 billion level in over 3,000 transactions. A key concern in any merger (or acquisition) is the legality of the purchase. The Department of Justice frequently issues guidelines for horizontal, vertical, and conglomerate mergers, such as the 1968 *Merger Guidelines*. These documents further define the interpretation that will be made in enforcing the Sherman Act and Clayton Act while strengthening the enforcement of Section 7 of the Clayton Act. Since the guidelines are extensive and technical, the entrepreneur should secure adequate legal advice when any issues arise.

Why should an entrepreneur merge? There are both defensive and offensive strategies for a merger, as indicated in Table 13–3. Merger motivations range from survival to protection to diversification to growth. When some technical obsolescence, market or raw material loss, or deterioration of the capital structure has occurred in the entrepreneur's venture, a merger may be the only means for survival. The merger can also protect against market encroachment, product innovation, or an unwarranted takeover. On a more offensive side, a merger can provide a great deal of diversification as well as growth in market, technology, and financial and managerial strength.[8]

---

[8]For a discussion of the impact of mergers, see M. Rockmore, "Life after a Corporate Merger," *American Way*, April 15, 1986, pp. 66–69.

How does a merger take place? It requires sound planning by the entrepreneur. The merger objectives, particularly those dealing with earnings, must be spelled out with the resulting gains for the owners of both companies delineated. Also, the entrepreneur must carefully evaluate the other company's management, if retained, to ensure that it would be competent in developing the growth and future of the combined entity. The value and appropriateness of the existing resources should also be determined. In essence, this involves a careful analysis of both companies to ensure that the weaknesses of one do not compound those of the other. Finally, the entrepreneur should work toward establishing a climate of mutual trust to help minimize any possible management threat or turbulence.

The same methods for valuing the entrepreneur's company (discussed in Chapter 10) can be used to determine the value of a merger candidate. This will result from assessing plant value, marketing opportunity, earnings potential, or owner's value. The process involves the entrepreneur looking at the synergistic product/market position, the new domestic or international market position, any undervalued financial strength, whether or not the company is skilled in a related industry, or any underexploited company asset. A common procedure for determining value is to estimate the present value of discounted cash flows and the expected after-tax earnings attributable to the merger. This should be done on optimistic, pessimistic, and probable scenarios of cash flows and earnings using various acceptable rates of return.

LEVERAGED BUYOUTS

Another financing alternative—the leveraged buyout (LBO)—has been popular at various times, depending on the availability of financing and junk bonds. In this form of acquisition, the assets of the acquired company are used as collateral to finance the deal. The entrepreneur can either put up the acquired company's assets as security for a loan to finance the transaction or arrange in advance to sell a part of the acquired company immediately upon the completion of the transaction. The assets of the acquired company in effect provide **leverage,** or the ability to borrow enough money to provide the additional equity needed for the acquisition. Frequently, the additional equity is a combination of the acquired company's assets and the finances of the entrepreneur and a venture capitalist. Though LBOs yield a lower return (about 30 percent ROI), venture capitalists have recognized the high probability of success in a well-structured one and are interested in financing them. Several factors constitute a well-structured LBO. One that involves no management changes is considered well structured and has very low risk, for example, a corporate divestiture to a management group that has been operating the division being divested. Not only is there no learning curve in this type of LBO, but there are hidden problems as management, being familiar with operations, has full knowledge of the division's strengths and weaknesses. When the LBO requires new management, the risk increases, but to a lesser extent if this new management has a successful track record in the same industry.

By its nature, a leveraged buyout provides an excellent opportunity for a manager to turn entrepreneur. The LBO can be finalized more quickly when the parent firm loans the new entrepreneur the money over a period of time—usually five years. The loan is secured by the assets, and the entrepreneur purchases the existing inventory over the next 90 days by profitably operating the division. The selling company can furnish such support services as accounting, purchasing, and personnel during this transaction period.

In growth situations, a leveraged buyout provides an excellent opportunity for the entrepreneur to build in-house capabilities, add new products or product lines, or enter new markets. A study of high-technology companies in Silicon Valley found that over 32 percent of the 250 firms were involved in some form of merger, acquisition, or leveraged buyout during the 20-year period investigated.[9] Most of this activity took place in companies involved in semiconductor components and materials, semiconductor devices, computers, computer peripherals, and software.

SUMMARY

There are special considerations confronting entrepreneurs in expanding their companies. Time management is important, especially during periods of growth and expansion. Effective time management increases productivity and job satisfaction, improves esprit de corps, reduces tension, and promotes better health. To achieve effective time management, the entrepreneur should analyze current use of time, develop efficient methods of dealing with routine tasks, and use prioritized planning. Effective use of time will improve efficiency throughout the organization.

Negotiation is another skill needed by entrepreneurs in expanding an organization. Understanding the underlying motivations is important in approaching a negotiation situation. When cooperation is possible, integrative bargaining occurs, with parties using rational decision making to solve a joint problem. The problem should be identified from the vantage point of each party; both parties then propose alternative solutions before agreeing on the best solution.

In competitive negotiation, techniques of distributive bargaining are employed. Since conflicting goals make this area of negotiation more difficult, the entrepreneur should learn as much as possible about the adversary, both directly

---

[9]A. Brune & A. Cooper, "Patterns of Acquisition in Silicon Valley," *Proceedings*, Babson Research Conference, April 1981, pp. 92–110.

and indirectly. The settlement range of the other party will determine the likelihood of reaching an agreement. In any negotiation situation the entrepreneur should follow eight steps: prepare, discuss, signal, propose, respond, bargain, close, and agree. Negotiation skills are particularly important in expansion through joint ventures, acquisitions, mergers, and leveraged buyouts.

Joint ventures are separate entities formed by two or more partners. Although the most common joint ventures are between private-sector companies, they can involve universities, other nonprofit organizations, and the public sector. Objectives include sharing technology, cutting costs, entering new markets, and entering foreign markets. The success of joint ventures depends on the relationships of the partners, the symmetry of the partners, reasonable expectations, and timing.

Another method an entrepreneur can use in expanding the business is acquisition. An acquisition is the purchase of a company so that it is completely absorbed by the acquiring company. The acquisition process involves evaluating a candidate business and structuring a final deal. The evaluation process involves analyzing the firm's financial data, the product line, research and development, marketing, the manufacturing process, and management. When a candidate passes the evaluation process, an appropriate deal needs to be structured.

A third method for expanding a company is through a merger. This transaction involves two or more companies, with only one company surviving. Motivations to engage in a merger include survival, protection, diversification, and growth.

An increasingly popular alternative for entrepreneurial expansion is the leveraged buyout. In this, assets of the acquired company are used to finance the deal.

Entrepreneurs facing expansion require skills in time management and negotiation in order to efficiently achieve growth in the marketplace. These skills and knowledge of joint ventures, mergers, acquisition, and leveraged buyouts can result in successful growth of the venture.

CHAPTER

Ending the Venture

CHAPTER OBJECTIVES

1. To illustrate differences in alternative types of bankruptcy under the bankruptcy act of 1978 (amended in 1984).

2. To illustrate rights of creditors and entrepreneurs in different cases of bankruptcy.

3. To provide the entrepreneur with an understanding of the typical warning signs of bankruptcy.

4. To illustrate how some entrepreneurs can turn bankruptcy into a successful business.

5. To describe the succession of a business to family or nonfamily members.

FRANK LORENZO

Although often surrounded by controversy, Frank Lorenzo was one of the real entrepreneurs in the airline industry. His reign in the industry spanned over two decades, during which he changed the industry's mode of operations, pioneering the wave of deregulation. A graduate of Harvard Business School, Lorenzo was among the first to capitalize on cheap fares. His use of low fares broke up the stable oligopoly of airlines and made air travel possible for many people. With this strategy, he transformed Texas Air Corporation from a small regional carrier into the nation's largest airline.

Starting out with an initial $25,000 investment in Texas International Airlines in 1971, Lorenzo proceeded to build his airline empire through leveraged acquisitions of Continental, People Express, Frontier, and Eastern, resulting in $8.6 billion in sales. During its peak in 1987, his company's estimated market value was put at $2.1 billion.

During the last decade, Lorenzo endured financial chaos, heated labor disputes, and bankruptcy proceedings, eventually bailing out in 1990. His many union disputes stemmed from his slashing of labor costs to maintain lower fares. In 1983, he broke the trade union contracts with Continental by taking the airline into Chapter 11 bankruptcy. This allowed him to reorganize without the unions. The uproar from this tactic actually led to legislation by Congress barring Chapter 11 as a means of negotiation. However, Lorenzo did not stop there. When Eastern's machinists went on strike in 1989, he again sought bankruptcy. While the strike continued, Lorenzo proceeded to replace striking workers.

At the same time, Lorenzo had already begun to cash in some of his holdings. When his empire reached its peak value in 1987, he gained about $7 million by dumping much of his common stock. He maintained a significant stake through his investment company, Jet Capital, which controlled 33 percent of the Texas Air vote through a special class of stock. By 1989, his airlines were laden with debt, particularly Continental, which was struggling to integrate Frontier. At the suggestion of Texas Air board member Carl R. Pohlad, Lorenzo negotiated a deal to sell Eastern to former baseball commissioner Peter V. Ueberroth for $464 million—a deal Ueberroth later aborted.

Lorenzo, known for his multiple negotiating, had also begun talking with Jan Carlzon, CEO of SAS, a Scandinavian airline. Lorenzo continued to dance through negotiations that slowed as business picked up for Eastern and Continental toward the end of 1989. However, by spring of 1990, the federal bankruptcy court in Manhattan removed Lorenzo from control of Eastern and appointed former Continental president Martin R. Shugrue as trustee to steer the airline out of bankruptcy. At this time, Lorenzo realized it was time for him to leave the airlines. By June, Lorenzo and Carlzon were deeply involved in negotiations for SAS's purchase of Lorenzo's interest in Texas Air, which finally led to a plan they presented to Texas Air's board.

The board, no longer under Lorenzo's thumb, severely trimmed the deal, allowing him to clear $30.5 million, a huge sum but much less than his stock's former value. An interesting clause in the deal prohibits Lorenzo from working in the industry until 1998. However, Lorenzo remains director of Continental Holdings, and he has indicated that he plans to be active.[1]

BANKRUPTCY—AN OVERVIEW

The above saga of Frank Lorenzo is probably not indicative of the average life of an entrepreneur. However, his failure is not uncommon in many new ventures. According to the Small Business Administration, about half of all new start-ups fail in their first years. In many cases, the entrepreneur could have prevented failure—which is personally painful—by paying more attention to certain critical factors in the business operation. Figure 14–1 compares incorporations and bankruptcies from 1981 to 1986. Each year represents the percentage change from the previous year. Thus, although the growth in establishing corporations is relatively stable (5 percent) the growth in bankruptcies is increasing. This chart does not include partnerships and proprietorships, which probably have higher failure rates because of an even greater lack of capitalization.

Bankruptcy is a term heard too often among entrepreneurs yet it doesn't always end their ambitions nor does it always have to result in the end of the business in question. Recently, four former entrepreneurs were interviewed regarding their views on bankruptcy. Each one had experienced bankruptcy at least once. Bill Lewis, founder and CEO of Federal Refunds Inc., had filed for bankruptcy twice. His new company, which assists buyers of petroleum products in recovering funds on overbilled accounts, reached sales of $1 million in 1990. John Koss, the founder of Koss Corp., a manufacturer of stereo headphones,

---

[1]M. Ivey and M. O'Neal, "Frank Lorenzo: The Final Days," *Business Week,* August 27, 1990, pp. 32–3; J. Castro, "Gone but Not Forgotten," *Time,* August 20, 1990, p. 48; and "Frank Lorenzo's Bumpy Landing," *U.S. News and World Report,* August 20, 1990, p. 14.

FIGURE 14–1 Incorporations and Bankruptcies

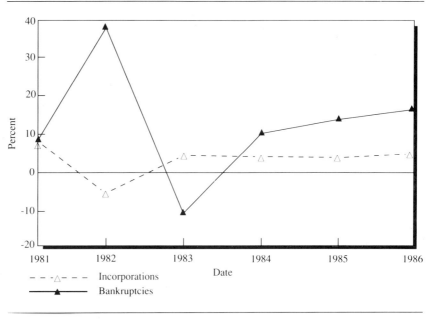

Source: U.S. Small Business Administration.

filed Chapter 11 in 1984 and, through a reorganization, the company reemerged almost one year later. In 1990, sales for this venture reached $27 million.

Paul Perkins, on the other hand, is now driving a school bus after his Voyages International Travel Co. went bankrupt in 1989. He is in the process of starting another new venture. A fourth entrepreneur became a partner and bankruptcy specialist at Peat Marwick. His company, Virtual Network Services Corp., a long distance telephone service provider, went bankrupt in 1986 (under Chapter 11) and was sold shortly thereafter.

All four entrepreneurs indicate how much they learned from the experiences of bankruptcy. Some of the lessons can be summarized as follows.[2]

- Many entrepreneurs spend too much effort and time to diversifying into markets they lack knowledge in. They should focus on known markets.
- Bankruptcy protects entrepreneurs only from the creditors, not from competitors.
- It's difficult to separate the entrepreneur from the business. They put every-thing into the company and worry about the future of employees.

---

[2]T. Richman, "The Lessons of Bankruptcy," *INC.* December 1989, pp. 29–38.

- Many entrepreneurs never think their business is going to fail until it's too late. They should file early.
- Bankruptcy is emotionally painful. Going into hiding after bankruptcy is a big mistake. Bankruptcy needs to be shared with employees and everybody else involved.

As the above examples indicate, bankruptcy is serious business and requires some important understanding of its applications. The Bankruptcy Act of 1978 (amended in 1984) was designed to ensure a fair distribution of assets to creditors, to protect debtors from unfair depletion of assets, and to protect debtors from unfair demands by creditors. The act provides three alternative provisions for a firm near or at a position of insolvency: (1) liquidation or Chapter 7 bankruptcy, (2) reorganization or Chapter 11 bankruptcy, and (3) extended time payment or Chapter 13 bankruptcy. All attempt to protect the troubled entrepreneur as well as provide a reasonable way to organize payments to debtors or to end the venture.

CHAPTER 11—REORGANIZATION

This is the least severe alternative to bankruptcy. In this situation, the courts try to give the venture time and "breathing room" to pay their debts. Usually this situation results because the venture has cash flow problems and the creditors begin to pressure the firm with lawsuits and so on. The entrepreneur feels that, with some time, the business can become solvent and liquid enough to meet its debt requirements.

A major creditor, a group of creditors, the entrepreneur, or any party of interest will usually present the case to the court. The entrepreneur then prepares a plan for reorganization, indicating how the business will be turned around. The plan will divide the debt and ownership interests into two groups: those that will be affected by the plan and those that will not. It then will specify whose interests will be affected and how payments will be made.

Once the plan is completed it must be approved by the court. All bankruptcies are now handled by the U.S. Bankruptcy Court, whose powers were restructured under the Bankruptcy Amendments Act of 1984.[3]

Approval of the plan also requires that all creditors and owners agree to comply with the reorganization plan as presented to the courts. The decisions made in the reorganization plan generally reflect one or a combination of the following:[4]

---

[3]R. A. Anderson, I. Fox, and D. P. Turney, *Business Law: Principles Cases Legal Environment* (rev. ed.), (Cincinnati, OH: South-Western Publishing, 1987), p. 777.

[4]K. R. Van Voorhis, *Enterprise and Small Business Management* (Boston, MA: Allyn & Bacon, 1980), p. 439.

1. *Extension*—This occurs when two or more of the largest creditors agree to postpone any claims. This acts as a stimulus for smaller creditors to also agree to the plan.
2. *Substitution*—If the future potential of the venture looks promising enough, it may be possible to exchange stock or something else for the existing debt.
3. *Composition settlement*—The debt is prorated to the creditors as a settlement for any debt.

All of the preceding decisions can succeed. If this alternative is not feasible, the entrepreneur may choose bankruptcy under Chapter 13.

CHAPTER 13—EXTENDED TIME PAYMENT PLANS

If the entrepreneur has a regular income, he or she can file for extended time payments as long as the unsecured debts are less than $100,000 and the secured debts are less than $350,000. Under this plan, the entrepreneur files a schedule for the installment payment of outstanding debts. If approved by the court, it binds the creditors even if they had not originally agreed to such installment payments.

The entrepreneur must file with the court a plan that basically budgets future income with respect to any outstanding debts. The plan must provide for the payment of all claims identified as having priority under the Bankruptcy Act. In addition, it will outline how much is to be paid until all payments have been completed.

The claims to be paid are in the following order of priority: (1) secured creditors, (2) administrative expenses, (3) claims arising from operation of the business, (4) wage claims up to $2,000 per person, (5) contributions to employee benefit plans, (6) claims by consumer creditors, (7) taxes, and (8) general creditors.[5]

CHAPTER 7—LIQUIDATION

The most extreme case of bankruptcy requires the entrepreneur to liquidate, either voluntarily or involuntarily, all nonexempt assets of the business.

If the entrepreneur files a **voluntary bankruptcy** petition under Chapter 7, it constitutes a determination that his or her venture is bankrupt. Usually the courts will also require a current income and expense statement.

---

[5]*Business Law*, pp. 785–86.

TABLE 14–1   Liquidation under Chapter 7 Involuntary Bankruptcy

Requirements	Number and Claims of Creditors	Rights and Duties of Entrepreneur	Trustee
Debts are not being paid as they become due	If 12 or more creditors, at least 3 with unsecured claims totaling $5,000 must sign petition.	Damages may be recovered if creditor files in bad faith.	Elected by creditors. Interim trustee appointed by court.
Custodian appointed within 120 days prior to filing of petition.	If less than 12 creditors, 1 creditor whose unsecured claim is at least $5,000 must sign the petition.	If involuntary petition is dismissed by court, costs, fees, or damages may be awarded.	Becomes by law owner of all property considered nonexempt for liquidation.
Considered insolvent when fair value of all assets is less than debts. Called a balance sheet test.	A proof of claim must be filed within 90 days after first meeting of creditors.	Must file a list of creditors with courts. Must file a current income and expense statement.	Can set aside petitions; transfer of property to a creditor under certain conditions.

Table 14–1 summarizes some of the key issues and requirements under the **involuntary bankruptcy** petition. As the table indicates, an involuntary bankruptcy can be very complicated and can take a long time to resolve. Sometimes, however, liquidation is in the best interests of the entrepreneur if there is no hope of recovering from the situation.

STRATEGY DURING REORGANIZATION

Normally the reorganization under Chapter 11 or an extended payment plan under Chapter 13 takes a significant amount of time. During this period, the entrepreneur can speed up the process by taking the initiative in preparing a plan, selling the plan to secured creditors, communicating with groups of creditors, and avoiding writing checks that are not covered.

The key to enhancing the bankruptcy process is keeping creditors abreast of how the business is doing and emphasizing the significance of their support during the process. Improving the entrepreneur's credibility with creditors will help the venture emerge from financial difficulties without the stigma of failure. Trying to meet with groups of creditors usually results in turmoil and ill will. These direct contact meetings in groups should be avoided.

Bankruptcy should be a last resort for the entrepreneur. Every effort should be made to avoid it and keep the business operating.

TABLE 14–2   Requirements for Keeping a New Venture Afloat

- Avoid excess optimism when business appears to be successful
- Always prepare good marketing plans with clear objectives
- Make good cash projections and avoid capitalization
- Keep abreast of the marketplace
- Identify stress points that can put the business in jeopardy

---

KEEPING THE VENTURE GOING

Any entrepreneur who starts a business should pay attention to, as well as learn from, the mistakes of others. There are certain requirements that can help keep a new venture going and reduce the risk of failure. We can never guarantee success but we can learn how to avoid failure.

Table 14–2 summarizes some of the key factors that can reduce the risk of business failure. The entrepreneur should be sensitive to each of these issues regardless of the size or type of business started.

Many entrepreneurs have confidence in their abilities, which is necessary for them to be successful in their field. However, there can be excessive optimism, which can be dangerous in a new venture. Inevitably, the overly optimistic entrepreneur becomes sloppy in managing the business and often misses important signals that the business needs help.

Kenneth J. Susnjara of Thermwood Corporation illustrates how optimism for his company's robotic paint sprayer almost led to a disaster. Susnjara left his post as CEO for three months to become a distributor for the paint sprayer. It gave him a completely different view of Thermwood and an understanding of how to market the sprayer. As a result of changes in strategy and policy, the new product will succeed. Thus, by having a different perspective on the business, Susnjara traded optimism for realism and incorporated significant changes in strategy.[6]

Preparing an effective marketing plan for a 12-month period is essential for the entrepreneur. The marketing plan discussed in Chapter 6 helps the entrepreneur prepare for contingencies and control his or her day-to-day activities.

Good cash projections are also a serious consideration for the entrepreneur. Cash flow was a serious problem at Eastern and is probably an issue in most bankruptcy situations. In preparing cash projections, many entrepreneurs require assistance from accountants, lawyers, or one of the federal agencies such as the SBA.

---

[6]N. L. Croft, "Keeping Your Business Afloat," *Nation's Business*, February 1987, pp. 16–17.

Many entrepreneurs avoid gathering sufficient information about the market. Information is an important asset to any entrepreneur, especially regarding future market potential and forecasting the size of the immediate attainable market. Entrepreneurs will often try to guess what is happening in the market and ignore the changing marketplace. This could spell disaster, especially if competitors are reacting more positively to the market changes.

In the early stages of a new venture it is helpful for the entrepreneur to be aware of stress points, that is, those points at which the venture is changing in size, requiring new strategies to survive. Early rapid rises in sales can be interpreted incorrectly, leading the venture to add plant capacity, sign new contracts with suppliers, or increase inventories. All these actions can result in shrinking margins and overleverage. To offset this situation, ventures often increase prices or weaken quality, which can lead to lower sales. This becomes a vicious circle that can lead to bankruptcy.

Stress points can be identified on the basis of amount of sales. For example, it may be possible to recognize that sales of $1 million, $5 million, and $25 million may represent key decision marks in terms of major capital investment and operational expenses (e.g., hiring new key personnel). Entrepreneurs should be aware of the burden of sales levels on capital investment and operational expenses.[7]

WARNING SIGNS OF BANKRUPTCY

Entrepreneurs should be sensitive to signals in the business and the environment that may be early warnings of trouble. Often the entrepreneur is not aware of what is going on or is not willing to accept the inevitable. Table 14–3 lists some of the key early warning signs of bankruptcy. Generally they are interrelated and one can often lead to the other.

For example, when the management of financial affairs becomes lax, companies tend to do anything to generate cash, such as reducing prices, cutting back on supplies to meet orders, or releasing important personnel like sales representatives. A new office furniture business catering to small or medium-sized businesses illustrates how this can happen. Top management of the firm decided that moving merchandise was its top priority. Sales representatives earned standard commission on each sale and were free to reduce prices where necessary to make the sale. Hence, without any break-even awareness, sales representatives often reduced prices to below direct costs. They still received their commissions when the price charged was below cost. Thus, the venture eventually lost substantial amounts of money and had to declare bankruptcy.

---

[7]*Nation's Business*, p. 18.

TABLE 14-3 Warning Signs of Bankruptcy

- Management of finances becomes lax, so that no one can explain how money is being spent
- Directors cannot document or explain major transactions
- Customers are given large discounts to enhance payments because of poor cash flow
- Contracts are accepted below standard amounts to generate cash
- Bank requests subordination of its loans
- Key personnel leave company
- Lack of materials to meet orders
- Payroll taxes are not paid
- Suppliers demand payment in cash
- Increase in customers' complaints regarding service and product quality

---

When an entrepreneur sees any of the warning signs in Table 14-3, he or she should immediately seek the advice of a CPA or an attorney. It may be possible to prevent bankruptcy by making immediate changes in the operation to improve the cash flow and profitability of the business.

STARTING OVER

Bankruptcy and liquidation does not have to be the end for the entrepreneur. History is full of examples of entrepreneurs who have failed many times before finally succeeding.

Gail Borden's tombstone reads "I tried and failed, and I tried again and succeeded." One of his first inventions was the Terraqueous Wagon, which was designed to travel on land or water. The invention sank on its first try. Borden also had three other inventions that failed to get patents. A fourth was patented but eventually wiped him out because of lack of capital and poor sales. However, Borden was persistent and convinced that his vacuum condensation process, giving milk a long shelf life, would be successful. At 56, Borden had his first success with condensed milk.

Over the years, other famous entrepreneurs have also endured many failures before finally achieving success. Rowland Hussey Macy (retailing—Macy's), Ron Berger (National Video), and Thomas Edison, to name a few, are examples of struggling entrepreneurs who lived through many failures.

The characteristics of entrepreneurs were discussed in Chapter 3. From that chapter we know that entrepreneurs are likely to continue starting new ventures even after failing. There is evidence that they learn from their mistakes, and investors often look favorably on someone who has failed previously, assuming that he or she will not make the same mistake again.[8]

---

[8]L. M. Lament, "What Entrepreneurs Learn from Experience," *Journal of Small Business Management* 10 (1972), p. 36.

Generally, entrepreneurs, in endeavors after failure, tend to have a better understanding and appreciation of the need for market research, more initial capitalization, and stronger business skills. Unfortunately, not all entrepreneurs learn these skills from their experiences; many tend to fail over and over again.

However, business failure does not have to be a stigma when it comes time to seek venture capital. Past records will be revealed during subsequent start-ups, but the careful entrepreneur can explain why the failure occurred and how he or she will prevent it in the future, restoring investors' confidence. As discussed in Chapter 5, the business plan will help sell the business concept to investors. It is in the business plan that the entrepreneur, even after many failures, can illustrate how this venture will be successful.

BUSINESS TURNAROUNDS

Too often we hear only about the business failures and overlook those who are able to survive bankruptcy or near bankruptcy and turn their business into a success. History provides some good examples of such turnarounds.

Many of the firms discussed below are large businesses that started small and grew through the efforts of their entrepreneurs. They demonstrate that Chapter 11 reorganization can give the entrepreneur time to resolve its financial problems without pressure from creditors.

Allegheny International, a business conglomerate, filed for Chapter 11 on February 20, 1988, when it was unable to meet its debt of $500 million even after divesting Wilkinson Sword. As part of the reorganization, Goldman Sachs bought the firm for $655 million and changed the company name to Sunbeam-Oster. The company emerged from Chapter 11 on September 28, 1990. However, it is still expecting losses of more than $43 million on sales of about $1 billion in 1990.

Baldwin-United, a financial services firm, filed for Chapter 11 on September 26, 1983, with $600 million of debt. During reorganization, the company settled more than 8,300 claims. Assets decreased from $9 billion to $490 million. The company, under a new name, was then acquired by Leucadia National. On November 13, 1986, the company emerged from bankruptcy. In 1990, its revenues were $350 million, with profits of $35 million.

Storage Technology is a true success story. It emerged from Chapter 11 bankruptcy without being acquired by another firm. In 1984, the computer hardware firm was unable to pay its debt of $645 million, so $60 million of its assets, including a computer chip factory, were sold. The business was refocused on computer storage, and on July 28, 1987, it emerged from Chapter 11 reorganization. In 1990, the firm had profits of $70 million on sales of $1.1 billion.[9]

---

[9]K. Ballen, "Life After Chapter 11 for Six Big Survivors," *Fortune*, February 11, 1991, p. 13.

In 1989, more than 18,000 U.S. companies filed for Chapter 11, in 1990 20,500 filed, and as many as 23,000 are expected in 1991. Thus, it seems that bankruptcy is becoming a more common strategy to protect businesses against creditors. How many of these companies will actually survive the bankruptcy is difficult to ascertain because many are acquired before the reorganization is complete. However, the stigma of being or having been in bankruptcy should not affect the entrepreneur's determination to make his or her venture successful.

If it becomes necessary to file for bankruptcy, the entrepreneur should seek the advice of attorneys, accountants, and investment bankers when appropriate. Although their fees may be high there is often no other alternative. An entrepreneur can minimize these fees by getting the creditors to preapprove any restructuring or reorganization, thus reducing the time the firm remains under Chapter 11 and the necessity of the advisors' services.

SUCCESSION OF BUSINESS

Many new ventures will be passed on to family members. If there is no one in the family interested in the business, it is important for the entrepreneur to either sell the business or train someone within the organization to take over.

Transfer to Family Members

Passing the business down to a family member can create internal problems. This often results when a son or daughter is handed the responsibility of running the business without sufficient training. A young family member can be more successful in taking over the business if he or she assumes various operational responsibilities early on. It is beneficial for the family member to rotate to different areas of the business in order to get a good perspective of the total operation. Other employees in these departments or areas will be able to assist in the training and get to know their future leader.

It is also helpful if the entrepreneur stays around for a while to act as an advisor to the successor. This can be helpful in the business decisions. Of course, it is possible that this can result in major conflicts if the personalities involved are not compatible. In addition, employees who have been with the firm since start-up may resent the younger family member assuming control of the venture. However, while working in the organization during this transition period, the successor can prove his or her abilities, justifying his or her future role.

Transfer to Nonfamily Members

Often a member of the family is not interested in assuming responsibility of the business. When this occurs the entrepreneur has three choices: train a key employee and retain some equity; retain control and hire a manager; or sell the business outright.

Passing the business on to an employee ensures that the new principal is familiar with the business and the market. The employee's experience minimizes transitional problems. In addition, the entrepreneur can take some time to make the transition smoother.

The key issue when passing the business on to an employee is ownership. If the entrepreneur plans to retain some ownership, the question of how much becomes an important area of negotiation. The new principal may prefer to have control, with the original entrepreneur remaining as a minority owner or a stockholder. The financial capacity and managerial ability of the employee will be important factors in the decision on how much ownership is transferred.

If the business has been in the family for some time and the succession to a family member may become more likely in the future, the entrepreneur may hire a manager to run the business. However, finding someone to manage the business in the same manner and with the same expertise as the entrepreneur may be difficult. If someone is found to manage the business, the likely problems are compatibility with the owners and willingness of this person to manage for any length of time without a promise of equity in the business. Executive search firms can help in the search process. It will be necessary to have a well-defined job description to assist in identifying the right person.

The last option, often referred to as **harvesting,** is to sell the business outright to either an employee or an outsider. The major considerations in this option are financial, which will likely necessitate the help of an accountant and/or lawyer. This alternative also requires a determination of the value of the business (see Chapter 11).

Harvesting Strategy

Businesses are not sold only as a last resort to bankruptcy. Many entrepreneurs choose to sell so that they can move on to new endeavors. Steven Rosendorf provides a good example of the considerations involved in any possible sale of the business. In 1976, his brother/partner died suddenly, leaving him alone with a $2 million costume jewelry business. At that point, Rosendorf began to plan for the eventual sale of the company. The plan included upgrading of showrooms and cost-cutting measures, including a reduction of his own salary. Within a few years, the company showed $2 million profits on sales of $13 million. With this,

Rosendorf felt it was time to sell the business, and within one year, he did so for $16 million.[10]

Unless the entrepreneur is desperate, putting a business up for sale may require time and planning, as Rosendorf's example indicates. Successful small businesses are in demand by larger firms that wish to grow by acquisition.

One of the important considerations of any business sale is the type of payment the buyer will use. Often buyers will purchase a business using notes based on future profits. If the new owners fail in the business, the seller may receive no cash payment and possibly find him or herself taking back the company that is struggling to survive.

As exemplified in the Rosendorf example, preparing for a sale may necessitate serious financial reconsiderations. Many entrepreneurs give themselves big salaries and large expense accounts that obviously cut into profits. This also makes the company's earning capacity appear to be much lower than it is. Thus, if the entrepreneur must or plans to sell the business, he or she should tighten spending, avoid large personal salaries and expenses, and reinvest as much profit as possible back into the business. This formula will likely result in a much better sale agreement.

Business brokers in some instances may be helpful since trying to actually sell a business will take time away from running it. Brokers can be discreet about a sale and may have an established network to get the word around. Brokers earn a commission from the sale of a business. Generally, these commissions are based on a sliding scale starting at about 10 percent for the first $200,000.

The best way to communicate the business to potential buyers is through the business plan. A five-year comprehensive plan can provide buyers of the business with a future perspective and accountability of the value of the company (see Chapters 6 and 7).

Involvement of Entrepreneur after Sale

Once the business is either sold or passed on to a family member or employee, the entrepreneur's role may depend on the sale agreement or contract with the new owner(s). Many buyers will want the seller to stay on for a short time to provide a smooth transition. Under these circumstances the seller (entrepreneur) should negotiate an employment contract that specifies time, salary, and responsibility. If the entrepreneur is not needed in the business, it is likely that the new owner(s) will request that the entrepreneur sign an agreement not to engage in the same business for a specified number of years. These agreements vary in scope and may require a lawyer to clarify details.

---

[10]T. Thompson, "When It's Time to Sell Out," *U.S. News & World Report*, June 28, 1989, pp. 62–4.

SUMMARY

This chapter deals with the decisions, problems, and issues involved in ending the venture. Even though the intent of all entrepreneurs is to establish a venture for a long time, many problems can cause these plans to fail. Since about one-half of all new businesses fail in their first four years of business, it is important for the entrepreneur to understand the options for either ending or salvaging a venture.

Bankruptcy offers three options for the entrepreneur. Under Chapter 11 of the Bankruptcy Act of 1978, the venture will be reorganized under a plan approved by the courts. Chapter 13 provides for an extended time payment plan to cover outstanding debts. Both of these alternatives are designed to help entrepreneurs salvage the business and keep it going. Under Chapter 7, the venture will be liquidated either voluntarily or involuntarily.

Keeping the business going is the primary intent of all entrepreneurs. Avoiding excessive optimism, preparing good marketing plans, making good cash projections, keeping familiar with the market, and being sensitive to stress points in the business all can help keep the business going.

Entrepreneurs can also be sensitive to key warnings of potential problems. Lax management of finances, discounting to generate cash, loss of key personnel, lack of raw materials, nonpayment of payroll taxes, demands of suppliers to be paid in cash, and increased customer complaints about service and product quality are some of the key factors that lead to bankruptcy. If the business does fail, however, the entrepreneur should always consider starting over. Failure can be a learning process as evidenced by the many famous inventors who succeeded after many failures.

One of the other venture-ending decisions that an entrepreneur may face is succession of the business. If the business is family-owned, the entrepreneur would likely seek a family member to succeed. Other options, if no family member is available or interested, include transferring some or all of the business to an employee or outsider or hiring an outsider to manage the business.

PART V SPECIAL ISSUES FOR THE ENTREPRENEUR

Legal Issues for the Entrepreneur

15

CHAPTER OBJECTIVES

1. To understand the nature of a patent and the rights it provides to the entrepreneur.

2. To recognize the differences between utility and design patents.

3. To illustrate the process for filing a patent.

4. To understand the purpose of a trademark and the procedure for filing.

5. To learn the purpose of a copyright and how to file for one.

6. To understand the value of licensing to either expand a business or to start a new venture.

7. To understand important issues related to product safety and liability.

8. To explain how to hire a lawyer.

EDWIN H. LAND

Edwin Land has been called one of the greatest living inventors and entrepreneurs. As a 22-year-old Harvard dropout living in New York, he used to sneak into the Columbia University labs to conduct research on an idea he had for polarizing light. Needing capital to start a business and continue research on his concept, he obtained $375,000 in capital from investors such as W. Averill Harriman, James P. Warburg, and several others. With this money he started Polaroid Corporation.

Initially, Land was intent on directing Polaroid's research effort at finding a solution for glare in automobile headlights by means of a polarizing lens. Unfortunately, the auto manufacturers were not interested in the lens, so Land turned to optic lenses, which were in demand during World War II.

After the war, the optic lens market dried up and Polaroid was on the verge of bankruptcy. Edwin Land then announced that he had discovered a near-magic process that would permit a camera to take a picture, develop it inside the camera, and produce a photo print in minutes.

In 1948, Polaroid Corporation unveiled the first sepia print instant camera. Land got the idea after one of his children asked why a picture could not be seen immediately after it was taken. He then spent the next few years developing the process before effectively mastering it. For the next 30 years, Land and Polaroid produced innovation after innovation, each one carefully protected by patents. Each innovation seemed to improve on the previous discovery and pushed photographic technology beyond the bounds of the average person's comprehension. By 1980, with the help of his many inventions, Land had built the company into $1.4 billion business. At that point, at age 70, he retired from the company.

Patents were very important to Polaroid because the company was so dependent on this single technology. Any failure to be at the leading edge of this technology could have bankrupted the company. Yet, over the years, Land and Polaroid continued to pioneer development in this field. With the innovation and development of many processes and products, the company successfully obtained nearly 2,000 patents. Edwin Land personally has his name on 537 U.S. patents, second only to Thomas Edison's 1,093.

Polaroid's existence under the direction of Edwin Land was not without its problems. A number of product failures, such as Polavision, as well as continued improvement in 35-mm cameras and processing, diminished the significance of instant photography to the ultimate user. Market activity restricted to the amateur market and a single-product line also caused some doubts as to the future of his company. Even threats from competitors such as Kodak caused concern over Polaroid's future.

One of Polaroid's major legal battles over patent rights was with Eastman Kodak, which introduced an instant camera to compete with Polaroid. With Kodak's strong distribution, film manufacturing capability, and image, Polaroid was believed to be in serious trouble. However, Land was not about to give up his success to anyone. Polaroid filed a patent infringement suit against Eastman Kodak, shocking the photography industry.

In October 1985, after nine years of litigation, a federal court judge ruled that Eastman Kodak was guilty of infringement on 7 of 10 patents named in the lawsuit. In the lawsuit, Polaroid claimed that Kodak had copied patents from its popular SX-70 camera introduced in 1972. Kodak, which had sold 16.5 million cameras and captured 25 percent of the instant market, was ordered to cease production on cameras and film. The problem then faced by Kodak was how to cushion the blow for its customers. To address this problem Kodak offered trade-ins, a hot line, and brochures outlining the options for customers.

With Kodak's market share dropping and consumer interest diminishing, the ruling by the courts seemed to be a blessing in disguise. However, the future of instant photography does not appear favorable because of the new 35-mm technology, fast photo services, improved video technology, and simple boredom with a process that is no longer unique.

In any event, patents can be an important means of protecting a new technology, process, and so on for an entrepreneur. Unfortunately, the nine years of litigation incurred by Polaroid and Kodak would not have been possible for a new venture. However, legal issues like patents are important concerns in any new venture. Good advice can save money, the entrepreneur's reputation, and the future existence of the business. This chapter provides some insight for the entrepreneur on such issues as patents, copyrights, trademarks, product liability, and insurance.[1]

NEED FOR A LAWYER

Since all business is regulated by law, the entrepreneur needs to be aware of any regulations that may affect his or her new venture. At different stages of the start-up, the entrepreneur will need legal advice. It is also likely that the legal expertise required will vary based on such factors as whether the new venture is

---

[1]See "Polaroid vs. Kodak: The Decisive Round," *Business Week*, January 13, 1986, p. 37, and "Instant Getaway," *Time*, January 20, 1986, p. 43.

a franchise, an independent start-up, a buyout, consumer versus industrial product, nonprofit, or involves exporting or importing.

Most lawyers have developed special expertise and the entrepreneur should carefully evaluate his or her needs before hiring one. Awareness and sensitivity to legal questions are also important for the entrepreneur. This chapter provides some insight into the areas that will probably require legal assistance. The form of organization, as well as franchise agreements, are discussed in Chapters 8 and 16, and will not be addressed here. Legal advice for these agreements (i.e., partnership, franchise, or articles of incorporation) is necessary to ensure that the most appropriate decisions have been made.

By being aware of when and what legal advice is required, the entrepreneur can save much time and money. In addition, the chapter concludes with some advice on how to select a lawyer and where to get legal advice and information regarding legal issues.

PATENTS

A patent is a contract between the government and an inventor. In exchange for disclosure of the invention, the government grants the inventor exclusivity regarding the invention for a specified amount of time. At the end of this time, the government publishes the invention and it becomes part of the public domain.[2]

Basically, the patent gives the owners a negative right because it prevents anyone else from making, using, or selling the defined invention. Moreover, even if an inventor has been granted a patent, in the process of producing or marketing the invention he or she may find that it infringes on the patent rights of others. The inventor also should recognize the distinction between utility and design patents.

- *Utility Patents*—When speaking about patents, most people are referring to utility patents. A utility patent has a term of 17 years, beginning on the date the Patent and Trademark Office (PTO) issued it. It grants the owner protection from anyone else making, using, and/or selling the identified invention and generally reflects protection of new, useful, and unobvious processes such as developing film, machines such as a copier, and articles of manufacture such as the toothpaste pump.

- *Design Patents*—Covering new, original, ornamental, and unobvious designs for articles of manufacture, a design patent reflects the appearance of an object. These patents are granted for a 14-year term and, like the utility patent, provide the inventor with a negative right excluding others from making, using, or selling an article having the ornamental appearance given in the drawings included in the patent.

---

[2]D. A. Burge, *Patent and Trademark Tactics and Practice*, 2nd ed. (New York: John Wiley and Sons, 1984), p. 25.

- *Plant Patents*—These are issued for 17 years on new varieties of plants. Very few of these types of patents are issued.

Patents are issued by the Patent and Trademark Office (PTO). In addition to patents, this office administers other programs. One of these is the Disclosure Document Program, whereby the inventor files disclosure of the invention, giving recognition that he or she was the first to develop or invent the idea. In most cases, the inventor will subsequently patent the idea. A second program is the Defensive Publication Program. This gives the inventor the opportunity to protect an idea for which he or she does not wish to obtain a patent. It prevents anyone else from patenting this idea but gives the public access to the invention.

The Disclosure Document

It is recommended that the entrepreneur first file a disclosure document to establish a date of conception of the invention. This document can be important when two entrepreneurs are filing for patents on similar inventions. In that instance, the entrepreneur who can show that he or she was the first one to conceive of the invention will be given the rights to the patent. Thus this disclosure is a vital step to proving the conception of the invention.

To file a disclosure document, the entrepreneur must prepare a clear and concise description of the invention. In addition to the written material, photographs may be included. A cover letter and a duplicate are included with the description of the invention. Upon receipt of the information, the PTO will stamp and return the duplicate copy of the letter to the entrepreneur, thus establishing evidence of conception. There is also a fee for this filing, which can be determined by telephoning the PTO.

The disclosure document is not a patent application. Before actually applying for the patent it is advisable to retain a patent attorney to conduct a patent search. After the attorney completes the search, a decision can be made as to the patentability of the invention.

The Patent Application

The patent application must contain a complete history and description of the invention as well as claims for its usefulness. In general, the application will be divided into the following sections:

- *Introduction*—This section should contain the background and advantages of the invention and the nature of problems that it overcomes. It should clearly state how the invention differs from existing offerings.
- *Description of Invention*—Next the application should contain a brief description of the drawings that accompany it. These drawings must comply with PTO requirements. Following this would be a detailed description of the inven-

tion, which may include engineering specifications, materials, components, and so on that are vital to the actual making of the invention.

- *Claims*—This is probably the most difficult section of the application to prepare since claims are the criteria by which any infringements will be determined. They serve to specify what the entrepreneur is trying to patent. Essential parts of the invention should be described in broad terms so as to prevent others from getting around the patent. At the same time, the claims must not be so general that they hide the invention's uniqueness and advantages. This balance is difficult and should be discussed and debated with the patent attorney.

In addition to the above sections, the application should contain a declaration or oath that is signed by the inventor or inventors. This form will be supplied by an attorney. The completed application is then ready to be sent to the PTO, at which time the status of the invention becomes patent pending. This status is important to the entrepreneur because it provides complete confidential protection until the application is approved. At that time the patent is published and thus becomes accessible for review by the public.

A carefully written patent should provide protection and prevent competitors from working around it. However, once granted, it is also an invitation to sue or be sued if there is any infringement.

The fees for filing an application will vary, depending on the patent search and claims made in the application. Attorney fees will also be a factor in completing the patent application. In general, the average cost of a patent seems to be about $1,500.

Patent Infringement

To this point we have discussed the importance and the procedure of filing for a patent. It is also extremely important for the entrepreneur to know if he or she is infringing on someone else's patent.

The fact that someone else already has a patent does not mean the entrepreneur must give up dreams of starting a business. Many businesses, inventions, or innovations are the result of improvements or modifications of existing products. Copying and improving on a product may be perfectly legal (no patent infringement) and actually good business strategy. If it is impossible to copy and improve the product to avoid patent infringement, the entrepreneur may try to license the product from the patent holder. Figure 15–1 illustrates the steps that an entrepreneur should follow as he or she considers marketing a product that may infringe on an existing patent. Each step is discussed in the following paragraphs.

First, an entrepreneur should confirm the existence of a patent. This can usually be accomplished by reviewing information on the company's package. Even if a patent is known to exist, the entrepreneur should find out exactly what it

FIGURE 15–1   Options to Avoid Infringement

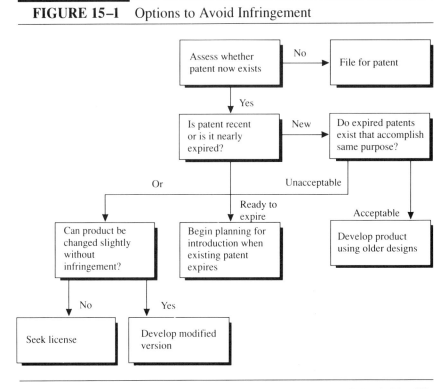

Source: Adapted from H. D. Coleman and J. D. Vandenberg, "How to Follow the Leader," *INC.*, July, 1988, pp. 81–82.

entails. If there is some doubt, a patent search may be necessary. Computer software is also available to provide the entrepreneur with information on existing patents that are in the same product category. If all else fails, the entrepreneur should consider hiring a patent attorney to perform a more thorough search.

Once the patent is found, it should be ascertained if the patent is new or is ready to expire. If it is new, the entrepreneur has two options: to try to modify the product without infringement of an existing patent or to identify older designs of a similar product whose patents have expired. If older designs are unacceptable or unavailable, it may be possible to modify the existing patented product without infringement. If modification is not possible, the entrepreneur may consider licensing, or offering the patent holder a proposal that would benefit both parties. Licensing is discussed later in this chapter.

If the original patent held by a competitor is ready to expire, the entrepreneur may either try to modify it or plan for the time when it can be legally copied. Once a patent has been granted, it becomes public information, which can be to the entrepreneur's advantage when considering the introduction of a similar product. In fact, a review of the proceedings that led to the granting of a patent can often suggest ways to modify the product to avoid infringement.

TRADEMARKS

A trademark may be a word, symbol, design, or some combination of such, or it could be a slogan or even a particular sound that identifies the source or sponsorship of certain goods or services. Unlike the patent, a trademark can last indefinitely, as long as it continues to perform its indicated function. The trademark is generally given an initial 20-year registration with 20-year renewable terms. In the fifth to sixth year, the registrant is required to file an affidavit with the PTO indicating that the mark is currently in commercial use. If no affidavit is filed, the registration is canceled.

Before filing an application for a trademark, the entrepreneur must actually use the mark on goods shipped or sold or on services rendered. Thus protection is granted based on actual use of the mark.

The protection awarded is dependent on the character of the mark itself. There are four categories of trademarks: (1) coined marks denote no relationship between the mark and the goods or services (e.g., Polaroid, Kodak) and afford the possibility of expansion to a wide range of products; (2) an arbitrary mark is one that has another meaning in our language (e.g., Shell) and is applied to a product or service; (3) a suggestive mark is used to suggest certain features, qualities, ingredients, or characteristics of a product or service (e.g., Halo shampoo). It differs from an arbitrary mark in that it tends to suggest some describable attribute of the product or services. Finally, (4) a descriptive mark must have become distinctive over a significant period of time and gained consumer recognition before it can be registered. The mark then is considered to have secondary meaning, that is, it is descriptive of a particular product or service, (e.g., Rubberoid as applied to roofing materials that contain rubber).[3]

Registering a trademark can offer significant advantages or benefits to the entrepreneur. Figure 15–2 summarizes some of these benefits.

Registering the Trademark

As indicated earlier, the PTO is responsible for the federal registration of trademarks. To file an application, the entrepreneur must complete the form illustrated in Figure 15–3. The application varies only in the address and applicant name if the business is a partnership or a corporation. For a partnership, names of all partners are included. In the case of a corporation, the corporation's name and address and the state of incorporation would be given.

Filing of the trademark registration must meet four requirements: (1) completion of the written form, (2) a drawing of the mark, (3) five specimens showing actual use of the mark, and (4) the fee. Each trademark must be applied for separately. Upon receipt of this information, the PTO assigns a serial number to the application and sends a filing receipt to the applicant.

---

[3]*Patent and Trademark Tactics*, pp. 124–25.

FIGURE 15–2   Benefits of a Registered Trademark

- It provides notice to everyone that you have exclusive rights to the use of the mark throughout the territorial limits of the United States.
- Entitles you to sue in federal court for trademark infringement, which can result in recovery of profits, damages, and costs.
- Incontestable rights are established regarding the commercial use of the mark.
- Right to deposit registration with customs to prevent importation of goods with similar mark.
- It entitles you to use the notice of registration ®.
- It provides a basis for filing trademark application in foreign countries.

The next step in the registering process is a determination by the examining attorney at the PTO as to whether the mark is suitable for registration. Within about three months, an initial determination is made as to its suitability. Any objections by the entrepreneur must be raised within six months or the application is considered abandoned. If the trademark is refused, the entrepreneur still has the right to appeal to the PTO.

Once accepted, the trademark is published in the *Trademark Official Gazette* to allow any party 30 days to oppose or request an extension to oppose. If no opposition is filed, the registration is issued. This entire procedure usually takes about 13 months from the initial filing.

COPYRIGHTS

A copyright protects original works of authorship. It does not protect the idea itself and thus someone else can use the idea or concept in a different manner.

The copyright law has become especially relevant to computer software companies. In 1980, the Computer Software Copyright Act was added to the Federal Code of Copyright Laws. It provided explanation of the nature of software protection under the copyright laws. Authors or publishers of software are protected similarly to artistic works. The idea of the software (e.g., spreadsheets) is not eligible for protection but the actual program to produce the spreadsheet is eligible.

Copyrights are registered with the Library of Congress and will not usually require an attorney. All that is necessary is that the completed form, illustrated in Figure 15–4, two copies of the work, and the appropriate fee be sent to the Register of Copyrights. The term of copyright is the life of the author plus 50 years. If the author is an institution, the term of the copyright is 75 years from publication.

Besides computer software, copyrights are desirable for such things as books, scripts, articles, poems, songs, sculptures, models, maps, blueprints, collages, printed material on board games, data, and music. In some instances, several

FIGURE 15–3

TRADEMARK APPLICATION, PRINCIPAL REGISTER, WITH DECLARATION (Individual)	MARK *(identify the mark)*
	CLASS NO *(if known)*

TO THE COMMISSIONER OF PATENTS AND TRADEMARKS:

NAME OF APPLICANT, AND BUSINESS TRADE NAME, IF ANY

BUSINESS ADDRESS

RESIDENCE ADDRESS

CITIZENSHIP OF APPLICANT

The above identified applicant has adopted and is using the trademark shown in the accompanying drawing for the following

goods: _____

and requests that said mark be registered in the United States Patent and Trademark Office on the Principal Register established by the Act of July 5, 1946.

The trademark was first used on the goods on _____ ; was first used on the goods in
                                                   (date)

_____ commerce on _____ ; and is now in use in such
       (type of commerce)   *(date)*

commerce.

The mark is used by applying it to _____

and five specimens showing the mark as actually used are presented herewith.

_____
(name of applicant)

being hereby warned that willful false statements and the like so made are punishable by fine or imprisonment, or both, under Section 1001 of Title 18 of the United States Code and that such willful false statements may jeopardize the validity of the application or any registration resulting therefrom, declares that he/she believes himself/herself to be the owner of the trademark sought to be registered; to the best of his/her knowledge and belief no other person, firm, corporation, or association has the right to use said mark in commerce, either in the identical form or in such near resemblance thereto as may be likely, when applied to the goods of such other person, to cause confusion, or to cause mistake, or to deceive; the facts set forth in this application are true; and all statements made of his/her own knowledge are true and all statements made on information and belief are believed to be true.

_____
(signature of applicant)

_____
(date)

FORM PTO-1476FB (REV. 4-87)   U.S. DEPARTMENT OF COMMERCE/Patent and Trademark Office

FIGURE 15-4

Filling Out Application Form TX

Detach and read these instructions before completing this form. Make sure all applicable spaces have been filled in before you return this form.

BASIC INFORMATION

When to Use This Form: Use Form TX for registration of published or unpublished non-dramatic literary works, excluding periodicals or serial issues. This class includes a wide variety of works: fiction, non-fiction, poetry, textbooks, reference works, directories, catalogs, advertising copy, compilations of information, and computer programs. For periodicals and serials, use Form SE.

Deposit to Accompany Application: An application for copyright registration must be accompanied by a deposit consisting of copies or phonorecords representing the entire work for which registration is to be made. The following are the general deposit requirements as set forth in the statute.

Unpublished Work: Deposit one complete copy (or phonorecord)

Published Work: Deposit two complete copies (or phonorecords) of the best edition

Work First Published Outside the United States: Deposit one complete copy (or phonorecord) of the first foreign edition

Contribution to a Collective Work: Deposit one complete copy (or phonorecord) of the best edition of the collective work

The Copyright Notice: For published works, the law provides that a copyright notice in a specified form "shall be placed on all publicly distributed copies from which the work can be visually perceived." Use of the copyright notice is the responsibility of the copyright owner and does not require advance permission from the Copyright Office. The required form of the notice for copies generally consists of three elements: (1) the symbol "©", or the word "Copyright," or the abbreviation "Copr.", (2) the year of first publication, and (3) the name of the owner of copyright. For example: "© 1981 Constance Porter." The notice is to be affixed to the copies "in such manner and location as to give reasonable notice of the claim of copyright."

For further information about copyright registration, notice, or special questions relating to copyright problems, write:

Information and Publications Section, LM-455
Copyright Office
Library of Congress
Washington, D.C. 20559

PRIVACY ACT ADVISORY STATEMENT Required by the Privacy Act of 1974 (Public Law 93-579)	PRINCIPAL USES OF REQUESTED INFORMATION • Establishment and maintenance of a public record
AUTHORITY FOR REQUESTING THIS INFORMATION • Title 17, U.S.C., Secs. 409 and 410	• Examination of the application for compliance with legal requirements
FURNISHING THE REQUESTED INFORMATION IS • Voluntary	OTHER ROUTINE USES • Public inspection and copying • Preparation of public indexes • Preparation of public catalogs of copyright registrations
BUT IF THE INFORMATION IS NOT FURNISHED • It may be necessary to delay or refuse registration	• Preparation of search reports upon request NOTE
• You may not be entitled to certain relief, remedies and benefits provided in chapters 4 and 5 of title 17, U.S.C.	• No other advisory statement will be given you in connection with this application • Please keep this statement and refer to it if we communicate with you regarding this application

LINE-BY-LINE INSTRUCTIONS

1 SPACE 1: Title

Title of This Work: Every work submitted for copyright registration must be given a title to identify that particular work. If the copies or phonorecords of the work bear a title (or an identifying phrase that could serve as a title), transcribe that wording *completely* and *exactly* on the application. Indexing of the registration and future identification of the work will depend on the information you give here.

Previous or Alternative Titles: Complete this space if there are any additional titles for the work under which someone searching for the registration might be likely to look, or under which a document pertaining to the work might be recorded.

Publication as a Contribution: If the work being registered is a contribution to a periodical, serial, or collection, give the title of the contribution in the "Title of this Work" space. Then, in the line headed "Publication as a Contribution," give information about the collective work in which the contribution appeared.

2 SPACE 2: Author(s)

General Instructions: After reading these instructions, decide who are the "authors" of this work for copyright purposes. Then, unless the work is a "collective work," give the requested information about every "author" who contributed any appreciable amount of copyrightable matter to this version of the work. If you need further space, request additional Continuation sheets. In the case of a collective work, such as an anthology, collection of essays, or encyclopedia, give information about the collective work as a whole.

Name of Author: The fullest form of the author's name should be given. Unless the work was "made for hire," the individual who actually created the work is its "author." In the case of a work made for hire, the statute provides that "the employer or other person for whom the work was prepared is considered the author."

What is a "Work Made for Hire"? A "work made for hire" is defined as (1) "a work prepared by an employee within the scope of his or her employment", or (2) "a work specially ordered or commissioned for use as a contribution to a collective work, as a part of a motion picture or other audiovisual work, as a translation, as a supplementary work, as a compilation, as an instructional text, as a test, as answer material for a test, or as an atlas, if the parties expressly agree in a written instrument signed by them that the work shall be considered a work made for hire." If you have checked "Yes" to indicate that the work was "made for hire," you must give the full legal name of the employer (or other person for whom the work was prepared). You may also include the name of the employee along with the name of the employer (for example: "Elster Publishing Co., employer for hire of John Ferguson").

"Anonymous" or "Pseudonymous" Work: An author's contribution to a work is "anonymous" if that author is not identified on the copies or phonorecords of the work. An author's contribution to a work is "pseudonymous" if that author is identified on the copies or phonorecords under a fictitious name. If the work is "anonymous" you may: (1) leave the line blank; or (2) state "anonymous" on the line; or (3) reveal the author's identity. If the work is "pseudonymous" you may: (1) leave the line blank; or (2) give the pseudonym and identify it as such (for example: "Huntley Haverstock, pseudonym"); or (3) reveal the author's name, making clear which is the real name and which is the pseudonym (for example: "Judith Barton, whose pseudonym is Madeline Elster"). However, the citizenship or domicile of the author **must** be given in all cases.

Dates of Birth and Death: If the author is dead, the statute requires that the year of death be included in the application unless the work is anonymous or pseudonymous. The author's birth date is optional, but is useful as a form of identification. Leave this space blank if the author's contribution was a "work made for hire."

Author's Nationality or Domicile: Give the country of which the author is a citizen, or the country in which the author is domiciled. Nationality or domicile **must** be given in all cases.

Nature of Authorship: After the words "Nature of Authorship" give a brief general statement of the nature of this particular author's contribution to the work. Examples: "Entire text", "Coauthor of entire text", "Chapters 11-14"; "Editorial revisions"; "Compilation and English translation"; "New text".

FIGURE 15–4 *(continued)*

3 SPACE 3: Creation and Publication

General Instructions: Do not confuse "creation" with "publication." Every application for copyright registration must state "the year in which creation of the work was completed." Give the date and nation of first publication only if the work has been published.

Creation: Under the statute, a work is "created" when it is fixed in a copy or phonorecord for the first time. Where a work has been prepared over a period of time, the part of the work existing in fixed form on a particular date constitutes the created work on that date. The date you give here should be the year in which the author completed the particular version for which registration is now being sought, even if other versions exist or if further changes or additions are planned.

Publication: The statute defines "publication" as "the distribution of copies or phonorecords of a work to the public by sale or other transfer of ownership, or by rental, lease, or lending"; a work is also "published" if there has been an "offering to distribute copies or phonorecords to a group of persons for purposes of further distribution, public performance, or pubic display." Give the full date (month, day, year) when, and the country where, publication first occurred. If first publication took place simultaneously in the United States and other countries, it is sufficient to state "U.S.A."

4 SPACE 4: Claimant(s)

Name(s) and Address(es) of Copyright Claimant(s): Give the name(s) and address(es) of the copyright claimant(s) in this work even if the claimant is the same as the author. Copyright in a work belongs initially to the author of the work (including, in the case of a work made for hire, the employer or other person for whom the work was prepared). The copyright claimant is either the author of the work or a person or organization to whom the copyright initially belonging to the author has been transferred.

Transfer: The statute provides that, if the copyright claimant is not the author, the application for registration must contain "a brief statement of how the claimant obtained ownership of the copyright." If any copyright claimant named in space 4 is not an author named in space 2, give a brief, general statement summarizing the means by which that claimant obtained ownership of the copyright. Examples: "By written contract"; "Transfer of all rights by author"; "Assignment"; "By will." Do not attach transfer documents or other attachments or riders.

5 SPACE 5: Previous Registration

General Instructions: The questions in space 5 are intended to find out whether an earlier registration has been made for this work and, if so, whether there is any basis for a new registration. As a general rule, only one basic copyright registration can be made for the same version of a particular work.

Same Version: If this version is substantially the same as the work covered by a previous registration, a second registration is not generally possible unless: (1) the work has been registered in unpublished form and a second registration is now being sought to cover this first published edition; or (2) someone other than the author is identified as copyright claimant in the earlier registration, and the author is now seeking registration in his or her own name. If either of these two exceptions apply, check the appropriate box and give the earlier registration number and date. Otherwise, do not submit Form TX; instead, write the Copyright Office for information about supplementary registration or recordation of transfers of copyright ownership.

Changed Version: If the work has been changed, and you are now seeking registration to cover the additions or revisions, check the last box in space 5, give the earlier registration number and date, and complete both parts of space 6 in accordance with the instructions below.

Previous Registration Number and Date: If more than one previous registration has been made for the work, give the number and date of the latest registration.

6 SPACE 6: Derivative Work or Compilation

General Instructions: Complete space 6 if this work is a "changed version," "compilation," or "derivative work," and if it incorporates one or more earlier works that have already been published or registered for copyright, or that have fallen into the public domain. A "compilation" is defined as "a work formed by the collection and assembling of preexisting materials or of data that are selected, coordinated, or arranged in such a way that the resulting work as a whole constitutes an original work of authorship." A "derivative work" is "a work based on one or more preexisting works." Examples of derivative works include translations, fictionalizations, abridgments, condensations, or "any other form in which a work may be recast, transformed, or adapted." Derivative works also include works "consisting of editorial revisions, annotations, or other modifications" if these changes, as a whole, represent an original work of authorship.

Preexisting Material (space 6a): For derivative works, complete this space and space 6b. In space 6a identify the preexisting work that has been recast, transformed, or adapted. An example of preexisting material might be: "Russian version of Goncharov's 'Oblomov'." Do not complete space 6a for compilations.

Material Added to This Work (space 6b): Give a brief, general statement of the new material covered by the copyright claim for which registration is sought. Derivative work examples include: "Foreword, editing, critical annotations"; "Translation"; "Chapters 11-17." If the work is a compilation, describe both the compilation itself and the material that has been compiled. Example: "Compilation of certain 1917 Speeches by Woodrow Wilson." A work may be both a derivative work and compilation, in which case a sample statement might be: "Compilation and additional new material."

7 SPACE 7: Manufacturing Provisions

General Instructions: The copyright statute currently provides, as a general rule, that the copies of a published work "consisting preponderantly of nondramatic literary material in the English language" be manufactured in the United States or Canada in order to be lawfully imported and publicly distributed in the United States. If the work being registered is unpublished or not in English, leave this space blank. Complete this space if registration is sought for a published work "consisting preponderantly of nondramatic literary material that is in the English language." Identify those who manufactured the copies and where those manufacturing processes were performed. As an exception to the manufacturing provisions, the statute prescribes that, where manufacture has taken place outside the United States or Canada, a maximum of 2000 copies of the foreign edition may be imported into the United States without affecting the copyright owners' rights. For this purpose, the Copyright Office will issue an Import Statement upon request and payment of a fee of $3 at the time of registration or at any later time. For further information about import statements, write for Form IS.

8 SPACE 8: Reproduction for Use of Blind or Physically Handicapped Individuals

General Instructions: One of the major programs of the Library of Congress is to provide Braille editions and special recordings of works for the exclusive use of the blind and physically handicapped. In an effort to simplify and speed up the copyright licensing procedures that are a necessary part of this program, section 710 of the copyright statute provides for the establishment of a voluntary licensing system to be tied in with copyright registration. Copyright Office regulations provide that you may grant a license for such reproduction and distribution solely for the use of persons who are certified by competent authority as unable to read normal printed material as a result of physical limitations. The license is entirely voluntary, nonexclusive, and may be terminated upon 90 days notice.

How to Grant the License: If you wish to grant it, check one of the three boxes in space 8. Your check in one of these boxes, together with your signature in space 10, will mean that the Library of Congress can proceed to reproduce and distribute under the license without further paperwork. For further information, write for Circular R63.

9,10,11 SPACE 9, 10, 11: Fee, Correspondence, Certification, Return Address

Deposit Account: If you maintain a Deposit Account in the Copyright Office, identify it in space 9. Otherwise leave the space blank and send the fee of $10 with your application and deposit.

Correspondence (space 9): This space should contain the name, address, area code, and telephone number of the person to be consulted if correspondence about this application becomes necessary.

Certification (space 10): The application can not be accepted unless it bears the date and the **handwritten signature** of the author or other copyright claimant, or of the owner of exclusive right(s), or of the duly authorized agent of author, claimant, or owner of exclusive right(s).

Address for Return of Certificate (space 11): The address box must be completed legibly since the certificate will be returned in a window envelope.

FIGURE 15–4 *(continued)*

FORM TX
UNITED STATES COPYRIGHT OFFICE

REGISTRATION NUMBER

TX   TXU

EFFECTIVE DATE OF REGISTRATION

Month   Day   Year

DO NOT WRITE ABOVE THIS LINE. IF YOU NEED MORE SPACE, USE A SEPARATE CONTINUATION SHEET.

1 TITLE OF THIS WORK ▼

PREVIOUS OR ALTERNATIVE TITLES ▼

PUBLICATION AS A CONTRIBUTION If this work was published as a contribution to a periodical, serial, or collection, give information about the collective work in which the contribution appeared. **Title of Collective Work ▼**

If published in a periodical or serial give **Volume ▼**   **Number ▼**   **Issue Date ▼**   **On Pages ▼**

2 NAME OF AUTHOR ▼   DATES OF BIRTH AND DEATH
                                                        Year Born ▼   Year Died ▼

Was this contribution to the work a   AUTHOR'S NATIONALITY OR DOMICILE   WAS THIS AUTHOR'S CONTRIBUTION TO
"work made for hire"?   Name of Country   THE WORK
☐ Yes   OR { Citizen of ▶ _____   Anonymous?   ☐ Yes ☐ No   If the answer to either
☐ No   { Domiciled in ▶ _____   Pseudonymous? ☐ Yes ☐ No of these questions is
                                                                                  Yes, see detailed
                                                                                  instructions

NOTE
Under the law, the author of a work made for hire is generally the employer, not the employee (see instructions). For any part of this work that was made for hire check "Yes" in the space provided, give the employer (or other person for whom the work was prepared) as "Author" of that part, and leave the space for dates of birth and death blank.

NATURE OF AUTHORSHIP Briefly describe nature of the material created by this author in which copyright is claimed. ▼

NAME OF AUTHOR ▼   DATES OF BIRTH AND DEATH
                                                        Year Born ▼   Year Died ▼

Was this contribution to the work a   AUTHOR'S NATIONALITY OR DOMICILE   WAS THIS AUTHOR'S CONTRIBUTION TO
"work made for hire"?   Name of Country   THE WORK
☐ Yes   OR { Citizen of ▶ _____   Anonymous?   ☐ Yes ☐ No   If the answer to either
☐ No   { Domiciled in ▶ _____   Pseudonymous? ☐ Yes ☐ No of these questions is
                                                                                  Yes, see detailed
                                                                                  instructions

NATURE OF AUTHORSHIP Briefly describe nature of the material created by this author in which copyright is claimed. ▼

NAME OF AUTHOR ▼   DATES OF BIRTH AND DEATH
                                                        Year Born ▼   Year Died ▼

Was this contribution to the work a   AUTHOR'S NATIONALITY OR DOMICILE   WAS THIS AUTHOR'S CONTRIBUTION TO
"work made for hire"?   Name of Country   THE WORK
☐ Yes   OR { Citizen of ▶ _____   Anonymous?   ☐ Yes ☐ No   If the answer to either
☐ No   { Domiciled in ▶ _____   Pseudonymous? ☐ Yes ☐ No of these questions is
                                                                                  Yes, see detailed
                                                                                  instructions

NATURE OF AUTHORSHIP Briefly describe nature of the material created by this author in which copyright is claimed. ▼

3 YEAR IN WHICH CREATION OF THIS   DATE AND NATION OF FIRST PUBLICATION OF THIS PARTICULAR WORK
      WORK WAS COMPLETED This information Complete this information Month ▶ _____ Day ▶ _____ Year ▶ _____
                          must be given   ONLY if this work
                    ◀ Year in all cases.   has been published.   ◀ Nation

4 COPYRIGHT CLAIMANT(S) Name and address must be given even if the claimant is the   APPLICATION RECEIVED
      same as the author given in space 2 ▼
                                                                          ONE DEPOSIT RECEIVED

See instructions   TWO DEPOSITS RECEIVED
before completing
this space
                                                                          REMITTANCE NUMBER AND DATE
      TRANSFER If the claimant(s) named here in space 4 are different from the author(s) named
      in space 2, give a brief statement of how the claimant(s) obtained ownership of the copyright. ▼

DO NOT WRITE HERE
OFFICE USE ONLY

MORE ON BACK ▶ • Complete all applicable spaces (numbers 5–11) on the reverse side of this page.   DO NOT WRITE HERE
                    • See detailed instructions.   • Sign the form at line 10.
                                                                                          Page 1 of _____ pages

FIGURE 15–4 *(concluded)*

EXAMINED BY _____

CHECKED BY _____

☐ CORRESPONDENCE
　 Yes

☐ DEPOSIT ACCOUNT
　 FUNDS USED

FORM TX

FOR
COPYRIGHT
OFFICE
USE
ONLY

DO NOT WRITE ABOVE THIS LINE. IF YOU NEED MORE SPACE, USE A SEPARATE CONTINUATION SHEET.

PREVIOUS REGISTRATION Has registration for this work, or for an earlier version of this work, already been made in the Copyright Office?
☐ **Yes** ☐ **No** If your answer is "Yes," why is another registration being sought? (Check appropriate box) ▼
☐ This is the first published edition of a work previously registered in unpublished form
☐ This is the first application submitted by this author as copyright claimant
☐ This is a changed version of the work, as shown by space 6 on this application
If your answer is "Yes," give: **Previous Registration Number** ▼ _____ **Year of Registration** ▼ _____

5

DERIVATIVE WORK OR COMPILATION Complete both space 6a & 6b for a derivative work; complete only 6b for a compilation
a. Preexisting Material Identify any preexisting work or works that this work is based on or incorporates. ▼

b. Material Added to This Work Give a brief, general statement of the material that has been added to this work and in which copyright is claimed. ▼

6

See instructions
before completing
this space

MANUFACTURERS AND LOCATIONS If this is a published work consisting preponderantly of nondramatic literary material in English, the law may require that the copies be manufactured in the United States or Canada for full protection. If so, the names of the manufacturers who performed certain processes, and the places where these processes were performed **must** be given. See instructions for details.
Names of Manufacturers ▼ _____ **Places of Manufacture** ▼ _____

7

REPRODUCTION FOR USE OF BLIND OR PHYSICALLY HANDICAPPED INDIVIDUALS A signature on this form at space 10, and a check in one of the boxes here in space 8, constitutes a non-exclusive grant of permission to the Library of Congress to reproduce and distribute solely for the blind and physically handicapped and under the conditions and limitations prescribed by the regulations of the Copyright Office: (1) copies of the work identified in space 1 of this application in Braille (or similar tactile symbols); or (2) phonorecords embodying a fixation of a reading of that work; or (3) both
　　　　a ☐ Copies and Phonorecords 　　b ☐ Copies Only 　　c ☐ Phonorecords Only

8

See instructions

DEPOSIT ACCOUNT If the registration fee is to be charged to a Deposit Account established in the Copyright Office, give name and number of Account.
Name ▼ _____ **Account Number** ▼ _____

9

CORRESPONDENCE Give name and address to which correspondence about this application should be sent. Name-Address-Apt-City-State-Zip ▼

_____ Area Code & Telephone Number ▶ _____

Be sure to
give your
daytime phone
◀ number

CERTIFICATION* I, the undersigned, hereby certify that I am the
　　　　　　　　　　　　Check one ▶
☐ author
☐ other copyright claimant
☐ owner of exclusive right(s)
☐ authorized agent of _____
　　Name of author or other copyright claimant or owner of exclusive right(s) ▲
of the work identified in this application and that the statements made by me in this application are correct to the best of my knowledge.

10

Typed or printed name and date ▼ If this is a published work, this date must be the same as or later than the date of publication given in space 3.
_____ date ▶ _____

✎ Handwritten signature (X) ▼

**MAIL
CERTIFI-
CATE TO**

Certificate
will be
mailed in
window
envelope

Name ▼ _____

Number Street Apartment Number ▼ _____

City State ZIP ▼ _____

Have you:
• Completed all necessary spaces?
• Signed your application in space 10?
• Enclosed check or money order for $10 payable to *Register of Copyrights?*
• Enclosed your deposit material with the application and fee?
MAIL TO: Register of Copyrights Library of Congress, Washington, D.C. 20559

11

* 17 U.S.C. § 506(e): Any person who knowingly makes a false representation of a material fact in the application for copyright registration provided for by section 409, or in any written statement filed in connection with the application, shall be fined not more than $2,500.

U.S. GOVERNMENT PRINTING OFFICE: 1985 491-560 20,011

December 1985—200,000

forms of protection may be available. For example, a trademark may be obtained for the name of a board game, the game itself protected by a utility patent, the printed matter or the board protected by a copyright, and the playing pieces covered by a design patent.[4]

TRADE SECRETS

In certain instances, the entrepreneur may prefer to maintain the confidentiality of an idea or process and sell or license it as a trade secret. The trade secret will have a life as long as the idea or process remains a secret.

A trade secret is not covered by any federal law but is recognized under a governing body of common laws in each state. Employees involved in working with an idea or process may be asked to first sign a confidential information agreement that will protect against their giving out the trade secret either while an employee or after leaving the organization. The entrepreneur should hire an attorney to help draw up any such agreement. The holder of the trade secret has the right to sue any signee who breaches such an agreement.

Unfortunately, protection against the leaking of trade secrets is difficult to enforce. More important, legal action can be taken only after the secret has been revealed. The effectiveness of a trade secret depends on how careful the entrepreneur is in giving information to employees and having legal support in setting up the confidential information agreement.

LICENSING

Licensing may be defined as an arrangement between two parties, where one party has proprietary rights over some information, process, or technology protected by a patent, trademark, or copyright. This arrangement, specified in a contract (discussed later in this chapter), requires the licensee to pay a royalty or some other specified sum to the holder of the proprietary rights (licensor) in return for permission to copy the patent, trademark, or copyright.

Thus, licensing has significant value as a marketing strategy for holders of patents, trademarks, or copyrights to grow their business in new markets when they lack resources or experience in those markets. It is also an important marketing strategy for entrepreneurs who wish to start a new venture but need permission to copy or incorporate the patent, trademark, or copyright with their idea.

A patent license agreement would specify how the licensee would have access to the patent. For example, the licensor may still manufacture the product but give the licensee the rights to market it under their label in a noncompetitive

---

[4]*How to Protect and Benefit from Your Ideas* (Arlington, VA: American Patent Law Association, 1981), p. 27.

market (e.g., foreign market). In other instances, the licensee may actually manufacture and market the patented product under their own label. This agreement must be carefully worded and should involve a lawyer to ensure the protection of all parties.

Licensing a trademark generally involves a franchising agreement. The entrepreneur operates a business using the trademark and agrees to pay a fixed sum for use of the trademark, pay a royalty based on sales volume, buy supplies from the franchisor (e.g., Shell, Exxon, Dunkin Donuts, Pepsi Cola or Coca Cola bottlers, or Midas Muffler), or some combination of these. Chapter 16 discusses franchising as an option for the entrepreneur to start a new business.

Copyrights are another popular licensed property. They involve rights to use or copy books, software, music, photographs, or plays, to name a few. In the late 1970s, computer games were designed using licenses from arcade games and movies. Television shows have also licensed their name for board games or computer games. Celebrities will often license the right to use their name, likeness, or image in a product (e.g., Andre Agassi tennis clothing, Elvis Presley memorabilia, or Mickey Mouse lunch boxes). Hit movies have resulted in a wave of new products. For instance, *Who Framed Roger Rabbit?* resulted in a licensing agreement with Hasbro to produce a line of plush dolls and with McDonalds to offer Roger Rabbit drinking glasses. In fact, the success of the movie resulted in nearly 50 license agreements.[5] Other movies, such as *Rambo, Willow, Crocodile Dundee,* have also resulted in numerous licensing agreements providing opportunities for entrepreneurs and a means to extend the profit potential of the movie company.[6]

Before embarking in a license agreement, the entrepreneur should ask the following questions:

* Will the customer recognize the licensed property?
* How well does the licensed property complement my products or services?
* How much experience do I have with the licensed property?
* What is the long-term outlook for the licensed property? (For example, the loss of popularity of a celebrity can result in an end to a business involving that celebrity's name.)
* What kind of protection does the licensing agreement provide?
* What commitment do I have in payment of royalties, sales quotas, and so on?
* Are renewal options possible and under what terms?

Licensing is an excellent option for the entrepreneur to increase revenues, without the risk and costly start-up investment. To be able to license requires the entrepreneur to have something to license, which is why it is so important to

---

[5]"Hit Movies Spark Licensing Tie-ins," *Playthings,* 99 (August 1988), pp. 56–7.

[6]M. Manley, "Let's Shake on That," *INC.,* June 1986, pp. 131–32.

seek protection for any product, information, name, and so on with a patent, trademark, or copyright. On the other hand, licensing can also be a way to start a new venture when the idea may infringe on someone else's patent, trademark, or copyright. In this instance, the entrepreneur has nothing to lose in seeking a license agreement from the holder of the property.

Licensing continues to be a powerful marketing tool. With the advice of a lawyer, entrepreneurs may find that licensing opportunities are a way to minimize risk, expand a business, or complement an existing product line.

PRODUCT SAFETY AND LIABILITY

It is very important for the entrepreneur to assess whether any product that is to be marketed in the new venture is subject to any regulations under the Consumer Product Safety Act. The act, passed in 1972, created a five-member commission that has the power to prescribe safety standards for more than 10,000 products.

In addition to setting standards for products, the commission is empowered to identify what it considers to be substantial hazards and bar products it considers unsafe. It is especially active in recognizing whether possible product defects may be hazardous to consumers. If this is the case, the commission will request the manufacturer, in writing, to take any corrective action.

The entrepreneur should ascertain whether his or her new product falls under the Consumer Product Safety Act. If it does, he or she will have to follow the appropriate procedures in meeting all the necessary requirements.

Product liability problems are complex, and they continue to be an important consideration for entrepreneurs in light of the increases in insurance premiums, legal fees, and legal cases. The entrepreneur must consult with an attorney and insurance agent to obtain satisfactory coverage and protection.

Claims regarding product liability usually fall under one of the following categories:

1. *Negligence*—Extending to all parts of the production and marketing process, this involves being negligent in the way a product is presented to a client, such as using deficient labels, false advertising, and so on.

2. *Warranty*—Consumers may sue if advertising or information overstate the benefits of a product or the product does not perform as stated.

3. *Strict Liability*—In this action, a consumer is suing on the basis that the product in question was defective prior to its receipt.

4. *Misrepresentation*—This occurs when advertising, labels, or other information misrepresent material facts concerning the character or quality of the product.

The best protection against product liability is to produce safe products and to warn consumers of any potential hazards. It is impossible to expect zero defects, so entrepreneurs should be sensitive to what kinds of product liability problems may occur.

INSURANCE

Some of the problems relating to product liability were discussed in the previous section. Besides being cautious, the entrepreneur should purchase insurance in the event that problems do occur. Service-related businesses such as day care centers, amusement parks, shopping centers, and so on have had significant increases in the number of lawsuits.

In general, most firms should consider coverage for those situations described in Figure 15–5. Each of these types of insurance provides a means of managing risk in the new business. The main problem is that the entrepreneur usually has

FIGURE 15–5 Types of Insurance and Possible Coverage

Type of Insurance	Coverage Possible
Property	• Fire insurance to cover losses to goods and premises resulting from fire and lightning. Can extend coverage to include risks associated with explosion, riot, vehicle damage, windstorm, hail, and smoke. • Burglary and robbery to cover small losses for stolen property in cases of forced entry (burglary) or if force or threat of violence was involved (robbery). • Business interruption will pay net profits and expenses when a business is shut down because of fire or other insured cause.
Casualty	• General liability covers the costs of defense and judgments obtained against the company resulting from bodily injury or property damage. This coverage can also be extended to cover product liability. • Automobile liability is needed when employees use their own cars for company business.
Life	• Life insurance protects the continuity of the business (especially a partnership). It can also provide financial protection for survivors of a sole proprietorship or for loss of a key corporate executive.
Worker's compensation	• May be mandatory in some states. Provides benefits to employees in case of work-related injury.
Bonding	• This shifts responsibility for employee or performance of a job. It protects company in case of employee theft of funds or protects contractor if subcontractor fails to complete a job within agreed-upon time.

limited resources in the beginning. Thus, it is important for the entrepreneur to determine not only what kind of insurance to purchase but also how much to purchase and from what company.

Seeking advice from an insurance agent is often difficult because the agent is trying to sell insurance. However, there are specialists at universities or the Small Business Administration who can provide this advice at little or no cost.

CONTRACTS

The entrepreneur, in starting a new venture, will be involved in a number of negotiations and contracts with vendors, landlords, and clients. It is very important for the entrepreneur to understand some of the fundamental issues related to contracts, while also recognizing the need for a lawyer in many of these negotiations.

Often, business deals are concluded with a handshake. Ordering supplies, lining up financing, reaching an agreement with a partner, and so on are common situations in which a handshake consummates the deal. Usually, when things are operating smoothly this procedure is sufficient. However, if there are disagreements, the entrepreneur may find that there is no deal and he or she may be liable for something never intended. The courts generally provide some guidelines based on precedence of cases. One rule is to never rely on a handshake if the deal cannot be completed within one year. For example, a company that trains salespeople asked another firm to produce videotapes used in the training. The training firm was asked to promise to use the tapes only for its own salesforce and not to sell the tapes to others. Some time after the original tapes were produced, this firm began to produce and sell the tapes under a newly formed company. The original developer of the tapes brought suit and the courts ruled that an oral agreement for more than one year is not enforceable. The only way that this could have been prevented was if the copying firm had signed a contract.

In addition to the one-year rule of thumb, the courts insist that a written contract exist for all transactions over $500. Even a quote on a specified number of parts from a manufacturer may not be considered a legal contract. For example, if an entrepreneur asked for and received a quote for 10 items and then only ordered one item, the seller would not have to sell that item at the original quoted price unless a written contract existed. If the items were all over $500, even the quoted price can be changed without a written contract.

Most sellers would not want to try to avoid their obligations in the above example. However, unusual circumstances may arise that force the seller to change his or her mind. Thus, the safest way to conduct business deals is with a written contract, especially if the amount of the deal is over $500 and is likely to extend beyond one year.

Any deal involving real estate must be in writing to be valid. Leases, rentals, and purchases all necessitate some type of written agreement.

Although a lawyer might be necessary in very complicated or large transactions, the entrepreneur cannot always afford one. Therefore, it is helpful for the entrepreneur to understand the four essential items in an agreement to provide the best legal protection.[7]

1. All of the parties involved should be named and their specific roles (e.g., buyer, seller, consultant, client, etc.) in the transaction specified.
2. The transaction should be described in detail (e.g., exact location of land, dates, units, place of delivery, payer for transportation, etc.).
3. The exact value of the transaction should be specified (e.g., installment payment with finance charges).
4. Obtain signature(s) of the person(s) involved in the deal.

HOW TO SELECT A LAWYER

Lawyers, like many other professionals, are specialists not just in the law but in specific areas of the law. The entrepreneur does not usually have the expertise or know-how to handle possible risks associated with the many difficult laws and regulations. A competent attorney is in a better position to understand all of the possible circumstances and outcomes related to any legal action.

In today's environment, lawyers are much more up-front with their fees. In fact, in some cases these fees, if for standard services, may even be advertised. In general, the lawyer may work on a retainer basis (stated amount per month or year) by which he or she provides office and consulting time. This does not include court time or other legal fees related to the action. This gives the entrepreneur the opportunity to call an attorney as the need arises without incurring high hourly visit fees.

In some instances, the lawyer may be hired for a one-time fee. For example, a patent attorney may be hired as a specialist to help the entrepreneur obtain a patent. Once the patent is obtained, this lawyer would not be needed, except perhaps if there was any litigation regarding the patent. Other specialists for setting up the organization or for purchase of real estate may also be paid on a service-performed basis. Whatever the fee basis, the entrepreneur should confront the cost issue initially so no questions arise in the future.

Choosing a lawyer is like hiring an employee. The lawyer with whom you work should be someone to whom you can relate personally. In a large law firm, it is possible that an associate or junior partner would be assigned to the new venture. The entrepreneur should ask to meet with this person to ensure that there is compatibility.

---

[7]Ibid., p. 132.

A good working relationship with a lawyer will ease some of the risk in starting a new business and will give the entrepreneur necessary confidence. When resources are limited, the entrepreneur may consider offering the lawyer stock in exchange for his or her services. The lawyer then will have a vested interest in the business and will likely provide more personalized services. However, in making such a major decision, the entrepreneur must consider any possible loss of control of the business.

SUMMARY

This chapter explores some of the major legal concerns in starting a new venture. It is important for the entrepreneur to seek legal advice in making all of the legal decisions required in the new venture. Lawyers have specialities that can provide the entrepreneur with the most appropriate advice under the circumstances.

A patent requires a patent attorney, who assists the entrepreneur in completing an application to the Patent and Trademark Office with the history and description of the invention, as well as claims for its usefulness. Patent fees will vary but in general will cost about $1,500. Infringement may also be a concern of the entrepreneur. An assessment of the existing patent(s) will help to ascertain whether infringement is likely and to evaluate the possibilities of modifying the patented product or licensing the rights from the holder of the patent.

Trademarks may be a word, symbol, design, or some combination or a slogan or sound that identifies the source of certain goods or services. Trademarks give the entrepreneur certain benefits as long as the following four requirements are met: (1) completion of the written application form, (2) submission of a drawing of the mark, (3) submission of five specimens showing actual use of the mark, and (4) payment of the required fee.

Copyrights protect original works of authorship. Copyrights are registered with the Library of Congress and do not usually require an attorney. They have become especially relevant to computer software firms.

Licensing is a viable means of starting a business using someone else's product, name, information, and so on. It is also an important strategy that the entrepreneur can use to expand the business without extensive risk or large investments.

The entrepreneur also should be sensitive to possible product safety and liability requirements. Careful scrutiny of possible product problems, as well as insurance, can reduce the risk. Other risks relating to property insurance, life insurance, workman's compensation, and bonding should be evaluated to ascertain any insurance needs.

Contracts are an important part of the transactions that the entrepreneur will make. As a rule of thumb, oral agreements are invalid for deals over one year and over $500. In addition, all real estate transactions must be in writing to be valid. It is important in a written agreement to identify all the parties and their respective roles, to describe the transaction in detail, to specify the value of the deal, and to obtain the signatures of the persons with whom you are doing business.

Franchising and Direct Marketing

CHAPTER OBJECTIVES

1. To present the opportunities of franchising for entrepreneurs

2. To contrast and compare the different types of franchises

3. To explain the risks in investing in a franchise

4. To identify the steps in evaluating a franchise opportunity

5. To understand the franchise agreement

6. To understand the opportunities and advantages of direct marketing

7. To identify important direct marketing start-up considerations

8. To explain the alternative techniques for direct marketing

RAY KROC

Ray Kroc, founder of McDonald's Corporation, was a pioneer in the fast-food franchise industry. The highly automated and efficient operations of the McDonald's restaurants surpassed the billion dollar sales mark in its 21st year of business. McDonald's has sales today of over $11 billion in 42 countries, with no sign of slowing down.

Kroc, the oldest of three children, was born on October 5, 1902, in Chicago, Illinois. Ray's father, a Western Union man with a modest income, lost his savings in real estate investments during the Great Depression. To survive, Ray's mother gave piano lessons and Ray always had odd jobs. One of Ray's pleasures was baseball. His affection for the game led, in 1974, to his acquisition of the San Diego Padres major league team for $10 million.

Kroc had only a 10th-grade education and insisted that hard work and persistence were the roots of success. Although Kroc's fame came from his McDonald's successes, his earlier years spent selling paper cups, malt mixers, and real estate were rewarding.

Kroc had entrepreneurial tendencies early in life. In 1917, at age 15, he and two other friends invested $100 apiece in a music store business. They sold sheet music and novelty instruments, while Kroc played the piano and sang. Unfortunately, Kroc and his friends did more singing than selling. He then falsified his age and was admitted as a Red Cross ambulance driver in World War I. He soon returned home and attended high school for a short time before dropping out. After playing the piano for various orchestras and bands, Kroc married, left the music business, and went to work as a paper cup salesman. As a salesman he was continuously initiating ideas to improve the business. When soda fountain owners objected to his soda take-out idea (using his Lily-Tulip paper cups, of course), he would arrange for 200 to 300 cups to be delivered for a trial period at no charge. Kroc's take-out idea was an immediate success.

Kroc then moved to Florida to sell swampland in the mid-1920s. Although he soon had financial rewards in Florida, they were short-lived. The boom collapsed in 1926, and he went back to work for Lily-Cup. In 1937, he came upon a new invention that could mix five milkshakes at a time. Kroc, who was continuously at odds with the Lily-Cup management, decided it was time to go into business for himself, so he became the exclusive U.S. distributor for the multimixer. After a couple of years of slow sales, the multimixer product finally took off.

In 1954, Kroc started hearing stories of a small hamburger diner, McDonald's in San Bernardino. He arrived at McDonald's around 10 A.M. and was surprised to find such a small restaurant, although the parking lot and other areas were immaculate and the employees were wearing nice uniforms. Soon people were arriving at McDonald's by the carload. There were families, construction workers, and teenagers. Kroc watched with fascination as the hamburgers, french fries, and milkshakes were prepared using an assembly line method. He asked several of the customers why and how often they ate at McDonald's. The usual response was that the food was good and cheap (didn't have to tip waitresses) and they normally ate there every day. People knew what to expect when they arrived at McDonald's—good, inexpensive food and fast service.

Kroc was thinking of all the multimixers he could sell if the McDonald brothers were to expand their operations. When Kroc approached Dick and Maurice McDonald with his idea, they were less than enthusiastic about opening additional restaurants. They didn't want the headaches of more restaurants and also couldn't think of anyone who would run the restaurants for them. Without much thought, Kroc said he could run the restaurants himself. An agreement was drawn up whereby the McDonald brothers would receive 0.5 percent gross revenues; in return Kroc would receive the right to copy the McDonald's business operations and use their name.

In 1955, at age 52, Kroc opened his first McDonald's store in Des Plaines, Illinois. By 1960, there were 228 restaurants and sales totaling $37 million. By 1973, there were 2,500 McDonald's restaurants. Today there are over 9,000 outlets across the world.

Ray Kroc attributes his success to several factors. One of these is what Kroc called the basics of the McDonald's operations, QSC&V (Quality, Service, Cleanliness, and Value). He insisted that quality was emphasized in every procedure, that each crew member was drilled on the McDonald's method of providing service, and that the restaurants were kept thoroughly clean. Kroc felt that quality, service, and cleanliness, combined with low prices, would result in a good value for their customers.

Franchise operators were required to go to Hamburger University. There, a specially trained staff would install QSC&V in all managers. By 1963, McDonald's had an extensive research and development laboratory in Addison, Illinois. The R&D lab continuously developed new equipment to aid in the operating efficiency of the McDonald's locations. McDonald's was a pioneer in the area of automating and standardizing operations in the fast-food industry.

Kroc instilled the entrepreneurial spirit in each franchise. McDonald's management style has been called "tight-loose." Operating controls are very stringent, but the atmosphere still allows individual creativity. The slogan for McDonald's operators is "In business for yourself, but not by yourself." This individual creativity is necessary for localizing the marketing methods. On occasion, a few menu modifications are allowed for certain markets.

Kroc was successful in creating a family atmosphere in his franchised McDonald's restaurants. He even made the decision early not to allow pay telephones, juke boxes, or vending machines. He felt that they created unproductive traffic and encouraged loitering that might disrupt customers.

Kroc died from heart failure January 14, 1984, at the age of 81. His personal fortune at the time of his death was estimated at $500 million. Although Kroc created a thriving restaurant franchise empire, he probably would have been successful at most anything.[1]

Ray Kroc proved that franchising could be a unique way to allow many other individuals to have their own businesses that could be supported by an effective management team (the franchisor). In addition to franchising, direct-mail marketing has recently become another popular method of starting a new business. Because both of these start-up alternatives are so important to entrepreneurs, and since they offer similar advantages, they are discussed in this chapter. Franchising and direct-mail marketing offer the entrepreneur the advantages of less start-up capital, lower risk, faster entry into the market, and a clearly defined target market. Advantages and disadvantages of each type of business are presented, as well as a discussion of how the entrepreneur should proceed if considering one of these alternatives.

UNDERSTANDING FRANCHISING

Franchising represents an opportunity for an entrepreneur to enter into business with the benefit of experience, knowledge, and support from the franchisor. Often the entrepreneur is beginning a new venture with little assurance that it will succeed. With a franchise, the entrepreneur will be trained and supported in the marketing of the business and will be using a name that has an established image.

Franchising is also an alternative strategy for an entrepreneur to expand his or her business, by having others pay for the use of the name, process, product, service, and so on. In 1989, George Naddaff bought the recipes and rights to use the name Boston Chicken from Arthur Cores and Steven "Kip" Kolow, two young chefs who independently owned and operated the Boston Chicken store. Naddaff realized that the restaurant was ideal for a franchising business. In less than nine months, 16 new Boston Chicken restaurants had been started in the New England area. In 1991, sales are expected to hit about $33 million.[2] Thus, franchising represents two opportunities: one is to franchise a business, and the second is to buy a franchise. In this chapter we will focus on the issues involved

---

[1] "McWorld?," *Business Week*, October 13, 1986, p. 80, and R. Kroc with R. Anderson, *Grinding It Out* (Chicago: Contemporary Books, 1977), p. 103.

[2] K. Fadel, "Different Strokes," *Entrepreneur*, April 1991, pp. 103–9.

in buying a franchise, but it should be remembered that regardless of which side of the arrangement you are on (buyer or seller), these factors are all important in the decision process.

During recent years, franchising businesses have been expanding rapidly and have found new areas of application. By 1990, there were 3,000 franchise companies representing over 500,000 franchises. These franchises accounted for more than $600 billion in sales. It is predicted that by 1999 the number of franchise companies will reach 9,000, which means there is an expected growth of 500 franchise start-ups per year.[3]

Any person who has the urge to own his or her own business may feel that a franchise is an easy solution. There are, however, some important risks involved that will be discussed later in this chapter. The important thing is that the entrepreneur should have a clear understanding of what a franchise is, its advantages, and potential risks.

Definition of Franchising

Franchising may be defined as "an arrangement whereby the manufacturer or sole distributor of a trademarked product or service gives exclusive rights of local distribution to independent retailers in return for their payment of royalties and conformance to standardized operating procedures."[4] The person offering the franchise is known as the **franchisor.** He or she probably has many years of experience in the business and knowledge of what is and what is not successful. The **franchisee** is the person who purchases the franchise and is given the opportunity to enter a new business with a good chance to succeed. However, there is risk in any new business, and there are some good franchise opportunities and some that are much less desirable.

Advantages of Franchising

One of the most important advantages of buying a franchise is that the entrepreneur does not have all the headaches associated with starting a business from scratch. The franchisor will usually provide a plan with clear directions for the operation of the business.

The franchisee is given advice or a defined location for the business. In retailing franchises, such as McDonald's, a location analysis is done to ensure that the business will reach needed goals. Assessment of traffic, demographics, growth of businesses in the area, competition, and so on make up an integral part of the decision as to where to locate the business. Often the franchise in-

---

[3]E. Kotite, "Franchising Comes Alive," *Entrepreneur,* April 1991, pp. 99–101.

[4]D. D. Seltz, *The Complete Handbook of Franchising* (Reading, MA: Addison-Wesley Publishing Co., 1982), p. 1.

TABLE 16–1	What You May Buy in a Franchise

1. Product or service with established market and favorable image
2. A patented formula or design
3. Trade names or trademarks
4. A financial management system for controlling the financial revenues
5. Managerial advice from experts in the field
6. Economies of scale for advertising and purchasing
7. Head office services
8. Tested business concept

volves an established name that will give the franchisee instant recognition in the market area. This doesn't ensure success, but it does provide the impetus to begin the business with a positive image.

One of the purposes of franchising a business is that the franchisor can benefit from extensive and rapid expansion without borrowing or taking significant financial risks. If the franchisor provides a strong opportunity for success, then he or she will also benefit from the royalty checks received from each franchisee. Thus, to ensure this, it is important to provide standardized accounting and operating procedures and retain control over store design, equipment, and supplies. These structural controls are actually advantageous to the franchisee since he or she will be benefiting from the years of trial and error and experience of someone else in these key decision areas.

Each individual franchise under normal circumstances would not be able to afford extensive media advertising. However, by pooling (contributions made by each franchisee based on volume), the entire organization can conduct major media advertising to strengthen the franchise name. Each individual franchise can then devote effort to any special local promotions within the constraints of the franchise agreement.

The franchisor may also provide management advice, tax information, and other business activities to the franchise. Thus, known successful management decisions are passed on to the franchisee to ensure their success. Table 16–1 summarizes all the possible advantages that the entrepreneur obtains by purchasing a franchise.

Types of Franchises

Basically there are three types of franchises available.[5] Variations may also exist as new innovations in franchising are developed. One type of franchise is dealerships, with many found in the automobile industry. Here, manufacturers use

---

[5]W. Siegel, *Franchising* (New York: John Wiley & Sons, 1983), p. 9.

franchises to distribute their product lines. These dealerships act as the retail stores for the automobile manufacturers. In some instances, they are required to meet quotas set by the manufacturers, but as any franchise, they benefit from the advertising and management support provided by the franchisor.

The most common type of franchise is that which offers a name, image, method of doing business, and so on, such as McDonald's, Kentucky Fried Chicken, Speedy Muffler, Dunkin' Donuts, and Holiday Inns. There are many of these types of franchises and their listing, with information, can be found in various sources.[6]

A third type of franchise offers services, such as personnel agencies, income tax preparation companies, and realtors. These services offer established names, reputations, and methods of doing business. In some instances, such as real estate, the franchisee has actually been operating a business and then applies to become a member of the franchise.

Recent franchising opportunities have evolved because of important changes in the environment. Some of the important trends that have contributed to the development of new franchises are as follows:[7]

• *Good health*—Today people are eating healthier food and spending more time keeping fit. Many new franchises have developed in response to this trend. For example Bassett's Original Turkey was created in 1983 in response to consumer interest in eating foods lower in cholesterol. Frozen yogurt franchises such as TCBY in New England and Nibble-Lo's in Florida have also been very successful. In Los Angeles, a unique restaurant, The Health Express, offers its customers a 100 percent vegetarian menu.

• *Time saving or convenience*—More and more consumers are finding that they prefer to have things brought to them rather than having to go out of their way to buy them. In fact, many food stores now offer home delivery services. In 1990, Auto Critic of America Inc. was started as a mobile car inspection service. At about the same time, Ronald Tosh started Tubs To Go, which offers the delivery of a jacuzzi to almost any location for an average of $100 to $200 per night.

• *Environmental consciousness*—Radon testing service franchises have grown as a response to the consumers' need to protect themselves and their families from dangerous radon gas. In 1987, Ecology House, a gift store, began to add more hands-on consumer products such as water-saving devices, rechargeable batteries, and energy-saving light fixtures.

• *The second baby boom*—Today's baby boomers are having babies themselves, which has resulted in a number of child-related service franchises. Child-care franchises such as Kinder Care and Living and Learning are thriving. In 1989 two attorneys, David Pickus and Lee Sandoloski, decided to open

---

[6]*Directory of Franchising Organizations* (Babylon, NY: Pilot Industries, 1985).

[7]K. Rosenberg, "Franchising, American Style," *Entrepreneur,* January 1991, pp. 86–93.

Jungle Jim's Playland. This is an indoor amusement park with small-scale rides in a 20,000 to 27,000 square-foot facility. One franchise, Computertots, teaches classes on computers to preschoolers. This franchise has spread to 25 locations in 15 states.

RISKS IN INVESTING IN A FRANCHISE

Franchising involves many risks that the entrepreneur should be aware of before considering such an investment. We hear of the success of McDonald's or Burger King, yet for every one of the successes there are many failures. Franchising, like any other venture, is not for the passive person. It requires effort, as any business would, since business decisions such as hiring, scheduling, buying, accounting, and so on are still the franchisee's responsibility. In many cases, long hours are required to ensure that the business operates effectively.

Certain steps can be taken to lower or minimize the risks in investing in a franchise. Each of these is discussed below.

Conduct a Self-Evaluation

The entrepreneur should do a self-evaluation to be sure that entering a franchise venture is right for him or her. Answering the following questions can help a person determine if this is the correct decision.

- Are you a self-starter?
- Do you enjoy working with other people?
- Do you have the ability to provide leadership to those who will work for you?
- Are you able to organize your time and the people who are employed in the business?
- Can you take risks and make good business decisions?
- Do you have the initiative to continue the business during its ups and downs?
- Do you have good health?

If you answered yes or maybe to most of the above questions then chances are you are making the right decision to enter a new franchise venture.

Investigate the Franchise

Not every franchise is right for each entrepreneur. He or she must evaluate the franchise alternatives (it is valuable to look at more than one) to decide which one is most appropriate. A number of factors should be assessed before making the final decision.

1. *Unproven versus proven franchise*—There are some trade-offs when investing in a proven or unproven franchise business. An unproven franchise will be less expensive as an investment. However, the lower investment is offset by a substantial amount of risk. In an unproven franchise, the franchisor is likely to make mistakes as the business grows. These mistakes could inevitably lead to failure. Constant reorganization of a new franchise can result in confusion and mismanagement. On the favorable side, a new and unproven franchise can offer more excitement and challenge and can lead to significant opportunities for large profits should the business grow rapidly.

A proven franchise offers lower risk of failure but requires a substantial financial investment. However, it should be remembered that there's always some risk, even in a mature franchise business.

2. *Financial stability of franchise*—The purchase of a franchise by an entrepreneur should entail an assessment of the financial stability of the franchisor. There are a number of factors that will help the entrepreneur ascertain the long-term stability and profitability of the franchise organization. The potential franchisee should ask the franchisor the following questions or should ascertain the answers from alternative sources.

- How many franchises are there in the organization?
- How successful are each of the members of the franchise organizations?
- Are most of the profits of the franchise a function of fees from sale of franchises or from royalties based on profits of franchisees?
- Does franchisor have management expertise in production, finance, and marketing?

Some of the above information can be obtained from profit-and-loss statements of the franchise organization. Face-to-face contact with the franchisor can also reveal a strong sense of success of the organization. It may also be worthwhile to contact some of the franchisees directly to determine their success and to identify any problems that have occurred. If the entrepreneur cannot effectively evaluate the financial statements, he or she should hire an accountant to provide this assessment. If financial information of the franchisor is unavailable, the entrepreneur may purchase a financial rating from a source such as Dun & Bradstreet. Generally, the following are good external sources of information.

- Franchise associations
- Other franchisees
- Government
- Accountants and lawyers
- Libraries
- Franchise directories and journals
- Business exhibitions

3. *Potential market for the new franchise*—It is important for the entrepreneur to evaluate the market area from which customers will be attracted to the new franchise. One simple starting point is to take a map of the community or local area and try to evaluate the traffic flow and demographics of the residents in the area. Traffic flow information may be observed by visiting the area. Direction of traffic flow, ease of entry to business, and amount of traffic (pedestrian and automobile) may be estimated by observation. The demographics of the area can be determined from census data, which can be obtained from local libraries or the town hall. It can also be advantageous to locate competitors on the map to determine their potential effect on the franchise business.

If the franchisor is willing or financing is available to undertake it, marketing research in the market area is helpful. Attitudes and interest in the new business can be assessed in the marketing research. If the resources are not available for a market research study, the entrepreneur may consider using local colleges or universities as part of a student project. In some instances, the franchisor will conduct a market study as a selling point to the franchisee.

4. *Profit potential for new franchise*—As in any start-up business, it is important to develop pro forma income, balance sheets, and cash flow statements. The franchisor should provide projections in order to calculate the needed information. Again, the entrepreneur may need assistance from an accountant to develop these statements. See Chapter 7 for specific information on how to prepare these statements.

In general, most of the above information should be provided in the disclosure statement or the prospectus. In 1979, the Federal Trade Commission's Franchise Rule became law. It requires franchisors to make full presale disclosure in a document that provides information about 20 separate aspects of a franchise offering.[8] The information required in this disclosure is summarized in Table 16–2. However, even though such a statement is required by law, it is often not made available until a few days before the signing of the franchise agreement. Thus, it is usually necessary for the entrepreneur to seek out much of the information as described above. The alternative is to request a disclosure agreement at the beginning of the negotiations. It is also important to realize that some of the information will be well written and comprehensive and some will be poorly written and very sketchy. There are always weaknesses that must be evaluated prior to making a commitment. The disclosure statement represents a good resource, but it is also important to evaluate the other services mentioned earlier in this chapter. If in doubt a lawyer and/or accountant may help.

As all of the information is assessed, the entrepreneur will eliminate some of the different franchise alternatives. It is often useful at this point for the entrepreneur to work in one or more of the franchises to get a better sense of whether

---

[8]D. J. Kaufmann & D. E. Robbins, "Now Read This," *Entrepreneur,* January 1991, pp. 100–5.

TABLE 16–2   Information Required in Disclosure Statement

1. Identification of the franchisor and its affiliates and their business experience.
2. The business experience of each of the franchisor's officers, directors, and management personnel responsible for franchise services, training, and other aspects of the franchise programs.
3. The lawsuits in which the franchisor and its officers, directors, and management personnel have been involved.
4. Any previous bankruptcies in which the franchisor and its officers, directors, and management personnel have been involved.
5. The initial franchise fee and other initial payments that are required to obtain the franchise.
6. The continuing payments that franchisees are required to make after the franchise opens.
7. Any restrictions on the quality of goods and services used in the franchise and where they may be purchased, including restrictions requiring purchases from the franchisor or its affiliates.
8. Any assistance available from the franchisor or its affiliates in financing the purchase of the franchise.
9. Restrictions on the goods or services franchises are permitted to sell.
10. Any restrictions on the customers with whom franchises may deal.
11. Any territorial protection that will be granted to the franchisee.
12. The conditions under which the franchise may be repurchased or refused renewal by the franchisor, transferred to a third party by the franchisee, and terminated or modified by either party.
13. The training programs provided to franchisees.
14. The involvement of any celebrities or public figures in the franchise.
15. Any assistance in selecting a site for the franchise that will be provided by the franchisor.
16. Statistical information about the present number of franchises; the number of franchises projected for the future; and the number of franchises terminated, the number the franchisor has decided not to renew, and the number repurchased in the past.
17. The financial statement of the franchisor.
18. The extent to which the franchisees must personally participate in the operation of the franchise.
19. A complete statement of the basis of any earning claims made to the franchisee, including the percentage of existing franchises that have actually achieved the results that are claimed.
20. A list of the names and addresses of other franchises.

---

he or she is well suited to this business. Front-end procedure fees, royalty payments, expenses, and so on should be compared to those of franchises in the same field, as well as in different business areas.

If one franchise looks good as an investment, the entrepreneur may request a franchise package from the franchisor. It should contain a draft franchise agreement or contract. Generally this package will require a deposit of $300 to $500.

The entrepreneur should not pay any more than this for the package and should be sure that it is fully refundable.

THE FRANCHISE AGREEMENT

The contract or franchise agreement is the final stage in becoming a franchisee. At this stage a lawyer experienced in franchising will be needed. The franchise agreement contains all of the specific requirements and obligations of the franchisee. Things such as the exclusivity of territory coverage will protect against the franchisor's granting another franchise within a certain radius of the business. The renewable terms will indicate the length of the contract and requirements for renewing it. Financial requirements will stipulate the initial price for the franchise, schedule of payments, royalties to be paid, and so on. Termination of franchise requirements should indicate the terms for ending the agreement with the franchisor. The terms should indicate what happens if the franchisee becomes disabled or dies and what provisions are made for the family. The problems with terminating a franchise generally result in more lawsuits than any other issue in franchising. These terms should also provide for the franchisee to obtain fair market value should the franchise be sold.

All of these items are important and require the assistance of a lawyer. Even though the agreement may be standard, the franchisee should try to negotiate any of the items that are important in risking the franchise investment.

As can be seen, the franchise can offer the entrepreneur an easier alternative to starting a new business than beginning from point zero. There are still risks but, given a careful assessment of the issues discussed in this chapter, an informative decision can be made.

DIRECT MARKETING

There is a growing interest in new ventures involving direct marketing. It offers advantages over other types of start-ups since the entrepreneur can usually risk less start-up capital and can benefit by focusing his or her marketing efforts on a well-defined customer group reachable through a direct-marketing technique. Since direct marketing is a unique entrepreneurial approach and since it offers some of the same advantages as franchising, it has been included in this chapter.

There is always argument as to where direct marketing actually started. However, with all the success of direct-mail-marketing ventures, most people regard the catalog giants of Montgomery Ward, Sears Roebuck, and Spiegel as the first major successes.

In 1893, a telegraph operator named Richard Warren Sears acquired a shipment of gold-filled watches that were undeliverable. Being an agent of the railroad, young Richard assumed that the best market for these watches would be other railroad employees. To reach this market, he obtained a mailing list of about 20,000 railroad employees. His business was so successful that in four years he had developed a catalog of more than 6,000 items. By 1902, the company achieved sales of more than $50 million.

Since the success of Sears, thousands of entrepreneurs have discovered the importance and profitability of reaching a specific market by direct mail or some other media. This growth has taken place in all markets from industrial equipment to services, including insurance, perishables such as cheeses, and unusual products such as flowers and trees. For the new venture, mail-order business or any other direct-marketing efforts can provide access to regional or national markets.

In 1990, consumers purchased $156.3 billion worth of merchandise through the mail. Television, radio, magazines, and newspapers contributed to the direct-marketing sales total. Catalog sales in 1990 were nearly $35 billion. All of this success is an important incentive for entrepreneurs who dream of selling their product by direct marketing.[9]

Bill Bruegman started his home-based toys and collectibles business in 1986 and targeted it to baby boomers using a catalog he designed himself. In 1990, his sales reached $100,000. Both Bill and his wife Joanne do all the shipping so that his costs are kept to a minimum. Alternatively, Biddy and Annie Hurlbut, a mother and daughter team, are seeking to expand to international markets with their classic fashions line made from alpaca and Peruvian pima cotton. In 1990, their sales reached $5 million with these imported handknit, crochet, and hand-wove clothing. Using advertising in *The New York Times Magazine,* they were able to generate 3,000 inquiries, which resulted in 300 customers. From this initial effort, the company now has a mailing list of 100,000 names that it has developed over the last 15 years.[10]

The list of success stories in direct marketing is long, yet the entrepreneur should not assume that it ensures the pot of gold at the end of the rainbow. Direct-marketing start-ups have many of the same risks as any other new venture. There is significant competition in this market that necessitates careful preparation and planning. Some of the important issues that the entrepreneur interested in this strategy must consider will be discussed in the remainder of this chapter.

Definition of Direct Marketing

Direct marketing has been called direct mail, mail order, and direct response, to name a few. All can be categorized as direct marketing since they all involve "the total of activities by which the seller effects the transfer of goods and ser-

---

[9]E. Kotite, "Who Will Buy?" *Entrepreneur,* February 1991, p. 92.

[10]K. McLaughlin, "Postal Notes," *Entrepreneur,* February 1991, pp. 111–18.

TABLE 16–3   Innovations Enhancing Growth of Direct
Marketing

1950s	Bank credit cards such as VISA and MasterCard were made available to privileged customers. Credit cards greatly enhanced the mail-order transaction, allowing customers to avoid cash payments.
1950s	The proliferation of computers allowed mail-order businesses to store and retrieve large amounts of data. Mailing lists were also refined to enrich the potential sales of products and services to appropriate market segments.
1960s	AT&T introduced the first "800" service, which provided direct-mail customers with access to mail-order businesses with toll-free long-distance telephone calling.
1960s and 70s	The growth of magazines and broadcast media allowed mail-order businesses to utilize these media for lists and for selling certain products and services. Cable, satellite, and interactive television also contributed to the opportunities to reach large audiences.
1970s and 80s	Major changes in the life-styles and demographics of the American consumer made direct marketing businesses more popular because of their speed and convenience. The growth of two-income households, rising energy costs, and the significance of time were but a few of these changes that enhanced direct marketing.

---

vices to the buyer [and] directs his efforts to a qualified audience using one or more media for the purpose of soliciting a response by phone, mail, or personal visit from a prospect or customer." [11]

This definition explains how direct marketing differs from other marketing techniques such as personal selling or general advertising. Other alternative marketing techniques do not involve the directness to a specific audience or the ability to bring about a transaction through the media.

Innovations That Enhanced the Growth of Direct Marketing

The growth of direct marketing has been enhanced by a number of key innovations and environmental changes. Table 16–3 summarizes some of the major innovations and how they enhanced interest among entrepreneurs in starting new

---

[11]R. S. Hodgson, *Direct Mail and Mail Order Handbook,* 3rd ed. (Chicago: The Dartnell Corporation, 1980), p. 24.

direct-mail businesses. As can be seen, many of these innovations made it simpler for the American consumer to purchase products and services without having to personally visit a store.

As the demographics of Americans in the 1990s, such as increases in education and income, continue to change, more and more interest has developed in the convenience and efficiency of direct marketing. A consumer can now use the telephone or mail to purchase anything from household necessities to luxury items such as vacations or jewelry.[12]

New technologies in the 1990s, such as videodiscs and video cassettes, may become the future sales tools of direct-marketing firms. The use of fax machines to order products or services and the growth of electronic data transmission and retrieval will allow firms to transmit a menu of products and services electronically. Videotex appears to be the most significant technology for direct marketers since it will allow the delivery of text and visual information directly to the consumer. The consumer will then be able to interact directly with the system by using a handheld keypad. Whatever the future holds, it is likely that direct marketing will continue to grow because it satisfies such important needs of the modern consumer.

ENVIRONMENTAL FACTORS AND THE SUCCESS OF DIRECT MARKETING

Besides the innovations discussed above, there were a number of environmental factors that changed the needs of the customer and enhanced the success of direct-marketing businesses. Probably the most significant factor has been the growth in dual-income households. They now account for nearly 65 percent of all families. In 1990, their average earnings rose 4.5 percent, to $894 a week. Because of their interest in saving time, dual-income families represent the most important segment of the market to direct-marketing firms.[13]

Single men and women have also grown in importance as direct-marketing customers mainly because marriages are occurring later and thus single men and women are getting good jobs, good salaries, and permanent addresses, which is particularly important to direct-mail businesses. Products such as clothing, records, tapes, giftware, and gardening supplies are most popular in this segment. Spiegel has been particularly successful with the single customer. About 10 years ago they took a gamble and changed the image to an upscale women's clothing catalog, in order to appeal to working women. As sales of these products grew, Spiegel expanded into men's and children's clothing, home accessories, furniture, and more.[14]

---

[12]M. Baier, *Direct Response Marketing* (New York: McGraw-Hill, 1983), p. 11.

[13]Kotite, *Entrepreneur,* February 1991, pp. 94–6.

[14]Ibid., p. 96.

The last factor that has contributed to the growth of direct marketing is that most people have been exposed to it in one way or another, so that shopping by mail or the telephone is no longer considered a major risk. Liberal return policies, better-quality catalogs, and personalized addressing are a few factors that have enhanced the image of direct marketing. While most people using direct marketing are buying more, they are also demanding more, as competition for the consumer's dollar rages on.

ADVANTAGES OF DIRECT MARKETING

The entrepreneur starting a new venture will have several advantages by beginning a direct-marketing business rather than some other approaches. Each of the advantages is discussed in this section.[15]

The most important advantages of direct marketing are the ease of the entry and low capital requirement. Anyone can enter a direct-marketing business without special licenses or educational skill requirements. For a mail-order start-up, the entrepreneur will need only a local business license. The U.S. Post Office will provide assistance since they benefit from mail-order sales. Thus, a mailing list with a catalog of products can be mailed easily to the appropriate customer. No other requirements are necessary to send the printed material through the mail.

In addition to the ease of entry, the capital required to enter a direct-marketing business is also minimal. No major facility, store front, or number of employees are needed to enter a direct-marketing business. Capital needed by the entrepreneur will be mostly for printing, mailing, and lists. All of this can also be accomplished on a part-time basis until the business has a built-in cash flow that can support the entrepreneur full-time. This is contrary to most other new ventures, where investors will require the entrepreneur to make a full-time commitment to the new venture.

Direct marketing also offers the entrepreneur the opportunity to reach the market quickly. Products and services can also be tested to determine customer interest at a minimal cost. If certain products or services are successful, the offerings can easily be expanded to meet the potential demand for those specific products.

Important Start-Up Considerations

As in any new venture, the entrepreneur will need to resolve certain important questions. Earlier it was mentioned that the entrepreneur can start a direct-marketing business part-time with little capital investment. Questions inherent

---

[15]W. A. Cohen, *Direct Response Marketing: An Entrepreneurial Approach* (New York: John Wiley & Sons, 1984), pp. 6–7.

in such a low-overhead beginning are whether to use a post office box or street address, to allow the use of credit cards, and to take advantage of a toll-free number.[16]

A street address gives the new venture credibility; for this reason alone it should be given priority over using a post office box. The street address may also give local customers an opportunity to see the product close-up.

In general, the use of credit cards increases the potential returns. It also adds credibility and provides an important convenience for the customer. This may be especially important for more expensive items since it gives the customer the opportunity to finance purchases.

The toll-free number is an added expense for the entrepreneur but does increase customer response because it makes it easier for the customer to order. The telephone company will provide toll-free service with a variety of plans. One option is to rent a toll-free line exclusively. This is the more expensive alternative, which usually has a base rate for so many hours of use and an additional fee for each hour over the base. The other option is to share a line with others who have rented a line from the telephone company.

Like the credit card and the street address, the toll-free line can also add credibility to the new venture. Credibility can be an important positive factor given the competitive environment in which the entrepreneur may operate.

LEGAL ISSUES

The Federal Trade Commission (FTC) now provides guidelines for pricing and special offers. Any questions on these practices should be resolved by requesting information from the FTC.

One important factor is the "30-Day Delay Delivery Rule" passed by the FTC in 1976. This rule requires that any product or service be shipped within 30 days of receiving an order. If this is not possible, the entrepreneur must clearly indicate how long shipment will take. If no statement is made as to the length of time, it is understood to be within 30 days.

Many frauds have tarnished the reputation of direct marketing. To avoid these, it is important to clearly state and/or picture what the consumer will receive for the stipulated price. Future business will be enhanced with an honest approach to the new venture. Any legal questions should be settled by a lawyer. Questions as to how to obtain legal advice were discussed in detail in Chapter 15.

---

[16]Ibid., pp. 32–33.

ALTERNATIVE TECHNIQUES FOR DIRECT MARKETING

A number of alternative strategies may be used by the entrepreneur in the start-up venture.

1. *Classified Advertising*—The simplest and least costly approach for the entrepreneur is the classified ads in newspapers and magazines. Magazines and newspapers should be identified that would reach the appropriate market for the products or services. In general, classified ads that are effectively placed can result in a high-profit return. Support or advice on the ad can also be provided by the medium in which the ad will be placed.

The major disadvantage in a classified ad is the limited space available. It is important, if this alternative is used, that the product or service can be communicated easily in the limited space available.

2. *Display Ads*—This type of advertising allows the entrepreneur to purchase space in a magazine or newspaper. It offers the opportunity to explain and picture the product or service more clearly. In addition, a coupon can be included in the display ad that the customer can cut out to send along with payment.

3. *Direct Mail*—This technique allows the entrepreneur the opportunity to send sales material directly to prospective customers. It requires the use of a mailing list, discussed later in this chapter. This technique should be used when there is a clearly defined product and market segment.

It is common for the direct-mail package to contain a sales letter, guarantee, testimonials, publisher's letter, and self-addressed and stamped envelope. It is most important that the direct-mail piece be opened and read by the potential customer; otherwise the mailing will not result in a sale.

4. *Catalog Sales*—The printing of a quality catalog can be an expensive investment for the entrepreneur. Although this may be easier than selling in a retail store, the catalog must be attractive and stimulate interest by the customer. The advantage is that catalogs can result in repeat sales since the catalog may be stored for future use.

There are many successful catalog businesses in the United States. Regular mailings to a selected customer list can provide a profitable alternative to marketing many products. There is the added advantage of important advice that can be obtained from any printing company to help determine the most cost-effective alternative.

5. *Media Direct-Response Marketing*—Radio, television, and the telephone may be considered as alternative approaches for marketing any products or services. Radio and television are considered broadcast media forms of advertising. In purchasing time rather than space, as in display ads, the entrepreneur is faced with some important differences. In buying time, no schedule is available, which makes it more difficult to plan. Costs will vary, depending on the time of day, the station, length of ad, and the size of the audience that may be reached. The entrepreneur should consult *Standard Rate and Data* for these cost differences.[17]

Telemarketing has also become a very popular method for selling products and services. Using WATS lines, costs can be kept at a minimum while still reaching a nationwide audience.

The advantage of telemarketing is that it provides immediate feedback to the user. Thus, the response rate is likely to be higher than that of other methods. The entrepreneur can identify communities by telephone exchanges that match the demographics for the most likely person to purchase a product or service. A good telephone personality is a must in being successful with this technique.

THE MAILING LIST

There are many sources for mailing lists. They can be purchased from mailing-list brokers, media, organizations of any type, directories, trade associations, municipalities, and so on. The list may be used for mailing or for telephone sales, depending on the availability of telephone numbers. It is important that the entrepreneur first determine which list will most effectively reach the desired market. In other words, the list should include the names of people or businesses that would probably be interested and hence are most likely to purchase the product or service.

Most lists, even those available from brokers, are relatively inexpensive, depending on how rigid your specifications are for identifying the names of potential customers. These brokers, some of which are listed in Table 16–4, will provide a catalog of all the lists available and the number of names in that list file. Thus, if you were interested in a mailing list of lawyers you might locate a page out of a broker's catalog that looks like Figure 16–1, which includes over 400,000 names. From this list you may decide that you need only lawyers practicing in one or a few specific states. This list would then be compiled and would be much smaller. If it is necessary to chose from a large list, it is possible to select every *n*th name or some other reasonable sequence.

In general, the mailing-list brokers have a minimal fee and charge prorated amounts for additional names. The costs are usually within $200 for a minimum of 2,000 names.

The mailing lists may be obtained as pressure-sensitive labels, tape, diskettes, index cards, sheet listing, chesire labels, or perforated gummed labels. These labels vary in cost on a per 1,000 name basis.

---

[17]For more information on general advertising and broadcast media see M. L. Rothchild, *Advertising* (Lexington, MA: D. C. Heath, 1987) and J. F. Engel, M. R. Warsaw & T. C. Kinnear, *Promotional Strategy,* 5th ed. (Homewood, IL: Richard D. Irwin, 1983).

TABLE 16–4   A Sample of Mailing-List Brokers

American Business Lists Inc. 5707 South 86th Circle P.O. Box 27347 Omaha, NE 68127 (402) 331-7169	Ed Burnett Consultants Inc. 2 Park Avenue New York, NY 10016 (800) 223-7777
Alvin B. Zeller 475 Park Avenue South New York, NY 10016 (800) 223-0814	R. R. Bowker 205 East 42nd Street New York, NY 10017 (212) 916-1698
Edith Roman Associates Inc. 875 Avenue of the Americas New York, NY 10001 (800) 223-2194	

Regardless of the mailing list used, it is important for the entrepreneur to maintain good records to ascertain which list is most effective in generating sales. Customers who buy should be placed in a file for future mailings since they would be experienced and, it is hoped, satisfied customers. This list should be updated and modified as needed to avoid duplication in mailings. As it is refined, this list will become the most important part of the entrepreneur's business.

It should be noted that direct-marketing approaches are not a guarantee for success. Motivation and commitment are necessary, just as in any other business. Research will be needed to identify those products or services most likely to succeed. Although the start-up investment is low, there is still risk involved. Failure to satisfy a customer need can result in a new-venture failure just as it would in any other start-up business.

SUMMARY

In this chapter we have discussed two very important and unique approaches for the entrepreneur to start a new business: franchising and direct marketing. Both offer possible unique advantages such as ease of entry, lower risk, and lower capital requirements.

In starting a franchise, the entrepreneur has the advantage of the experience of the franchisor to help in getting the business underway. An established name, advertising strength, and management advice all help to reduce the risk in the new venture.

FIGURE 16–1 Example of Broker's List

S.I.C. Code	List Title	Approx U.S. Count	State Count Page
9924F	LOUVERS (WHOLESALE & MANUFACTURERS)	180	1
5172G	LUBRICANTS (WHOLESALE)	1458	1
3569J	LUBRICATING DEVICES & SYSTEMS	911	1
7538J	LUBRICATING SERVICE-MOBILE	313	1
5948B	LUGGAGE REPAIRING	914	1
5948A	LUGGAGE RETAIL	1752	1
5099N	LUGGAGE WHOLESALE & MANUFACTURERS	356	1
4212K	LUMBER CARRIERS	83	1
2411D	LUMBER MANUFACTURERS	594	1
2421C	LUMBER MILL REPRESENTATIVES	61	1
5211E	LUMBER RETAIL	21630	31
2491A	LUMBER TREATING	419	1
5931Z	LUMBER USED	140	1
5031A	LUMBER WHOLESALE	6102	27
	M		
20[illegible]	MACARONI (MANUFACTURERS)	147	1
5080R	MACHINE SHOP SUPPLIES	141	1
3599A	MACHINE SHOPS	35790	26
5084P	MACHINE TOOLS (WHOLESALE)	3716	29
3599D	MACHINE TOOLS REPAIRING & REBUILDING	661	1
1796A	MACHINERY-MOVERS & ERECTORS	1463	1
5084W	MACHINERY-NEW	2321	29
3599E	MACHINERY-REBUILDING & REPAIRING	1519	1
3599F	MACHINERY-SPECIALLY DESIGNED	1827	1
5092A	MACHINERY-USED	1309	1
5949J	MACRAME SUPPLIES (RETAIL)	46	1
5931Q	MAGAZINES-BACK NUMBER	192	1
5994B	MAGAZINES-DEALERS	2358	36
5199S	MAGAZINES-DISTRIBUTORS	588	1
5963F	MAGAZINES-SUBSCRIPTION AGENTS	387	1
7929D	MAGICIANS	755	1
5945U	MAGICIANS SUPPLIES	312	1
9211B	MAGISTRATES	111	1
3694B	MAGNETOS (WHOLESALE & MANUFACTURERS)	330	1
3499F	MAGNETS & MAGNETIC DEVICES	332	1
7349L	MAID & BUTLER SERVICE	2359	39
7331B	MAIL ADDRESS SERVICE	1727	1
3469C	MAIL BOXES	564	1
3444D	MAIL CHUTES	1	1
5961A	MAIL ORDER & CATALOG SHOPPING	3063	35
7290M	MAIL RECEIVING SERVICE	1928	1
7331A	MAILING LISTS	2083	1
5081R	MAILING MACHINES & EQUIPMENT	1009	1
7331D	MAILING SERVICES	2395	38
7231K	MAKE-UP STUDIOS	575	1
5190Q	MALTS & HOPS (WHOLESALE)	69	1
6531E	MANAGEMENT-BUILDING & PROPERTY	25456	37
7392A	MANAGEMENT CONSULTANTS	17643	39
7231D	MANICURING (SERVICE)	18813	37
	MANUFACTURERS LISTS	381916	48
5099C	MANUFACTURERS AGENTS & REPRESENTATIVES	20054	30
2741F	MAPS (PRINTERS)	1154	1
1741F	MARBLE CONTRACTORS	242	1
5039Q	MARBLE-CULTURED (WHOLESALE)	1320	1
5039F	MARBLE-NATURAL (WHOLESALE)	1648	1
5030I	MARBLE-SYNTHETIC (WHOLESALE)	36	1
2079A	MARGARINE (WHOLESALE)	20	1
4469A	MARINAS	5082	27
1629E	MARINE CONTRACTORS	1672	1
7629U	MARINE ELECTRIC SERVICE	212	1
5088G	MARINE ELECTRONIC EQUIPMENT & SUPPLIES	851	1
5088B	MARINE EQUIPMENT & SUPPLIES (WHOL)	5459	29
5088H	MARINE EQUIPMENT & SUPPLIES WHOL & MFRS	194	1
4469H	MARINE REPAIRS	279	1
4469D	MARINE SURVEYORS & ADJUSTORS	1111	1
7392I	MARKET RESEARCH & ANALYSIS	4543	39
7392J	MARKETING CONSULTANTS	6205	39
7392W	MARKETING PROGRAMS & SERVICES	934	1
5411F	MARKETS	10969	31
3953B	MARKING DEVICES	455	1
9943Q	MARKING SERVICE-METAL, RUBBER, ETC	13	1
8321B	MARRIAGE & FAMILY COUNSELORS	39568	43
7999C	MARTIAL ARTS-INSTRUCTION	911	1
5941Z	MARTIAL ARTS-SUPPLIES & EQUIPMENT	188	1
5082E	MASON CONTRACTORS EQUIPMENT & SUPPLIES	1011	1
1741A	MASONRY CONTRACTORS	10971	25
7299P	MASSAGE (SERVICE)	3453	38
9925B	MASSAGE EQUIPMENT & SUPPLIES	135	1
3999F	MATCHES (MANUFACTURERS)	537	1
5084E	MATERIAL HANDLING EQUIPMENT (WHOL/MFRS)	5299	29
5621C	MATERNITY APPAREL (RETAIL)	2322	32
9925D	MATS & MATTING (WHOLESALE & MFRS)	878	1
5712D	MATTRESSES (RETAIL)	8380	33
7600L	MATTRESSES RENOVATING	277	1
5021M	MATTRESSES WHOLESALE	525	1
5999G	MAUSOLEUMS	8775	36
2035A	MAYONNAISE & SALAD DRESSINGS	47	1
5147C	MEAT BROKERS	316	1
3551B	MEAT CHOPPERS & GRINDERS	85	1
5423E	MEAT CUTTING SERVICE	532	1
5147E	MEAT JOBBERS	103	1
2011A	MEAT PACKERS	3995	25
5081Q	MEAT PACKERS EQUIPMENT & SUPPLIES	365	1
2011A	MEAT PROCESSING	3995	25
5423A	MEAT RETAIL	19731	32
3551G	MEAT SAWS	62	1
5147A	MEAT WHOLESALE	7002	30
1711H	MECHANICAL CONTRACTORS	4681	24
8090J	MECHANOTHERAPISTS DM	59	1
7300G	MEDIATION SERVICES	903	1
6321B	MEDICAL & SURGICAL PLANS	57	1

S.I.C. Code	List Title	Approx U.S. Count	State Count Page
8081B	MEDICAL & SURGICAL SVC ORGANIZATIONS	992	1
7392G	MEDICAL BUSINESS ADMINISTRATION	746	1
8081Q	MEDICAL CENTERS	185	1
9925J	MEDICAL ELECTRONICS	227	1
5086E	MEDICAL EQUIPMENT & SUPPLIES (WHOL)	4647	29
7690T	MEDICAL EQUIPMENT REPAIRING	128	1
8081H	MEDICAL GROUPS	1605	1
8071A	MEDICAL LABORATORIES	6042	42
7392D	MEDICAL MANAGEMENT CONSULTANTS	216	1
5210G	MEDICINE CABINETS (RETAIL)	135	1
5912D	MEDICINES-PATENT & PROPRIETARY	640	1
9925M	MEDITATION INSTRUCTION	319	1
5999G	MEMORIAL TABLETS	8775	36
5611A	MEN'S CLOTHING & FURNISHINGS RETAIL	21890	32
5136B	MEN'S CLOTHING & FURNISHINGS WHOL/MFRS	1900	1
8081S	MENTAL HEALTH CLINICS	242	1
8321J	MENTAL HEALTH SERVICES	9193	43
8321K	MENTAL RETARDATION INFORMATION CENTERS	580	1
9925N	MENU SERVICE	364	1
9925P	MERCHANDISE BROKERS	261	1
7492H	MERCHANDISING SERVICE	170	1
7399K	MESSAGE RECEIVING & FORWARDING SERVICE	8838	39
7399G	MESSENGER SERVICE	3052	39
9925R	METAL CLEANING	234	1
9925S	METAL CLEANING EQUIPMENT	29	1
3541E	METAL CUTTING MACHINES	66	1
5051K	METAL DISTRIBUTORS	66	1
1791D	METAL FABRICATORS	2342	25
3471C	METAL FINISHERS	1948	1
3559C	METAL FINISHERS-EQUIPMENT & SUPPLIES	233	1
5732H	METAL LOCATING EQUIPMENT	844	1
3471A	METAL POLISHING	283	1
3499A	METAL PRODUCTS (WHOLESALE & MFRS)	143	1
9925V	METAL ROLLING & FORMING	342	1
5051D	METAL SPECIALTIES	1131	1
3469D	METAL SPINNING	310	1
9944L	METAL SPRAYING	81	1
3469A	METAL STAMPING	3027	26
3599B	METALLIZING	407	1
5051Q	METALS-BASE	450	1
9925Y	METALS-PRECIOUS SHEET WIRE TUBING ETC	112	1
9926A	METAPHYSICIANS	107	1
5063N	METERS (WHOLESALE)	1172	1
9926B	METERS REPAIRING	236	1
5812M	MEXICAN FOOD PRODUCTS (RETAIL)	2830	34
5141F	MEXICAN FOOD PRODUCTS-WHOLESALE & MFRS	129	1
5990D	MEXICAN GOODS (RETAIL)	178	1
7399H	MICROFILMING SERVICE-EQUIPMENT/SUPPLIES	2392	39
5733N	MICROPHONES (RETAIL)	155	1
5086N	MICROSCOPES (WHOLESALE)	465	1
3662B	MICROWAVE COMMUNICATIONS EQUIP/SYSTEMS	313	1
5722K	MICROWAVE OVENS (RETAIL)	6997	34
7629Y	MICROWAVE OVENS REPAIRING	1132	1
8049W	MIDWIVES	383	1
5611B	MILITARY GOODS	3331	32
5451C	MILK	4416	32
9926F	MILK DISPENSERS	8	1
5143A	MILK PRODUCTS-WHOLESALE	1971	1
5631D	MILLINERY-RETAIL	228	1
	MILLIONAIRES		56
2431A	MILLWORK	3645	25
1796D	MILLWRIGHTS	606	1
9926G	MINERALOGISTS	7	1
9942Q	MINERALS	296	1
5945L	MINIATURE ITEMS FOR COLLECTORS	751	1
1499A	MINING COMPANIES	1975	1
7392U	MINING CONSULTANTS	395	1
1629D	MINING CONTRACTORS	206	1
5082L	MINING EQUIPMENT	2006	1
5719F	MIRRORS (RETAIL)	7925	33
7600M	MIRRORS-RESILVERING	192	1
9926J	MISSILE & ROCKET RESEARCH & DEVELOPMENT	49	1
7300W	MISSING PERSONS BUREAUS	67	1
8321M	MISSIONS	733	1
3531A	MIXING & AGITATION MACHINERY	299	1
5271D	MOBILE HOME DEALERS-USED	222	1
6515A	MOBILE HOME PARKS	18466	37
5271A	MOBILE HOMES-DEALERS	9547	31
2451A	MOBILE HOMES-DISTRIBUTORS & MFRS	500	1
5271C	MOBILE HOMES-EQUIPMENT & PARTS	2792	31
7519A	MOBILE HOMES-RENTING & LEASING	1105	1
7349E	MOBILE HOMES-REPAIRING & SERVICE	5841	38
4213A	MOBILE HOMES-TRANSPORTING	2657	26
5271B	MOBILE OFFICES & COMMERCIAL UNITS	697	1
5065T	MOBILE TELEPHONE EQUIPMENT & SUPPLIES	1583	1
4811E	MOBILE TELEPHONE SERVICE	631	1
9926L	MOBILE TELEPHONE UNITS	28	1
7990R	MODEL CAR RACING CENTERS	98	1
3999G	MODEL MAKERS	1112	1
7362A	MODELING AGENCIES	1621	1
8299E	MODELING SCHOOLS	927	1
7342A	MOISTURE CONTROL (PEST CONTROL SVCS)	15225	38
5190M	MOLASSES (WHOLESALE)	86	1
3079S	MOLD MAKERS	200	1
5031K	MOLDINGS (WHOLESALE)	777	1
3544E	MOLDS (MANUFACTURERS)	2850	26
3313A	MOLYBDENUM (MANUFACTURERS)	11	1
6052C	MONEY BROKERS	95	1
6059C	MONEY ORDER SERVICE	2716	36
5949D	MONOGRAMS (SERVICE)	2547	35
8211A	MONTESSORI SCHOOLS	54	1
5999G	MONUMENTS	8775	36

S.I.C. Code	List Title	Approx U.S. Count	State Count Page
4463D	MOORAGES	59	1
5571B	MOPEDS (DEALERS)	943	1
5087Q	MOPS (WHOLESALE)	273	1
9926U	MORTAR (WHOLESALE)	73	1
6162A	MORTGAGES	46179	36
5030J	MOSAICS (WHOLESALE)	92	1
5081T	MOTEL & HOTEL EQUIPMENT & SUPPLIES	590	1
7392R	MOTEL & HOTEL MANAGEMENT	203	1
6531G	MOTEL BROKERS	95	1
7011B	MOTELS & HOTELS*	73068	37
7011D	MOTELS & HOTELS-RESERVATIONS	1523	1
7342J	MOTHPROOFING	257	1
7813C	MOTION PICTURE CONSULTANTS	47	1
5043E	MOTION PICTURE EQUIP & SUPPLIES	629	1
7394K	MOTION PICTURE EQUIP & SUPPLIES RENTING	832	1
9926Y	MOTION PICTURE EQUIP & SUPPLIES REPAIR	197	1
5043D	MOTION PICTURE FILM	96	1
7823A	MOTION PICTURE FILM-DISTRS & EXCHS	690	1
7819B	MOTION PICTURE FILM-EDITING	311	1
7829A	MOTION PICTURE FILM-LIBRARIES	312	1
7819C	MOTION PICTURE LABORATORIES	213	1
7813A	MOTION PICTURE PRODUCERS & STUDIOS	3488	41
7813D	MOTION PICTURE REPRESENTATIVES	71	1
8299X	MOTIVATIONAL/SELF IMPROVEMENT TRAINING	552	1
4121A	MOTOR FREIGHT LINES	18617	26
5561C	MOTOR HOMES (DEALERS)	1239	1
5561K	MOTOR HOMES EQUIPMENT & PARTS	116	1
7519F	MOTOR HOMES RENTING & LEASING	572	1
7690B	MOTOR HOMES REPAIRING & SERVICE	695	1
5571A	MOTORCYCLES & MOTOR SCOOTERS DEALERS*	7804	32
7690C	MOTORCYCLES & MOTOR SCOOTERS REPAIR/SVC	4349	41
5571E	MOTORCYCLES & MOTOR SCOOTERS SUPPLIES	3513	32
5012C	MOTORCYCLES SUPLS & PARTS WHOL & MFRS	565	1
5031K	MOULDINGS (WHOLESALE)	777	1
5941Y	MOUNTAIN CLIMBING EQUIPMENT	476	1
2789C	MOUNTING & FINISHING (JEWELERS)	126	1
7699M	MOUNTING (TAXIDERMISTS)	3400	41
4214A	MOVERS*	13070	26
9927J	MOVING SELF-SERVICE	451	1
4214A	MOVING SERVICES-LABOR & MATERIALS*	13070	26
7513B	MOVING SUPPLIES & EQUIPMENT	638	1
7394P	MOVING SUPPLIES & EQUIPMENT RENTING	3609	39
0782F	MOWING SERVICE	197	1
1389A	MUD JACKING CONTRACTORS	169	1
7539E	MUFFLERS & EXHAUST SYSTEMS ENGINE*	17467	40
5013U	MUFFLERS/EXHAUST SYSTS ENGINE WHOL/MFRS	99	1
2499D	MULCHES	424	1
5990L	MURALS (RETAIL)	411	1
8411A	MUSEUMS	4384	43
0182A	MUSHROOMS	336	1
8999K	MUSIC ARRANGERS & COMPOSERS	446	1
7399Q	MUSIC BACKGROUND	966	1
5945M	MUSIC BOXES (RETAIL)	440	1
5733H	MUSIC DEALERS	2323	34
8299F	MUSIC INSTRUCTION-INSTRUMENTAL	5802	43
8299G	MUSIC INSTRUCTION-VOCAL	754	1
2741G	MUSIC PUBLISHERS	837	1
5733A	MUSICAL INSTRUMENTS DEALERS	7808	34
7494M	MUSICAL INSTRUMENTS RENTAL	994	1
7699T	MUSICAL INSTRUMENTS REPAIRING	3602	41
3931A	MUSICAL INSTRUMENTS SUPLS/ACCESS MFRS	53	1
5733G	MUSICAL INSTRUMENTS SUPPLIES & ACCESS	868	1
5931P	MUSICAL INSTRUMENTS USED	466	1
5099P	MUSICAL INSTRUMENTS WHOLESALE & MFRS	527	1
7929B	MUSICIANS	2061	1
6211B	MUTUAL FUNDS	4366	36
	N		
7231D	NAIL SALONS	18813	37
5039N	NAILING MACHINERY (WHOLESALE & MFRS)	656	1
5051R	NAILS & TACKS (WHOLESALE)	273	1
3993D	NAME PLATES (WHOLESALE & MFRS)	1877	1
8090B	NAPRAPATHS	159	1
9711C	NATIONAL GUARD	168	1
8049X	NATUROPATHIC PHYSICIANS	329	1
5088I	NAUTICAL INSTRUMENTS (WHOLESALE)	98	1
8910B	NAVAL ARCHITECTS	259	1
5611J	NECKWEAR RETAIL	96	1
2323A	NECKWEAR WHOLESALE & MANUFACTURERS	136	1
3926A	NEEDLES	60	1
5949B	NEEDLEWORK/NEEDLEWORK MATERIALS RETAIL	5058	35
2395A	NEEDLEWORK/NEEDLEWORK MATLS WHOL & MFR	198	1
	NEW BUSINESS NAMES		59
	NEW HOME OWNERS (MONTHLY)		58
5994A	NEWS DEALERS	1727	1
2721B	NEWS PUBLICATIONS-TRADE, ASSN, ETC	283	1
7351A	NEWS SERVICE	794	1
5963E	NEWSPAPER DELIVERY	169	1
5199G	NEWSPAPER DISTRIBUTORS	831	1
2711A	NEWSPAPERS	16280	25
5813B	NIGHT CLUBS	10813	34
9927T	NOISE CONTROL CONSULTANTS	87	1
2098A	NOODLES (MANUFACTURERS)	155	1
8999C	NOTARIES PUBLIC	9439	44
5949H	NOTIONS RETAIL	867	1
5134K	NOTIONS WHOLESALE & MANUFACTURERS	257	1
5947H	NOVELTIES RETAIL	1763	1
5199H	NOVELTIES WHOLESALE & MANUFACTURERS	867	1
5072H	NOZZLES (WHOLESALE)	77	1
3579C	NUMBERING MACHINES (MANUFACTURERS)	139	1
5199Z	NURSERIES-PLANTS, TREES, ETC WHOLESALE	3121	31
8351D	NURSERY SCHOOLS & KINDERGARTENS	2046	1

Before entering a franchise agreement, the entrepreneur should conduct a self-evaluation to be sure that the franchise form of business is right for him or her. In addition, it is important to investigate the franchise carefully, especially if it is unproven. The financial stability, market potential, and profit potential should all be considered in the investigation. After investigating the franchise, an agreement will be signed. At this point the entrepreneur should consult a lawyer to avoid any future legal problems.

Direct marketing, also sometimes referred to as direct mail, mail order, or direct response, is a growing area for entrepreneurial activity. Growing at a fast rate, direct-mail business alone totaled $156.3 billion in 1990.

Direct marketing also has important unique advantages. It offers ease of entry, low capital, low risk, and initially no full-time commitment. Major questions as to the mode of direct marketing, that is, telephone, advertising, or mail, should be evaluated. Classified ads or display ads may be placed in newspapers or magazines that reach the appropriate market segments. Catalogs, direct mail, or broadcast media are also options for selling products or services.

A mailing list is the most important marketing tool for the entrepreneur in this type of venture. Brokers, media, organizations, directories, trade associations, or municipalities are but a few of the sources for obtaining lists. Over time, the list should be refined to ensure efficiency in reaching that customer most interested in purchasing the product or service.

CHAPTER 17

Intrapreneurship

CHAPTER OBJECTIVES

1. To identify the reasons for the interest in intrapreneurship.

2. To explain the organizational environment conducive for intrapreneurship.

3. To discuss the differences between corporate and intrapreneurial cultures.

4. To identify the general characteristics of an intrapreneur.

5. To explain the process of establishing intrapreneurship in an organization.

JOE WILLIAMS

Joe Williams is used to grappling with big ideas and high risk. He is chairman of the board and chief executive officer of The Williams Companies, a diversified firm with 1987 revenues of $1.78 billion and income from continuing operations of $24 million. Although the company started small, as all do, the founders were not afraid to take a big risk. In 1966, while Joe was working in Iran as project manager for the Williams Brothers Trans Iranian Pipeline, his cousin John was buying the Great Lakes Pipeline Company for $287.5 million, the largest cash transaction in corporate America up to that time. The small Williams Brothers Company, engaged in the construction but not the ownership of pipelines, was about to enter a new field. In this transaction, the company spent only $1.6 million of its own money, financing the rest.

In 1967, Joe Williams was asked to come home to Tulsa to help run the newly expanded company, becoming president of The Williams Companies in 1971. As the company expanded into areas of agriculture (Agrico, fertilizer), natural resources (Edgcomb Metals and Peabody Coal), and real estate (Williams Realty), Joe encouraged new ideas and simultaneously fostered growth of the company through diversification. These efforts changed the company from a small pipeline construction concern to a large multiproduct firm with revenues averaging over $2 billion and assets over $4 billion from 1983 to 1986.

But Joe's diversification plan had not stabilized the company as well as expected. When energy and agriculture hit a recession simultaneously, the company's profits plunged. By 1982, profits had fallen 69 percent and the company's stock was selling at about one-third its book value. Joe began looking for, as he called it, "the fourth leg on the stool," to stabilize the other three areas of the company's business (energy, agriculture, and real estate).

Joe's management style could be characterized as a task force mentality with an "open door at the executive level." This philosophy encouraged executives to think creatively and to develop their skills through external programs, such as Harvard's executive management program. Sending Roy Wilkens, president of Williams Pipeline, to the Harvard session for four months indicated Joe's willingness to bet on people and to promote an intrapreneurial attitude within the company.

On returning to Williams Pipeline, Williams was eager to maximize the company's assets. He created a task force to study possible uses for unused pipelines. The result was the establishment of a network of pipelines for telecommunications. MCI executives showed such great interest in the company's telecommunications proposal that Wilkens approached Joe Williams about the company entering the telecommunications field on its own. Not many executives would listen to a proposal to compete with a giant like AT&T in an area about which the company knew nothing, but, as Wilkens described Joe, "You are dealing with an executive who will listen to anything you have to say."

While telecommunications offered The Williams Companies the growth Joe was looking for in a fourth subsidiary—the fourth leg of the stool—it entailed taking on a high level of risk—$200 million of increased exposure to the company. There was little time for study as the Bell System was breaking up and the technology in fiber optics was increasing; the window of opportunity was open but closing fast. Joe had to decide over the Christmas holidays. By New Year's Day, the company gave its approval and WilTel was born.

Roy Wilkens is now President of WilTel, which is the number four telecommunications business in America. Their own 11,000 mile fiber-optic network was expanded to 25,000 miles in 1990 through an asset exchange agreement with MCI. In 1989, it reported an operating profit of $59.5 million and gross revenue of $300 million. The future looks bright for WilTel, since fiber optics is the carrier of choice for the up-and-coming high-definition television industry.

Making WilTel succeed demanded the long hours and dedicated effort necessary for any successful new venture. In WilTel, the management team was composed of people who were high risk-takers. What was the major incentive for a person to accept this challenge? Wilkens felt the answer was in the intrapreneurship spirit: The situation created its own rewards in its dynamic and exciting atmosphere. Joe Williams's accessibility to his employees and his interest in growth through intrapreneurship have continued to carry The Williams Companies through periods of economic difficulty to a more promising future.

What Joe Williams realized in the case of The Williams Companies is what hundreds of executives are also becoming aware of in their own organizations—it is important to keep or instill the entrepreneurial spirit in an organization in order to innovate and grow. This realization is threatening to revolutionize American management and economic thinking. In a large organization, problems often occur that thwart creativity and innovation, particularly in activities not directly related to the organization's main mission. When an organization finally does recognize the importance of these secondary activities, it frequently takes too long to plan and implement them, in part because the established plans lack the needed flexibility. The growth and diversification that can result from this flexibility is particularly critical since large, vertically integrated, diversified corporations are often more efficient in a competitive market than smaller firms.

Internally administered coordination in a large corporation can often be more effective than the coordination achieved through market mechanisms.[1]

The resistance against flexibility, growth, and diversification can in part be overcome by developing a spirit of entrepreneurship within the existing organization. This spirit, called **intrapreneurship,** is discussed in terms of its causes, new venture creation and the necessary management transition, differences between corporate cultures, environment for intrapreneurship, characteristics of the intrapreneur, procedures for implementing intrapreneurship in an organization, and intrapreneurial strategy and strategy guidelines.

CAUSES FOR RECENT INTEREST

The interest in intrapreneurship shown by existing organizations has resulted from a variety of events occurring in the United States on social, cultural, and business levels. On a social level, there is an increasing interest in "doing your own thing" and doing it on one's own terms. Individuals who believe strongly in their own talents frequently desire to create something of their own. They want responsibility and have a strong drive for individual expression and more freedom in their present organizational structure. When this freedom is not forthcoming, frustration can develop that can lead to the individual becoming less productive or even leaving the organization to achieve self-actualization elsewhere. This new search for meaning, and the impatience involved, has recently caused more discontent in structured organizations than ever before. When meaning is not provided within the organization, individuals often search for an institution that will provide it. Intrapreneurship is one method for stimulating and then capitalizing on individuals in an organization who think that something can be done differently and better.

Simultaneous with the increase in the social and cultural pressures for intrapreneurship has been an increase in business pressures brought on by severe competition. Hypercompetition both at home and abroad have forced U.S. companies to have an increased interest in such areas as new product development, diversification, and increased productivity. The increased productivity has caused some reductions in the company's labor force. During a recent five-year period, employment in Fortune 500 companies decreased by 2.2 million people.

---

[1]These concepts are developed in D. Chandler, *The Visible Hand: The Managerial Revolution in American Business* (Cambridge: Harvard University Press, 1977) and O. E. Williamson, *Markets and Hierarchies: Analysis and Antitrust Information* (New York: The Free Press, 1975).

Yet, these and new individuals are being absorbed in the work force. Where has this employment occurred? Basically, in small businesses and particularly start-up efforts. In 1985, almost 700,000 new companies were formed compared to 200,000 in 1965 and only 90,000 in 1950.[2] In addition to these 700,000, there were about 400,000 new partnerships and 300,000 newly self-employed people. These 1.4 million new entities correspond to the average annual 1.4 million new private-sector jobs created each year in the economy.

In 1989, there were about 20 million firms in the United States; 25 percent of these were farms, 25 percent solo self-employed, 25 percent part-time, and 25 percent companies with employees. These 20 million firms varied greatly in terms of revenue; 6 million firms generated between $25,000 and $100,000 in revenue; 1.2 million firms generated $100,000 to $1 million in revenue; and only .8 million firms generated revenues greater than $1 million.

This increasing shift away from large corporations to small ones is indicated in the plot of real growth in gross national product (GNP) against the number of new incorporations each year. Since 1975, an increasing number of businesses have become involved in increasing the GNP of the United States. An analysis of the net change in firms entering and exiting versus the growth in GNP reveals that the higher the net change in firms entering versus exiting, the higher the growth in GNP. Since exit rates remain about the same, this increase in growth in GNP is due to the increase in the number of new businesses being started.

VENTURE GROWTH AND MANAGEMENT TRANSITION

As the statistics on the size of the businesses within the United States indicate, most firms are not growing. The ability to grow is affected by many factors, including the degree of competitiveness in the industry, the nature and geographical location of the company and its initial market, the degree of the company's success, the company's protectability, the universality of the product and its unique selling proposition, the company's financial capability, and the desire and capabilities of the entrepreneur and the management team. Not all companies are able or willing to grow, but this does not necessarily mean failure. While growth is not automatic for a new venture, when it does occur it goes through various stages: start-up, rapid growth, competitive turbulence, and decline. The **growth patterns** of new ventures are indicated in Figure 17–1. These growth patterns generally occur across all industries while some deviations do occur. The few firms that drive high start-up and high growth are ones that achieve $25 million in sales in the first year and increase sales at least $1 million per year. These instances indicate that growth of a venture depends on two factors more

---

[2]D. L. Birch, "The Atomization of America," *Inc.*, March 1987, p. 21.

FIGURE 17–1   Possible Growth Patterns of New Businesses

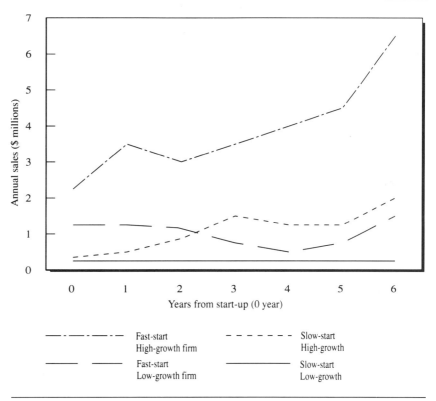

than any other: market factors, particularly the size of the market and the window of opportunity, and management factors such as the desire and drive for growth and the ability to manage it. Classifying firms on these two management factors—the propensity and ability to grow—yields four types of firms. Marginal small firms are those that have a low ability for managing growth. Successful small firms have a low propensity for growth but a high ability to manage it. High-growth firms have both a high propensity and a high ability to manage growth. High-growth firms can have either a slow or fast start.

To successfully grow a venture requires a flexible, capable entrepreneur and management team. Several success themes for growth have been identified.[3]

[3]A study indicating these success themes is D. C. Hambrick and L. M. Crozier, "Stumblers and Stars in the Management of Rapid Growth," *Journal of Business Venturing* 1 (Winter 1985), pp. 31–46.

CORPORATE VERSUS INTRAPRENEURIAL CULTURE

Business and sociological conditions have given rise to a new era in American business—the era of the entrepreneur. The positive media exposure and success of entrepreneurs is threatening to some established corporations, who notice that smaller, aggressive, entrepreneurially driven firms are developing more new products and becoming dominant in certain markets. Recognizing the positive results brought about by employees of large corporations who catch the "entrepreneurial fever," some companies are attempting to create the same spirit, culture, challenges, and rewards of entrepreneurship in their organizations. What are the differences between corporate and entrepreneurial cultures? Between managers, entrepreneurs, and intrapreneurs?

The typical **corporate culture** has a climate and reward system that favors conservatism in decision making. Emphasis is on gathering a large amount of data on which to base a rational decision and to use as justification if the decision does not produce optimal results. Risky decisions are often postponed until enough hard facts can be gathered or a consultant hired to "illuminate the unknown." Frequently there are so many sign-offs and approvals required for a large-scale project that no individual feels personally responsible.[4]

The traditional corporate culture differs significantly from an **intrapreneurial culture.** The guiding principles in a traditional corporate culture are: follow the instructions given; do not make any mistakes; do not fail; do not take initiative but wait for instructions; and stay within your turf and protect your backside. This restrictive environment is of course not conducive to creativity, flexibility, independence, and risk taking—the jargon of intrapreneurs. The guiding principles of an intrapreneurial culture are quite different: develop visions, goals, and action plans; be rewarded for actions taken; suggest, try, and experiment; create and develop regardless of the area; and take responsibility and ownership. This environment supports individuals in their efforts to create something new.

There are also differences in the shared values and norms of the two cultures. The traditional corporation is hierarchical in nature, with established procedures, reporting systems, lines of authority and responsibility, instructions, mandates, standardized hours, and control mechanisms. These support the present corporate climate and inhibit new-venture creation. The culture of an intrapreneurial firm is in stark contrast to this established one. Instead of hierarchical structure with all the accompanying problems, an intrapreneurial climate has a flat organizational structure with networking, teamwork, sponsors, and mentors abounding. Close working relationships help establish an atmosphere of trust and counsel that facilitates the accomplishment of visions and objectives. The tasks are viewed as fun events, not chores, with participants gladly putting in the number of hours necessary to get the job done. Instead of building barriers to protect turfs, individuals make suggestions within and across functional areas and divisions, resulting in a cross fertilization of ideas.

---

[4]For a discussion of this aspect, see N. Fast, "A Visit to the New Venture Graveyard," *Research Management* 22 (March 1979), pp. 18–22.

As would be expected, these two different cultures produce different types of individuals and management styles. A comparison of traditional managers, entrepreneurs, and intrapreneurs reveals these differences (see Table 17–1). While **traditional managers** are motivated primarily by promotion and typical corporate rewards, entrepreneurs and intrapreneurs thrive on independence and the ability to create. The intrapreneurs expect their performance to be suitably rewarded.

The differences are also reflected in the time orientation of the three groups, with managers emphasizing the short run, entrepreneurs the long run, and intrapreneurs somewhere in between. Similarly, the primary mode of activity of in-

TABLE 17–1 Comparison of Entrepreneurs, Intrapreneurs, and Traditional Managers

	Traditional Managers	*Entrepreneurs*	*Intrapreneurs*
Primary motives	Promotion and other traditional corporate rewards, such as office, staff, and power	Independence, opportunity to create, and money	Independence and ability to advance in the corporate rewards
Time orientation	Short run—meeting quotas and budgets, weekly, monthly, quarterly, and the annual planning horizons	Survival and achieving 5–10-year growth of business	Between entrepreneurial and traditional managers, depending on urgency to meet self-imposed and corporate timetable
Activity	Delegates and supervises more than direct involvement	Direct involvement	Direct involvement more than delegation
Risk	Careful	Moderate risk taker	Moderate risk taker
Status	Concerned about status symbols	No concern about status symbols	Not concerned about traditional corporate status symbols—desires independence
Failure and mistakes	Tries to avoid mistakes and surprises	Deals with mistakes and failures	Attempts to hide risky projects from view until ready
Decisions	Usually agrees with those in upper management positions	Follows dream with decisions	Able to get others to agree to help achieve dream
Who serves	Others	Self and customers	Self, customers, and sponsors
Family history	Family members worked for large organizations	Entrepreneurial small-business, professional, or farm background	Entrepreneurial small-business, professional, or farm background
Relationship with others	Hierarchy as basic relationship	Transactions and deal making as basic relationship	Transactions within hierarchy

Source: An extensively modified version of table in G. Pinchot, *Intrapreneuring* (New York: Harper & Row, 1985) pp. 54–6.

trapreneurs falls between the delegation activity of managers and the direct involvement of entrepreneurs. While intrapreneurs and entrepreneurs are moderate risk takers, managers are much more cautious about taking any risks. Protecting the backside and turf is a way of life of many traditional managers. These managers attempt to avoid mistakes and failures at almost any cost. On the other hand, most entrepreneurs usually fail at least once and intrapreneurs learn to conceal risky projects from management until the last possible moment.

While the traditional managers tend to serve those at a higher level in the organization, entrepreneurs serve self and customers, with intrapreneurs adding sponsors to these two entrepreneur categories. This aspect is reflected in their respective backgrounds. Managers tend to come from families who have worked for large organizations and intrapreneurs and entrepreneurs from entrepreneurial or professional families. Instead of building strong relationships with those around them the way entrepreneurs and intrapreneurs do, managers tend to follow the relationships outlined in the organizational chart.

CLIMATE FOR INTRAPRENEURSHIP

How can the climate for intrapreneurship be established in an organization? In establishing an intrapreneurial environment, certain factors and leadership characteristics need to be operant.[5] The overall characteristics of a good intrapreneurial environment are summarized in Table 17–2. The first of these is that the organization operates on the frontiers of technology. Since research and development is a key source for successful new product ideas, it must operate on the cutting edge of the industry's technology, encouraging and supporting new ideas instead of discouraging them as frequently occurs in firms that require rapid return on investment and high sales volume.

Second, experimentation—trial and error—needs to be encouraged. Good new products or services do not appear fully formed but usually evolve after many iterations. It took time and some product failures before the first marketable computer appeared. A company wanting to establish an intrapreneurial spirit has to establish an environment that allows mistakes and failures in developing new innovative products. While this is in direct opposition to the established career and promotion system of the traditional organization, without the opportunity to fail, few if any corporate intrapreneurial ventures will be undertaken. Almost every entrepreneur has experienced at least one failure before establishing a successful venture.

Third, an organization should make sure that there are no initial **opportunity parameters** inhibiting creativity in new product development. Frequently in an organization, various "turfs" are protected, frustrating attempts by potential in-

---

[5]For a thorough discussion of the factors important in intrapreneurship, see R. M. Kanter, *The Change Masters* (New York: Simon & Schuster, 1983) and G. Pinchot III, *Intrapreneuring* (New York: Harper & Row, 1985).

TABLE 17–2   Intrapreneurial Environment

- Organization operates on frontiers of technology
- New ideas encouraged
- Trial and error encouraged
- Failures allowed
- No opportunity parameters
- Resources available and accessible
- Multidiscipline teamwork approach
- Long time horizon
- Volunteer program
- Appropriate reward system
- Sponsors and champions available
- Support of top management

---

trapreneurs to establish new ventures. In one Fortune 500 company, the attempt at establishing an intrapreneurial environment ran into problems and eventually failed when the potential intrapreneurs were informed that a proposed new product and venture was not possible because it was the domain of another division.

Fourth, the resources of the firm need to be available and easily accessible. As one intrapreneur stated, "If my company really wants me to take the time, effort, and career risks to establish a new venture, then it needs to put money and people resources on the line." Often, insufficient funds are allocated to the task of creating something new, with available resources being committed instead to solving problems that have immediate effect on the bottom line. And, when resources are available, all too often the reporting requirements make it so difficult to obtain them that frustration and dissatisfaction occur.

Fifth, a multidiscipline teamwork approach needs to be encouraged. This open approach, with participation by needed individuals regardless of area, is the antithesis of the corporate organizational structure and theory. An evaluation of successful cases of intrapreneurship indicated that one key to the success was the existence of "skunkworks" involving key people. Some companies can facilitate internal venturing by legitimizing and formalizing the skunkworks already occurring. Developing the needed teamwork for a new venture is further complicated by the fact that a team member's promotion and overall career within the corporation is related to job performance in the current position, not to the extent of contribution to the new venture being created.

Besides encouraging teamwork, the corporate environment must establish a long time horizon for evaluating the success of the overall program as well as the success of each individual venture. If a company is not willing to invest money with no expectation of return for 5 to 10 years, it should not attempt to create an intrapreneurial environment. This patient attitude toward money in the corporate setting is no different than the investment/return time horizon used by venture capitalists and others in the risk-capital market when investing in an entrepreneurial effort.

Sixth, the spirit of intrapreneurship cannot be forced on individuals; it must be on a volunteer basis. There is a difference between corporate thinking and intrapreneurial thinking, with individuals performing much better on the latter side of the continuum. Most managers in a corporation are not capable of being successful intrapreneurs. Those who do emerge from this self-selection process must be allowed the latitude to carry a project through to completion. This is not consistent with most corporate procedures for new product introduction, where different departments and individuals are involved in each stage of the development process. An individual willing to spend the excess hours and effort to create a new venture needs have the opportunity and the accompanying reward of carrying the project through to completion. An intrapreneur falls in love with the newly created internal venture and will do almost anything to help ensure success.

The seventh characteristic is a **reward system.** The intrapreneur needs to be appropriately rewarded for all the energy and effort expended in the creation of the new venture. These rewards should be based on the attainment of established performance goals. An equity position in the new venture is one of the best methods for motivating and eliciting the amount of activity and effort needed for success.

Eighth, a corporate environment favorable for intrapreneurship has sponsors and champions throughout the organization who not only support the creative activity and resulting failures but have the planning flexibility to establish new objectives and directions as needed. As one intrapreneur stated, "For a new business venture to succeed, the intrapreneur needs to be able to alter plans at will and not be concerned about how close they come to achieving the previously stated objectives." Corporate structures frequently measure managers on their ability to come close to objectives, regardless of the quality of performance reflected in this accomplishment.

Finally, and perhaps most important, the intrapreneurial activity must be wholeheartedly supported and embraced by top management, both by physical presence and by making sure that the personnel and financial resources are readily and easily available. Without top management support, a successful intrapreneurial environment cannot be created.

INTRAPRENEURIAL LEADERSHIP CHARACTERISTICS

Within this overall corporate environment, there are certain individual characteristics needed for a person to be a successful intrapreneur. As summarized in Table 17–3, these include understanding the environment, being visionary and flexible, creating management options, encouraging teamwork while employing a multidisciplined approach, encouraging open discussion, building a coalition of supporters, and persisting.

An entrepreneur needs to understand the environment and all its many aspects. Part of this ability is reflected in the individual's level of creativity. Creativity, perhaps at its lowest level in large organizations, generally tends to

---

TABLE 17–3 Intrapreneurship Leadership Characteristics

- Understands the environment
- Visionary and flexible
- Creates management options
- Encourages teamwork
- Encourages open discussion
- Builds a coalition of supporters
- Persists

---

decrease with age and education. To successfully establish a successful intrapreneurial venture, the individual must be creative and have a broad understanding of the internal and external environments of the corporation.

The person who is going to establish a successful new intrapreneurial venture must also be a visionary leader—a person who dreams great dreams. Although there are many definitions of leadership, the one that best describes that needed for intrapreneurship is: "A leader is like a gardener. When you want a tomato, you take a seed, put it in fertile soil, and carefully water under tender care. You don't manufacture tomatoes, you grow them." Another good definition is that "leadership is the ability to dream great things and communicate these in such a way that people say yes to being a part of the dream." Martin Luther King said "I have a dream" and thousands followed, in spite of overwhelming obstacles. To establish a successful new venture, the intrapreneurial leader must have a dream and overcome all the obstacles to achieve it by "selling" the dream to others.

The third needed characteristic is that the intrapreneur must be flexible and create management options. An intrapreneur does not mind the store as is frequently taught in many business schools but is playful and irreverent. By challenging the beliefs and assumptions of the corporation, an intrapreneur has the opportunity to create something new in the largely bureaucratic organizational structure.

The intrapreneur must possess another characteristic—the ability to encourage teamwork and use a multidisciplined approach. This also violates the organizational practices and structures taught in most business schools and that end up being incorporated in the established corporate plan. Every new company formation requires a broad range of business skills—engineering, production, marketing, and finance. Obtaining these skills in forming a new venture usually requires crossing the established departmental structure and reporting systems. To minimize the negative effect of any disruption caused, the intrapreneur must be a good diplomat.

Open discussion must be encouraged to develop a good team for creating something new. Many corporate managers have forgotten the frank, open discussion and disagreements that were a part of their educational process. Instead, they spend time building protective barriers and insulating themselves in their corporate empires. A successful new intrapreneurial venture can be formed only when the team involved feels the freedom to disagree and critique an idea to reach the best solution. The degree of openness obtained depends on the degree of openness of the intrapreneur.

Openness leads to the establishment of a strong coalition of supporters and encouragers. The intrapreneur must encourage and affirm each team member, particularly during the problem times. This encouragement is very important, as the usual motivators of career paths and job security are not operational in establishing a new intrapreneurial venture. A good intrapreneur makes everyone a hero.

Last, but not least, is persistence. Throughout the establishment of any new intrapreneurial venture, frustration and obstacles will occur. Only through the intrapreneur's persistence will a new venture be created and successful commercialization result.

ESTABLISHING INTRAPRENEURSHIP IN THE ORGANIZATION

An organization desiring to establish an intrapreneurial environment must implement a procedure for its establishment. Although this can be done by its employees, frequently an organization finds it easier to use an outside consultant to facilitate the process. This is particularly true when the organization's environment is very traditional and has a record of little change and few new products being introduced.

The first step in this process is to secure commitment to intrapreneurship in the organization by top management and the upper and middle management levels. Without **top management commitment** the organization will never be able to go through all the cultural climate changes necessary for implementation. Once the top management of the organization has committed to intrapreneurship for a sufficient period of time (1–3 years), the concept is introduced throughout the organization. This can be best accomplished through seminars where the aspects of intrapreneurship are introduced and strategies developed to transform the organizational culture into an intrapreneurial one. General guidelines need to be established for intrapreneurial venture development. Once the initial framework is established and the concept embraced, intrapreneurial leaders need to be identified, selected, and trained. This training needs to focus on obtaining resources within the organization, identifying viable opportunities and their markets, and developing the appropriate business plan.

Ideas and general areas that top management are interested in supporting should be delineated, along with the amount of risk money that is available to develop the concept further. Also, overall program expectations and the target results of each intrapreneurial venture should be established. As much as possible, these should specify the time frame, volume and profitability requirements for the new venture, and the impact on the organization. Along with the intrapreneurial training, a mentor/sponsor system needs to be established. Without sponsors or champions, there is little hope that the culture of the organization can be transformed into an intrapreneurial one.

Following the initial commitment and training, the organization can firmly establish an intrapreneurial culture by using a group of interested managers to train and share their experiences with other members. The training sessions should be conducted one day per month for eight months. Informational items about intrapreneurship in general and the specifics of the company's activities should be disseminated throughout the company either directly or through the company's house organ.

These activities will help establish role models and intrapreneurial ventures. The organization should institute concrete activities through which ideas can be developed into marketable products or services that are the basis of new business venture units. This will require the intrapreneurial team to develop a business plan, obtain customer reaction and some initial intentions to buy, and learn how to coexist within the organizational structure.

Finally, the organization needs to establish a strong support structure for intrapreneurship. This is particularly important since intrapreneurship is a secondary activity in the organization, not a primary one. Since they do not immediately affect the bottom line, intrapreneurial activities can be easily overlooked and receive little funding and support. Providing the investment funds necessary for an intrapreneurial venture to develop and compete in external markets is critical for the success of the program. To be successful, these ventures require flexible, innovative behavior, with the intrapreneurs having total authority over expenditures. When the intrapreneur has to justify expenses on a daily basis, it is really not a new internal venture but merely an operational extension of the funding source.[6]

The support must also involve tying the rewards to the performance of the intrapreneurial unit. This encourages the team members to work harder and compete more effectively since they will benefit directly from their efforts. Because the intrapreneurial venture is a part of the larger organization and not a totally independent unit, the equity portion of the compensation will be difficult to administer along with the salary. Incentives should also be established to reward cooperation with other areas of the company.

Finally, the organization needs to implement an evaluation system that allows successful intrapreneurial units to expand and unsuccessful ones to be eliminated. Just as occurs in an entrepreneurial firm, when a good job is done, an intrapreneurial unit should be allowed to expand to fill market demands as warranted. The organization can establish constraints to ensure that this expansion does not run in juxtaposition with the corporate mission statement. Similarly, inefficient intrapreneurial venture units should not be allowed to exist just because of vested interests in perpetuating them. To have a successful intrapreneurial environment, the organization must allow some ventures to fail even as it allows more successful ones to expand. However, some ventures may be contin-

---

[6]For a discussion of this aspect, see R. Peterson & D. Berger, "Entrepreneurship in Organizations," *Administrative Science Quarterly* 16 (August 1971), pp. 97–106; and D. Miller & P. Friesen, "Innovation in Conservative and Entrepreneurial Firms: Two Models of Strategic Momentum," *Strategic Management Journal* 3 (May 1982), pp. 1–25.

ued, even if unprofitable, if the venture is subsidizing some other part of the larger organization, blocking some competitive entrance, or laying the groundwork for entering some new strategic business area.

PROBLEMS AND SUCCESSFUL EFFORTS

Intrapreneurship, or what is alternatively called corporate venturing, is not without its problems. One study found that new ventures started within a corporation performed worse than those started independently by entrepreneurs.[7] The reasons cited for this were the corporation's difficulty in maintaining a long-term commitment, lack of freedom to make autonomous decisions, and a constrained environment. These findings were supported by another study which found that every obstacle to the successful creation of a new corporate venture presented less of an obstacle for an alternative—establishing a joint venture.[8] Although joint ventures are not without their own obstacles, they have fewer problems and do provide the opportunity to gain some experience in a different development process before attempting new-venture creation. Companies do tend to become more adept at overcoming the obstacles involved, but this frequently does not occur until the fourth attempt at creating a new internal venture.

Given the many obstacles, high failure rate, and learning curve necessary for successful intrapreneurship to occur, an organization should consider all alternative growth strategies before selecting intrapreneurship. These include joint venturing, acquisitions, and internal product development using the established corporate procedures. As was the case with joint venturing, independent, venture-capital-based start-ups by entrepreneurs tend to outperform corporate start-ups significantly. On average, not only did the independents become profitable twice as fast, they ended up twice as profitable.[9]

However, these findings should not deter organizations committed to intrapreneurship from starting the process. There are numerous examples of companies that, having understood the environmental and intrapreneurial characteristics necessary, have adopted their own version of the implementation process previously discussed to successfully launch new ventures. One of the best known of these firms is Minnesota Mining and Manufacturing (3M). Having had many successful intrapreneurial efforts, 3M in effect allows employees to devote 15

---

[7]N. Fast, "Pitfalls of Corporate Venturing," *Research Management* March 1981, pp. 21–24.

[8]I. C. MacMillan, Z. Block, & P. N. Subba Narasimha, "Obstacles and Experience in Corporate Venturing," *Proceedings,* Babson Research Conference (April 1984), pp. 341–63.

[9]For complete information on the relative performance, see R. Biggadike, "The Risky Business of Diversification," *Harvard Business Review,* May-June 1979, pp. 103–11; L. E. Weiss, "Start-up Business: A Comparison of Performances," *Sloan Management Review,* Fall 1981, pp. 37–53; and N. D. Fast & S. E. Pratt, "Individual Entrepreneurship and the Large Corporation," *Proceedings,* Babson Research Conference (April 1984), pp. 443–50.

percent of their time to independent projects. This enables the divisions of the company to meet their goals of a significant percent of sales coming from new products introduced within the last five years. One of the most successful of these intrapreneurial activities was the development of Post-it by intrapreneur Arthur Fry. This effort developed out of Fry's annoyance that pieces of paper marking his church hymnal constantly fell out when he sang. As a 3M chemical engineer, Fry knew about the discovery by a scientist, Spencer Silver, of a very low sticking-power adhesive, which to the company was a poor product characteristic. However, this characteristic was perfect for Fry's problem; a marker with lightly sticking adhesive that is easy to remove provided a good solution. But, Fry had to obtain approval to commercialize the idea. This proved to be a monumental task until the samples made and distributed to secretaries within 3M, as well as other companies, created such a demand that the company eventually began selling the product under the name Post-it. Sales have reached more than $500 million.

Another firm committed to the concept of intrapreneurship is Hewlett-Packard. After failing to recognize the potential of Steven Wozniak's proposal for a personal computer (which was the basis for the intrapreneurial venture called Apple Computer Inc.), Hewlett-Packard has taken steps to ensure that it will be recognized as a leader in innovation and not miss future opportunities. Even with this being the case, the road to commercialization in the company is not always an easy one. This was the case for Charles House, an engineer who went far beyond his intrapreneurial duty when he ignored an order from David Packard to stop working on a high-quality video monitor. The monitor, once developed, was used to track NASA's manned moon landings, and in heart transplants as well. Although projected to achieve sales of no more than 30 units, more than 17,000 of these large-screen displays (about $35 million in sales) have already been sold.

Even the computer giant, IBM, some seven years ago decided that intrapreneurship would help spur corporate growth. The company developed the independent business unit concept in which each unit is a separate organization with its own mini-board of directors and autonomous decision-making authority on many manufacturing and marketing issues. The more than 11 business units have developed such products as the automatic teller machine for banks, industrial robots, and the IBM Personal Computer. The latter business unit was given a blank check with a mandate to get IBM into the personal computer market. Intrapreneur Philip Estridge led his group to develop and market the PCs, both through IBM's sales force and the retail market, breaking some of the most binding operational rules of IBM at that time. This independent business unit has grown into a division with more than 10,000 employees and yearly sales exceeding $5 billion.

These and other success stories indicate that the problems of intrapreneurship are not insurmountable and that the concept can lead to new products, growth, and the development of an entirely new corporate environment and culture.

SUMMARY

Social and business pressures have caused an increase in new venture creation both outside and inside existing corporate structures. Within existing corporate structures, this entrepreneurial spirit and effort is called intrapreneurship.

To develop successful innovation, a corporation should establish a conducive organizational procedure. This will differ greatly from the traditional corporate climate. Traditional managers tend to adhere more strictly to established hierarchical structures, to be less risk-oriented, and to emphasize short-term results. This tends to inhibit the creativity, flexibility, and risk required for new ventures. Organizations desiring an intrapreneurial climate need to encourage new idea and trial and error efforts, eliminate opportunity parameters, make resources available, promote a teamwork approach and voluntary intrapreneurship, and establish a long time horizon, an appropriate reward system, and top management support.

The intrapreneur must also have appropriate leadership characteristics. In addition to being creative, visionary, and flexible, the intrapreneur must be able to work within the corporate structure. Intrapreneurs need to encourage teamwork and work diplomatically across established structures. Open discussion and strong support of team members is also required. Finally, the intrapreneur must be persistent in order to overcome the inevitable obstacles.

The process of establishing intrapreneurship within an existing organization requires the commitment of management, particularly top management. The organization must carefully choose intrapreneurial leaders, develop general guidelines for ventures, and delineate expectations of the program before the intrapreneurial program begins. Training sessions are an important part of the process. As role models and intrapreneurial ventures are introduced, the organization must establish a strong organizational support system, along with incentives and rewards to encourage team members. Finally, it should establish a system to expand successful ventures and to eliminate unsuccessful ones.

Intrapreneurship can be fraught with perils. Studies have cited problems with corporate ventures due to lack of commitment, lack of freedom, and a constrained environment. For companies not willing to commit to intrapreneurship, joint ventures offer an alternative for growth and diversification. However, the numerous examples of successful intrapreneurial ventures prove that the concept is indeed doable. Intrapreneurship is becoming a recognized component for growth and innovation within established corporations in response to the new challenges and hypercompetitive environment confronting American business.

18

International Business and Entrepreneurship

CHAPTER OBJECTIVES

1. To identify the aspects of international business and its importance to economies and firms.

2. To explain the similarities and differences between domestic and international business.

3. To identify the important strategic issues in doing international business.

4. To identify the available options for entering international markets.

5. To discuss the recent research on international entrepreneurship.

BERNARD TAPIE AND WANG YONG XIAN

No one knows better that entrepreneurship is a risky business than Bernard Tapie, a Frenchman who runs, among other things, his own holding company, Bernard Tapie Finance, S.A.[1] Raised in a working-class neighborhood in a suburb of Paris, Tapie is native to a culture that is among the most risk-averse in Europe. The social stigma associated with bankruptcy and business failure is so strong that most French citizens choose to work for someone else rather than take the risks and reap the rewards of starting their own business.

Not so for Tapie, who began his career at age 18 as a door-to-door television salesman. While working as a business consultant in the 1960s, he was convinced he had the skills to run his own company. However, Tapie's debut as an entrepreneur ended in a business reversal and a conviction for false advertising. Although the conviction was retracted on appeal, the negative publicity from the affair made for a less than auspicious beginning.

Since 1977, Tapie has been in the business of buying and revitalizing well-known companies that find themselves in difficulty. "Group Tapie" is composed of 45 firms, including Wonder-Mazda, a battery maker; Look, a company that was until recently in the sports industry; Terraillon, a maker of scales for personal and kitchen uses; and La Vie Claire, a chain of health food stores.[2]

This billion dollar holding company has brought him more than financial success; his high profile in the media has made him a cultural hero to the nation's young and a symbol of individual success. For example, he hosts a quarterly television show called "Ambitions" that addresses the special issues of business start-up.[3]

Business success is not the only element contributing to this man's celebrity status. In 1986, Tapie bought ownership of the Marseille Soccer Team— "Le Club Olympique de Marseille" (OM)—which was then floundering but has since become the heavyweight team in France and a contender for the European championship.[4]

---

[1]For more in-depth information on this company and the founder, see P. Sherrid, J. P. Shapiro, M. Wechsler, & M. Lord, "America's Hottest New Export," *U.S. News and World Report,* July 27, 1987, pp. 39–40.

[2]A. Cressatti, "Bernard Tapie a la Rescousse d'Adidas," *Journal Francais d'Amerique* 12, no. 16 (July 27–August 23, 1990), p. 8.

[3]R. I. Kirkland Jr., "Europe's New Entrepreneurs," *Fortune,* April 27, 1987, p. 258.

[4]H. Haget, "Voyage au Coeur de l'OM," *L'Express,* September 14, 1990, p. 36.

Tapie has also become involved in France's political arena. Elected to the parliament in 1988 and seated among the socialists in the National Assembly, he has taken on a challenging position in southern France, a region beset by a host of problems associated with immigration. One of his concerns, shared by a number of French people, is the growing support in southern France for the far-right political leader of the "National Front": Jean-Marie LePen. The issues in the south are such a public concern that in December, 1989, Tapie and LePen held a televised debate. Tapie has since announced a plan to create a political forum—multipartisan in nature—to reduce the clout of his opponent's party. Tapie's tough stance on racism and his bold, confrontational way with Le Pen have won him favor and respect in much of France.[5]

In the meantime, Tapie has managed to close a deal with Adidas, giving him 80 percent ownership of the German sporting-goods concern. Financing for the purchase was arranged using a combination of short-term loans and stock and bond issues.[6] Following the death of Chairman Horst Dassler in 1987, Adidas lost its grip on the number one spot in the world of sports footwear, reporting a loss for 1989 amounting to 120 million marks, or $72 million, on 4.6 billion marks in sales.[7] Of course, Tapie has plans to change all that.

Tapie is one of a growing number of people who are making entrepreneurship work in a variety of cultures and contexts throughout the world. Since 1973, there have been 8 million new jobs created in the United States, largely due to the growth of small businesses. Other nations, witnessing the stability and dynamism of the U.S. economy, are turning to entrepreneurship as a new solution for old economic solutions.

In contrast to the life-style of Tapie in France is Wang Yong Xian, who, in his blue denim Mao jacket and trousers, does not look out of place on Canton's busy streets. A 49-year-old plant manager of a shipyard, Wang has worked his way up from a mechanic's position. During the Cultural Revolution, Wang said, "no one bothered me because I was only a junior manager." In 1974, while in Peking at the Sixth Ministry of Machine Building, which supervises shipyards, Wang helped negotiate the contract for a container plant. He then became its manager.

Wang initiated a work bonus plan by first seeking his employees' advice. The employees developed a plan based on individual contributions to increasing productivity. Wang refined the plan and established quotas that needed to be surpassed to earn extra money. His workers get an average $25 bonus each month in addition to their regular pay of $31 to $38. In theory, the bonus system will allow some to double their normal earnings, receiving as much as Wang—about $75 a month. Wang himself is not eligible for a bonus.

---

[5]D. de Montvalon, "Tapie Peut-il Briser Le Pen?" *L'Express*, June 22, 1990, pp. 24–30.

[6]E. S. Browning, "Tapie Discloses Loan Package to Raise $289 Million to Buy 80% of Adidas AG," *Wall Street Journal*, July 18, 1990, p. A6.

[7]V. Beaufils, "Comment Reussir a Perdre Adidas," *L'Express*, August 3, 1990, p. 17.

Wang also makes sure that the government helps the shipyard attain the self-sufficiency needed in a Chinese factory like the container plant, which has been equipped to make its own machine parts, carpenters' aprons, and even ice-cream bars.

In addition to government and employees' intervention, Wang willingly adopts other good suggestions. For example, when one engineer pointed out that many employees lingered outside the plant after their lunch break, Wang had a gong installed to summon them back to work promptly. Wang's managerial style is surprising. When an office employe had nowhere to leave her 19-month-old child, Wang spent part of the day cheerfully bouncing the toddler on his lap. Immediately after that, he was a tough negotiator in a business meeting.

As the Soviet Union moves toward market orientation, it needs to consider the "second economy," which is outside that once controlled by the state. Run by entrepreneurs ranging in importance from peasants who till tiny gardens to rich manufacturers, the second economy has not been all underground. Its most important legal product is the crops and livestock that Soviet citizens raise on private plots and sell at public markets. These tiny farms, averaging less than an acre, were cultivated by people moonlighting from farm and factory jobs alike. While the plots represented only 3 percent of Soviet farmland, farmed with entrepreneurial zeal, they produced one-fourth of all Soviet farm products. Soviet doctors who worked for the state are also allowed to treat patients at home for fees set low and taxed heavily by the government. The incorporation of this second economy into the new market-oriented one is a critical aspect of achieving a strong unified economy for the Soviet Union.

As indicated in these vignettes, the importance of international business and entrepreneurship is becoming increasingly obvious. More developed countries like the United States, Japan, Great Britain, and Germany must sell their products in a variety of new and different market areas. From Rome to Stalingrad to Rio de Janiero, the familiar red and white of Coca-Cola can be found. And, rival Pepsi has a significant market position in the Soviet Union and Hungary as well as throughout Europe, Latin America, Africa, and Asia. L'Oreal has a significant share of the world's cosmetics market. Simultaneously, the U.S. markets have been successfully penetrated by international firms, particularly those from Japan and Germany. Toyota, Datsun, and Honda have captured significant shares of the U.S. automobile market.

As countries become more developed, the distinction between foreign and domestic markets becomes less. What was once only produced domestically is now produced internationally. For example, Yamaha pianos are now manufactured in the United States. Digital Equipment Company has plants in Puerto Rico. Nestle's chocolates are made in Europe. This blurring of national identities will continue to accelerate as more and more products are introduced outside domestic boundaries.

THE NATURE OF INTERNATIONAL BUSINESS

What is international business? Simply stated, international business is the process of conducting business activities across national boundaries. It is exporting, licensing, opening a sales office in another country, or something as simple as placing a classified advertisement in the Paris edition of the *Herald Tribune*. All of those activities necessary for ascertaining and satisfying the needs and wants of target consumers often take place in more than one country. When a company executes its business in more than one country, it is engaged in international business.

With a commercial history of only 300 years, the United States is a relative newcomer to the arena of international business. As soon as settlements had been established in the "New World," the new Americans began an active international trade with Europe. Foreign investors helped build much of the early industrial trade with Europe as well as much of the early industrial base of the United States. The future commercial strength of the United States will depend on the ability of U.S. industry to take advantage of markets outside its borders.

THE ECONOMIC EFFECT OF INTERNATIONAL BUSINESS

At one point, the value of goods and services being traded between the countries of the world amounted to approximately $1 trillion. The United States' share of this trade amounted to approximately $170 billion or 17 percent of the world's exports. The comparable figures for Japan and the United Kingdom were $70 billion and $46 billion. These numbers indicate that the preservation of active engagement in world trade is necessary for the preservation of the world economy. The volume of international trade is critical to the political and economic stability of large areas of the globe. The actual trade between countries varies greatly, depending in part on the economic and political circumstances involved. Table 18–1 indicates the imports and exports between the United States, Europe, Eastern Europe, the USSR, China, and Taiwan for a period of five years. While U.S. exports to Europe increased from $67,512 million in 1980 to $87,995 million in 1988, imports from Europe to the U.S. increased at an even faster rate—from $46,602 million in 1980 to $100,515 million in 1988. Since 1985, the United States has imported more from Europe than it has exported to Europe, leaving a negative balance of trade. The same negative balance occurred in 1988 for each of the other areas listed in Table 18–1, with the exception of the USSR, where U.S. exports were $2,768 million and imports were $578 million. The U.S. government is very interested in trying to achieve a positive balance of trade with every country and will provide a great deal of assistance and information to any entrepreneurs wanting to export or in any way engage in interna-

TABLE 18–1 U.S. Imports and Exports by Country or Region*

	Exports					Imports				
	1980	*1985*	*1986*	*1987*	*1988*	*1980*	*1985*	*1986*	*1987*	*1988*
Europe	$ 67,512	$ 56,763	$ 61,642	$ 69,718	$ 87,995	$ 46,602	$ 79,756	$ 89,825	$ 95,496	$100,515
Eastern Europe†	2,347	792	741	720	882	983	1,527	1,443	1,498	1,580
USSR	1,513	2,423	1,248	1,480	2,768	454	409	558	425	578
China (Taiwan)	4,337	4,700	5,524	7,413	12,130	6,854	16,396	19,791	24,622	24,804
Total	$220,783	$213,146	$217,304	$252,866	$320,385	$244,871	$345,276	$369,961	$405,901	$441,282

*Statistics are in millions of dollars.
†This includes Bulgaria, Czechoslovakia, East Germany, Hungary, Poland, Rumania, and other Communist areas in Europe.
Source: *Statistical Abstract of the United States*, 1990 edition.

tional business. Besides the wealth of data already collected and special reports of doing business in certain countries, a limited amount of original research data can often be obtained through the U.S. embassy in the particular country.

Focusing on imports and exports highlights only one part of the economic effect of international business. Firms headquartered in the United States have made direct investments outside the country and sales by the majority-owned foreign affiliates of U.S. companies increase each year. There is also significant foreign direct investment in the United States. A traditional estimate is that $3.50 of sales occurs for each dollar of investment. It is clear that the world's standard of living would be greatly reduced if international business activity were to cease.

International business provides the systems framework through which the buyers and sellers of the goods and services described above are matched. International marketing has been described as the delivery system for a country's standard of living. Without a doubt, business and marketing play a crucial role in the delivery of the world's standard of living.

THE IMPORTANCE OF INTERNATIONAL BUSINESS TO THE FIRM

International business has become increasingly important to firms of all sizes. No longer are international sales only important for the survival and growth of some of the largest U.S. firms. Each firm is now competing in a global economy.

There can be little doubt that today's entrepreneur must be able to move in the world of international business. The successful entrepreneur will be someone who fully understands how international business differs from purely domestic business and is able to act accordingly. The entrepreneur considering entering the international market should answer the following questions:

Is managing international business different from managing domestic business?

What are the strategic issues to be resolved in international business management?

What are the options available for engaging in international business?

How should one assess the decision to enter into an international market?

INTERNATIONAL VERSUS DOMESTIC BUSINESS MANAGEMENT

Whether international or domestic, a company has the same basic strategic decisions: sales, costs, and profits. What differentiates domestic from international business is the variation in the relative importance of the factors being considered in each decision. International business decisions are more complex than domestic business decisions. The uncontrollable factors of economics, politics, culture, and technology create enormous complexity in the formulation of international business programs.

Economics

When a company designs a domestic business strategy, it is dealing with a single country at a specified level of economic development. The varied regions of this single country are affected by the same balance of payments and the entire country is almost always organized under a single economic system. Creating a business strategy for a multicountry area means dealing with different levels of economic development, varying degrees of balance of payments problems, and possibly vastly different economic systems. These differences manifest themselves in each aspect of the international business plan.

Stage of Economic Development

The United States is an industrially developed nation with regional variances in relative income, but it has no region that would be classified as less developed or developing. While needing to adjust the business plan according to regional differences, a manager with domestic U.S. responsibility does not have to worry about the lack of infrastructure items such as roads, electricity, communication systems, banking facilities, adequate educational systems, and well-developed justice systems.

When General Motors decided to introduce a Basic Transportation Vehicle (BTV) in Asia, its product development group had to deal with a set of unique problems created because much of Asia is economically underdeveloped. The BTV is a combination of private car, light truck, and taxi cab, with a power train designed for and marketed in an area with a limited road system, few licensed drivers, and widespread illiteracy.

Balance of Payments

With the switch to a system of flexible exchange rates, a country's balance of payments (the difference between the value of a country's imports and exports over time) situation is quickly reflected in the value of its currency. The automobile industry again provides an example of how an economic variable will affect an international business program. At one time, Italy's chronic balance of payments deficit led to a radical depreciation in the value of the lira. Fiat responded to this by offering significant rebates on cars sold in the United States. These rebates cost very little because fewer dollars purchased many more lira due to the depreciation in value of the lira.

Type of System

Pepsi-Cola began considering the possibility of marketing in the Soviet Union as early as the 1959 visit of then Vice President Nixon to the Soviet Union. When Premier Nikita Khrushchev expressed his approval of Pepsi's taste, the slow wheels of East-West trade began moving, with Pepsi entering the Soviet Union 13 years later. Instead of using its traditional type of franchise bottler in this entry, Pepsi used a barter type arrangement that satisfied both the Soviet socialized system and the U.S. capitalist system. In return for receiving technology and syrup from Pepsi, the Soviet Union provided the company with Soviet vodka and the right to distribute it in the United States. Many such **barter** or **third-party arrangements** have been used to increase the amount of business activity with the Soviet Union and Eastern Bloc countries. Now direct foreign investments and joint ventures are used, with some or all of the profits being taken home in the form of currency.

There are still many difficulties in establishing joint ventures in Eastern Europe and the USSR. In the USSR, only 10–12 percent of the 1,400 registered joint ventures are actively operating. Some of the reasons are gaps in the Soviets' basic knowledge of the Western system regarding business plans, product promotion, marketing, and profits; widely variable rates of return; nonconvertibility of rubles, which necessitates finding a countertrade item; differences in the accounting system; and nightmarish communications.[8]

Political-Legal Environment

The multiplicity of political and legal environments in the international market create vastly different business problems. For example, U.S. environmental standards have eliminated the possibility of importing several models of European cars. In addition, as part of a political arrangement Japanese businesses have agreed to reduce the volume of their exports to the United States. Perhaps the most significant events in the political-legal environment involve the price fluctuations in oil reflecting the oil embargo, overproduction of oil, and the Iraq invasion of Kuwait.

Each element of the business strategy in a multinational firm has the potential to be affected by the multiplicity of legal environments. Pricing decisions in a country that prohibits resale price maintenance is in direct conflict with those decisions made by the same company in a country with resale price maintenance. Advertising strategy is affected by the limitations and variations of what can be said in the copy. For example, justification for advertising claims varies

---

[8]R. Cooper, "Much Ventured, Little Gained," *Euromoney*, February 1990, pp. 21–3.

dramatically between countries. Production decisions are affected by legal requirements on labeling, ingredients, and packaging. Amount and type of ownership and organizational forms vary widely not only in the United States but throughout the world. The laws governing these types of arrangements also vary in the over 150 different legal systems and sets of national laws.

Cultural Environment

The impact of culture on business programs and strategies is also significant. Firms must make sure that each element in the business plan has some degree of congruence with the local culture. For example, in some cultures point of purchase displays are not allowed in the country's retail stores as they are in stores in the United States.

Respect for the local culture is most necessary at the headquarters of the business. The entire debate over the degree of adaptation and standardization in worldwide plans revolves around the concept of culture. This is an important issue that must be resolved by each company doing international business.

Technological Environment

Technology, like culture, varies significantly across countries. The variations in and availability of technology are often surprising, particularly to a manager from a developed country. Many Americans, for example, have a difficult time understanding how a technologically advanced military economy like the USSR could have shortages of food and consumer goods. Many major multinational food companies have experienced the effect of crop variation on production and marketing. U.S. farms produce mostly standardized, relatively uniform products that can be sorted to meet industry standards. This standardization minimizes changes in product taste or formulation.

New products in a country are often created on the basis of self-referential criteria and assumptions about technology or its related output. For example, U.S. car designers can assume wide roads and, one at a time, inexpensive gasoline when designing the next year's domestic models. When these same designers had to work on transportation vehicles for other parts of the world, they had to alter their assumptions significantly. For many products, the assumptions built into their design are subtle and not apparent on superficial reflection.[9]

---

[9]J. A. Lee, "Cultural Analysis in Overseas Operations," *Harvard Business Review,* March–April 1966, pp. 106–14.

Strategic Issues

Four strategic issues are of paramount importance to the international manager. These are (1) the allocation of responsibility between headquarters and subsidiary management; (2) the nature of the planning, reporting, and control systems to be used throughout the international business system; (3) the appropriate organization structure for conducting international business; and (4) the degree of adaptation or standardization encouraged in the worldwide business program.

The problems of allocation of responsibility between headquarters and subsidiary is essentially the degree of decentralization that can be tolerated. As companies move through their experience with international business, they tend to change their approach to the allocation of responsibility. This frequently occurs in the following progression.

- *Stage 1*—When making its first moves into international business, a firm typically follows a highly centralized decision-making process. Since the firm generally has a limited number of individuals with international experience, it tends to use a centralized decision-making network. The attitude is often: "What do those people from another country know about our product and its needs? We better do it all from here."

- *Stage 2*—When success occurs, a Stage 1 firm finds it can no longer use a completely centralized decision-making process in running an international operation. The multiplicity of environments faced by the firm become far too complex to handle from a central headquarters. In response, the firm often goes to the other extreme and decentralizes its entire international operation. The philosophy at this point can be summed up as follows: "There's no way we're ever going to be able to understand the differences between all of those markets. Let them make their own decisions."

- *Stage 3*—The process of decentralization carried out in a Stage 2 firm becomes intolerable once the firm attains further success. Individual corporate units within the different countries end up in conflict with each other. Corporate headquarters become the last to receive information about problems in which they should be actively involved. When this occurs, limited amounts of power, authority, and responsibility are pulled back to headquarters. A balance between headquarters having reasonably tight control on major strategic marketing decisions and the subsidiary having the responsibility for the tactical implementation of corporate strategy is usually achieved.

Planning, reporting, and control systems in the multinational firm are very important aspects of international success. They allow management to identify and evaluate the worth of markets, to monitor the company's performance in those markets already entered, and to make any necessary changes in the operations.

To understand what is required for effective planning, reporting, and control for multinational business, the firm should consider the following questions:

Environmental Analysis

1. What are the unique characteristics of each national market? What characteristics do each market have in common with other national markets?

2. Can we cluster national markets for operating and/or planning purposes? What dimensions of markets should we use to cluster markets?

Strategic Planning

3. Who should be involved in marketing decisions?

4. What are our major assumptions about target markets? Are they valid?

5. What needs are satisfied by our products in target markets?

6. What customer benefits are provided by our product in target markets?

7. What are the conditions under which our products are used in the target markets?

8. How large is the ability to buy our products in target markets?

9. What are our major strengths and weaknesses relative to existing and potential competition in target markets?

10. Should we extend, adapt, or invent products, prices, advertising, and promotion programs for target markets?

11. What are the balance-of-payments and currency situations in target markets? Will we be able to remit earnings? Is the political climate acceptable?

12. What are our objectives given the alternatives open to us and our assessment of opportunity, risk, and company capability?

Structure

13. How do we structure our organization to optimally achieve our objectives, given our skills and resources? What is the responsibility of each organizational level?

Operational Planning

14. Given our objectives, structure, and assessment of the market environment, how do we implement effective operational marketing plans? What products will we market, at what prices, through what channels, with what communications, and in which markets and market clusters?

Controlling the Marketing Program

15. How do we measure and monitor plan performance? What steps should be taken to ensure that marketing objectives are met?[10]

One key to successful marketing planning is an appreciation of the market phase. Questions 1 and 2 in the preceding list of 15 questions focus in on this

---

[10]W. J. Keegan, "A Conceptual Framework for Multinational Marketing," *Journal of World Business,* November–December 1972, p. 75.

dimension of the planning process. The first step in identifying markets and clustering countries is to analyze data on each country of interest along the following seven vectors:

1. Market Characteristics
    a.   Size of market; rate of growth
    b.   Stage of development
    c.   Stage of product life-cycle; saturation levels
    d.   Buyer behavior characteristics
    e.   Social/cultural factors
    f.   Physical environment
2. Marketing Institutions
    a.   Distribution systems
    b.   Communication media
    c.   Marketing services (advertising, research, etc.)
3. Industry Conditions
    a.   Competitive size and practices
    b.   Technical development
4. Legal Environment
    (laws, regulations, codes, tariffs, taxes, etc.)
5. Resources
    a.   Manpower (availability, skill, potential, cost)
    b.   Money (availability, cost)
6. Financial Environment
    (balance of payments, foreign exchange rate, regulations, etc.)
7. Political Environment
    a.   Current government policies and attitudes
    b.   Long-range political environment

ENTREPRENEURIAL ENTRY INTO INTERNATIONAL BUSINESS

A wide range of choices are available to the firm that wants to enter into international business and market its products internationally. The choice of entry method or the mode of operating overseas is very much dependent on the goals of the company and the company's strengths and weaknesses. The modes of entering or engaging in international business can be divided into three categories: exporting, nonequity ventures, and direct investment.

Exporting

As a general rule, firms gain their first contact with international business through exporting. Exporting normally involves the sale and shipping of products manufactured in one country to a customer located in another country. Since there are many different methods of executing an export operation, it is helpful to divide them into two categories, direct and indirect.

Indirect Exporting. This involves a foreign purchaser in local market. For certain commodities and manufactured goods, foreign buyers actively seek out sources of supply and have purchasing offices in markets throughout the world. A firm wishing to take advantage of the overseas markets for its products can deal with one of these buyers. In this way, the entire transaction is handled as though it were a domestic transaction, but the seller knows that his or her goods are going to be shipped out of the country. This method of entering exporting involves the least amount of risk for the seller.

Export management firms are located in almost every commercial center. For a fee, these companies will provide representation in foreign markets. This type of management firm will put together a group of manufacturers from the same country it is located in who have no interest in becoming directly involved in exporting. The management firm handles all of the selling and technical problems involved in the export process.

Direct Exporting. Independent foreign distributors often handle products for firms seeking relatively rapid entry into a large number of foreign markets. This involves the firm in direct contact with a foreign purchaser and in all of the technicalities of arranging for export documentation and financing.

Many firms do not like to give up the control over their marketing efforts that the hiring of independent distributors entails. These firms tend to open their own overseas sales offices and hire their own salesmen to provide market representation. When the firm is very new to exporting, it may even send a U.S. or domestic salesperson to represent it in a foreign market. As firms with overseas sales offices become more involved in their foreign markets, they tend to open warehouses in the countries where they have the offices. They may even start a local assembly process if overseas sales attain a high enough level.

Second-Generation Exporting. So far we have been describing the export activities of firms new to international business. A large amount of exporting is done by firms who have a long history of involvement in international business. Once firms have set up manufacturing operations in foreign markets they then use the output from these factories to export to many other markets. Intracompany exports, that is, shipments from one division of a company to another, have also become more prevalent as multinational firms try to rationalize their worldwide manufacturing systems.

Nonequity Arrangements

Three forms of nonequity arrangements are most popular: licensing, turn-key projects, and management contracts. Each of these forms of engaging in international business allows the firm to gain income without a direct equity investment in a foreign market. Firms who either cannot export or make direct investments or those who simply choose not to engage in those activities still have the possibility of entering into nonequity arrangements.

Licensing. Licensing involves a domestic manufacturer (licensee) giving a foreign manufacturer (licensor) the right to use a patent, trademark, technology, or similar product in return for the payment of a royalty. The licensing arrangement is used when a company has no immediate intention of entering a particular market on their own either through exporting or direct investment. Many perceive the process as being very low in risk and an easy way to generate incremental income. If entered into after careful analysis, a licensing arrangement can be very beneficial. Unfortunately, many companies have entered into these arrangements after little or no investigation. They then find they have licensed their largest competitor into business or that they are investing large sums of time and money in aiding the licensor to adopt the technology or know-how he has licensed.

Wolverine World Wide Inc. opened a Hush Puppies store in Sofia, Bulgaria, in the summer of 1988, through a licensing agreement with a combine named Pikin. Negotiations with the Soviets began at about the same time; in June 1989, Wolverine signed a licensing agreement with a Soviet shoe combine called Kirov and hopes to open a Hush Puppies store both in Moscow and one outlying city. In the meantime, Wolverine has opened 30 other stores throughout Bulgaria.[11]

Turn-Key Projects. The underdeveloped or lesser developed countries of the world have recognized their need for manufacturing technology and infrastructure. They have also recognized that they do not want to turn over substantial portions of their economy to foreign domination. The solution to this dilemma has been to have a foreign firm build a factory or other facility, train the workers to operate the equipment, and train the management to run the installation. Once the operation is on line, it is turned over to its local owners.

Firms that would otherwise be blocked out of a foreign market have found the turn-key an attractive alternative. They can make the initial profit the turn-key project. In addition, such projects can be a major stimulus to follow-up export sales. The turn-key is also attractive as it provides cash flow throughout the entire project. Financing is often provided by the local owner and periodic payments are made over the entire period of construction and training.

---

[11]J. A. Cohen, "Footwear and the Jet Set," *Management Review,* March 1990, pp. 42–5.

Management Contracts. It has often been stated that the most advanced parts of American industry are its management techniques and managerial skills. Several firms have begun the practice of contracting their personnel to run noncompany-owned facilities in other countries. These contracts often follow up a turn-key project where the foreign owner wants to maintain the management of the turn-key supplier.

The management contract allows the purchasing country to gain foreign expertise without turning ownership of its resources over to a foreigner. To the supplier of the management contract it is another way of entering into markets that would otherwise be closed. It is also another means of reaping a profit without the need of a large equity investment.

Direct Foreign Investment

The wholly owned foreign subsidiary has been the preferred mode of ownership for U.S. firms making a direct foreign investment. Joint ventures and minority and majority equity positions have also been used as vehicles for making direct foreign investments. The percentage of ownership desired is closely related to the nationality of the foreign investor, the amount of overseas experience that investor has had, the nature of the industry, and the pressures exerted by the host government.

Minority Interests. Japanese multinationals have been frequent users of the minority equity position in direct foreign investment. The minority position provides the firm with either a source of raw materials or a relatively captive market for its products. Firms have frequently used minority positions to gain a foothold or experience in a market before making a major commitment. If the minority shareholder has something of value to offer to the organization, his ability to influence its decision making process is often far in excess of his shareholding.

Joint Ventures. The joint venture can take on many forms. In its most traditional form, two firms (for example, one U.S. firm and one German firm) get together and form a third company in which they share the equity. Another mode is for a U.S. firm to simply purchase 50 percent of the equity in a foreign firm.

Joint ventures have been used most frequently in two situations. First, they provide a convenient form of investment when the U.S. firm wants to purchase local knowledge and an already established marketing or manufacturing facility. Second, when rapid entry into a market is needed, a joint venture is often the only plausible path available to the investing firm. Often joint ventures are dissolved, with the U.S. firm taking over 100 percent ownership to control the marketing program.

Even though entering into a joint venture is a key strategic decision, the motivations or keys to success have not been well understood. The reasons for forming a joint venture today are different than those in the past. In the past, joint ventures were viewed as partnerships, according to the law, and often involved firms whose stock was owned by several other firms. Originally, joint ventures were used for trading purposes and as such were one of the oldest ways of transacting business. Merchants of ancient Babylonia, Egypt, and Phoenicia used joint ventures to conduct large trading operations. This use continued through the 15th and 16th centuries when merchants in Great Britain used joint venturing to trade all over the world, particularly in the Americas and India.

The use of joint ventures in the United States took a somewhat different form, being used by mining concerns and railroads as early as 1850. The largest, and perhaps best known, joint venture during this period was the formation of ARAMCO by four U.S. oil companies to explore and develop oil reserves. The use of joint ventures increased significantly during the 1950s with more than 350 domestic joint ventures of the 1,000 largest U.S. corporations in operation. These were often vertical joint ventures that shared the output of the supply facility—the original reason for the joint venture. In this way, the two firms could absorb the large volume of output where neither one could handle it alone or afford the diseconomies associated with a smaller size of plant.

While joint ventures actively continued at a rapid pace during the 60s and 70s in the United States and even more so in the European Community, the use of joint ventures accelerated further in 1980 with the advent of globalization, technological advances, and the need for product innovation. While 63 domestic joint ventures occurred in the United States in 1980, 54 occurred in both 1981 and 1982. The numbers exploded in 1983, with 260 joint ventures recorded. This number decreased to 99 in 1984. Since 1984, the activity level of joint ventures has increased radically. As is indicated in Table 18–2, the activity level of all forms of mergers and acquisitions (including joint ventures) during the period we are most interested in (1985–1990) was significant in the United States with 3,437 occurring in 1985, 4,381 in 1986, 3,920 in 1987, and 3,487 in 1988. In 1988, the activity level was highest in the finance, insurance, and real estate industry (658), followed by services (516), transportation and public utilities (300), retail trade (210), and wholesale trade (206).

What has caused this significant increase in the use of joint ventures, particularly since not all of them have worked well? The studies of success and failure rates of joint ventures have revealed many different motives for their formation, and the proper motive is necessary for success.

Probably, the most frequent reason for forming a joint venture is to share the costs and risks of a very uncertain project. Projects where new technology is involved frequently need resource sharing, allowing each firm to concentrate on its strengths. They can be particularly beneficial to smaller firms who do not have the financial resources to engage in capital intensive activities. In some cases, these large scale projects avoid the problems and costs that inefficient small scale plants experience, such as duplication of facilities.

Another frequent reason for forming a joint venture is the **synergy** between the firms. This may be in the form of people, inventory, or plant and equipment. The synergy provides leverage for each firm in the market. The extent of the

TABLE 18–2 Business Enterprise

No. 883. MERGERS AND ACQUISITIONS—SUMMARY: 1980 TO 1988

[Covers transactions valued at $1 million or more. Values based on transactions for which price data revealed. **All activity** includes mergers, acquisitions, acquisitions of controlling interest, divestitures, and leveraged transactions that result in a change in ownership. **Divestiture:** sale of a business, division, or subsidiary by corporate owner to another party. **Leveraged buyout:** acquisition of a business in which buyers use mostly borrowed money to finance purchase price and incorporate debt into capital structure of business after change in ownership]

ITEM	Unit	1980	1981	1982	1983	1984	1985	1986	1987	1988
All activity: Number	Number	1,560	2,329	2,298	2,391	3,164	3,437	4,381	3,920	3,487
Value	Mil. dol	32,883	70,064	60,698	52,691	126,074	145,464	204,895	177,203	226,643
Divestitures: Number	Number	104	476	562	661	792	1,037	1,413	1,192	1,090
Value	Mil. dol	5,090	10,171	8,362	12,949	30,556	43,524	72,320	57,519	80,103
Leveraged buyouts: Number	Number	11	100	164	231	253	254	335	270	318
Value	Mil. dol	236	3,870	3,452	4,519	18,697	19,634	45,160	36,069	42,914
Form of payment: All cash	Percent	(NA)	42	55	53	37	40	44	54	59
All stock	Percent	(NA)	22	14	16	12	10	11	11	7
Combination cash, stock, debt, other	Percent	(NA)	19	20	25	26	24	20	17	19
Undisclosed [1]	Percent	(NA)	17	11	6	26	26	25	18	15
Ownership status of acquisition targets:										
Public acquired company:										
Number	Number	398	668	687	553	832	817	853	995	874
Value	Mil. dol	11,948	49,675	46,701	31,891	85,724	91,513	108,894	102,829	125,195
Private acquired company:										
Number	Number	1,059	1,198	1,064	1,192	1,550	1,588	2,123	1,683	1,477
Value	Mil. dol	15,911	11,215	6,400	8,335	10,007	10,376	24,059	14,853	19,867

NA Not available.   [1] Price was given but form of payment was not.

No. 884. MERGERS AND ACQUISITIONS—NUMBER AND VALUE OF TRANSACTIONS, BY INDUSTRY: 1988

[See headnote table 883]

SIC[1] code	INDUSTRY	TOTAL		U.S. COMPANY ACQUIRING U.S. COMPANY		FOREIGN COMPANY ACQUIRING U.S. COMPANY		U.S. COMPANY ACQUIRING FOREIGN COMPANY	
		Number	Value (mil. dol.)	Number	Value (mil. dol.)	Number	Value (mil. dol.)	Number	Value (mil. dol.)
	Total activity [1]	**3,487**	**226,643**	**2,882**	**159,326**	**447**	**60,818**	**158**	**6,500**
(A)	Agriculture, forestry, fishing	16	580	12	579	4	(²)	–	(²)
(B)	Mining	141	10,460	112	7,942	17	1,744	12	774
(C)	Construction	33	2,257	30	587	3	1,670	–	(²)
(D)	Manufacturing:								
20	Food and kindred products	136	22,991	100	17,849	24	4,884	12	258
22	Textile mill products	26	2,736	18	2,186	7	501	1	49
23	Apparel, other textile products	34	1,307	28	1,288	3	19	3	(²)
24	Lumber and wood products	28	4,690	24	4,682	1	8	3	(²)
26	Paper and allied products	39	5,438	34	5,329	1	57	4	53
27	Printing and publishing	133	9,625	98	1,523	32	8,102	3	(²)
28	Chemicals and allied products	133	12,318	87	10,849	31	1,245	15	224
30	Rubber and plastic products	53	7,749	43	1,040	5	2,934	5	3,774
32	Stone, clay, glass, and concrete	42	3,545	26	2,379	12	1,143	4	23
33	Primary metals industries	43	3,248	33	3,109	7	118	3	21
34	Fabricated metal products	95	4,666	85	3,500	8	1,165	2	1
35	Industrial machinery, computer equipment	197	11,724	148	8,090	39	3,631	10	3
36	Electrical and electronic equipment	149	9,665	117	5,877	22	3,572	10	217
37	Transportation equipment	56	1,896	44	1,270	7	421	5	204
38	Instruments and related products [4]	189	5,038	139	3,417	42	1,587	8	33
(E)	Transportation and public utilities	300	16,128	276	15,350	17	753	7	26
(F)	Wholesale trade	206	2,896	162	2,529	31	358	13	9
(G)	Retail trade	210	29,481	191	21,308	13	8,097	6	76
(H)	Finance, insurance, real estate	658	32,535	596	21,635	53	10,766	9	134
(I)	Services	516	17,360	436	12,821	59	4,416	21	123

– Represents zero.   [1] Standard Industrial Classification; see text, section 13.   [2] Includes other industries, not shown separately.   [3] Transaction price data not revealed.   [4] Data have been revised since publication release.

Source of tables 883 and 884: MLR Publishing Company, *Mergers and Acquisitions*, 1988 (copyright). Publication contains extract from database, M&A Database.

Source: *Statistical Abstract of the U.S.* (1990 ed.), p. 534.

synergy is related to how beneficial the joint venture will be for both companies involved. This synergy frequently allows a reduction in inventory as neither company has to carry a safety stock. Synergy can also allow each firm to leverage their information without any duplication of efforts.

Another frequent purpose of joint ventures is to obtain a competitive advantage. A joint venture can preempt competitors, allowing a company to access new customers and expand its market base. It can also result in an entity that is more effectively competitive than the original company. Hybrids of companies tend to possess the strengths of each of the joint venture partners and are therefore stronger than either one alone.

Joint ventures are probably most frequently used in economies that are difficult to enter. This has been the case with the countries of Eastern Europe and the USSR. The rules and strategic aspects of joint ventures in these countries vary greatly (see Table 18–3). For example, it is easier to establish a joint venture in Hungary than in other Eastern European countries because of fewer registration requirements, but Hungary's tax rate on the joint venture as a percentage of profits is higher. The ease of establishing a joint venture has made Hungary the Eastern Bloc country with the most joint venture activity (80), as indicated in Table 18–4. However, the Soviet Union, with its massive size and economic turmoil, has more with 99.

Majority Interests.   In a technical sense, anything over 50 percent of the equity in a firm should provide complete managerial control. The majority interest allows the investing firm to gain managerial control while keeping its capital outlay to a minimum. It is also useful when the maintenance of a local identity is important.

Firms that have initially taken small majority positions have had a tendency to increase the ownership to 100 percent. This is because of the tight regulation in many countries over the rights of minority shareholders. The move to 100 percent ownership also reduces any possible conflict with the local owner.

100 Percent Ownership.   With 100 percent ownership comes complete control. For a variety of reasons, U.S. firms have had a history of desiring complete ownership and control over their foreign investments. Perhaps the most obvious reason for this is the elimination of the need for a foreign partner. If the U.S. firm has the capital, technology, and marketing skills required for successful entry into a market, it does not make a great deal of sense to share ownership.

As has been mentioned, U.S. multinationals try to standardize large segments of their marketing programs and attempt to standardize the marketing planning process utilized throughout their foreign subsidiaries. This standardization of activity becomes much easier to accomplish when dealing with wholly owned subsidiaries.

One form of 100 percent ownership that has been used significantly in international business as well as within the United States is mergers and acquisitions.

TABLE 18–3 Rules Governing the Establishment of Joint Ventures in Eastern Europe

	Bulgaria	Czechoslovakia	Yugoslavia	Poland	Romania	Soviet Union	Hungary
Year of first joint venture	1980	1985	1968	1976	1971	1988	1972
Number of joint ventures	41	20	230	170	5	685	628
Permit issuing authority	Council of Ministers	Individual ministries, following consultation with other authorities	Varies according to republic; in special cases, the federal government	Agency dealing with foreign investments	Council of Ministers	Council of Ministers	Ministry of Commerce and finance if the foreign share exceeds 50%, otherwise registration is sufficient
Tax rate as a percentage of profits	30	40	10	40	30	30	Up to 3 million forints—40 Over 3 million forints—50
Special deals for establishing joint ventures	Special tax-free status can be requested for first five years	—	—	First three years are tax free, an additional three can be requested. Value of new investments can be deducted from tax base	The first year is tax free. Second year 15% tax and 20% reduction if the profit is not taken out of the country	First 2 (3 in the far eastern areas) years are tax free. Lower taxes in far east later as well	Depends on amount of capital, percentage of foreign capital, type of activity. The special reduction can even be 100% in the first 5 years
Tax on dividends as a percentage	10–15	—	—	30	10	20—Special reduction possible	20—Private individuals pay personal income tax, economic organizations do not pay
Repatriation of profits	Only hard currency portion	Only hard currency portion	Only hard currency portion	85% of surplus export	Only hard currency portion	Profit covered by convertible export	The entire profit can be changed to hard currency and taken out of the country with no limitations

TABLE 18–4   Soviet and East European Investments in the West by Country, October 1987

Host Country	Bulgaria	Czechoslovakia	East Germany	Hungary	Poland	Romania	USSR	Total
Austria	2	1	6	26	8	2	4	49
Belgium	2	3	6	1	5	0	13	30
Canada	1	5	0	1	1	1	5	14
Finland	0	0	1	1	1	0	7	10
France	4	3	3	3	8	6	12	39
Italy	5	3	4	5	2	5	8	32
Netherlands	1	1	3	2	3	0	2	12
Spain	1	0	1	3	2	1	5	13
Sweden	0	3	2	2	5	0	3	15
Switzerland	2	2	1	4	2	2	4	17
United Kingdom	6	9	10	6	12	5	13	61
United States	1	2	1	7	12	1	4	28
West Germany	12	3	0	20	15	7	11	68
Others	5	0	4	5	4	2	8	28
Total	42	35	42	86	80	32	99	416

Source: United Nations, Economic Commission for Europe, *East-West Joint Ventures: Economic, Business, Financial and Legal Aspects*, 1988, p. 71.

Mergers and acquisitions have varied in use as a strategic option. Some of the most significant mergers and acquisitions for 1989 are indicated in Table 18–5. During periods of intense merger activity, financial managers spend significant time searching for a firm to acquire and then developing the appropriate deal for the transaction before another firm makes the acquisition. The deal itself should reflect basic principles of any capital investment decision and should make a net contribution to shareholders' wealth. The merits of a merger are difficult to determine. Not only must the firm determine the benefits and costs of a merger, it must address special accounting, legal, and tax issues. In addition, the firm needs to have a general understanding of the benefits and problems of mergers as a strategic option and of the complexity of integrating an entire company into its present operations.

There are five basic types of mergers: horizontal, vertical, product extension, market extension, and diversified activity. A **horizontal merger** is the combination of two firms that produce one or more of the same or closely related products in the same geographical area. They are motivated by economies of scale in marketing, production, or sales such as occurred with 7-Eleven Convenience Stores acquiring Southland Stores.

A **vertical merger** is the combination of two or more firms in successive stages of production that often involve a buyer-seller relationship. This form of merger stabilizes supply and production and offers more control of these critical areas. An example is McDonald's Corporation or Phillips Petroleum acquiring their store and gas station franchisees, making them company-owned stores.

TABLE 18-5 Significant Mergers and Acquisitions in 1989

Deal	Value (000) Percentage of Book Value	Transaction	Financial Intermediaries (Client)	Fee (000)	Fee as Percentage of Deal
Bristol-Myers (pharmaceuticals) acquires Squibb (pharmaceuticals) and changes name to Bristol-Myers Squibb	$12,656,271 852%	Acquisition for stock, October 4	Goldman Sachs Shearson Lehman Hutton (Bristol-Myers) Morgan Stanley (Squibb)	$25,000 $ 3,500 $23,900	.20 % .03 % .19 %
Beecham Group and SmithKline Beckman (pharmaceuticals companies) merge to form SmithKline Beecham	$ 8,253,000 519%	Merger by exchange of stock, July 26	Kleinwort Benson Wasserstein Perella (Beecham Group) Goldman Sachs J.P. Morgan (SmithKline Beckman)	N.A. N.A. $15,000 $15,000	— — .18 % .18 %
Time (broadcasting, publishing) acquires 50.6% of Warner Communications (entertainment, broadcasting, publishing)	$ 7,000,000 656%	Cash tender offer, July 24, as part of a $14 billion acquisition due to close January 1990	Merrill Lynch Shearson Lehman Hutton Wasserstein Perella (Time) Alpine Capital Group Goldman Sachs Lazard Freres Merrill Lynch (Warner Communications)	$ 1,500 $16,000 $16,000 $ 6,000 $ 1,000 $20,000 $ 1,000	.01 % .11 % .11 % .04 % .007% .14 % .007%

TABLE 18–5 (concluded)

Deal	Value (000) Percentage of Book Value	Transaction	Financial Intermediaries (Client)	Fee (000)	Fee as Percentage of Deal
Grand Metropolitan (British beverage company) acquires Pillsbury (restaurants, foods)	$ 5,757,917 430%	Acquisition for cash January 9	Morgan Stanley S. G. Warburg (Grand Metropolitan) Drexel Burnham Lambert First Boston Kleinwort Benson Shearson Lehman Hutton Wasserstein Perella (Pillsbury)	$14,200 $ 7,100 $10,000 $10,000 $ 1,000 $10,000 $10,000	.25 % .12 % .17 % .17 % .02 % .17 % .17 %
Imperial Oil (70% owned by Exxon) acquires Texaco Canada (78% owned by Texaco)	$ 4,149,595 250%	Acquisition for cash and stock, February 28	First Boston Gordon Capital (Imperial Oil) Morgan Stanley Scotia McLeod Wasserstein Perella (Texaco)	$ 100 $ 6,672 N.A. N.A. N.A.	.002% .16 % — — —
Dow Chemical acquires 67% of Marion Laboratories (pharmaceuticals)	$ 3,800,000 320%	Cash tender and merger of Marion Laboratories and Merrell Dow Pharmaceuticals to form Marion Merrell Dow, December 2	Morgan Stanley (Dow Chemical) Shearson Lehman Hutton (Marion Laboratories)	$16,000 $17,000	.42 % .45 %

Transaction	Value / Premium	Type & Date	Advisors	Fees	%
Sony (electronic equipment) acquires Columbia Pictures Entertainment (movies, TV production and distribution)	$ 3,400,000 / 320%	Acquisition for cash, November 6	Blackstone Group (Sony) / Allen & Co. (Columbia Pictures Entertainment)	$ 9,900 / $30,000	.29% / .88%
Ford Motor acquires First Capital (finance company) from Paramount Communications (entertainment)	$3,350,000 / N.A.	Acquisition for cash, October 31	Goldman Sachs / Shearson Lehman Hutton / Lazard Freres / Morgan Stanley (Paramount Communications)	N.A. / N.A. / N.A. / N.A.	— / — / — / —
Panhandle Eastern (gas, oil) acquires Texas Eastern (gas, oil)	$ 3,223,799 / 199%	Acquisition for cash and stock, June 28	Kidder Peabody (Panhandle Eastern) / Dillard Read / First Boston / James Capel / Wasserstein Perella (Texas Eastern)	$14,500 / $ 1,750 / $12,900 / $ 1,250 / $ 7,500	.45% / .05% / .40% / .04% / .23%
Black & Decker (power tools, household appliances) acquires Emhart (industrial, consumer products)	$ 2,670,000 / 275%	Acquisition for cash, July 18	Salomon Brothers (Black & Decker) / Shearson Lehman Hutton / Wasserstein Perella (Emhart)	$ 5,000 / $ 5,000 / $ 5,000	.19% / .19% / .19%
BSN (French food and beverage company) acquires RJR Nabisco's five European food businesses from RJR Holdings (Kohlberg Kravis Roberts)	$ 2,500,000 / N.A.	Acquisition for cash, June 6	Lazard Freres (BSN) / Morgan Stanley / Wasserstein Perella (RJR Holdings)	N.A. / N.A. / N.A.	— / — / —

A **product extension merger** occurs when acquiring and acquired companies have related production and/or distribution activities but not products that compete directly with each other. Examples are Miller Brewing being acquired by Phillip Morris and Western Publishing, a publisher of children's books, being acquired by Mattel Toy Company.

A **market extension merger** is when the acquiring and acquired firms produce the same products but sell them in different geographic markets. The motivation is that the acquiring firm can economically combine its management skills, production, and marketing with that of the acquired firm. An example is Dayton Hudson (a Minneapolis retailer) acquiring Diamond Chain (a West Coast retailer).

The final type is a **diversified activity merger.** This is a conglomerate merger involving the consolidation of two essentially unrelated firms with as limited a transfer of skills and activities as possible. Usually the acquiring firm is not interested in actively running and managing the acquired company. An example is Hillenbrand Industries (caskets and hospital furniture manufacturer) acquiring American Touristers (a luggage manufacturer).

Mergers are the best strategic option when synergy is present. Synergy is the qualitative effect on the rates of return of the acquiring firm brought about by complementary factors inherent in the firm being acquired. What makes two firms worth more together than apart? Several factors cause synergy to occur, increasing the value of the two-firm combination to more than the value of the separate entities. The first factor, economics of scale, is probably the most prevalent reason for mergers. Economies of scale can occur in production; coordination and administration; sharing central services such as office management and accounting executive development; financial control; and upper level management. Economies of scale increase the operating, financial, and management efficiency, resulting in better earnings.

The second factor is taxation or, more specifically, unused tax shields. Sometimes a firm has a loss but not enough profits to take tax advantage of the loss. Corporate income tax regulations allow the net operating losses of one company to reduce the taxable income of another when they are combined. By combining a firm with a loss with one with a profit, the tax-loss carry-over can be used.

The final important factor for mergers is the benefits received in combining complementary resources. Many large firms will merge with smaller ones to ensure a source of supply for key ingredients, to obtain the smaller firm's new technology, or to keep the smaller firm's product from being a competitive threat. It often is quicker and easier for a firm to merge with another that already has new technology developed, combining the innovation with the acquiring firm's ample engineering and sales talent, than to develop the technology from scratch. Some of the largest mergers and acquisitions of 1989 are indicated in Table 18–5. They have ranged from the nearly $12.7 million merger of Bristol-Myers and Squibb to form Bristol-Myers Squibb to the $2.7 million acquisition of Emhart by Black and Decker.

For example, Pan American World Airways and the Soviet Airline Aeroflot formed a joint venture in 1988 called the Soviet Pan Am Travel Effort. Initially the 50/50 agreement was put together to provide nonstop U.S./USSR service, but the carriers have since begun expanding operations into the hotel/convention center arena. A joint venture was arranged between the two airlines, Sheraton, and Mossoviet (the Moscow City Council) for two new hotels in Moscow.[12]

RECENT RESEARCH ON INTERNATIONAL ENTREPRENEURSHIP

Much research has been undertaken on international entrepreneurship in Europe, the Far East, and various areas with controlled economies.

Europe

Europe has not long been hospitable to the growth of entrepreneurship. Risk taking in general is discouraged by European culture since business failure is considered a social disgrace and is difficult to surmount financially. Recently however, several changes in the social and political climate have conspired to change this traditional, security conscious culture. Successful entrepreneurs, some of whom have become cultural heroes, are breaking through the stigma associated with striking out on one's own. In the political arena, in spite of the overregulation common to most Old World economies, new tax laws are providing incentives to would-be entrepreneurs that were previously lacking.[13]

One group that exemplifies the latest among these newcomers are academics, especially scientists and engineers. European academic circles typically hold great distaste for the world of commerce. Even for those scientists and engineers working in commercial enterprises, entrepreneurship is not very enticing; the private corporations and public research organizations where they are presently employed offered secure, well-paid, risk-free careers. For these same reasons, small European companies have difficulty attracting people with a knowledge of innovative management techniques and the know-how to launch high-technology products.

In spite of these disincentives, there are those in both academic circles and large companies who are looking for a challenge, and finding it in entrepreneurship. New government policies are making it easier to raise money for starting up businesses.[14] Britain and France are the European leaders in entrepreneurship with an abundance of venture capital; in West Germany and Italy, two major

[12]L. Fried, "Footwear and the Jet Set," pp. 42–5.

[13]R. I. Kirkland Jr., "Europe's New Entrepreneurs," *Fortune*, April 27, 1987, p. 253.

[14]D. Dickson, "An Entrepreneurial Tree Sprouts in Europe," *Science* 245 (September 8, 1989), pp. 1038–40.

obstacles for entrepreneurs are the lack of venture capital and limited access to bank credit for financing growth.[15]

In 1983, the United Kingdom government created the Business Expansion Scheme (BES) to provide external capital to new and small business ventures. Investors in the BES receive a tax break on their investments in "unquoted" enterprises.[16]

The French government is also trying to develop entrepreneurial enterprises as part of an overall strategy to stimulate their economy, but several economic and social factors in France create difficulties for aspiring entrepreneurs. In the first place, French venture capital is managed by bankers who are risk averse and have little understanding of the needs of small businesses and little regard for entrepreneurial expertise. A second major hurdle for entrepreneurs is the French contempt for both failure and success. Inherited fortunes are respected, but created wealth is generally considered unsavory, regardless of the money's origin.[17]

Significant research in Ireland and Sweden has produced a general profile of entrepreneurs in Ireland and of women entrepreneurs in Sweden. A survey of 272 entrepreneurs in Ireland found that the average age of their enterprises was 7 years old. The industry with the largest percentage of firms, 31 percent, was manufacturing; 45 percent of the businesses surveyed did not export, but among those that did, exportation accounted for 20 percent of total business.

In-depth personal interviews with a sample of the entrepreneurs from this survey indicated that the typical entrepreneur is a 40-year-old man who was the first born in his middle-class family. This person usually felt closer to his mother growing up, but often resembles his father in character. He is married, with three children. Although his parents are not educated, he completed high school and has experience in the field in which he is operating. This individual tends to be independent, energetic, goal-oriented, competitive, and flexible.[18]

One 1988 study on Northern Ireland supports the findings of this previous research regarding the personal attributes of entrepreneurs. The United Kingdom allocates $1 billion per year for the education and financial support of entrepreneurs, in an attempt to alleviate the 21 percent unemployment rate in Northern Ireland. Despite this and other efforts made by the Industrial Development Board and the Northern Ireland Economic Council, entrepreneurship has not taken

---

[15]C. Gaffney, "Hot Start-ups from Hong Kong to Hamburg," *Business Week,* May 23, 1988, p. 135.

[16]R. T. Harrison, and C. M. Mason, "Risk Finance, The Equity Gap and New Venture Formation in the United Kingdom: The Impact of the Business Expansion Scheme," *Frontiers on Entrepreneurship Research,* 1988, pp. 595–611.

[17]Jean-Louise Gassee, "The French Connection," *Across the Board* 24 (July–August 1987), p. 35.

[18]R. D. Hisrich, and B. O'Cinneide, "The Irish Entrepreneur: Characteristics, Problems and Future Success," *Frontiers of Entrepreneurship Research,* 1986, pp. 66–75.

roots. Many people are hesitant to start new businesses because, in addition to a volatile political situation, they must contend with high taxes, the high cost of capital, and customs regulations.[19]

In Sweden, a 1980 national survey of 1,500 female entrepreneurs and 300 male entrepreneurs broke down the population into three subclasses: single women (16%), married women (37%), and coentrepreneurs, or women in business with their husbands (47%). The percentage of single women in this group is low in comparison to the marital status of all Swedish women. Compared to the general population, female entrepreneurs were also found to have more children. Female entrepreneurs, ranging in age from 19 to 65, were found in almost every line of business, in every geographic location. Compared to men, female entrepreneurs in Sweden tend to be active in areas of retail, restaurants, and service, and are found less often in the manufacturing, construction, and transportation industries. These female entrepreneurs come from traditional backgrounds with the mother being a housewife and the father privately employed. Described as "adaptable," they often choose an entrepreneurial lifestyle to combine private and working life for family reasons. The desire to be their own boss was the number one reason given for starting up a business on their own.[20]

Other research refines the profile of an entrepreneur by outlining a new approach to explaining entrepreneurial behavior. This model relies more on prospect and attribution theories than on the personality profiles of entrepreneurs. It indicates that the familiar assumptions that entrepreneurs are risk takers, have an internal locus of control, and are motivated by a need for achievement result from the entrepreneur's positive perception of risk.[21]

A comparison study of high-technology firms with retail, manufacturing, and repair industries in Sweden was conducted through 15-minute telephone interviews with 540 firms. Typically, the high-technology firms were found to be younger than the others, their managers having a higher level of formal education and no entrepreneurial role models in their personal histories.[22]

Another research study of more than 400 Swedish concerns with 2–20 employees in the same industries analyzes factors that encouraged or deterred growth in small businesses. The factors found to influence entrepreneurs' will-

[19]R. D. Hisrich, "The Entrepreneur in Northern Ireland: Characteristics, Problems and Recommendations for the Future," *Journal of Small Business Management*, pp. 32–9.

[20]C. Holmquist, and E. Sundin, "Women as Entrepreneurs in Sweden: Conclusions from a Survey," *Frontiers of Entrepreneurship Research*, 1988, pp. 626–42.

[21]P. Davidsson, "On the Psychology of Continued Entrepreneurship in Small Firms," Paper presented at Second Workshop on Recent Research on Entrepreneurship in Europe, EIASM, Vienna, December 5–6, 1988.

[22]P. Davidsson, and K. Brynell, "Small High-Tech Firms and Conventional Small Firms—Similarities and Differences," Paper presented at Second Workshop on Recent Research on Entrepreneurship in Europe, EIASM, Vienna, December 5–6, 1988.

ingness to let their businesses grow were an anticipated loss of control over the enterprise (deterrent), increased independence as a result of growth (motivator), and financial gains (motivator). [23]

The Far East

The success of entrepreneurship in the Asian countries also varied greatly depending on the culture and the political and economic systems in place. Malaysia and Singapore, for example, are very close geographically and share some common history. Although both were once a part of the British Empire, they have evolved in very different ways.

The people of the Malaysian peninsula converted to Islam in the 15th century, not long before the advent of a European rule that lasted more than 400 years. First the Portuguese, then the Dutch, and finally the British governed the Malay people until independence in 1957. The natives traditionally lived in rural areas and left the cities to the dominant foreign powers, causing industrialization to occur late. There is still a lack of social mobility in this country, with women required to be covered in public and not allowed to hold positions of authority. The government established the Malaysian Industrial Development Authority to promote and coordinate efforts to eradicate poverty and restructure the social environment through economic development and stability. Unfortunately, the agency hasn't accomplished much. Another equally unhelpful agency, the New Investment Fund of Malaysia, which was established by the Ministry of Finance, actually has a lending rate higher than the base rate of the commercial banks.

The roots of entrepreneurship in Singapore reach as far back as the 14th century. More recently, in 1819, Sir Stamford Raffles bought the island and transformed it into a refuge for entrepreneurs, establishing a free port open to merchants of any ethnic background. When Singapore claimed its independence from Malaysia in 1965, the island once again became ethnically pluralistic, wrote secularism into its constitution, and gave tax incentives to entrepreneurs. In 1985, the Small Enterprise Bureau of Singapore was established to provide information and guidance to entrepreneurs in starting and expanding their enterprises. Social mobility is high and entrepreneurial success is greatly esteemed. [24]

Japan is a country whose social structure does not encourage entrepreneurship. Large corporations have dominated the economy for some time, and most Japanese entrepreneurial activity is limited to the service and information-

---

[23]P. Davidsson, "Entrepreneurship—and After? A Study of Growth Willingness in Small Firms," *Journal of Business Venturing* 4 (May 1989), pp. 211–26.

[24]L. P. Dana, "Entrepreneurship and Venture Creation—An Entrepreneurial Comparison of Five Commonwealth Nations," *Frontiers of Entrepreneurship Research,* 1987, pp. 573–89.

technology industries.[25] Even though these giant organizations encourage innovation and invention in their employees, the research findings of a 1987 study indicate that the five most important motivators for starting a high-technology firm in Japan were all centered on desires for self-actualization and creativity.[26] This is one need not addressed by this concensus-oriented society. In a culture where "the nail that sticks out gets hammered down," the growing interest in entrepreneurship and the increase in venture funds being appropriated for that purpose is somewhat surprising.

Perhaps in this culture too, trailblazers like Wataru Ohashi and Kazuhiko Nishi are breaking down the psychological barriers necessary to encourage entrepreneurship. Ohashi began a parcel-delivery service in 1981 that has since evolved into an enterprise that directly markets luxury items. Footwork, as the company is called, makes nearly half of its $115 million in earnings from the sales of items like melons, fresh salmon, caviar, and furs.[27]

At age 20, Nishi left the highly acclaimed Waseda University to start his own company. In 1978, he teamed up with William Gates of Microsoft. Within a few years, Nishi's company, ASCII, became the biggest PC software supplier in Japan.[28]

Hong Kong is also seeing a rise in entrepreneurial activity. Many of this country's entrepreneurs were previously managers of large companies before they broke away to start their own businesses.[29]

Hong Kong, a center for venture capital, has produced some of the wealthiest men in the world. Sir Yu Pao, driven out by Chinese Communists in 1948, worked initially to establish his family in the import/export business. In the mid-1980s, he bought his first ship, a coal-burning steamer. Since that time, Pao has built his fleet to become the world's largest private/independent shipowner and has amassed a personal fortune of over $1 billion. Kuang-Piu Chao is another refugee of communist China who left in the 1950s. Chao runs one of Hong Kong's largest textile operations, which in 1987 claimed a 4 percent share of Hong Kong's knitwear exports market. Li Ka-Shing arrived in Hong Kong with his parents at the age of 12. When his father died two years later, Li became the family breadwinner. By 20, Li was factory manager at the plastics factory where he first went to work, and several years later he had enough money to start his own plastic flower factory. Today, with an estimated net worth of $320 million, Li has a controlling interest in companies that are valued at $1 billion.[30]

[25]C. Gaffney, 1988, p. 135.

[26]D. M. Ray, "Factors Influencing Entrepreneurial Events in Japanese High-Technology Venture Business," *Frontiers of Entrepreneurship Research*, 1987, pp. 557–72.

[27]T. Holden, "Deliverymen Who Always Ring Twice," *Business Week*, May 23, 1988, p. 135.

[28]S. M. Dambrot, "Tensaiji: Whiz Kid Wins Business—Even in Japan," *Scientific American*, January 1990, p. 104.

[29]C. Gaffney, 1988, p. 135.

[30]"Hong Kong's Entrepreneurs on a Winning Streak," *Euromoney*, November 1987, pp. 44, 46, 48.

Controlled Economies

China's centralized, planned economy is known for not encouraging entrepreneurship. But there have been some changes wrought in the economic system since the reforms of December 1978. Guau Guarymei, a worker from Benxi, is a case in point. Guarymei leased eight government-run shops in 1985 and rapidly changed them from businesses operating at a loss to profitable enterprises. How did she do it? Guarymei reduced the managerial staff by 50 percent, devised a method of pay that made wages a function of performance, and instituted a system of fines for those who broke discipline. Controversy occurred over the amount of Guangmei's income as it was 20 times the wage of an average salesperson. This income level stands in opposition to the egalitarian socialist system in which every person enjoys equal benefits, regardless of the amount and quality of his/her contribution. These old values are slowly giving way to the idea of a socialist society that rewards those making contributions.[31]

Guan Guangmei is an example of the rising number of woman entrepreneurs in China. From a study of 50 woman entrepreneurs, a profile was created. Chinese woman entrepreneurs are mainly in the textile and clothing industries (48%). Seventy-six percent of the enterprises have been operating for 10 or more years; 64 percent of the entrepreneurs came from the coastal area of China, 36 percent from the interior. The majority of the woman entrepreneurs are between the ages of 40 and 50 (60%), with most having run their businesses less than 15 years (56%). Sixty percent of the women surveyed had received secondary technical training or higher education and 96 percent were members of the Communist party.[32]

Although the educational level of woman entrepreneurs in China is lower than their counterparts in other countries, the problems they encounter are much the same. Capital is lacking. There is a need for training and education in management, administration, and coordination of personnel. Finally, the needs for reform and implementation of countrywide policies are concerns shared with entrepreneurs in other countries with controlled economies, such as the USSR and those in Eastern Europe.

In Poland, the transitional upheaval and lack of adequate reform has led to a thriving black market, particularly in hard currency. One man who saw an opportunity was Bogdan Chosna, a 36-year-old Polish manager and co-owner of Promotor, a trading company based in Warsaw. In the 1980s, Chosna made a fortune by using investors' stashes of hard Western currency to buy cheap personal computers from Taiwan and Singapore. He then sold them to businesses at a premium in local currency, the zloty. Chosna gave his clients something to buy with the zloty, circumventing the slow-moving official channels. He ex-

---

[31]L. Delysin, "The Case of an Entrepreneur," *World Press Review,* January 1988, pp. 23–4.

[32]R. D. Hisrich, and Zhang Fan "Women Entrepreneurs in the People's Republic of China: An Exploratory Study," *Journal of Managerial Psychology* 6, no. 1 (March/April, 1991).

changed the vast profits in zlotys for dollars on the black market. With hyper-inflation and competition taking much of the profit out of the business, Chosna has become a sales agent for Western firms importing goods into Poland.

Another successful entrepreneur is Leonid Melamed from Riga, Latvia, in the USSR. Melamed began his professional life as a military lawyer, but since the advent of perestroika he has established 15 businesses—among them, three newspapers, a stainless steel cutlery operation, and a business devoted to women's lingerie. In 1988, when the Soviet government began allowing joint ventures, Melamed promptly reinvested four million rubles of his earnings in a joint venture with a Polish company and later found other partners in West Germany and the United States.

The economic reforms taking place in the Soviet Union and Eastern Europe have inspired the U.S. government to use the Overseas Private Investment Corporation (OPIC) to promote U.S. private-sector investments in those areas. OPIC, launched in 1969, has traditionally invested in Latin America, Africa, and South Asia. With the opportunities in Eastern Europe opening up, OPIC started there in the summer of 1989. OPIC provides a number of services. It sells political risk insurance that covers currency inconvertibility, appropriation, and political violence (long-term policies, up to 20 years). It offers direct loans—up to $6 million to individuals with a total outlay of $20 million—and it can guarantee up to $200 million. The agency organizes overseas missions through which U.S. business people can explore investment possibilities. It also provides investor information services.

One country ripe for the investment opportunities provided by OPIC is Hungary. The reforms in this country have supported decentralization, private initiative, and a market-oriented economy. In 1990, Hungary had 678 registered joint ventures; this number is second in Eastern Europe only to the Soviet Union's 685. This large number reflects the very favorable joint venture conditions established by the Hungarian government, including the ease of obtaining governmental permission. One major advantage Hungary has over other Eastern European countries in the establishment of joint ventures is that the profits earned can be changed to hard currency and taken out of the country. Only the hard currency portion of profits is allowed to be repatriated in the USSR. A survey of 46 Hungarian entrepreneurs found that most of them were between the ages of 30 and 50. The sample was equally spread among three educational levels: craftsman school, high school, and university. There were a variety of motivations for starting the new venture: to put their experience to work, to gain financial independence, or simply to work for themselves. Most of the entrepreneurs are operating in the service sector, with firm size being generally small, although the total variation in number of employees ranges from 1 to 300.[33]

---

[33]J. Vecsenyi, and R. D. Hisrich, "Entrepreneurship and the Hungarian Transformation: An Entrepreneurial Perspective," *Journal of Managerial Psychology* 5 (1990), pp. 11–16.

Some of the businessmen who were in leadership roles before the reunification of East and West Germany have left their positions since the event. Others have somehow managed to keep hold of the reins and are guiding the GDR into a market economy and union. Five such men are Heinz Warzecha, Erwin Rohde, Dieter Resch, Rudolf Staderman, and Helmut Krausser. Warzecha, the chief executive of a machine-tool manufacturer, is a pace-setter for East German industrialists. Rohde is a university professor and disillusioned Communist party member who has been teaching Western financial concepts since 1975. He was one of the first outspoken advocates of currency union on a one-to-one parity with West Germany. Resch, Deputy Editor-in-Chief of the *Berliner Zeitung* and a student of economics, sees his journal as an interpreter between the East and West. Staderman, an entrepreneur who began a microprocessor chips manufacturing business in his garage in 1981, is currently president of a newly formed organization for entrepreneurs called the Businessman's Association. Krausser is Department Head of the Deutche Aussenhandelsbank and a key player in East German banking.[34]

SUMMARY

The movement of the once planned economies to market orientation is necessary for economic revitalization. Entrepreneurship must take a leading role in the decentralization and privatization of these economies. There is need for the development of educational, business, and government infrastructures that will allow new venture creation and growth.

Entrepreneurship is increasing worldwide largely because of the understanding that individual initiative and new venture creation is a key to economic development. Of the approximately 18 million jobs created between 1977 and 1985 in the United States, 89 percent were generated by companies with fewer than 100 employees. This kind of dynamism has inspired the decentralization and privatization of business from Europe to China and may very well be the United States' best preparation for the future. Entrepreneurship is indeed an international occupation that facilitates the growth and diversification of an economy regardless of its ideology or geographic location.

GLOSSARY

accrual method of accounting An accounting method that records income and expenses when incurred, not when cash is received, thereby ignoring cash inflows and outflows.

acquisition financing Financing used for such activities as traditional acquisitions, leveraged buyouts, and going private.

acquisitions The purchase of an entire company or part of it so that the acquired entity is completely absorbed by the acquiring company and no longer exists as a separate business.

aftermarket support The managing underwriter's readiness to purchase or sell the stock to stabilize the market, helping to prevent the price from going below that of the initial public offering.

assets Everything of value owned by the business. Value is based on the actual cost or amount expended for the asset. Assets are categorized as fixed or current, based on the length of time they will be used.

asset base for loans The entity of value pledged against the loan, ensuring a reasonable expectation of repayment. Usually the loan is based on accounts receivable, inventory, equipment, or real estate.

balance of payments The difference between the value of the goods and services imported into a country and those exported, which is reflected in the value of the country's currency.

barter Trading of goods or services without the exchange of money.

birth order A concept that the relative position of one sibling versus another in a family affects the entrepreneurial tendency of an individual.

blue sky laws The securities of a company going public must be qualified under the laws of each state in which they will be offered for sale.

book value Acquisition cost minus liabilities.

break-even The point in the operation where total revenue equals total costs. Each additional unit sold after break-even results in a profit equal to the difference between the selling price and variable cost per unit.

breakthrough innovations The few innovations that, if successful, with either radically change an existing industry or create an entirely new one.

business angels An "invisible" group of individual, informal investors who are looking for equity-type investment opportunities. They provide funds needed in all stages of financing.

business plan A concise, written document prepared by the entrepreneur describing the present venture and market situation, future directions, and implementation strategies. The major purposes of the plan are supporting the financing needs for the entrepreneur and guiding the future direction of the venture.

cash method of accounting An accounting method where income and expenses are recorded only when cash is received or disbursed, making the results more consistent with cash flow.

C corporation This is the typical corporation, where the owners are the stockholders. Unlike the proprietorship and partnership, it is treated as a separate legal entity for tax and liability purposes.

competitive negotiation A situation involving directly competing claims on a fixed, limited economic resource. It requires concessions in allocating shares in order for a settlement to be reached.

contract A written, legally binding agreement specifying the parties, their roles, and value of transaction.

controlled economies Centralized, planned economies that are the opposite of a competitive market economy.

conventional bank loans Business loans such as lines of credit, installment loans, straight commercial loans, long-term loans, and character loans.

cooperative negotiation A situation where two parties bargain by working with each other to obtain a mutually beneficial solution.

copyright A protection of the original works of authorship for a term of the life of the author plus 50 years, or if an institution, 75 years from the date of publication.

deal structure The terms of the transaction between the entrepreneur and the funding source.

deficiency letter A letter informing the company that the preliminary prospectus covering the information contained in the final prospectus needs some modifications before being approved.

departure point The time when dissatisfaction and frustration with his or her present job causes the entrepreneur to consider leaving to form a new venture.

description of venture The part of the business plan that discusses the product/service, business location, plan and equipment, and qualifications of entrepreneurs.

desirability of new venture formation The desire to form a new venture resulting from an individual's culture, subculture, family, teachers, and peers.

developmental financing The second basic financing type in which capitalists play an active role in providing funds.

direct exporting Exporting through the use of Independent Foreign Distributor and Overseas Sales Offices.

direct foreign investment A foreign company buying assets in any economy, usually in the form of putting money or its equivalent in a company in a foreign economy.

direct marketing Seller's use of one or more media for purposes of soliciting a response by phone, mail, or personal visit.

disclosure document The document sent to the Patent and Trademark Office to establish a date of conception of an invention. Used to prove that the inventor was the first to conceive of the invention.

distributive bargaining A situation where one party is not allowed to achieve his or her goals; therefore, there is no trust between the two parties, and a solution can only be reached through a series of modified positions of compromise and concessions.

diversified activity merger A conglomerate merger involving the consolidation of two essentially unrelated firms with as limited a transfer of skills and activities as possible.

due diligence Assessing the upside potential and downside risk as well as the markets, the industry, financial analysis, customers, and management capability before making an investment.

early-stage financing Two types of financing occur during this difficult stage for raising capital: seed capital and start-up.

earnings approach The most widely used method of valuing a company as it provides the potential investor with the best estimate of the probable return on investment.

entrepreneur as an innovator To reform or revolutionize a present pattern by opening a new source of supply or new outlets, reorganizing a new industry, or undertaking some other innovative activity.

entrepreneur decision process The decision to leave a present career or life-style because the entrepreneurial venture being considered is desirable and external and internal factors make the venture possible.

entrepreneurial career Dynamic stages in the life of an entrepreneur, with each stage reflecting and interacting with other stages and events in the individual's life.

entrepreneurial domain Pressures on a business to manage in a looser entrepreneurial manner caused by such factors as diminishing opportunity streams and rapidly changing technology, consumer economics, social values, and political rules.

entrepreneurial process The four distinct phases of creating a new venture, including: (1) identifying and evaluating the opportunity, (2) developing the business plan, (3) determining the resources required, and (4) managing the resulting entity.

entrepreneurship The process of creating a new venture of value. Involves devoting the necessary time and effort, assuming the accompanying financial, psychic, and social risks, and receiving the resulting rewards of monetary and personal satisfaction.

equity participation Having an ownership position in an organization as a result of contributing some resource, usually money.

equity pool A sum of money accumulated for investing in various situations.

exporting The sale and shipping of products manufactured in one country to a customer located in another country.

external funds Money obtained outside the company. It is usually one of two types: debt financing or equity financing.

factor approach An approach used to determine the value of a venture using one of three major factors: earnings, dividend-paying capacity, and book value.

factors in valuating a business Eight factors that indicate the importance of using the value of other corporations engaged in the same or similar line of business in valuing the business venture at hand.

FIFO Method of inventory costing called first-in-first-out. As an item is sold, the cost of goods is based on the cost of producing the oldest item in inventory.

financial plan A plan involving pro forma statements for cash flow, income, and balance sheet. Indicates the potential investment and possible sources of funds.

firm growth pattern Each industry has established track records by which a firm grows.

form S–1 A registration form used in an initial public offering. Provides information to purchasers to assess the company's cash flow from internal and external sources.

form S–18 The appropriate registration form for a small initial public offering.

foundation companies Firms created from research and development that lay the foundation for a new industry.

franchise Arrangement whereby manufacturer or sole distributor of a trademarked product or service gives exclusive rights to an entrepreneur in return for payment of royalties and conformance to standard operating procedures.

franchise agreement Written document that contains all of the specific requirements and obligations of the franchisee.

franchisee The person or entrepreneur who purchases the right to use, manufacture, or sell any trademark, copyright, or patent.

franchisor The seller of a franchise. Has ownership of trademark, patent, or copyright that is offered to someone in return for royalties.

full disclosure Making sure that all pertinent facts and figures about a company are made public.

general valuation method One approach an entrepreneur can use to determine how much of the company a venture capitalist will want for a given investment.

general partner The sponsoring company that secures the needed limited partners to develop the technology.

going public The transformation of a closely held corporation into one where the general public has a proprietary interest.

government as innovator One method for commercializing the results of the interaction between a social need and technology.

high-potential venture The type of new company that receives the greatest investment interest and publicity. It frequently goes public or is purchased by a larger company.

horizontal merger A merger of two firms that produce one or more of the same or closely related products in the same geographical area.

indirect exporting Exporting through the use of a foreign purchaser in a local market and export management firm.

industry analysis An assessment of historical achievements, trends, major competitors and their strategies, market segments, and future forecasts of a particular industry.

industry—university agreement A type of joint venture agreement for the purpose of doing research. Takes on a variety of forms, depending on the parties involved and the subject of the research.

informal risk-capital market One type of risk capital that is composed of a virtually invisible group of investors who are looking for equity-type investment opportunities in a wide variety of entrepreneurial ventures.

initial public offering The first stock offering of a once privately owned company.

integrative bargaining A form of negotiation involving cooperation between the parties negotiating.

internal funds Money generated from the operations of a company. Includes profits, sale of assets, reduction in working capital, credit from suppliers, and accounts receivable.

international business The process of conducting business activities across national boundaries.

intrapreneurial culture Instilling the entrepreneurial spirit in an existing organization in order to innovate and grow.

intrapreneurial leadership characteristics These include understanding the environment, being visionary and flexible, creating management options, encouraging teamwork, encouraging open discussion, building a coalition of supporters, and persistence.

intrapreneurship Entrepreneurship within an existing business structure.

inventor A person who has family, education, and occupational experiences that contribute to creative development and free thinking; a problem solver who loves to create new things.

job description It should specify the details of the work to be performed by the person holding the position.

job specifications These identify the requirements needed by the person applying for a job. Included might be skills, experience, education, and so on.

joint venture A separate entity involving two or more active participants as partners.

leverage The ability to borrow enough money to provide the additional equity needed for the acquisition.

leveraged buyout Occurs when the assets of the acquired company are used as collateral to finance the deal.

leveraged buyout financing The money involved in acquiring a company with the assets of the acquired company being used as collateral.

liabilities The amount a company owes to creditors. They are categorized as current or long term, depending on whether they are due within a year or longer.

license An arrangement between two parties, where one party has proprietary rights based on a patent, trademark, or copyright. Licenses are formed by contract, with a royalty or fixed sum being paid in return for permission to use the patent, trademark, or copyright.

life-cycle approach A conceptualization of entrepreneurial careers in nine major categories: educational environment, individual personalities, childhood family environment, employment history, current work situation, the individual's current perspective, and the current family situation.

life-style firm A privately held firm achieving only modest growth. It primarily supports the owners and has little opportunity for significant growth and expansion.

LIFO Method of inventory costing called last-in-first-out. As an item is sold, the cost of goods would be based on the cost of producing the most recent item in inventory.

limited partner A partner having limited liability yet not a totally taxable entity.

liquidation covenant A provision in an agreement allowing the investor to require registration, sale, or other disposition of the securities given certain conditions occur.

liquidation value The amount that would be received if the corporation liquidated.

locus of control The internal-external control dimension of an individual.

majority interests Having a large enough ownership position in a firm to have control. This usually means owning over 50 percent.

management contract A method allowing the purchasing country to gain foreign expertise without acquiring ownership of the company's resources; this allows a profit to be obtained without the need of a large equity investment.

managerial (administrative) domain Pressures on a business to manage in a more hierarchical fashion caused by such factors as power, status, financial rewards, performance measurement criteria, risk reduction, inertia, organizational culture, and planning systems.

managing underwriter The lead firm in forming the underwriting syndicate for the issuance of stocks or bonds of a company.

market extension merger An agreement reached between acquiring and acquired firms that produce the same products but sell them in different geographic markets.

marketing goals and objectives Written statements in the marketing plan that describe where the company is gong in the next 12 months.

marketing mix The interaction of four major controllable variables in the marketing system: product/service, pricing, distribution, and promotion.

marketing-oriented organization This is an organization where the management philosophy is to determine the consumer's needs and then develop and deliver products and services that will effectively meet them.

marketing plan   A written guide within the business plan, usually for a 12-month period, which describes the market, industry, competition, and the plan to be implemented to achieve future sales and profits. Describes how the product(s) or service(s) will be distributed, priced, and promoted, with specific forecasts and projected profitability.

marketing system   A description of the interrelationships between the external and internal environment with decisions on product, pricing, distribution, and promotion.

merger   A transaction involving two or more companies in which only one survives.

minority interest   Having a small investment in a company to gain a foothold or experience in a market before making a major commitment.

moral-support network   A cheering squad of family and friends that provide advice, encouragement, understanding, and even assistance to the entrepreneur.

motivation   The drives and desires to become an entrepreneur.

need for achievement   An individual's desire for responsibility for solving problems, setting goals, and reaching goals.

need for independence   An individual's desire to do things in his or her own way and time. Such a person may have a difficult time working for someone else.

negotiation approach   The process by which parties attempt to resolve a conflict by agreement. If a resolution is not possible, the critical issues in the disagreement are identified. This is done in eight steps: prepare, discuss, signal, purpose, respond, bargain, close, and agree.

nonequity arrangements   These are agreements that involve no financial commitment. The three most popular forms are licensing, turn-key projects, and management contracts.

opportunity identification   After formulating a general idea about the type of company desired, entrepreneurs use informal and formal mechanisms for identifying the best opportunity to become involved in.

opportunity parameters   Boundaries of creativity in a new product development.

ordinary innovation   New products or services with little uniqueness or technology.

organization culture   The atmosphere and working environment of a particular organization.

organizational plan   A part of the business plan describing the venture's form of ownership, terms of agreement, management team, roles and responsibilities of the team, and compensation for each member.

owner equity   The excess of all assets over all liabilities. It is the net worth of the business.

partnership   In this legal form of business, there is more than one owner, each with responsibility for the operation of the venture. The partnership agreement stipulates the responsibility of the owners and their liability. A partnership may have general or limited partners.

patent   A contract between the government and an inventor whereby the government grants the inventor exclusivity on the material presented for a specified amount of time.

possibility of new venture formation   The factors that contribute to the creation of a new venture such as governments, background, marketing, role models, and finances.

preliminary screening   An investigation of the economy of the industry. Includes an assessment of the appropriateness of the knowledge and ability of the venture capitalist.

present value of future cash flow   A method of valuation that adjusts the value of the cash flow of the business for the time value of money and the business and economic risks.

pricing amendment   The information contained in the final prospectus made available before the effective date. Includes offering price, underwriters' commission, and amount of proceeds.

primary data   New unpublished information collected for a specific need or purpose. It usually involves the development of a market research study to collect the data.

private offering   A formalized approach for obtaining funds from private investors that is faster and less costly than other approaches.

private placement   A method for obtaining money from private investors, who may be family and friends or wealthy individuals.

private venture capital firm   One type of venture capital firm usually involving a general operating partner and limited partners who have supplied the capital.

production plan   A part of the business plan that describes the manufacturing process and its costs, any subcontractors used, machinery and equipment needed, raw materials needed, potential sources of supplies, and layout of plant and manufacturing process.

product/market opportunity   A unique growing market opportunity where the company's offering has a differential advantage.

product evolution process   The process through which an innovation is developed and commercialized through entrepreneurial activity stimulating economic growth.

product-extension merger   An agreement between the acquiring and acquired companies having related production and/or distribution activities that do not compete directly with each other.

Product Safety and Liability Commission   Empowered under the Consumer Product Safety Act, a five-member commission prescribes safety standards for more than 10,000 products. This commission identifies products considered substantial hazards and, where appropriate, will request the manufacturer to take corrective action.

professional-support network   Advice obtained from a mentor, business associates, trade associations, or personal affiliations.

pro forma balance sheet   Forecasts the asset, liability, and owner equity balance of a venture based on the pro forma income and cash flow statements.

pro forma cash flow   Projection of cash balance sheet at the end of a specific time period based on projected cash receipts and cash disbursements from the income statement.

pro forma income statement   Projection of a venture's earnings and expenses from operations. It should be prepared on a monthly basis for the first year and then on an annual basis thereafter.

pro forma sources and applications of funds   Projects the disposition of earnings from operations and from other financing. Indicates how the money for operation of a company will be obtained.

proprietorship   The simplest form of business. The owner is the individual who starts the business and has full responsibility for its operations.

prospectus   A legal offering document normally prepared as a brochure or booklet for distribution to prospective buyers.

publicity   This is free advertising in which a trade magazine, newspaper, magazine, radio, or TV program finds it of public interest to do a story on the new venture.

quiet period   The period of time from when the decision to go public is made to 90 days following the date of becoming effective.

rational decision model   The type of negotiation flow that moves from establishing objectives, to establishing criterion, to analyzing cause-and-effect relationships involved, to developing and evaluating alternatives, and then to selecting an alternative and an action plan. The final step must be the measuring of the outcomes upon implementation.

red herring   The preliminary prospectus. Its purpose is to show how income was used to increase assets or pay off debt.

referral sources   Information on potential deals from such sources as business associates, friends, active personal research, investment bankers, and business brokers.

registration statement   Supplemental information to the prospectus, which is available for public inspection at the office of the SEC.

Regulation D   Contains a number of broad provisions designed to simplify the private offering.

replacement value   A valuation method used for insurance purposes or in very unique circumstances whereby the valuation of the venture is based on the amount of money it would take to replace that asset.

reporting requirements   One of the negative aspects of going public. The company must carefully observe each requirement since mistakes can have significant negative consequences.

research and development limited partnership An agreement that the sponsoring company will develop the technology and the limited partnership will provide the funds.

restrictive covenant Section of an investment agreement that protects the investor and allows the investment to be profitably liquidated at a later date.

reward system Ensures that an intrapreneur receives rewards for attaining established performance goals.

risk assessment A section of the business plan that identifies the potential risks in the venture and strategies that might be implemented to deal with them.

risk-capital market The market where financing can be obtained for new and growing companies. It has three primary parts: informal risk capital industry, the formal venture capital industry, and the public stock market.

risk taking of an entrepreneur A calculated risk that an entrepreneur takes in order to make a profit by establishing a new venture.

role models Parents, brothers, sisters, other relatives, successful entrepreneurs in the surrounding community, or nationally touted entrepreneurs who entrepreneurs emulate to varying extents.

S corporation This is a special type of corporation, where the income (and losses) are declared as personal income by the shareholders. There are restrictions on who can elect this form of business.

secondary data Information that already exists in a published form. It may be purchased from an outside source or it may be available in a library.

settlement range The area of values in a negotiation procedure where a mutually agreeable decision can be reached.

situation analysis A description of the historical perspective of the new venture including background on the entrepreneur, the product/service, and the industry. It answers the question, Where have we been?

Small Business Innovation Research (SBIR) grants An opportunity for small businesses to obtain research and development money through a uniform method by which each participating agency solicits, evaluates, and selects the research proposals for funding.

Small Business Investment Company (SBIC) firms The first firms that started of the formal venture-capital industry.

social status The status placed on an individual or family by society, which is reflected in their behavior and value systems.

stage of economic development The different stages of economic development a country goes through, from being very undeveloped to very developed and achieving a better standard of living.

state-sponsored venture-capital firm A venture-capital firm sponsored by a state. The size and investment thrust varies from state to state. Each is required to invest a certain percentage of the funds in companies in the particular state.

strong management team A good team of managers having solid experience and background, commitment to the company, capabilities in their specific areas of expertise, the ability to merge challenges, and flexibility.

synergy Any situation where the whole is greater than the sum of parts and therefore worth joining together. A particularly important characteristic for a successful joint venture.

target market A subset of the total market identified by the entrepreneur as having the greatest opportunity for success.

technological innovation A new product or service having advances in science and technology.

third-party payments Payments to a party other than the ones directly involved in the transaction.

time management Managing your time effectively by focusing on the areas most important in accomplishing the goal.

top management commitment The first step in the process of establishing intrapreneurship in an organization is to secure commitment by top management. Without this commitment the organization will never be able to go through all the cultural climate changes necessary for implementation.

trademark A word, symbol, design, or some combination of such, or a slogan or sound that identifies the source or sponsorship of certain goods and services. It is granted by the Patent and Trademark Office for renewable 20-year periods. In the sixth year an affidavit is filed to prove that the mark is in use.

trade secret The protection available when the entrepreneur prefers to maintain an idea or process as confidential and not copyright or patent it. Not covered by any federal law but is recognized under a governing body of common laws in each state.

traditional managers Motivated primarily by promotion and typical corporate rewards. They tend to adhere strictly to established hierarchical structures, to be less risk-oriented, and to emphasize short-term results.

turn-key projects A company built by a foreign company that trains the workers and managers and then turns the operation over to the local owners.

underwriting syndicate The group of investors who have gotten together to issue the stock or bonds of a company.

venture-capital decision process The process by which the typical venture-capital firm decides to invest in a particular investment opportunity.

venture-capital market One of the three types of risk capital that has formal companies making investment decisions in a variety of business areas.

vertical merger A merger of two or more firms in successive stages of production that often involve a buyer-seller relationship. This stabilizes supply and production and offers more control of these critical areas.

windows of opportunity The length of time a market is available for a new product or service idea.

work history The documentation of an individual's jobs and accomplishments over time. This is an important aspect in obtaining external financing.

INDEX